TITANIC
AND THE MYSTERY SHIP

TITANIC
AND THE MYSTERY SHIP

SENAN MOLONY

The
History
Press

For my parents

First published in 2006 by Tempus Publishing

Reprinted in 2010 by
The History Press
The Mill, Brimscombe Port,
Stroud, Gloucestershire, GL5 2QG
www.thehistorypress.co.uk

Reprinted 2012, 2017

British Library Cataloguing in Publication Data.
A catalogue record for this book is available from the British Library.

ISBN 978 0 7524 3743 9

Typesetting and origination by
Tempus Publishing Limited
Printed in Great Britain by TJ International ltd, Padstow, Cornwall

CONTENTS

Then water was washing us away,
A torrent running right over us;
Running right over us then
Were turbulent waters.

Psalm 124

THE AUTHOR

Senan Molony is the Political Editor of the *Irish Daily Mail*. He has over twenty years' experience in covering all forms of civil and criminal trials, parliament, judicial tribunals and inquiries. He was born in 1963.

His uncle was a Merchant Marine Captain in the Second World War whose vessels were sunk by enemy action on two occasions. Another uncle became Flag Officer of the Irish Naval Service. Mr Molony, whose other books include *The Irish Aboard Titanic* and *Lusitania: An Irish Tragedy*, lives in Dublin with his wife Brigid and three children.

ILLUSTRATIONS AND ACKNOWLEDGEMENTS

All illustrations in this volume are credited to the original copyright holder. Reproduction fees paid to Southampton City Council; the *Illustrated London News* library; The National Maritime Museum, Greenwich; the Peabody Museum of Salem; Dundee City Archives; and the Mariners' Museum, Newport News, Virginia. Permission to make use of a photograph from the Fr Browne Collection gratefully acknowledged to the Wolfhound Press and Society of Jesus, Dublin Provincialate. Crew images from the Public Record Office granted use with attribution. Pictures from defunct newspapers are deemed in the public domain.

The author expresses gratitude to the following for the use of pictures within their possession or other assistance with illustrations: Günter Bäbler; Joe Carvalho; Chris Dohany; George Fenwick; Charles Haas; Library of Congress; Stanley Tutton Lord estate; Martin Maher; Jeff Newman; Inger Sheil; Joanne Smith; Southampton Archive Services; 20th Century Fox; Claes Göran Wetterholm; J. & C. McCutcheon. Other images by the author. Any alteration to an image is stated in accompanying captions. In addition, any authorial comment within an extract is enclosed by square brackets.

Mr Paul Slish of Buffalo, NY, USA, proof-read the manuscript and also provided notable refinements and technical improvements. The author hereby acknowledges his significant contribution to the finished work. The author also wishes to thank Alec Dubber of Tempus Publishing for his editorial efforts.

INTRODUCTION

They are buoyed on a boundless ocean. From horizon to horizon, the slick surface of the sea is black and unbroken. The darkness is over the deep, and the nearest point of land is 800 miles away.

The glory of their gilded cage now seems a mockery. Instead of being safe and warm in the singing romance of a ship at sea, the 2,200 people aboard the RMS *Titanic* find to their surprise that she is sinking beneath their feet.

Immersion in freezing seawater is a cruel way to die. The pitiless seizure of limbs and sudden slowing of senses will speedily siphon all life away in the ultimate loneliness of the mid-Atlantic.

The disaster claimed more than 1,500 lives, equivalent to thirty busloads packed with individuals. It was a waste of talent, wisdom and potential on a massive scale. A liner trumpeted as 'practically unsinkable' went down in more than 2 miles of water off the coast of Newfoundland, and did so on her maiden voyage. Only 712 escaped.

It was not glorious, nor noble, nor in any way civilized, but a repulsive roulette that separated husbands from wives, fathers from children, and whole families from the veil of life. It was very far indeed from its modern reinterpretation as a deliciously exclusive way to die.

The *Titanic* went down because she was steaming too fast to avoid an iceberg. She had lifeboat spaces for 1,200 passengers and crew at the very most, which meant at least 1,000 were doomed to lose their lives, unless help could be summoned from somewhere.

In the two hours and forty minutes from impact to sinking, the *Titanic* sent out unceasing and increasingly desperate appeals for aid by wireless. The captain and officers in that time managed to launch sixteen boats and two collapsible craft. Two other collapsibles were swept off at the terrible end and provided temporary haven for 'lucky' swimmers who reached them in the dark.

Yet it could all have been so different.

There *was* another ship there.

A ship that could have undoubtedly alleviated the unfolding nightmare. This vessel, known as the 'mystery ship', approached from over the horizon and stopped when between 5 and 6 miles from the *Titanic*.

The joy on the White Star liner when she first appeared can be imagined. Second Officer Lightoller, in charge of loading lifeboats on the port side, saw that other vessel on the port bow. He admitted in his memoirs that he reassured the *Titanic*'s passengers that the other ship was on her way to their succour.

It is probable that the clear sighting of a ship's light impeded the filling of lifeboats. Men could afford to indulge their bravado at the sight of a saviour so close. Women had a reason to refuse to risk life and limb by attempting to enter a 'cockleshell' in the dark, 70ft up.

All unconsciously remembered the great wireless rescue of barely three years earlier. In 1909, Jack Binns, the Marconi operator of another White Star liner, the *Republic*, had been able to conjure a variety of ships to the rescue through the magic of the ether. It appeared the recent invention of wireless had all but banished the spectre of major sinkings.

It was a misplaced trust. Wireless operators need sleep, and many in the vicinity, like Cyril Evans on the *Californian*, had gone to bed by midnight, long before the *Titanic* began tapping out her death rattle. None of the ships that did pick up the SOS were in a position to render assistance prior to the maiden voyager vanishing beneath the waves.

Except the mystery ship. This vessel seemed to promise deliverance. Why was she coming the 'wrong way' on an essentially westbound shipping track if she had not picked up the distress message?

If she *had* picked it up, why did she not use her own wireless in turn to communicate with the *Titanic*, which was by then firing a fusillade of rockets to attract her attention, and signalling constantly with Morse lamps?

Perhaps she did not have wireless. Perhaps she was herself stuck in ice invisible to the *Titanic*, and unable to make progress. If so, why did she not instead answer the *Titanic*'s Morse communications? Why did she, in fact, take no action whatsoever?

But she did take action. The action she took was to eventually steam away, crushing the hope of all those on the *Titanic* who had pinned their trust to her so forlornly.

Without knowing the identity of the craft in question (*Titanic* Fourth Officer Boxhall judged her to be a three or four-masted steamer) it is impossible to answer these questions. Why did she steam away? If it was to look for a way through impeding ice, why did she not take that action sooner? Could she really have missed all the rockets? If not, what did she think they signified?

And we are brought in turn to the most chilling question of all: Is it possible that fellow seafarers, bound in the brotherhood of all who occupy their business in great waters, would knowingly discern distress and yet do nothing?

Monumental callousness!

It was for all these reasons that the first inquiry into the *Titanic* disaster, convened by the US Senate Subcommittee on Commerce, was anxious to pin down the identity of the mystery ship. It eventually settled on the *Californian*, a medium-sized tramp steamer of just over 6,200 tons, a workhorse of the Leyland Line, built in Dundee in 1901.

Like the *Titanic*, she was bound west that night, but for Boston, not New York. Her captain was Stanley Lord, a thirty-five-year-old shipmaster of extensive experience, who had qualified for command at a very early age. He signed a completed crew agreement on 1 April 1912 that named his chief officer as thirty-four-year-old George Stewart, with Herbert Stone and Charles Groves, both twenty-four, the other officers among a complement of fifty-five.

At 6 a.m. on 5 April 1912, the *Californian* left Victoria Docks, London, carrying a general cargo. It would be Captain Lord's last full voyage as her commander. The British Inquiry, settling on the same verdict as that handed down in America, would soon see to that.

But was the mystery ship the *Californian*?

Doubts, argument and agitation persisted for the rest of the twentieth century. This book will, for the first time, examine the totality of evidence – particularly in light of the discovery of the *Titanic*'s actual wreck site in 1985, a location crucially unknown to the official investigations of seventy-three years earlier.

Great care has been taken to write this book for the ordinary reader, and it is hoped the voyage will therefore prove rewarding and revealing. Most of all, however, it is hoped that it will appeal to your common sense, in suspension of the instant judgement dispensed on both sides of the Atlantic in the wake of an appalling catastrophe.

1

CALIFORNIAN STOPS

The story begins with the *Californian*. Bound for Boston on the evening of Sunday 14 April 1912, she had been following the course of the liner *Parisian* and knew from wireless warnings that field ice lay ahead in her path. *Californian's* captain, Stanley Lord, had seen three icebergs to his southward that early evening and passed this intelligence by wireless to other shipping – including *Titanic*.

At 10.20 p.m. that night, Captain Lord spotted an icefield ahead and ordered his helm hard over, reversing engines. He came to a stop one minute later, with the *Californian's* head (bow) pointing north-east. Her bow had obviously been pointing due west, until she took avoiding action to escape the ice and ended up 'heading about northeast true' (Lord, US p.732). A current was operating that night which would gradually bring her bow around clockwise to point due east and eventually to point due south over some hours.

For now, all that needs to be known is that the *Californian* was stopped. She was to remain stationary, drifting absolutely imperceptibly (the current was half a knot per hour) for the whole of that fateful night...

EVIDENCE THAT THE *CALIFORNIAN* WAS STOPPED

Unimpeachable evidence that the *Californian* was at a standstill comes from her courtesy message to the *Titanic*, transmitted at 11 p.m. that night, which began 'Say Old Man, we are stopped and surrounded by ice' and which was coldly rebuffed by the *Titanic's* senior operator Jack Phillips. *Californian* had no reason to lie about being at a standstill, and this message was transmitted before *Titanic* struck her iceberg.

The following evidence was given by the *Californian's* captain, Stanley Lord, to the British Inquiry, in response to question number 6701:

> Later on did you have to stop on account of ice? — I had to stop and reverse engines.
> 6702. Would you tell us what time that was? — 10.21 p.m.
> 6713. Until? — 6 o'clock next morning. 5.15 a.m. we moved the engines for a few minutes and then we stopped on account of the news we received, and waited 'til 6 o'clock.

There is no suggestion that the *Californian* engaged her engines at any time that night. The British Board of Trade took depositions from all of her crew on their return at Liverpool and none suggested any navigation by the *Californian* from 10.21 p.m. to 6 a.m., when she began to move, in response to the dreadful news of the *Titanic* sinking, which she had just received by wireless.

Her original intention was to wait for morning before attempting to negotiate the ice barrier confronting her. A number of *Californian* crew witnesses called to the official inquiries testified to the point that their vessel was stopped that night. They included the apprentice officer, James Gibson:

> 7422. When you came on duty at midnight, did you find that your ship had stopped? —Yes.
> 7423. We have been told she stopped some time before half-past ten? —Yes.

Second Officer Herbert Stone also came on duty at midnight:

> 7809. Did you find the ship stopped and surrounded by ice? —Yes.

Third Officer Charles Victor Groves, who was on duty until midnight, when relieved by Stone, also answered questions:

> 8116. And we know your steamer stopped because she got among the ice? —Yes.
> 8117. At 10.26 was it? —Yes, at 10.26...

Chief Officer George Frederick Stewart was also called:

> 8572. Did you go on duty at 4 a.m.? —Yes.
> 8575. Did you find that your ship was stopped? —Yes.

And Wireless Operator Cyril Evans gave the following answers:

> 8976. We know she did [stop], about 10.25, your ship's time? —Yes.
> 8977. Did you go on deck when you found the ship had stopped? —Yes.
> 8978. I think you found the Captain and the Chief Engineer discussing the matter? —Yes.

Captain Lord and W/O Evans also gave evidence in the US Inquiry, similarly claiming that the *Californian* was stationary that night.

Californian witnesses are unanimous in this regard. Absolutely no-one makes any suggestion to the contrary. This is important, as we shall see in due course.

Meanwhile it should be borne in mind that the 11 p.m. wireless warning to the *Titanic* – 'we are stopped and surrounded by ice' – independently confirms the *Californian's*

POSTAL TELEGRAPH COMMERCIAL CABLES

CLARENCE H. MACKAY, President.

TELEGRAM

The Postal Telegraph-Cable Company (Incorporated) transmits and delivers this message subject to the terms and conditions printed on the back of this blank.

COUNTER NUMBER.	TIME FILED.	CHECK.	

Send the following message, without repeating, subject to the terms and conditions printed on the back hereof, which are hereby agreed to.

```
412  NY  79  GOVT              Received 6pm   4-25 1912
   WASHINGTON DD AML 25-12      Served on Captain Lord and
                                    Mr Evans 7pm
     Guy Murchie, Esq.,
        U. S. Marshal, Boston, Mass.

You are hereby authorized and deputized to serve subpoena on the

Captain and Wireless Operator of the Steamship California now at

Boston and scheduled to sail Saturday Evening next and to bring

with them the log of the Steamship California to appear forthwith

before subcommitte on Commerce U. S. Senate, Washn. D. C.   Will

   hear them promptly and will not detain them.   Answer.

                              D. M. Ransdell,

                         Sergeant at Arms, U. S. Senate.



A True Copy
   Attest:-        Guy Murchie

        United States Marshal for Massachusetts.
```

A telegraph from the Senate in Washington to the US Marshal at Boston, instructing him to serve subpoenas on the captain and wireless operator of the California *(sic). The instruction was carried out at 7 p.m. on 25 April 1912, an hour after receipt of this message.*

immobility, and does so in advance of *Titanic*'s collision. The evidence indicates that the Leyland liner SS *Californian* was stopped all night. To suggest otherwise is to suspect a mass conspiracy to deceive by every single man aboard *Californian*, when in fact her witnesses would tell very different stories in relation to their individual sightings that night.

There was no 'agreed story', except on one very salient fact: the *Californian* was immobile. This is a single important certainty on a night of myriad uncertainties.

2

THE SHIP NOT SEEN BY *TITANIC*

The ship seen by the *Titanic* in her throes of distress became known as the 'mystery ship'. She is the vessel charged by *Titanic* survivors with not going to their assistance at a time when the *Titanic* must have been brilliantly visible to the stranger and was both flashing Morse lamps and firing rockets to summon assistance.

The first thing to be said about the mystery ship, however, is that she was not discernible before the *Titanic* had her emergency, nor when she had completed her failed attempt to evade the iceberg, and had come to rest. Thus the mystery ship was initially not seen by *Titanic*, and this is a point worthy of particular and careful note.

It was the duty of the *Titanic's* lookouts to report anything they saw. This might seem obvious but it needs to be reinforced. Frederick Fleet (one of the lookouts when she struck the iceberg and for up to forty-five minutes afterwards) stated that 'We are only up there to report anything we see' (US Inquiry, p.318). Senator Smith (Chairman of the US Inquiry) pursued this statement, pressing Fleet on the issue:

> Smith: But you are expected to see – and report – anything in the path of the ship, are you not?
> Fleet: Anything we see – a ship, or anything.
> Smith: Anything you see?
> Fleet: Yes; anything we see.

Fred Fleet and Reginald Lee, the other lookout, did not see another ship or light on the horizon before, during, or after the collision until their shift was relieved at 12.23 a.m. They were serving an extended watch because the *Titanic's* clocks were due to be put back that night.

If the *Californian* was the *Titanic's* mystery ship, it ought to have been seen by Fleet and Lee, as the *Californian* was stationary, and had been for over an hour at this point. Fleet was adamant, however:

> Senator Smith: Were there lights of any other vessels in sight when you came down from the crow's nest?

Fleet: There was NO lights AT ALL when we was up in the crow's nest. This is after we was down and on the boats; *then* I seen the light.

Fleet was pressed on this point at the British Inquiry too. Here is his emphatic denial:

17429. Did you see this light on the port bow before you left the crow's nest? — No, it must have been about 1 o'clock.

17430. Did you observe it before you left the *Titanic*?

17430a. [The Commissioner] He says he saw it at 1 o'clock. [To the Witness]: When did you leave the *Titanic,* at what time?

Fleet: I think I got into the water in the boat about 1 o'clock.

17431. And it was about that time that you saw this light? — Or just a little before it; about that time.

Reg Lee, Fleet's lookout colleague in the crow's nest, did not see a light either while on duty:

2419. Before half-past eleven on that watch had you reported anything at all, do you remember? — There was nothing to be reported.

Yet Captain Lord of the *Californian* stated this:

7118/9. How far do you think your [masthead] lights would be observable by another ship? — I suppose the masthead lights you would see 7 or 8 miles. 8 miles I should think.

7120. Suppose the *Titanic* was 7 or 8 miles from you between 11.30 and 12 o'clock, would those on her bridge have been able to see your lights? — Easily.

Captain Lord said the officers on the *Titanic*'s bridge ought 'easily' to have seen lights if the *Californian* had indeed been 7 and 8 miles away. If it would have been an easy task on the bridge, how much easier would it have been from the lofty crow's nest, where the lookouts were stationed? The crow's nest was about 20ft higher than the bridge (question 2616) in order to give the lookouts just such an advantage over the bridge in surveying the full sweep of sea and sky.

It should be noted here that the limit of the visible horizon on this night would have been of the order of 10 to 12 miles – possibly more, since it was a spectacularly clear night.

Consider what the *Titanic*'s senior surviving officer, Second Officer Charles Lightoller, testified about lookout abilities on clear nights:

14309. The [lookout] man may, on a clear night, see the reflection of [a] light before it comes above the horizon. It may be the loom of the light and you see it sometimes sixty miles away.

If the mystery ship soon to be seen by the *Titanic* was the *Californian*, let us re-state then, that she, the *Californian*, was absolutely stationary. And if the *Californian* was the mystery ship, and stationary, then she should have been seen in advance of the collision by Fleet and Lee, the lookouts.

But she was not seen.

The lookouts, if indeed the *Californian* was to be the mystery ship, should have seen her as a light on the horizon long before the collision with the 'berg. *Titanic* observers, when they finally noticed the mystery ship, put her at an average distance of 5 miles. Less than halfway to the horizon!

If this light had always been stationary, only to be subsequently seen at 5 miles, and if the *Titanic*'s visible horizon was always a minimum of 10 miles (as it assuredly was), then at a pre-crash speed of 22 knots, the *Titanic* ought to have seen the light prior to impact for up to fifteen minutes! This is simple maths.

But no such light was seen. Not before impact, and not for a considerable time thereafter. Remember, it was the lookouts' duty to report lights all over the horizon. 'Anything we see', was the phrase Fleet used to describe their responsibilities. Before the impact, he and Lee had been 'looking all over the place, all around' (US, p.322). After the *Titanic* struck, it would have been particularly important for them to scan the 360 degree horizon. For a light! They should have been looking for precisely that: another ship. And they stayed on duty, diligently looking out, after the collision (US, p.319):

Fleet: I kept staring ahead again.
Senator Smith: You remained in the crow's nest?
Fleet: I remained in the crow's nest until I got relief.

They were relieved at 12.23 a.m., almost three-quarters of an hour after the collision at 11.40 p.m. And they had seen no light.

3

THE SHIP SEEN BY *TITANIC*

At last we come to the mystery ship, not previously seen, which now approached the *Titanic*, in the words of a senior surviving witness, *Titanic* Fourth Officer Joseph Groves Boxhall. Boxhall was the officer who watched this vessel, initially through binoculars, as she came ever closer to the stricken *Titanic*. He was adamant until his death that the ship he saw had ventured towards the RMS *Titanic* until the visitor next turned and stopped. This is what he stated at the US Inquiry (p.236):

> Senator Smith: Were the two masthead lights the first lights that you could see?
> Boxhall: The first lights.
> Sen. Smith: And what other lights?
> Boxhall: And then, as she got closer, she showed her side light, her red light.
> Sen. Smith: So you were quite sure she was coming in your direction?
> Boxhall: Quite sure.

Elsewhere in the inquiry, Boxhall declares (US Inquiry, p. 235):

> Boxhall: I saw his masthead lights and I saw his side light.
> Sen. Smith: In what direction?
> Boxhall: Almost ahead of us.

And later, he offers more details (US Inquiry, p.910) :

> Boxhall: She was headed toward us, meeting us.
> Senator Fletcher: Was she a little toward your port bow?
> Boxhall: Just about half a point off our port bow.

And, from the British Inquiry:

> Boxhall: I submitted the [SOS] position to the Captain first, and he told me to take it to the Marconi room.

15392. And then you saw this light which you say looked like a masthead light? — Yes, it was two masthead lights of a steamer.

15393. Could you see it distinctly with the naked eye? — No, I could see the light with the naked eye, but I could not define what it was; but by the aid of a pair of glasses I found it was the two masthead lights of a vessel, probably about half a point on the port bow, and in the position she would be showing her red if it were visible, but she was too far off then.

15394. Could you see how far off she was? — No, I could not see, but I had sent in the meantime for some rockets ... I was sending rockets off and watching this steamer. Between the time of sending the rockets off and watching the steamer approach us I was making myself generally useful...

Boxhall was sure that the mystery ship was 'approaching', 'coming', 'meeting us', getting closer, 'headed toward' *Titanic*. The *Californian* was stationary. The mystery ship was not. When did he see her first?

The evidence shows that it was after he had reckoned a revised SOS position (41° 46' N, 50° 14' W), a wireless position that was transmitted and heard by other ships, at what the British Inquiry decided was 12.25 a.m. *Titanic* time. Boxhall gave the following responses:

15388. Before I saw this light I went to the chart-room and worked out the ships position.

15389. Is that the position we have been given already – 41° 46' N, 50° 14' W? — That is right [Boxhall had earlier estimated a position of 41° 44' N, 50° 24' W, which the *Titanic* had been sending out from 12.15 a.m., until this position was revised ten minutes later].

Boxhall had first discerned a ship some time after revising the distress position at 12.25 a.m. It is likely therefore that the far-off light was not seen before 12.30 a.m., since lookouts Fleet and Lee had descended from the crow's nest, their shift having ended at 12.23 a.m. with nothing seen.

It is important to emphasise that there was no light seen for three-quarters of an hour between the time of impact, 11.40 p.m., and at least 12.23 a.m., when Fleet and Lee left the crow's nest.

Crew duty watches were due to change at this time, with a plan to put back *Titanic*'s time to midnight once 12.23 a.m. was reached. The clocks were to go back forty-seven minutes that night and it was to be done in two stages – twenty-three minutes and twenty-four minutes, at the end of elongated midnight and 4 a.m. watches. This was to allow for *Titanic*'s noon to be approximately correct as the vessel steamed ever westward.

The following is from the US Inquiry (p.460), when Quartermaster Robert Hichens was called:

Senator Smith: You left the wheelhouse that Sunday night at?
Hichens (interposing): Twenty-three minutes past 12.

Sen. Smith: Your watch had not expired?

Hichens: My watch had expired; yes.

Senator Smith also questioned Fleet on the issue:

Sen. Smith: How long a watch did you have?

Fleet: Two hours; but the time was going to be put back that watch.

Sen. Smith: The time was to be set back?

Fleet: Yes, sir.

Sen. Smith: Did that alter your time?

Fleet: We were to get about 2 hours and 20 minutes. (On watch from 10 p.m. to 12.23 a.m.)

Meanwhile Lee, Fleet's crow's nest colleague, would testify that he left the crow's nest at 12 a.m. – which time it was indeed, by the changed clock (see US Inquiry, p. 317).

Boxhall, we know, first saw the mystery ship at half a point off the port bow, virtually straight in front of the ship and the lookout cage or crow's nest. Yet it was only the relief lookouts who took over from 12.23 a.m. who later reported the remote light, said Fleet.

So, what does half a point off the port bow mean? There are thirty-two points on a compass, that is, eight in each quadrant, a quadrant being the area delineated by, for example, west and north. To understand 'half a point off the port bow,' imagine a place halfway between 11 and 12 on a clock face – effectively the position of the hour hand when the time is at 11.30. 'One point' is actually closer to 12, or the bow of a ship, than this. And half a point is closer again. It is the compass equivalent of just one minute to midnight on a clockface, therefore representing just a tiny amount off the port bow.

This mystery ship will eventually move from 'half a point' to two points and more off the port bow when further observed, which is indicative of movement, since the *Titanic* has stopped after impact, although she may drift slowly thereafter. Furthermore, this strange ship has come from being non-existent before 12.23 a.m., to being close enough for a single light to be spotted by Boxhall, then closer still, so that two masthead lights are discernible, until finally being so close that a port-side red light is discernible along with all other lights .

That's movement. The *Californian*, according to the evidence of her crew, was stationary.

A note about side lights: ships carried them to indicate what side they were presenting. A red light was carried on the port side and a green one to starboard. Side lights will become important again later in this analysis, but for now the only salient fact for this argument is that visible side lights indicate closeness.

The question of how close a side light needs to be in order to be visible is answered by some of those called to the inquiries. Charles Groves, Third Officer on SS *Californian*, was questioned on the issue (question 8419): 'What is the average range of an ordinary ship's side light? — Two miles'. William Lucas, *Titanic* AB, was also called, and suggested (question 1802): 'Could you see a side light eight or nine miles distant? — A night like that I could'.

Boxhall suggested in the US Inquiry (p.934):

> …I have already stated, in answer to a question, how far this ship was away from us, that
> I thought she was about 5 miles, and I arrived at it in this way. The masthead lights of
> a steamer are required by the Board of Trade regulations to show for 5 miles, and [side
> lights] are required to show for 2 miles.
>
> Senator Burton: You could see that distance on such a night as this?
>
> Boxhall: I could see quite clearly.
>
> Sen. Burton: You saw not only the mast light but the side lights?
>
> Boxhall: I saw the side lights. Whatever ship she was, she had beautiful lights. I think we
> could see her lights more than the regulation distance…

It should be noted again that the visible horizon from the *Titanic's* boat deck this starlit
night would have been of the order of 10 to 12 miles. A light high out of the water could
be seen for another few miles.

In summary then, Boxhall saw the red side light of that mystery vessel, and concluded
she was 'about 5 miles away', this mystery vessel having approached over the horizon,
from an unseen position, to stop halfway to *Titanic*. And *Californian* was stationary.
All night.

Boxhall was not alone on the *Titanic* in witnessing the strange ship approaching. Able
Seaman Edward Buley offers the following information (pp.611-612, US Inquiry):

> …Yes, sir; I saw it (the light) from the ship. That is what we told the passengers.
> We said, 'There is a steamer coming to our assistance'. That is what kept them quiet,
> I think.
>
> Senator Fletcher: Did that boat seem to be getting farther away from you?
>
> Buley: No; it seemed to be coming nearer.
>
> Sen. Fletcher: You are possessed of pretty good eyes?
>
> Buley: I can see … 21 miles, sir.
>
> Sen. Fletcher: Did she come toward you bow on?
>
> Buley: Yes, sir; bow on toward us, and then she stopped…

Boxhall said she approached bow on, eased to starboard and stopped, showing her red
light broadside.

Third class passenger Olaus Abelseth (p.1037, US Inquiry):

> I could not say, but it [a light off the port bow] did not seem to be so very far. I thought
> I could see this mast light, the front mast light. That is what I thought I could see. A little
> while later there was one of the Officers who came and said to be quiet, that there was a
> ship coming. That is all he said.

Second Officer Lightoller later wrote of reassuring passengers in this way.

BOXHALL AND CAPTAIN SMITH

We know Fleet and Lee, the lookouts, did not see the light of a ship during their watch, which ended twenty-three minutes after midnight. But if the *Californian* was stationary nearby, then she ought to have been seen. Yet it seems to have been the relieving pair, the 'other lookout', who first reported the light. This appears to have happened around 12.30 a.m. or shortly thereafter. Boxhall had computed a new SOS position before seeing the light, he testified, and this new position was first transmitted by the *Titanic* at 12.25 a.m., meaning he first saw the light only after this time. Fleet testifies (US Inquiry, p. 328):

> Fleet: There was no lights at all when we was up in the crow's nest. This is after we was down and on the [life]boats; *then* I seen the light.
> Senator Smith: Where did you see it?
> Fleet: On the port bow. The other lookout reported it.
> Sen. Smith: How far ahead?
> Fleet: It was not ahead; it was on the bow, about four points.
> Sen. Smith: I am not speaking of that. I wanted to know whether you saw ahead, while you were on the watch, on the lookout, Sunday night, after the collision occurred or before, any lights of any other ship.
> Fleet: No, sir.
> Sen. Smith: You saw no lights at all?
> Fleet: No, sir.

Fleet had been on duty with Reginald Lee, but we know that the phrase 'other lookout' does not refer to his crow's nest partner, because Lee testified to seeing nothing during the time when he was either on duty, or on deck, with Fleet:

> 2564. When the steamer struck, was there any light of any other vessel to be seen? — [Lee] No.
> 2574. Does that mean that you only saw that light after the *Titanic* sank? — After I was in the (life) boat, after leaving the ship.
> 2576. Before she sank had you seen that light? — No. It was only after being in the boat and away from the ship that we saw that light.

If Lee didn't report the light to Fleet, then it is most likely that Fleet's remark about the 'other lookout' means the relief pair of Alred Hogg and Frank Evans who ascended the crow's nest to take over lookout duty at 12.23 a.m. Slated to stay in the crow's nest until 2 a.m., they instead came down after twenty minutes on watch.

Hogg gave evidence at both inquiries, but incredibly was never asked whether he had seen a ship's light – whether in the nest, or later on deck. He says he did telephone the bridge after noticing confusion on deck, but received no answer.

The British Inquiry never teased out the point about when the mystery light was first seen, and in fact it failed to call Evans, Hogg's partner, at all. Hogg himself was treated only as a witness in relation to the lifeboat he eventually joined!

Let us recap: if the *Californian* was this light that appeared, then that light was necessarily stationary – and the relief lookouts should have seen it at once, even allowing for bizarre blindness on the part of Fleet and Lee. But the impression from the evidence is that some further time elapsed before the light that would become the mystery ship was first reported.

Let us briefly re-examine Boxhall before seeing which other witnesses corroborate his version of a ship that approaches so close that even the colour of her side lights can be discerned.

The following is a transcript of Boxhall at the British Inquiry:

> 15400. Did you watch the lights of this steamer while you were sending the rockets up? —Yes.
>
> 15401. Did they seem to be stationary? — I was paying most of my attention to this steamer then, and she was approaching us; and then I saw her side lights. I saw her green light and the red. She was end on to us. Later I saw her red light. This is all with the aid of a pair of glasses up to now. Afterwards I saw the ship's red light with my naked eye, and the two masthead lights. The only description of the ship that I could give is that she was, or I judged her to be, a four-masted steamer.
>
> 15403. Did the ship make any sort of answer, as far as you could see, to your rockets? — I did not see it. Some people say she did, and others say she did not. There were a lot of men on the bridge. I had a Quartermaster with me, and the Captain was standing by, at different times, watching this steamer.
>
> 15404. Do you mean you heard someone say she was answering your signals? — Yes, I did, and then she got close enough, and I Morsed to her – used our Morse lamp.

And slightly later in the Inquiry:

> 15408. Then you thought she was near enough to Morse her from the *Titanic*? — Yes, I do think so; I think so yet.
>
> 15409. [The Commissioner] What distance did you suppose her to be away? — I judged her to be between 5 and 6 miles when I Morsed to her, and then she turned round – she was turning very, very slowly – until at last I only saw her stern light, and that was just before I went away in the boat.

The *Californian* was stationary. But it is clear that Boxhall saw a ship approaching head on, corroborating Buley's statement, showing both her side lights, until this 'four-masted steamer' turned to starboard, easing away to the left as the *Titanic* watched, showing her port (left) side light – the red one – to the *Titanic*.

'At last' she showed her stern light, which is always white, and the mystery ship eventually moved away.

Boxhall says the captain of the *Titanic*, E.J. Smith, 'was standing by, at different times, watching this steamer'. Smith, a vastly experienced mariner, the most senior captain of the White Star Line, thus implicitly agrees with Boxhall that the mystery ship was initially coming closer. More than that, Captain Smith instructed Boxhall to send Morse code flashes with the message 'come at once, we are sinking'. This was no mere SOS, but a detailed transmission, sent with the expectation that the other ship would be able to read and understand the detail due to its close proximity.

Boxhall states (US Inquiry, p.235):

…She got close enough, as I thought, to read our electric Morse signal, and I signalled to her; I told her to come at once, we were sinking; and the Captain was standing… I told the Captain about this ship, and he was with me most of the time when we were signalling.
Senator Smith: Did he also see it?
Boxhall: Yes, sir.
Sen. Smith: Did he tell you to do anything else to arrest its attention?
Boxhall: I went over and started the Morse signal. He said, 'Tell him to come at once, we are sinking'.

This is a Morse lamp, which flashes dots and dashes in Morse and can typically be seen for a range of 5 miles. Boxhall says, in answer to question 15409: 'I judged her to be between 5 and 6 miles when I Morsed to her'.

Stanley Lord of the *Californian* would tell the US Inquiry that his vessel had 'a very powerful Morse lamp', adding: 'I suppose you can see that about 10 miles' (p.729). The *Titanic's* Morse lamp, in other words, would certainly have been visible to the new arrival, especially on such a clear night. One Morse lamp was mounted on top of each bridge-wing, with its flashes operated from a keyboard located below.

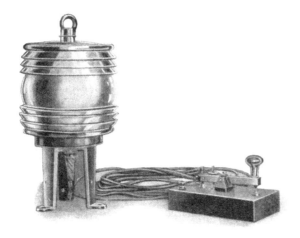

A ship's Morse lamp was a powerful communications tool. The Titanic *had two, located on top of the wing-cabs on either side of the bridge. The flashes ought to have been easily discernible, but* Titanic's *appeals were ignored by the mystery ship. Captain Lord testified that the* Californian's *own lamp could be read at a distance of 10 miles. He ordered repeated sessions of signalling to his vessel's nearby steamer, but it too remained unresponsive.*

Yet despite the *Titanic* being only 5 or 6 miles distant from the mystery ship in the estimate of Boxhall (and in the implied agreement of Captain Smith), the officers aboard the critically-wounded new luxury liner could not detect any positive response whatsoever to their Morsing:

15412. Did [anyone on *Titanic* see the mystery ship] Morsing in answer to your Morse signals? —
[Boxhall] They did not say she Morsed, but they said she showed a light. Then I got the Quartermaster [George Rowe] who was with me to call her up with our lamps, so that I could use the glasses to see if I could see signs of any answer; but I could not see any.
15413. You could not see any with the glasses? — No; and Captain Smith also looked, and he could not see any answer.
15414. He also looked at her through the glasses? — Yes.

It will be shown later that the *Californian*, coincidentally, could also see an unknown ship in her own location. This is a coincidence too far for some, but will be closely examined later. Meanwhile it is important to note that the *Californian's* evidence was that she herself flashed a Morse lamp repeatedly at her own stranger and never received an answer.

Those who were Morsing the neighbouring vessel from *Californian* said their stranger was a small to medium-sized cargo steamer only 5 miles away. But if the *Californian*, with her 'powerful' Morse lamp, really lay only 5 to 6 miles from *Titanic*, then her visual signals ought to have been clearly seen on the *Titanic* on a night of brilliant visibility. After all, Captain Smith of the RMS *Titanic* imagined that his mystery ship could read a complicated message: 'come at once, we are sinking'. *Californian's* Morse light, being very powerful, should have been seen at 'about ten miles'. The *Titanic*, lying 5 to 6 miles away from a puzzling presence, could detect no Morse replies.

Since neither inquiry ever disputed the evidence that the *Californian* repeatedly Morsed a vessel that approached her and stopped, the implication must be, once again, that the stationary yet Morsing *Californian* was not the RMS *Titanic's* approaching and uncommunicative stranger.

Let us return to the suggestion from the evidence that Captain Smith shares Boxhall's conviction that the *Titanic's* mystery ship has moved close. Bedroom steward Alfred Crawford separately provides corroboration of Captain Smith's conclusion that the mystery ship was close enough to Morse by lamp. Crawford went away in boat No.8, one of the early boats, launched from the port side at 1.10 a.m. He said he was ordered to use his oars to row to the nearby vessel! In question 17964 at the British Inquiry, Commissioner Mersey suggested: 'The gentleman who gave you that order must, I suppose, have thought that the lights that were visible were close to? Did Captain Smith say to you "Make for those lights"?' Crawford replied: 'He did'. Mersey went on to ask whether Smith ordered Crawford to 'Put your passengers on board that ship with those lights and then come back here' (17965). Crawford replied 'Yes, my Lord'. The Commissioner continued: 'Then I presume – I do not know – that he must have thought those lights were close to. I do not at present think he is right about that'.

The first part of this observation by the President of the British Inquiry makes sense, and is in accordance with the evidence. The latter part indicates, perhaps, a desire that it should be the other way! Commissioner Mersey would eventually convict the *Californian* of being the mystery ship.

Seaman Thomas Jones and passenger Mrs J. Stuart White were both also in boat No.8, and back up Crawford (US Inquiry, p.570):

> Jones: This No.8 boat was there… I jumped in the boat. The Captain asked me was the plug in the boat, and I answered, 'Yes, sir'… He told me to row for the light, and land the passengers and return to the ship. I pulled for the light, and I found that I could not get near… I had to carry out the Captain's orders and pull for that light; so I did so.
> Senator Newlands: Who was the officer on the port side who gave you your directions? — The Captain.
> Sen. Newlands: The Captain himself? — Yes, sir.

And Mrs White's evidence follows (US Inquiry, p.1007):

> Mrs White: We simply rowed away. We had the order, on leaving the ship, to do that. The officer who put us in the boat – (I do not know who he was whether an officer or the Captain) – gave strict orders to the seamen, or the men, to make for the light opposite and land the passengers and get back just as soon as possible. That was the light that everybody saw in the distance.

Further corroboration is given by the Countess of Rothes in an interview with *The Journal of Commerce*, 24 April 1912:

> Captain Smith stood next to me as we got in, and told Tom Jones, a sailor who acted nobly, to row straight for those ship lights over there, land the passengers aboard, and return as soon as possible.
> For three hours we pulled steadily for the lights seen three miles away; then we saw a port light vanish and the masthead lights grow dimmer until they disappeared.

The Countess is clearly talking about ship lights that subsequently moved away. The *Californian*, by the evidence of all aboard, did not move at all during this timeframe.

Meanwhile, Captain Smith was still giving those same orders later, to boat No.6, launched after No.8. Mrs Lucian P. Smith recalled that: 'The Captain looked over to see us… there was a small light on the horizon that we were told to row towards' (US Inquiry, p.1150); Quartermaster Robert Hichens states: 'I think I got in No.6 boat, sir; put in charge of her by the second officer, Mr Lightoller. We lowered away from the ship, sir, and were told to "Pull toward that light"' (US Inquiry, p.451).

Nightwatchman James Johnson was saved with Fourth Officer Boxhall in boat No.2, whose departure was officially put at 1.45 a.m. He suggested Captain Smith could still see the light at this late stage:

> 3677. Did you hear any order given by the Captain as to the sending away of your boat?
> — I think it was the Captain told us to make for that light and come back again.
> 3678. Did you hear him tell the fourth officer to go away? —Yes, and come back.

And, from the US Inquiry affidavit of Mrs Mahala Douglas (p.1101):

> Mr Boxhall was trying to get the boat off, and called to the Captain on the bridge, 'There's a boat coming up over there'. The Captain said 'I want a megaphone'...

So Captain Smith agreed with Boxhall that the ship had approached, and he believed her to be coming closer; indeed, so close that he might finally be able to hail her to issue instructions. Such closeness is simply inconsistent with both *Titanic* and *Californian* missing Morse.

TITANIC'S OTHER OFFICERS

Three considerations, arguably, ought to guide the reader on the movement question surrounding the *Titanic's* mystery ship.

Firstly, most credibility should be given to those who watched that ship, being tasked to that essential duty if all aboard *Titanic* were to be saved, rather than to those who commented on the basis of casual glances or impressions. Essentially this means concentrating on Fourth Officer Boxhall, whose account is unwavering about an approaching ship, and who finds implied support in his account from Captain Smith (who did not survive) as well as specific support from fellow officers who were saved.

Secondly, weight must be placed where it properly resides for observations at sea at night: with those trained to the task. This means officers of the watch and lookouts. Fred Fleet testified that he and Lee saw no other ship before or after the collision until a light was reported after they had climbed down from the crow's nest and were on duty at the boats.

Thirdly, we should favour observations from the boat deck of the *Titanic*, with its 70ft vantage point above sea level, rather than impressions gained from the hopelessly unreliable sea level viewpoint of a person in a lifeboat.

To recap a moment: Do we imagine *both* lookouts could have missed the stationary *Californian* over forty-five minutes? And do we also imagine that Boxhall is next in error by managing to see the immobile *Californian*, yet somehow imagining her to be moving instead of stationary? Do we further imagine that Captain Smith of the *Titanic*, while not making the 'invisible' mistake of Fleet and Lee, happens to make a different mistake about that ship, yet the same mistake as Boxhall, which led Boxhall to believe that Smith fully agreed with his assessment of the mystery ship's approach?

These four glaring 'mistakes' by key eyewitnesses must each happen in turn, it would appear, if the *Californian* is to be even considered as the mystery ship. Lookouts Fleet and Lee, Officer Boxhall and Captain Smith must all, separately and together, be mistaken on that night in 1912 if we are to believe those who later equated the *Californian* with the mystery ship. The *Californian* cannot have been moving: she was indeed stopped. So if she was stopped, the lookouts should have seen her. And when Boxhall and Smith saw her to be moving, they should instead have seen her as stationary. By far the greater likelihood, one would imagine, is that Fleet, Lee, Boxhall and Smith are correct, as the testimony (or implied witness) of all four is consistent with the late appearance of a moving ship and nothing else.

Let us examine now the evidence of those men to whom we must give the greatest weight in evidence. Not *Titanic* cooks or bedroom stewards, nor barbers nor greasers, nor even landlubber passengers. But the other officers of the RMS *Titanic*.

Chief Officer Wilde, First Officer Murdoch and Sixth Officer Moody were all lost in the disaster and offered no evidence to the inquiries. Captain Smith was lost too, but we have second-hand accounts of his attitude and behaviour. What of the surviving officers? Take these prime survivors in order: Second Officer Charles Lightoller, Third Officer Herbert Pitman, Fourth Officer Joseph Boxhall (already mentioned), and Fifth Officer Harold Lowe.

Second Officer Charles Herbert Lightoller saw:

14138. A white light about two points on the port bow; whether it was one or two lights I could not say. As to whether it was a mast-head light or a stern light, I could not say. I was perfectly sure it was a light attached to a vessel, whether a steamship or a sailing ship I could not say. I could not distinguish any other coloured lights, but merely it was a white light, distinct and plain.

14140. [The Commissioner] Can you form any estimate of the distance of the light from the *Titanic*? —Yes, my Lord; certainly not over 5 miles away.

And a little later in the Inquiry:

14145. Did you observe it yourself, or was your attention called to it? — No, I noticed it.

14147. Other people saw it, too, I suppose. Did you continue to see it when you looked from that time forward until the ship went down, or did it disappear?

Lightoller — I cannot say how long I noticed it. I saw it perhaps half an hour, probably about half an hour. I can recollect seeing it for about half an hour.

Lightoller elsewhere insisted this vessel was stationary - which it could have been, by the time he saw it, and he noticed it for just half an hour. Lightoller, who was phenomenally busy all night, also mentions a stern light. Boxhall's mystery ship, having been stationary, eventually turned until all he could see was a stern light, going away, as he told the British Inquiry, in reponse to question 15409.

Third Officer Herbert Pitman, who also saw the light as stationary, stated:

15061. Whilst you were in the (life)boat and before the ship sank, did you see any light or lights which you took to be the light or lights of another steamer? — [Pitman] I saw a white light which I took to be the stern light of a sailing ship.

15062. How far away did you judge it to be? — I thought it was about five miles.

15063. That would be a good distance to see a stern light, would it not? — Yes, it may have been less.

15064. Was it a good night for seeing a light; for seeing a good stern light? — An excellent night.

This is the evidence of Fifth Officer Harold Lowe:

15825. Did you look for any lights at this time at all? — [Lowe] As I was getting the emergency boat ready, No. 1, Mr Boxhall was firing the detonators, the distress signals, and somebody mentioned something about a ship on the port bow, and I glanced over in that direction casually and I saw a steamer there.

15826. What did you see of her? — I saw her two masthead and her red side lights.

Fifth Officer Lowe therefore agrees with Fourth Officer Boxhall. He too saw a red side light. Lowe was working at boat No. 1 at the time, which went off around 1.10 a.m. Pitman and Boxhall would seem to agree on seeing a late stern light. Lightoller could only distinguish a vessel near at hand.

So here we are: *all* the surviving *Titanic* officers – Lightoller, Lowe, Boxhall and Pitman – see a *close* ship, at an average estimation of 5 miles away. That ship was not seen previously. The surviving officers all first see her long *after* the iceberg collision. And Boxhall, like Captain Smith, observed her with binoculars. Boxhall, who survived, said he was 'absolutely sure' about the steamer's approach.

Consider Boxhall's critical duty and onerous responsibility at this time of emergency. Would he really report his time-consuming observations utterly incorrectly? He needs glasses to make out the light at first, but later says he can see her side light with his naked eye, just as Lowe (and other crew, as we shall see) can also see it and identify its colour with their naked eyes, all in complete agreement. And this, after lookouts previously couldn't see *any* light, never mind anything as close as red or green side lights (designed to be visible at 2 miles).

It is submitted that there can only be one conclusion, based on the evidence: That the mystery ship was moving at some stage. Yet it is uncontested that the *Californian* was stationary all night.

4

A RED LIGHT'S IMPORTANCE

The official verdict in 1912 – that the *Titanic's* mystery ship was the *Californian* – pays no attention to the testimony about the mystery ship eventually showing a stern light, as outlined by the officer witnesses in the previous chapter.

Yet because the *Californian* was pointing north-east when she stopped at 10.21 a.m. (see the beginning of this book), and knowing her rate of drift, it is inescapably true that she would *never* have shown her stern light to the *Titanic* that night. Pointing north-east, and drifting very slowly in a clockwise direction, the *Californian* would have shown any observer to the southward and eastward a *green* side light, on her starboard side (red light showing to port). And it is known from the location of the wreck site that the *Titanic* was indeed both to the south and east of the *Californian's* cited stop position. Therefore the *Titanic* ought to have seen the *Californian's* green side light, not her red. It is critically important to grasp this irreducible verity.

A ship has two side lights. The *Californian* pointing north-east would have thrown light like this '%', the circles to either side of the percentage sign representing her port and starboard lights. The port light, left side, was red. The starboard light, right side, was green. If the mystery ship was the *Californian*, then not only should she have been stopped instead of moving, but she should also have shown the *Titanic* her green light, not her red.

Boxhall (US Inquiry, p.933) states:

> I saw the masthead lights first, the two steaming lights; and then, as she drew up closer, I saw her side lights through my glasses, and eventually I saw the red light. I had seen the green, but I saw the red most of the time. I saw the red light with my naked eye.

And it is clear that use of the word 'eventually' refers only to the mystery steamer turning to starboard as she came closer, thus showing her red. The following extract shows that Boxhall saw the red light almost from the beginning (US Inquiry, p.236):

> Senator Smith: Were the two masthead lights the first lights that you could see? — The first lights.

Sen. Smith: And what other lights? — And then, as she got closer, she showed her side light, her red light.

Sen. Smith: So you were quite sure she was coming in your direction? — Quite sure.

In other words, the red light that Boxhall sees arrives too quickly to be the product of the *Californian* drifting clockwise interminably until she finally shows the red light on her port side. Officer Lowe, we have established, also saw a red light when he casually glanced up at the stranger while working at lifeboat No.1 at 1.10 a.m.

So, who else saw a red light on the mystery ship? Nightwatchman James Johnson:

3482. Did you see that light from the deck of the *Titanic*? — I should think we saw it for about twenty minutes on the port bow…

3486. I should consider it would be about eight or ten miles off…

And later:

3503. When we got away it disappeared altogether.

3504. What coloured light was it? — I think it was red. I think there were two lights, in fact, a red and a white light.

3505. [The Commissioner] Are you sure? — I can discern any sort of colour, racing, a mile and a quarter off, and I think I could see a red light.

3506. Are you sure? — I am certain.

Quartermaster Walter Wynn:

13336. While you were in the (life)boat did you see any light or lights? — I did.

13337. What did you see? — I saw a red light first, and then the red light disappeared, and I saw a white one.

13338. What did you think the red light was? — I could not say; I put it down to a steamer.

13339. You thought it was the port light of a steamer? — Yes.

13350. …It went away, and then I saw the white light about 10 or 15 minutes afterwards again in the same direction.

13351. I think you mean this, do you not, that you assumed that the white light you saw on the later occasion was the white light you had been seeing before? — Or it might have been a stern light.

And Steward Alfred Crawford gives the following evidence:

17847. And before you left the ship's side did Captain Smith give you any directions with regard to a light? — Yes, he pointed to a light on the port side…

17850. I should say she was 5 to 7 miles away from us…

17852. The Captain gave the directions? —Yes, he pointed the ship out...

17870. Did you yourself ever see any side-lights? —Yes...

17872. What side-light or side-lights of that steamer did you see? — There was the red and the green light.

17873. You saw them both? —Yes...

17968. [The Commissioner] This was about one o'clock in the morning? — About 1 a.m., yes...

18000. At what time was it you first saw her? — Just after one, when the Captain pointed it out.

18001. And how long had you her under observation? — Nearly all the night.

18002. What happened to her afterwards; did she come nearer to you, or did she disappear? — I could not say. We saw the *Carpathia* coming up, and we turned round and made for that one.

The evidence of AB William Lucas follows:

1566. Did you see any light? —Well, I did see a light, a faint side light of another ship...

1569. Where was it? — Off my port hand as I was in the boat.

1570. Do you mean it was a port light? Was it a red or a green light? — A red light, a side light.

And Bathroom Steward Charles Donald Mackay gave the following responses:

10803. Did you see what you thought was a light? —Yes, we thought there was a ship's stern light.

10804. Was it a white light or a coloured light? — It was a reddish light [he thinks on the starboard side of the *Titanic*].

Only Assistant Cook John Collins thought he saw a green light alone (US Inquiry, p.629):

...I looked back at her [*Titanic's*] stern end and I saw a green light.

Senator Bourne: What did you think it was, one of your own boats?

Collins: No, sir; I did not really think of what it was until the firemen and sailors came up and said that it was a boat.

Sen. Bourne: That is, a ship?

Collins: Yes, sir.

Sen. Bourne: What became of it?

Collins: Sir, it disappeared.

Sen. Bourne: How long was it visible?

Collins: About 20 minutes or half an hour, I am sure it was.

How far away, would you think, from the *Titanic*? — I guess it would be about 4 miles; I am sure, 3 or 4 miles.

Some of *Titanic's* lifeboats had green lights. However Collins is the only *Titanic* witness to specify a ship showing solely a green light. Later in his testimony he reveals:

> We were drifting about there; we drifted, I am sure, a mile and a half from the *Titanic*, from where she sank, and there was some lifeboat that had a green light on it, and we thought it was a boat after the *Titanic* had sunk. We thought this green light was some boat, and we commenced to shout. All we saw was the green light. We were drifting about for two hours, and then we saw the lights of the *Carpathia*.

Green flares were burned during the night by Officer Boxhall in lifeboat No.2. The cumulative evidence shows that the mystery ship was showing her red light for a long time. There is no evidence whatsoever from *Titanic* witnesses that the mystery ship was showing simply a green side light. Yet, if the mystery ship was to be the *Californian*, she should have been showing her green light from the very start; a green light alone, and still a green light until all hope of rescue was cruelly extinguished.

WHY COULDN'T THEY REACH A STATIONARY SHIP?

A number of *Titanic* witnesses say the light, at the time they saw it, was 'stationary,' or 'always seemed the same distance away'. It was even said to be 'there all night'. Of course, if it was there, and never moved at all, then it must have been even more visible in daylight! How is it then, that a vessel, stationary all night, was not seen in the morning? Why did all boats turn around and head for the *Carpathia*?

This is not an academic point. It is pure common sense. A stationary ship, whose red light and masthead lights had already been seen, *must* be visible in the morning after hours of pulling towards her, if she remained stationary (as *Californian* did until 6 a.m.). Dawn broke on the morning of 15 April 1912, no later than 4.30 a.m., three quarters of an hour before the *Californian* engaged engines for the first time (5.15 a.m. engines started). Daylight thus came a full hour and a half before the *Californian* began to move. Alfred Crawford gives the following evidence relating to the time of daybreak (US Inquiry, p.114):

> Senator Smith: What time did the day break on Monday?
> Steward Alfred Crawford: About 4 o'clock, I should say, it began to get light.

And here is James Gibson, Apprentice Officer aboard SS *Californian*:

> 7594. If it was twenty minutes to four it was not very far off the beginning of dawn, was it? — No, dawn was just breaking.

Harold Cottam, wireless operator aboard SS *Carpathia*, states (US Inquiry, p.109):

About 20 to half past 4, ship's time, just as the dawn was coming on; about half past 4 in
the morning.
Senator Smith: It was nearing dawn?
Mr Cottam: Yes, sir.

Arthur Rostron, captain of the *Carpathia* (question 25551) claimed that 'it was daylight
at about 4.20 a.m.' Herbert Pitman, *Titanic* Third Officer, gave the following evidence
(US Inquiry, p.292):

Yes; that must have been about 4 o'clock.
Senator Smith: Daybreak?
Pitman: It was just breaking day; yes.

And passenger Major Arthur Peuchen agreed (US Inquiry, p.350):

Senator Newlands: What time did the dawn come?
Peuchen: We could just commence to distinguish light, I think, about near 4 o'clock.

The *Californian* was stationary in the after-dawn (up to 6 a.m.), as it had been stationary
all night. Not a single person in any lifeboat gave sworn evidence of seeing the mystery
ship in daylight after hours of hard rowing in her direction. If she was still there, they
might at least have carefully marked her funnel colour, the most basic aid to identification.
The *Californian*'s funnel was pink. But nobody saw anything of the ship they had pursued.
Crawford, quoted above about the dawn, was in boat No.8. He and his occupants had
made most progress of all towards the light, and were *furthest* from the *Carpathia*, the ship
which eventually arrived to rescue survivors.
    Crawford is questioned below:

18052. You have not told us what distance you rowed in the direction of these lights? — I
should say between 3 and 4 miles [see *Titanic* officer estimates of the ship being around 5
miles away]. By the time the morning came we were furthest away from the *Carpathia*.
18053. Did they [the lights] ever appear to get any nearer? — No.

Lookout Reginald Lee said (question 565): 'There was a ship apparently ahead of the
Titanic, as she was then, but that ship was supposed to have disappeared. Anyway, we did
not see her in the morning.'
    Passengers could, however, see icebergs; survivor Arthur Peuchen estimating one to
be 5 miles away, while *Titanic* Third Officer Herbert Pitman saw the lights of the even-
tual rescue vessel *Carpathia* 'about half past three, as near as I can recollect... we could
see the masthead light over five miles on a clear night'. They had rowed strenuously
towards a mystery light, and now with a clear view in daylight, they could not see any
other steamer.

Perhaps, like Fleet, Lee, Captain Smith, Fourth Officer Boxhall, Fifth Officer Lowe, and so many others, they were all mistaken. How many mistakes of blindness would that be? There were 712 survivors, therefore 712 'mistakes'… Yet the 712 did not make any mistake in seeing the smoke, then the funnel, then the faint shapes, then the reality of the *Carpathia*. They should have seen two ships. They should have had a choice. They only saw one ship – *Carpathia* – and had no choice.

Think about the *Carpathia*, with a huge height advantage over the lifeboats. If there was a stationary ship within a 5 mile radius, the *Carpathia* could not have helped but see her. And, unlike the *Titanic*, there was nothing to stop her eventually reaching such a vessel, as would be required, to check whether she had any survivors, being so close to the scene. But the arriving *Carpathia* saw no such ship in the vicinity. That ship had gone.

The problem is summed up by Crawford in boat No.8 (US Inquiry, pp.829-830):

Senator Fletcher: But you could see the lights very distinctly?

Crawford: Very distinctly; yes, sir.

Senator Fletcher: How was it that when day broke, and the sun rose, you could not see any ship?

Crawford: I could not say. We saw the other ship coming to us, and we turned around for it.

Senator Fletcher: But you could see nothing in the way of a ship or vessel, or anything, where these lights were?

Crawford: No, sir.

The same dilemma confronted Quartermaster Arthur Bright in collapsible 'D' (US Inquiry, p.838):

Senator Fletcher: You did not see any ship or vessel of any sort next morning, in the direction of the light that you had seen during the night?

Bright: No. That seemed to disappear all at once. The next we saw was the *Carpathia*, just before daylight.

Sen. Fletcher: How far were you from her when you first saw the *Carpathia*?

Bright: About 4 miles.

Sen. Fletcher: You say that was before daylight?

Bright: Just before daylight, she came in sight.

The mystery ship was not there all night because she was demonstrably not there in the morning. She had moved. *Californian* did not move. Therefore *Californian* is not the mystery ship.

An alternative is, as many puzzled and exhausted passengers and crew came to believe, that the mystery light was 'imaginary', a figment of nature, or a star. If this is the case, then it automatically exculpates the *Californian*. But stars do not have red and green lights and masthead lights and they certainly do not approach.

The 'imaginary light' suggestion cannot explain what was patiently watched by experienced officers who were using binoculars on the boat deck. And so it must be found that a close ship, with coloured lights, did indeed exist and did indeed come very close at one point to the sinking *Titanic*.

We should also bear in mind that a light on the horizon will always look stationary from a lifeboat – until it disappears. This is like watching a ship from the beach on a trip to the seaside, except that at night there are no visible landmarks by which to check progress. There is also the point that, for some of the night at least, the mystery ship, having approached, *was* stationary (in Boxhall and Buley's expressed view) before pulling away.

Some of the 'stationary' evidence undoubtedly backs up Boxhall, but fails to mention the disappearance, and the reasons for this can only be guessed at. However, it can be readily observed that the quality of being stationary can be a moveable feast – a witness who says 'the light was stationary' does not inherently exclude the possibility that it later vanished, as indeed it did and must have done.

It is perhaps wise to beware of inexperienced witnesses giving impressions from a hopeless vantage point, as is the case with the accounts of civilian passengers in lifeboats. Yet those who insist *Californian* must be the mystery ship would have us believe the impressions of just some of these members of the British and American public, untrained in observation, sitting flat on the sea, who say 'the light was stationary' as if this were a categorical position the whole night. Because 'morning-after evidence' refutes it completely.

No, surely it is preferable to rely on the night-before accounts of Joseph Boxhall and his experienced fellow officers. These were trained men, with long years of night observations behind them, and with Boxhall and Smith using binoculars. And all the officers had a better vantage point: *Titanic*'s deck, 70ft up. Now consider the poor vantage point of the lifeboats, whose limited field of vision will prove a key point in the debate. Those in the *Titanic* lifeboats continued to see not just the masthead light, but the red side light of the mystery ship even after they got down on the water. This kills the idea that the mystery ship was any distance away other than the closeness described by *Titanic* officers.

The horizon of the lifeboats is small. How can occupants of such craft, set adrift on the New York track, see a vessel on the Boston track (Boston-bound *Californian* being labelled the mystery ship)?

The mystery ship was *near*. Quartermaster Walter Wynn (lifeboat No.9) claims:

13336. While you were in the (life)boat did you see any light or lights? — I did.

13337. What did you see? — I saw a red light first, and then the red light disappeared, and I saw a white one.

13338. What did you think the red light was? — I could not say; I put it down to a steamer.

The side light was below the bridge of the ship observed, far below the masthead light! AB William Lucas (collapsible 'D') gives the following responses:

1566. Did you see any light? — Well, I did see a light, a faint side light of another ship.

1569. Where was it? — Off my port hand as I was in the (life)boat. Do you mean it was a port light? Was it a red or a green light? — A red light – a side light.

To recall the evidence of nightwatchman James Johnson (lifeboat No.2):

3502. Then you had not gone very far towards the light? — A mile and a half. I am certain we pulled that.

3503. Did this light seem to get fainter or did it disappear suddenly?—When we got away it disappeared altogether.

3504. What coloured light was it? — I think it was red. I think there were two lights, in fact, a red and a white light.

3505. [Lord Mersey] Are you sure? — I can discern any sort of colour, racing, a mile and a quarter off, and I think I could see a red light.

3506. Are you sure? — I am certain.

And, in addition, here is the evidence of Bathroom Steward Charles Mackay (lifeboat No.11):

10802. Did you see a light while you were in the [life]boat? — A supposed light do you mean?

10803. Well, I do not know whether it was a supposed light or not. Did you see what you thought was a light? —Yes, we thought there was a ship's stern light.

10804. Was it a white light or a coloured light? — It was a reddish light.

10805. And you thought it was the stern light of a ship? —Yes.

10809. And did you row towards that light? — For a matter of about two hours as hard as we could row.

To develop this point further: the height of the crossbench or 'thwart' in a *Titanic* lifeboat was less than 2ft (most chair seats are only 18in high). Imagine that a man is standing up on the thwart – and furthermore that he happens to be the tallest man in the world at the time, a strapping 7½ft tall. Lop off 6in to get 7ft as the height of his eye. Plus 2ft for the thwart height, gives 9ft off the water. Now we will find the mileage from the lifeboat to the horizon, which has retracted sharply from standing on the *Titanic* because of the reduced height of the observer. An age-old formula says it is 1.17 times the square root of the height of one's eye (9ft in this case). Square root is three. Three times 1.17 is 3.51 nautical miles. The lifeboat horizon for the world's tallest man, then, is a maximum of 3½ miles. This must be added to 7.8 miles (the *Californian's* own visible horizon) for any element of a ship the height of the *Californian* to be seen. This amounts to 11.3 miles. For the tallest man in the world, standing up on a thwart, just glimpsing the looming of a masthead light, with everything else hull down. Any further and nothing at all will be seen. Just the darkness.

But a side light is much further down than a masthead light, and the lifeboat occupants are of average height, sitting down. They continued to see the red light of the mystery ship from the lifeboats. The realistic distance to that ship is thus of the order of 5 miles – until she disappears.

Let us now recap what is indicated by testimony thus far. Firstly, the mystery ship was *moving*. Yet the *Californian* was stationary. Secondly, the mystery ship showed her *red* light 'most of the time'. Yet the *Californian*, if she were indeed the mystery ship, would have been showing *Titanic* her *green* light. Thirdly, the lifeboats could not make any progress to the mystery ship, nor see her in the morning; if the mystery ship was indeed the *Californian*, they should have made progress *and* seen her after dawn. Lastly, we can observe that the mystery ship came very near at one point, because even her red sidelight, below the bridge, could be seen from the lifeboats. In short, the evidence thus far from *Titanic* observers is against the mystery ship being the *Californian*. And it is worth repeating – the issue is the *Titanic's* mystery ship. *Titanic* witnesses have no reason to lie!

5

THE MYSTERY SHIP GOES AWAY

We can recall that some *Titanic* witnesses claimed that the light was 'stationary', 'there all night', and 'always seemed the same distance away'. For the record, it should be indicated that this was by no means the universal feeling. And we know that the mystery ship was quite evidently not there in the morning.

It is argued here that Boxhall, the Fourth Officer charged with observing the mystery ship, got it right when he saw a light approach, develop into two masthead lights, become a ship showing both red and green side lights, and then turn to starboard, and lie apparently stationary there for some time, showing only the red light (port side) 'most of the time' to the *Titanic*. What happened later?

Let us see how Boxhall describes that mystery ship arrive, turn, then appear to move slowly, but inexorably, away (US Inquiry, pp.933-934):

Boxhall: I think I saw the green light before I saw the red light, as a matter of fact. But the ship was meeting us. I am covering the whole thing by saying the ship was meeting us.
Senator Burton: Your impression is she turned away, or turned on a different course?
Boxhall: That is my impression.
Sen. Burton: At a later time, when you were in the boat after it had been lowered, what light did you see? [Boxhall went away in boat No.2 around 1.45 a.m., more than an hour after he first saw the light]
Boxhall: I saw this single light, which I took to be her stern light, just before I went away in the boat, as near as I can say.
Sen. Burton: How long did you see this stern light?
Boxhall: I saw it until I pulled around the [*Titanic's*] stern [to the starboard side, blocking his view]. I had laid off a little while on the port side, on which side I was lowered, and then I afterwards pulled around the ship's stern, and, of course, then I lost the light, and I never saw it anymore.
Sen. Burton: Her course, as she came on, would have been nearer to your course; that is, your course was ahead, there, and she was coming in toward your course?
Boxhall: Yes, sir; she was slightly crossing it, evidently. I suppose she was turning around slowly.

Sen. Burton: Is it your idea that she turned away?

Boxhall: That is my idea, sir…

Sen. Burton: She kept on a general course toward the east, and then bore away from you, or what?

Boxhall: I do not think she was doing much steaming. I do not think the ship was steaming very much, because after I first saw the masthead lights she must have been still steaming, but by the time I saw her red light with my naked eye she was not steaming very much. So she had probably gotten into the ice, and turned around.

Sen. Burton: What do you think happened after she turned around? Do you think she went away to avoid the ice?

Boxhall: I do not know whether she stayed there all night, or what she did. I lost the light. I did not see her after we pulled around to the starboard side of the *Titanic*.

Sen. Burton: Then you lost track of her?

Boxhall: Yes.

Sen. Burton: And you saw her no more after that?

Boxhall: No, sir.

First class passenger Archibald Gracie remained on deck after Boxhall had left and, indeed, after all the lifeboats were gone. He wrote in his 1913 book *The Truth About the Titanic*:

> To reassure the ladies of whom I had special charge, I showed them a bright white light of what I took to be a ship about five miles off and which I felt sure was coming to our rescue. Colonel Astor heard me telling this to them and he asked me to show it, and I pointed the light out to him… but instead of growing brighter the light grew dim and less and less distinct and passed away altogether.

There now follows a sample of *Titanic* witnesses who felt the ship or light went away. If they are correct and the ship was underway, then she was not the *Californian*. But do not necessarily rely on these accounts, as no witness in a lifeboat can be realistically relied upon. These extracts are intended merely to show that it was not universally agreed that the *Titanic*'s mystery ship was 'there all night', 'stationary' or 'always the same distance away'. Let us now leave it with experienced seafarers, not civilian passengers, and hear the opinions of crew only. Firstly, AB George Symons:

> 11712. Did you row towards the light that you had mentioned? — We were rowing for the light. The light bearing roughly on our port beam when we were rowing away from the ship.
>
> 11715. Did you appear to be catching it up at all? — No I thought my own self she was gradually going away from us.

We also have the evidence of Quartermaster Robert Hichens:

1183. Could you tell at all whether the light was moving or whether it was still? — The light was moving, gradually disappearing. We did not seem to get no nearer to it.

1184. As I understand you, it seemed to get further away from you? — Yes, sir.

Lookout Fred Fleet states the following (US Inquiry, p. 326):

> We pulled for it, but we did not seem to get any nearer to it...
> Senator Smith: How close could you get to it?
> Fleet: She was getting away off...

Able Seaman Frank Osman (US Inquiry, p. 539):

> Senator Burton: When did you last have a sight of that light? – About an hour afterwards.
> What do you think about it? Did it sail away? – Yes, sir; she sailed right away.

Here is Seaman William Lucas:

> 1804. You saw nothing more of the vessel to which those lights belonged? — No; the light went further away every time we looked at it.

Nightwatchman James Johnson claims:

> 3503. Did this light seem to get fainter or did it disappear suddenly? — When we got away it disappeared altogether.

Steward Alfred Crawford (US Inquiry, p. 828):

> Senator Smith: Did you see any more of that light than you have now described?
> Crawford: No. At daybreak it seemed to disappear. We came around and came back.

Quartermaster George Rowe responded as follows (US Inquiry, p. 524):

> Senator Burton: Do you think there was a sailing boat there?
> Rowe: Yes, sir.
> Sen. Burton: And was she going away from you?
> Rowe: Toward daylight the wind sprung up and she sort of hauled off from us.

Able Seaman Edward Buley gives an extensive account (US Inquiry, p. 611):

> There was a ship of some description there when she struck [this 'when she struck' is a lazy phrase: Buley was 'sitting in the mess reading when she struck', in his own evidence (US Inquiry, p. 603), and he first saw the light 'when turning the boats out' after midnight (p. 612)]

and she passed right by us. We thought she was coming to us; and if she had come to us, everyone could have boarded her. You could see she was a steamer. She had her steamer lights burning...

Senator Fletcher: How far away was she?

Buley: Three miles, sir, I should judge... No; we could not see anything of her in the morning when it was daylight. She was stationary all night; I am very positive for about three hours she was stationary, and then she made tracks.

Sen. Fletcher: Did you see that ship before you were in the water?

Buley: Yes, sir; I saw it from the ship. That is what we told the passengers. We said: 'There is a steamer coming to our assistance'. That is what kept them quiet, I think.

Sen. Fletcher: Did she come toward you bow on?

Buley: Yes, sir; bow on toward us; and then she stopped, and the lights seemed to go right by us.

Sen. Fletcher: If she had gone by you, she would have been to your stern?

Buley: She was stationary there for about three hours, I think, off our port [side] there, and when we were in the boat we all made for her, and she went by us. The northern lights are just like a searchlight, but she disappeared.

The quality of Buley's eyesight – 'I can see a distance of 21 miles, sir' (US Inquiry, p.612) may perhaps be attested by his graphic account of the *Titanic* breaking in two before she sank. This was a fact disbelieved by the British Inquiry, which declared that 'the ship did not break in two' (Final Report, p.34). Buley's account was verified seventy-three years on, however, after the discovery of the two halves on the sea bed. He had this to say in 1912 (US Inquiry, pp.609-610 – the four answers are here compressed):

She went down as far as the after funnel, and then there was a little roar, as though the engines had rushed forward, and she snapped in two, and the bow part went down and the afterpart came up and stayed up five minutes before it went down... We could see the afterpart afloat, and there was no forepart to it. I think she must have parted where the bunkers were. She parted at the last, because the afterpart of her settled out of the water horizontally after the other part went down. First of all you could see her propellers and everything. Her rudder was clear out of the water... You could hear the rush of the machinery, and she parted in two, and the afterpart settled down again, and we thought the afterpart would float altogether. She uprighted herself for about five minutes, and then tipped over and disappeared... You could see she went in two, because we were quite near to her and could see her quite plainly.

Buley must be an excellent witness, possessing the sharp vision that he claimed to have. His account, along with all the other evidence, suggests that the mystery ship approached, turned, showed a red side light while lying stationary, and later showed a stern light as she turned once more to starboard and cruelly fled the scene. The *Californian*, by contrast, did not move all night.

WHAT WAS SHE?

Boxhall thought that the mystery ship he saw was a three-mast or four-mast steamer. He is the best witness to this point. He had the ship under observation, with glasses, for the longest period. The *Californian* was a four-masted steamer, but an immobile one. Yet not all agreed with Boxhall's observations. There is confusion, and even contradiction, in the numerous attempts to identify the mystery ship. There are passengers who think that the light was a fishing boat, but it is quite obvious folly to place any reliability whatsoever on passenger identification of a light at sea at night. We will look only at crew, ranked in order of seniority. Second Officer Lightoller states:

> 13894. I had already been calling many of the passengers' attention to it, pointing it out to them and saying there was a ship over there, that probably it was a sailing ship...
>
> 14138. I was perfectly sure it was a light attached to a vessel, whether a steamship or a sailing ship I could not say.

Third Officer Pitman seems more certain:

> 15061. Did you see any light or lights which you took to be the light or lights of another steamer? — I saw a white light which I took to be the stern light of a sailing ship.

Quartermaster Hichens guessed at the type of vessel sighted:

> 1339. We expected it to be a steamer from the ship, but when I got into the boat and could not get nearer to it, and being calm weather, then we expected it to be a fishing boat, a cod-banker, as we call it.

Quartermaster Bright was confident of sail, not steam (US Inquiry, p.836):

> It looked to me like a sailing ship – like a fishing boat. There were no lights to be seen about the hull of the ship, if it was a ship.

Quartermaster Rowe had little doubt about what he saw (US Inquiry, p.524):

> Do you think there was a sailing boat there? — Yes, sir. I think there was a ship there. Indeed, I am sure of it, and that she was a sailer.

Yet, Lookout Lee was not certain:

> 2568. The light disappeared. Whether it was a fishing vessel or a steamer, or what she was, I do not know.

Lookout Fleet was similarly reluctant to speculate (US Inquiry, p.358):

> It might have been a fisher sail, or something; it was only just one bright light. I could not say what it was.

At the British Inquiry, he offered no more information (question 17453):

> I could not tell what it was, it might have been a sailing ship, or it might have been a steamer.

AB Symons (question 11478) said: 'I took the light to be that of a cod-bankman – or fishing vessel'. And AB Frank Osman opined (US Inquiry, p.538): 'I thought it was a sailing vessel from the banks'.

Nine separate crewmen then, including two ranking officers, suggest that the vessel might possibly have been a fishing craft. They must all be mistaken if the mystery ship is to be the *Californian*. And there is separate evidence that fishing boats were in the vicinity.

FISHING VESSELS ON THE SCENE

On 18 April 1912, the *Belfast Newsletter* reported a *Reuters* story that:

> The Captain of the *Ultonia* [of the Cunard Line], which arrived at New York at midnight on the 16th instant, reported that he passed over the *Titanic's* route and had seen a number of fishing boats near where the disaster occurred.

The Dow Jones news agency had also reported:

> The Captain of Leyland Line freighter *Etonian*, which was not equipped with wireless and which docked in North River last night, reports that he passed along [the] route taken by *Titanic* and that a number of fishing boats were in the vicinity of the disaster at the time. He says he thinks many of the passengers if they secured life preservers may have been rescued by crews of fishing vessels.

But let us choose to ignore these claims and instead place reliance on Fourth Officer Boxhall who, it must be remembered, was armed with time, height, and binoculars. At the US Inquiry, the prime witness made clear his settled opinion (p.911):

> Senator Fletcher: She could not have been a fishing vessel?
> Boxhall: No, sir.
> Sen. Fletcher: Was she a sailing vessel?
> Boxhall: No, sir; a sailing vessel does not show steaming lights, or white lights.

And, later: 'She might have been a four-mast ship or might have been a three-mast ship, but she certainly was not a two-mast ship'. It must thus be assumed, as the key evidence indicates, that the mystery ship was indeed a steamer, and one of some size.

CHOICES AND SIGNPOSTS

First the good news – we are finished for now with *Titanic* witnesses. Soon we shall examine what happened on the *Californian* that night. It is undoubtedly right that we should not rush away from the *Titanic* witnesses to get to the *Californian*. That haste in 1912 prevented the British and US Inquiries from properly analysing the evidence of the *Titanic* witnesses about a vessel that was, after all, their perplexing nearby ship, the one close enough to effect a rescue and to save hundreds of lives. The *Titanic* witnesses claim that their strange ship was moving and showed a red side light for most of the time she was present. It appears she could have shown a stern light as she later 'made tracks'.

In deciding whether *Californian* could have been the *Titanic*'s mystery ship, we are now at a crossroads. We can take one of two routes. Either we can trust that Boxhall and others are correct, in which case *Californian* is not the mystery ship. Or we can believe that they are wrong, which still leaves the *Californian* as a potential mystery ship.

A reader having followed the thread of evidence to this point, concentrating on the *Titanic* witness testimonies, could be forgiven for already having severe doubts as to any possibility of the *Californian* being the mystery ship. Yet we must go down *both* routes signposted above, and see where they lead us. It may be noted that those in 1912 who rushed to label the *Californian* as the mystery ship seemed to feel no inclination to make any scenic tour in the other direction.

The inquiries effectively ignored the most credible *Titanic* witnesses, deeming them mistaken, and disregarded the preponderance of *Titanic* evidence as somehow irrelevant. A patient reader would certainly form a contrary impression.

So let us walk a hundred yards down the 'Believing Boxhall' road for a quick look at the vista it affords, before returning to take the short-cut to the *Californian*'s guilt.

If Boxhall and others are right, *Californian* is not the mystery ship. The corollary of this, of course, is that some other vessel is the mystery ship, and that the *Californian* is unseen by *Titanic*. Therefore the *Californian* lay over the visible horizon. If this is the case, she must have been at least 17 miles away (and probably more) according to unimpeachable scientific formulae. This is because 17 miles is the maximum observable mileage over the curvature of the earth for someone at 70ft, the height of *Titanic*'s bridge looking at an object the height of the *Californian*. If the distance becomes any larger than this, any object (such as a mastlight) disappears. The ship is said to be 'hull down' over the horizon, and unseen. The corpus of *Titanic* evidence, by marked contrast, puts the mystery ship approaching and visibly closing to 5 or 6 miles away, well inside the horizon. If Boxhall and others are right, then it makes perfect sense that the *Titanic*'s distant rockets should only rise halfway towards the masthead light of a ship which had stopped close to the *Californian*, and which was under observation by her.

This is what the *Californian* says she observed. Boxhall's direct opposite number on the *Californian* was Second Officer Herbert Stone. He spent the longest time observing his vessel's own nearby ship and was the only one to witness *all* the rockets seen by the *Californian* (although whether *Californian* saw all the rockets fired by the *Titanic* is another story, as we shall see). The *Californian*'s very own 'Boxhall' then, Second Officer Herbert Stone, testified that the rockets he saw 'did not go very high', rising about halfway up to the masthead light of the *Californian*'s unknown ship. Stone was quite specific in his evidence:

> 7921. Tell me what you said to the Chief Officer? — I have remarked at different times that these rockets did not appear to go very high; they were very low lying; they were only about half the height of the steamer's masthead light and I thought rockets would go higher than that.

Only accepting Boxhall and other *Titanic* witnesses as creditworthy makes sense of what Stone says he saw. Only if the *Titanic* lies over the horizon from the *Californian* and a considerable distance away will those rockets rise halfway to the masthead light. And let it be said that halfway to the masthead light does not mean 'halfway up the mast'. The masthead light could be located typically about two-thirds distance up the mast. Either way, the rockets he saw rose *less* than halfway up the mast of the nearby ship – 'very low lying' indeed.

Now think about this sheer absurdity: if that near ship in plain view of the *Californian* was actually the monster *Titanic*, then it is ridiculous for her rockets to rise only a small distance up her own masts! And when we look at the *Titanic* evidence we find no record of such damp squibs. There follows a quick sample of what the *Titanic* officers said about their own rockets. Here is the evidence of Fourth Officer Boxhall:

> 15397. Can you describe what the effect of those rockets is in the sky; what do they do?
> —You see a luminous tail behind them and then they explode in the air and burst into stars.

And in the US Inquiry (p.237), Boxhall states: 'They go right up into the air and they throw stars'.

Second Officer Lightoller provides similar reponses:

> 14153. What sort of light do they show? — A shell bursts at a great height in the air, throwing out a great number of stars.
> 14155. How are they discharged; are they discharged from a socket? — ...the pulling of this wire... fires the charge at the base of the cartridge. That, exploding, throws the shell to a height of several hundred feet, which is nothing more or less than a time shell, and explodes by time in the air.

Great height is simply inconsistent with Stone's description of what he saw. Several hundred feet? *Titanic*'s masts rose to a maximum of 130ft above the boat deck (although 205ft above the waterline). Therefore, if Stone's nearby steamer was indeed the *Titanic*, firing rockets that rose to only half the height of a mast, let alone half the height of a masthead light, then the *Titanic*'s rockets would travel not 'several hundred feet', but less than seventy. The height of the *Titanic*'s foremast light, meanwhile, was 85ft from the boat deck, or just a little above the 72ft funnels (the masts themselves ran on for another 45ft).

If Stone's description of the rockets reaching only 'half the height of the masthead light' is correct, this would mean the *Titanic* rockets rose only 42½ft from where they were fired. Barely over the roof of the average suburban house! Such a miserable performance would surely be remarked upon with dismay by *Titanic* survivors. It would be widely criticised and made a prime focus for investigation at any subsequent inquiry – if only their distress rockets could have gone higher!

But the *Titanic* seems to have had no such problem with rockets. Clearly Mrs Mahala Douglas is speaking for all the passengers when she describes how 'We watched the distress rockets sent off – they rose high in the air and burst...' (US Inquiry, p.1101). In other words, *Titanic*'s rockets performed as they were intended to do. They *did* rise several hundred feet, as one would expect. Senator Smith specifically asked about rockets at the US Inquiry (p.237). Did they work satisfactorily? 'Oh, yes', Boxhall readily confirmed, 'they were quite satisfactory'.

And it was spelt out clearly once more:

Sen. Smith: The failure to arouse the attention of this ship was not due to any impaired or partial success of these signals [the rockets]?
Boxhall: Not at all, sir.

This evidence seems to contradict Stone's account quite clearly. But why would Stone lie about the height of rockets? Once he has seen a rocket at all the fact of seeing it is the major concession. If a lie is to be attempted, it would be surely far better to deny seeing *any* rockets!

To summarise for the moment: for the *Californian* to be the mystery ship, not only must *Titanic*'s prime witness, Joseph Groves Boxhall, be mistaken; but his direct counterpart Herbert Stone, *Californian*'s prime nearby ship witness, must *also* be mistaken.

The unlikelihoods may be mounting to 'titanic' proportions, but we will return from that experimental walk on the side of Boxhall (and Stone) being correct, and go down the road that says they must be wrong. Of course, if they are wrong, *Californian* is potentially the mystery ship.

6

CALIFORNIAN'S OWN MYSTERY SHIP

The first one aboard the Leyland liner to discern a possible ship approaching was her Captain, Stanley Lord:

6715. Now close upon 11 o'clock [*Californian* time] did you see a steamer's light? — I did.

6716-19. …After we had stopped. It was approaching me from the eastward [thus heading west]. I did not get the bearings of it; I was just noticing it casually from the deck. It was on the starboard side.

6720. What did you see, what light? — I just saw a white light to commence with.

6721. Did you then ask your wireless operator what ships he had? — Yes I went to his room and I asked him what ships he had.

6723. What did he say? — 'Nothing, only the *Titanic*.'

6724. Did you think that the vessel approaching you was the *Titanic*? — No, I remarked at the time that [she] was not the *Titanic*.

6725. How could you tell that? — You can never mistake those ships – by the blaze of light.

6726. I am not quite sure that I understand you – you told us you had seen one light? — First.

6727. Then as she was approaching you, did you see more? — I saw more lights.

6728. Did you see any side lights? — I saw a green light [on her starboard side, consistent with a ship heading from east to west, seen from the north].

6725. And did you see any deck lights? — A few.

6730. It was sufficiently close for that? — Oh, yes, she was getting closer all the time.

6731. About what distance approximately did you consider she was from you? — At 11 o'clock? I suppose she was six or seven miles away. That is only approximately.

6733. Will you tell us what lights you saw at the time you had this conversation with the Marconi operator? — I saw one masthead light and a few other white lights, but I do not say I noticed the green light then, I was not paying a great deal of attention.

6734. [The Commissioner] Were the white lights bearing from east on your starboard side? — Coming from the eastward on our starboard side, my Lord.

6735. And you saw some other lights. What were they? — They might have been anything – lights from the portholes, doorways, or anything.

6736. But no coloured light? — I did not notice any then.

6737. [Attorney General] You said it was not the *Titanic*. Did you give him any directions? Did you tell him to let the *Titanic* know? — I said, 'Let the *Titanic* know that we are stopped, surrounded by ice'.

6738. Do you remember at what time that message was sent? — About 11 o'clock.

6739. About 11 o'clock that night, ship's time? — Ship's time [*Californian* time].

The importance of this, quite apart from Lord seeing a ship that had *no* blaze of light like a big passenger ship but only 'a few other white lights', is that Lord's own vessel, the *Californian*, would have been visible at 'six or seven miles away' to the lookouts on the other vessel. This is substantially before *Titanic's* collision.

Titanic's lookouts, we know, did not report the light of any other vessel either before or for over three-quarters of an hour after their collision. Lord's sighting of the light is the earliest recognition of a ship by the *Californian*, and is verified by the timing of the message sent by Cyril Evans, the *Californian's* wireless operator. Below is the information given by Evans:

8975. There is nothing more, as I follow you, until your ship stops? — No.

8976. Which we know she did, about 10.25 – your ship's time? — Yes.

8977. Did you go on deck when you found the ship had stopped? — Yes.

8978. I think you found the Captain and the Chief Engineer discussing the matter? — Yes.

8979. And then did the Captain make a communication to you and ask you to do something? — Well, Sir, he was talking about the ice then, he was talking to the Chief Officer [it may be that Evans means the Chief Engineer]... I asked him [captain] if anything was the matter, and if he wanted me. A little after that, he came along to my cabin to talk to me.

8980. What did he want to know? — He asked me what ships I had got.

8982. What did you say? — I said, 'I think the *Titanic* is near us. I have got her'.

8983. Did you say, 'I think the *Titanic* is 'near us' or 'is nearest'? — Near us.

8984. [The Commissioner] 'Nearer' is it you are saying? — She was 'near us'.

8985. [The Solicitor General] As far as you know, was there any ship with Marconi apparatus that was nearer you at this time than the *Titanic*? — Not as far as I know. I hadn't the *Titanic's* position.

8986. [The Commissioner] What time was this; about what time? — Five minutes to eleven.

8987. [The Solicitor General] Ship's time? — Yes.

8988. What did the Captain say when you said that? — He said, 'You had better advise the *Titanic* we are stopped and surrounded by ice'.

8989-91. Did you call up the *Titanic*? — Yes, 11 o'clock ship's time.

8992. What did you say? — I said, 'We are stopped and surrounded by ice'.

8993. Did you get an answer from the *Titanic*? — They said, 'Keep out'.

8994. Just explain to us, will you, what that means? — Well, Sir, he was working to Cape Race at the time. Cape Race was sending messages to him, and when I started to send he could not hear what Cape Race was sending.

8995. Does that mean that you would sound louder than Cape Race to him? —Yes, and he did not want me to interfere.

If Wireless Operator Cyril Evans had the *Californian's* stop position to hand, he did not initially offer it, nor did he have the chance to transmit it once the conversation was closed (the *Californian's* ice warning was not the only one ignored by *Titanic's* senior operator, Jack Phillips, that night; one from the *Mesaba*, specifying ice directly in the *Titanic's* path, never made it to the bridge).

The *Californian's* Third Officer, Charles Victor Groves, who was on duty until midnight, had also noticed the light of a ship drawing closer, although he appears to have noticed it later than his Captain. Here is what Third Officer Groves has to say:

8135. Now, what did you see, and when? — As I said before, the stars were showing right down to the horizon. It was very difficult at first to distinguish between the stars and a light, they were so low down. About 11.10 ship's time, I made out a steamer coming up a little bit abaft our starboard beam.

8141. When had you last looked at the clock? — Ten twenty-six – well, I had looked at my watch; we had no clock on the upper bridge.

8142. You saw a steamer? —Yes.

8143. What lights did you see? — At first I just saw what I took to be one light, one white light, but, of course, when I saw her first I did not pay particular attention to her, because I thought it might have been a star rising.

8144. When do you think you began to pay particular attention to her? —About 11.15.

8145. About five minutes after you first saw her? — About five minutes after I first saw her.

8146. Did you then see more lights than one? — About 11.25, I made out two lights – two white lights.

8148. Did you make out any other lights then? — Not at the time, no.

8149. You said that she was a little abaft your starboard beam? —Yes.

8150. How were you heading? — At that time we would be heading NE when I saw that steamer first, but we were swinging all the time because when we stopped the order was given for the helm to be put hard-a-port, and we were swinging, but very, very slowly [which is why the *Californian* could not have shown her red side light on the port side to a vessel to the south]…

8160. Could you form any judgment how far off she was? —When I saw her first light I should think she would be about 10 or 12 miles.

8161. Judging by the look of the light? — By the look of the light and the clearness of the night.

8162. …When you saw the one light? —Yes, when I say she was 10 to 12 miles away.

8163. Did she appear to get nearer? —Yes.

8164. The lights clearer? —Yes, all the time.

8167. Did you report… to the Captain? —Yes, because, as I said before, he left orders to let him know if I saw any steamers approaching.

8168. You went down to him? — I went down to the lower bridge, which is part of the saloon deck.

8169. [The Commissioner] Would this be something after 11 o'clock? — Yes, my Lord, when I went down to him it would be as near as I could judge about 11.30.

Groves would go on to testify that the nearby steamer seemed to put her lights out at 11.40 p.m. *Californian* time. The *Titanic* struck an iceberg at 11.40 p.m., but 11.40 p.m. *Titanic* time.

It has been suggested that the apparent loss of light by Groves' nearby ship – if she were the *Titanic* – could be explained by her turning suddenly (to avoid the berg), ending up facing the *Californian* bow-on, instead of broadside. This is a hypothesis that will be examined in detail later. But at this stage it is important to say that *Californian* and *Titanic* ship times were not identical. How they related to each other is not known. The issue is a quagmire, and there are many theories, all of which have inconsistencies. The British Inquiry used the simple expedient of regarding the times of the two ships as identical — which arguably suited the purpose of treating the *Californian* as the *Titanic's* mystery ship. But the truth is that no-one knows for sure how the time on one ship differed from that on the other. Perhaps they could have differed by up to half an hour, but it is no solution to regard them as indistinguishable.

TIME ON A SHIP

Time on a ship is set each day at local noon. Clocks are corrected to noon (whatever their time) when observations confirm that the sun is at its zenith. Local noon depends on longitude. London is further to the east, where the sun rises, and will therefore see noon five hours earlier than New York. Ships on the Atlantic in 1912 daily corrected their noon depending on where they were. One belief (and an erroneous one) is that the *Californian's* clock was twelve minutes behind the time kept on the RMS *Titanic*. So the argument runs that when it was noon on the *Titanic*, it was only 11.48 on the *Californian*.

Twelve minutes later, when it was noon on the *Californian*, time had also run on for the *Titanic*, where it was now 12.12. Hence the *Californian*, while located 'ahead' of the faster ship that would catch her up, was *apparently* behind her pursuer in time, although she could more properly be said to be ahead of her in the westward race for 'earliness'.

It was stated by Captain Lord in his US evidence that *Californian* time was one hour and fifty minutes ahead of New York time at his local noon of 14 April. He gave his longitude at noon as 47° 25' W, which confirms the following calculation: each hour of time west from Greenwich is 15 degrees (since twenty-four hours multiplied by 15 degrees equals 360 degrees, a day being the time the earth takes to make one complete rotation). Meanwhile, 45 degrees from Greenwich is three hours. Two further degrees (to 47 degrees) is eight minutes of time, since there are four minutes per degree as the earth rotates (360 degrees multiplied by four minutes equals 1,440 minutes, which, when divided by sixty equals twenty-four hours in a day).

A further twenty-five minutes of longitude makes 100 seconds of time, being twenty-five sixtieths of one four-minute period. So a longitude of 47° 25' is three hours, nine minutes, forty seconds, which Captain Lord has rounded to three hours ten minutes behind Greenwich time. New York is five hours behind Greenwich. So *Californian* time after noon on 14 April was one hour and fifty minutes ahead of New York.

The 'twelve-minute theory' would therefore have the *Titanic* two hours and two minutes ahead of New York Time, by comparison with the *Californian* time. The problem here is that the *Titanic*'s last transmission was heard by the *Virginian* at 12.27 a.m. NY time. Adding two hours and two minutes to this (to obtain the *Titanic*'s time) produces a last message sent at 2.29 a.m., even though that ship foundered nine minutes earlier at what was 2.20 a.m. her time!

The US Inquiry heard from officers Boxhall and Lightoller of a New York/*Titanic* time difference of one hour thirty-three minutes. It also noted a wireless message from the rescue ship *Carpathia* to the White Star liner *Olympic*: '*Titanic* foundered 2.20 a.m., 5.47 GMT...'

We can calculate that 5.47 in Greenwich Mean Time equals 0.47 NY time. Between 0.47 NY and 2.20 a.m. there is one hour and thirty-three minutes. This, it is suggested, is the margin by which *Titanic* time was ahead of New York.

Captain Lord's longitude and ship's time one hour fifty minutes ahead of New York would suggest an on-board time seventeen minutes ahead of *Titanic* (before midnight at least, when it was common to put clocks back in anticipation of the next local noon). When *Titanic* was striking an iceberg at 11.40 p.m. her time, therefore, it was three minutes before midnight on the *Californian*.

Lord confirmed this one hour fifty minutes in his British evidence. But *Californian* Wireless Operator Cyril Evans claimed on the other hand that the ship was one hour and fifty-five minutes ahead of New York (not one hour fifty minutes). It would appear Evans is mistaken, since he did not have direct access to navigational calculations.

After midnight, *Titanic* time seems to have generally run on (although it was due to go back), whereas *Californian* time might have gone back ten minutes to put her just seven minutes ahead of perceived time for many on the White Star liner during the period when rockets were fired.

We did say it was a quagmire! Presumably the *Carpathia*, sending that message on the morning after disaster, was relying on surviving *Titanic* officers – and checking watches against New York time.

Officer Pitman timed the sinking at 2.20 a.m. by his wristwatch, partly supporting his brother officers. The situation is complicated, and we cannot be certain of the time difference between *Californian* and *Titanic*. So let us return to the narrative, knowing only that time on both ships was not the same.

Captain Lord, who saw only one masthead light on the stranger, in contrast to Groves' two, had been carrying out his own observations from a lower deck, unseen by Groves (US Inquiry, p.728):

When I came off the bridge, at half past 10, I pointed out to the officer that I thought I saw a light coming along, and it was a most peculiar night, and we had been making mistakes all along with the stars, thinking they were signals. We could not distinguish where the sky ended and where the water commenced. You understand, it was a flat calm. He said he thought it was a star, and I did not say anything more. I went down below. I was talking with the engineer about keeping the steam ready, and we saw these signals coming along, and I said 'There is a steamer passing. Let us go to the wireless and see what the news is'. But on our way down I met the operator coming, and I said, 'Do you know anything?' He said: 'The *Titanic*'. So, then, I gave him instructions to let the *Titanic* know. I said: 'This is not the *Titanic*; there is no doubt about it'. She came and lay at half past 11 alongside of us, until, I suppose, a quarter past; within 4 miles of us.

Lord talks of pointing out the light at 10.30 p.m. to an officer at a time when it was Third Officer Groves' watch. In a 1959 affidavit, Lord said he pointed out the light to Groves, who thought it was a star. Groves admits to confusion about low-lying stars but does not mention the light being pointed out to him by Captain Lord at 10.30 p.m., before he himself saw a ship approaching at 11.10 p.m.

There is a big difference here. Lord says he spotted the light as early as 10.30 p.m. and mentioned it to Groves. But Groves said in evidence that he first noticed a ship approaching at 11.10 p.m., forty minutes later.

Yet Lord did see a ship at his earlier time, because he spoke first to the Chief Engineer about it and then to the wireless officer. A wireless message warning of ice was sent out ten minutes before Groves, who was on watch, says he noticed another steamer in the vicinity.

The crux is clear – the *Californian*'s own mystery ship was seen at 10.30 p.m. by the *Californian*, and if their near ship was the *Titanic* as claimed, then the *Titanic* in turn *must* have seen the *Californian*'s lights, particularly as she had far greater observation height.

Even at a minimum time difference between the ships, such a visual encounter is happening an hour or more before the *Titanic*'s collision. Yet the *Titanic* saw nothing. Recall Lord's evidence:

> 7120. Suppose the *Titanic* was 7 or 8 miles from you between 11.30 and 12 o'clock, would those on her bridge have been able to see your lights? — Easily.

Meanwhile Lord says he remained on the deck (which was lower than the bridge, where Groves was) watching this mystery steamer himself for quite a while.

This is a very important point. Somehow the myth has grown up that Lord never saw the *Californian*'s own approaching ship and was not interested in finding out about her. The evidence however shows that not only did Lord see her earliest of all – a tribute to his eyesight – but he then deployed his concentration for a considerable period in studying the visitor:

6749. Did you continue to watch the approaching, vessel? [Lord] Yes.

6750. Till what time? — Half-past 11 [*Titanic* collided at 11.40 her time]. I was standing on deck watching it.

6751. All this time you were stopped? — We were stopped.

6752. What size steamer did she appear to you – can you give us some idea? — She was something like ourselves. [*Californian* 6,233 tons, *Titanic* 46,000 tons!]

6753. Something like yourselves? — Yes.

6754. Medium size? — A medium size steamer.

6755. Did you see your Third Officer attempt to communicate with him? — I did.

6758. How? — By Morse lamp.

6758. Did he get any reply? — No [*Titanic* flashed her stranger with 'Come at once, we are sinking', but saw no reply].

6759. By this time had you been able to detect her side lights at all? — I could see her green light then.

6760. How far do you judge she was when you could see her green light? — Well, I saw it some time between 11 and half-past; I do not know exactly.

6761. What distance do you think she was from you when you could see the lights? — About five miles.

6762. As much as that? — About that, I should think.

It should be noted that Lord believed the ship he was watching came to a stop at 11.30 p.m. This was his cue for leaving the deck and going inside. This move coincides with Groves' visit down from the bridge to tell Lord about the ship he has recently noticed. Groves says:

8169. …when I went down to him [Lord] it would be as near as I could judge about 11.30.

8170. What did you say to him? — I knocked at his door and told him there was a steamer approaching us, coming up on the starboard quarter.

Size Comparison

Ship	GRT	Length (ft)	Beam (ft)	Hull depth (ft)	Electric lights
Titanic	46,328	882.5	92	60.5	10,000
Californian	6,223	447.5	53	30	260

Lord knew this already. What he didn't expect was Groves' next claim that the vessel was a *passenger steamer*. It is worth quoting Groves in full:

> 8174. [You] said 'She is evidently a passenger steamer'? —Yes, my Lord.
>
> 8175. You added something to that answer? — 'Coming up on the starboard quarter'.
>
> 8176. Did you say why you thought she was a passenger steamer? —Yes, I told him that I could see her deck lights and that made me pass the remark that she was evidently a passenger steamer…
>
> 8178. How many deck lights had she? Had she much light? —Yes, a lot of light. There was absolutely no doubt her being a passenger steamer, at least in my mind…
>
> 8182. Now is that all you said to the Captain before he said something to you? —Yes. He said, 'Call her up on the Morse lamp, and see if you can get any reply'.

Lord had personally witnessed only minutes earlier what he called a 'medium steamer', 'something like ourselves', with 'a few white lights'. Now Groves was insisting that he told the captain that what was coming close to the *Californian* was 'evidently a passenger steamer'. Lord ought to have been *astonished* at this claim, and one might imagine him straight away going out to check again that his eyes were not playing tricks.

But Lord denied that Groves had imparted any such information: 'Did he say to you that she was evidently a passenger steamer? — No' (6830).

Lord's prescription of Morse lamp signalling and his lack of special interest in the other ship at this point are common to both accounts. Whose account of the visitor does that tally with best? Would a captain mutely accept an assurance from an underling that the captain's privately formed opinion was utterly wrong?

We will look later at Groves' description of the course being adopted by his 'passenger steamer', but at this point there is a clear disparity between Groves' ship, reported at 11.30 p.m., and the one Lord had seen up to an hour earlier and personally viewed for some time.

It will be remembered that wireless operator Cyril Evans gave evidence of seeing Lord talking to the 'Chief Officer' shortly after 10.25 p.m., which matches Lord's evidence. The Morsing ordered by Lord now took place. The first attempt began immediately – just after 11.30 p.m., we may suppose. Very soon thereafter Lord came up to the bridge for another look, by Groves' evidence, because Groves was still Morsing when Lord appeared:

> 8481. When did he (the Captain) come up? —About 11.45 onto the bridge.
>
> 8482. You reported to the Captain at 11.30? —About 11.30.
>
> 8483. And then the Captain at some time looked at her and said: 'That does not look like a passenger steamer'? —That was about 11.45 on the bridge.
>
> 8484. What lights was she then showing? —Two masthead lights and a side light, *and a few minor lights* [author's italics].
>
> 8485. Some deck lights? —A few deck lights, yes, that is what I could see.
>
> 8486. Is that before or after you say the deck lights had gone out? —That was after the deck lights went out.

How do we square 'a few minor lights' with the *Titanic's* 10,000 electric lights all told, quite apart from her additional oil-burning lamps? The *Titanic* had eight decks of light, the upper decks particularly bright. The sheer layering of lights, if that ship was the *Titanic*, ought to have been unmistakable! Groves' shipmate, apprentice officer James Gibson seems to be referring to deck after deck of brightness on large passenger vessels when he later describes (in his response to question 7720) how 'a passenger boat is generally lit up from the water's edge' when the one he could see *was not*.

He could tell the difference between cargo boats and large liners at night by the sheer quantity of lights in the latter leviathans (question 7802). Groves says the vessel is a passenger steamer, and said previously that she had 'a lot of light', yet he is also the person who does not now see a quantity of lights but instead only 'a few minor lights'. Groves suggests that this is because the vessel has for some reason quenched her main lights. It is difficult to see how he can have it both ways – the *Titanic* passengers watched her lights burning brightly to the end, even from lifeboats 1 and 2 miles away. They saw line after line of shining portholes. There seems no possibility of the *Titanic* displaying only 'a few deck lights' either before her collision or in its aftermath, having doused her 'deck lights'. Dousing did not happen. Again, a hypothesis aimed at making Groves' ship the *Titanic* suggests that the *Titanic* somehow turned obliquely to the *Californian*, thus showing little light. But read Groves again. He can see the side light – meaning some of the broadside! Indeed the sheer shining spectacle of the sinking *Titanic* was one of the enduring memories for many disaster survivors. The lights burned to the very last; there are accounts telling how lights were still showing in the stern even when the bow had disappeared. And those lights went out suddenly at the death – unlike the gradual declining later seen from *Californian*, consistent with a steaming away.

By the time he came to give his testimony, Groves, 'from what I have heard subsequently', had become convinced that the ship he saw was the *Titanic*. And Lord insisted that Groves first declared that the ship he saw was in his opinion the *Titanic*, only after the *Californian* had made her return journey to Liverpool.

Yet Groves' vessel does not seem to have the vertical height needed to be the *Titanic* from his rather prosaic description. Instead it arguably seems much how his own ship, the *Californian*, might appear to an observer. The *Californian* regularly carried up to forty-seven paying customers. Does that make her a 'passenger steamer'? This brings us to another point: at no time did Groves ever describe his ship as 'large' or 'big'. The only suggestion of size comes from the subtle impression created by the phrase 'passenger steamer'.

To return to the narrative; Groves testified (question 8206) that Captain Lord had not been on the bridge since about 10.35 p.m., but reappeared at 11.45 p.m. when a burst of Morsing was underway.

8207. You went on the bridge after he had told you to signal with the Morse light?
Groves: Yes.
8208. And you did signal and then, as I understand, the Captain came on to the bridge?
— Not until after I was Morsing. I was actually Morsing when he came up.

8209. Very well, he came up and he remarked to you: 'She does not look like a passenger steamer'? — That is so.

8210. And you said: 'It is'? — Yes.

Groves in his evidence above is repeating what he said was his earlier assertion to the captain when below that a 'passenger steamer' was approaching. Captain Lord, having denied the earlier imparting of such a claim, would testify (question 6830) that Groves did *not* announce the nearby vessel as a passenger steamer when he came on the bridge again shortly before midnight. Therefore Lord had no reason to state, and says he did not state, that 'She does not look like a passenger steamer'.

There is a direct clash on this point between the two men. However both will leave the scene shortly and observations of *Californian's* nocturnal visitor will be taken over by two other men. It will be interesting to see whose interpretation of the vessel they favour.

Groves continues:

8211. Now you said something about the lights going out; what was it? — Well he said to me: 'It does not look like a passenger steamer'. I said: 'Well, she put her lights out at 11.40' — a few minutes ago that was [Groves seeks to explain, or arguably to dilute, his previous 'it is' insistence].

8212. Then had she put her lights out before the Captain came on the bridge? — Yes, my Lord.

8213. When did she put her lights out? — At 11.40.

8214. And you told the Captain this, did you? — Yes.

8215. What did he say to that; did he say anything? — When I remarked about the passenger steamer he said: 'The only passenger steamer near us is the *Titanic*'.

8216. He said that, did he? — Yes, my Lord.

8217. What makes you fix the time 11.40 for her lights going out? — Because that is the time we struck one bell to call the middle watch.

8219. Did the steamer continue on her course after that? — No, not so far as I could see.

8220. She stopped? — She stopped.

8221. Was that at the time when her lights appeared to go out? — That was at the time that her lights appeared to go out.

8222. Were the lights you saw on her port side or her starboard side? — Port side.

8223. I want to ask you a question. Supposing the steamer whose lights you saw turned two points to port at 11.40, would that account to you for her lights ceasing to be visible to you? — I quite think it would.

It is here being suggested by counsel that Groves' 'passenger steamer' was the *Titanic* and would have turned at or after impact – thereby facing due north – shutting in her lights and making her appear like a small tramp to Lord. The nominal similarity of times – 11.40 p.m. – proves irresistibly attractive. But Groves is actually agreeing with a suggestion that a steamer turned at a time which, according to the 'twelve-minute theory' turns out to be twelve minutes *after* the *Titanic* hit her berg (*Californian* time being behind that of the *Titanic*, as the theory suggests).

By the alternative time difference theory (the one accepted by the US Inquiry), the *Californian* was seventeen minutes ahead of the *Titanic's* time. In applying this version, Groves would have seen a very strange manoeuvre on the other ship at 11.23 p.m. *Titanic* time, or seventeen minutes before she struck the berg! Let us resist making both ships' times directly interchangeable, for the one thing we do know is that they were *not* the same, both ships being in different locations when they set their clocks to local noon.

Let us instead get back to a vessel which makes a turn, thereby shutting in her lights by counsel's version, or physically extinguishes them in Groves' account. While Groves has somehow missed the turn that results in a westbound vessel suddenly showing him her port side, it should be noted that Captain Lord was also watching this vessel, from below, before joining Groves at 11.45 p.m.

Lord was studying the ship independently from the lower deck just prior to ascending the bridge (question 6766: 'I was up and down off the bridge till 12 o'clock'). He did not see any lights go out on the vessel:

6864. Were you on deck about 20 minutes to 12? — I was on deck, yes [Groves, on the bridge above, said it was 11.40 p.m. when the lights went out – see question 8213, above. This is five minutes before Groves said Lord joined him on the bridge].
6866. Did you see that the deck lights of this vessel appeared to go out? — Not to me.

Nor did he see any turn. In fact Lord repeatedly offered his belief that the stranger had stopped at 11.30 p.m., ten minutes before Groves suggests she did. If she stopped when Lord says she did, then she cannot turn for Groves in order to hide her 'passenger steamer' lights.

A cynical person could make the argument that Groves' sudden change in the vessel's appearance is merely a fig-leaf to allow him to have seen her as both a 'passenger steamer' and an ordinary vessel, with few lights, like Lord. A cynic, indeed, might view this as a desperate defence.

Lord now ascends the bridge at 11.45 p.m. and continues to find himself looking at a vessel which he did not consider a passenger steamer, but 'something like ourselves':

6829. A quarter to 12 was the first time I ever mentioned anything to him about the steamer, that I recollect.
6830. Did he say to you that she was evidently a passenger steamer? — No.
6831. And did you say to him: 'The only passenger steamer near us is the *Titanic*'? — I might have said that with regard to the steamer, but he did not say the steamer was a passenger steamer.

It will be recalled however that Groves claims (question 8484), passenger steamer or no, that he can see the stranger's port side light. Lord too could see a side light, a different one, a green one, when he believed the stranger stopped at 11.30 p.m., fifteen minutes earlier. Yet, whatever their colour, side lights are to be visible under regulation for 2 miles. They might be seen at much greater distance, especially on a clear night such as this. And if *Californian* witnesses can see the side light of their nearby vessel – and if that vessel is the RMS *Titanic* – then surely those witnesses cannot miss that vessel's immense size? Read Groves again; what impression of size does he have? Groves mentions only (question 8178) that his steamer had 'a lot of light' – a claim he allows to be retracted by the doubt-ridden circumstances he subsequently describes. Furthermore, would a sudden turn by the largest moving object ever made really be missed by both Groves and Lord and, secondly, result in her closing in all her main lights to appear as a small steamer?

Another point to note in this context is that Captain Lord had previously seen the *Titanic*'s sister ship, the RMS *Olympic*, from a distance of 5 miles (US Inquiry, p.724):

> Senator Smith: Have you ever seen the *Olympic*?
> Lord: Only at a distance; about 5 miles away.

So, of the two men, Lord is the only one we know had seen a *Titanic*-class ship at the relevant range. Would he know what he was looking at? Would Groves?

Of course it might be contended that the vessel turned while the two men were discussing her down below. But this does not assist Groves, because he strongly suggests that he saw the lights go out on the strange steamer while he was watching her, having come back from talking to the captain:

> 8211. He [Lord] said to me: 'It does not look like a passenger steamer'. I said, 'Well, she put her lights out at 11.40 – a few minutes ago that was'.

If Groves seemed, by the time he reached the witness box, to be in two minds about this ship ('a lot of light' versus 'a few minor lights'), his captain was in no doubt at any stage. Here is further evidence from Lord:

> 6989. Does not it strike you now that that steamer you saw sending up rockets [NB: Lord saw the steamer, but like Groves never personally saw any rockets; counsel is being sly] must have been the *Titanic*? — No.
> 6990. Not now? — No, I am positive it was not the *Titanic*.
> 6991. Why are you positive it was not? — Because a ship like the *Titanic* at sea is an utter impossibility for anyone to mistake.
> 6992. That must depend upon the distance you are from her? — Well, my distance, according to my estimate, is 4 to 5 miles.
> 6993. But might not she have been a good deal further off? — I do not think so. I do not think we would have seen her side lights [if that were the case].

A good point, perhaps…

All the *Californian* witnesses, including Groves himself, could see a side light with their naked eyes – again confirming their average distance of around 5 miles, or 4 to 7 miles as would be specified by later witness Gibson. Groves thought she was 'about five to seven miles away' (question 8385).

Yet the *Californian's* powerful Morse lamp (Lord's US evidence: 'I suppose you can see that about 10 miles, and she was about 4 miles off') had meanwhile gone unanswered or proved ineffectual at this intermediate range. After Groves went off watch at midnight, *Californian's* Apprentice Officer James Gibson and Second Officer Herbert Stone watched their mystery ship for two hours. Both thought she was a 'small' to 'medium' steamer. In other words, they agreed with Lord. Not with Groves.

Let the question be asked again: is the RMS *Titanic*, at an estimated distance of 4 to 7 miles, going to look like a small coaster with a few minor lights? Her size in tonnage is *eight* times that of the *Californian* (*Titanic* 46,000 tons, *Californian* 6,200 tons). Surely the *Titanic* would indeed have been 'an utter impossibility for anyone to mistake'?

Groves became convinced, from what he learned subsequently, that the steamer he saw was the *Titanic*. Gibson and Stone would take a contrary view; they stood on the decks of the *Californian* and watched a nondescript tramp steamer 4 to 7 miles off, using glasses on and off for more than two hours, whereas Groves noticed her casually for only an hour at most. Are these next two men mistaken?

Groves said (question 8241) Lord remained on the bridge for three minutes at the outside, meaning the Captain descended again at 11.48 p.m. Groves stayed for the short remainder of his watch, adding (question 8244): 'After I had tried ineffectually to Morse her I did not pay any particular attention to her'. But Groves, before he goes off watch, has one more strange tale to tell. It concerns the attempt to Morse the stranger:

8188. Did you get any reply [to the Morse lamp]? — Not at first, no reply whatsoever.

8189. Did you afterwards? — Well, what I took to be a reply. I saw what I took to be a light answering, and then I sent the word 'What?' meaning to ask what ship she was. When I sent 'What?' his light was flickering. I took up the glasses again and I came to the conclusion it could not have been a Morse lamp.

8190. [The Commissioner] Is the long and short of it this, that you did not get a reply, in your opinion? — In my opinion, no.

8191. You thought at first you had? — Yes, I thought at first I had.

8192. But you satisfied yourself that you were wrong? — That is so.

8193. Did you go down again to the Captain? — No, he came to the bridge [11.45pm].

8194. Was there anyone else there except you and he? — Not on the bridge.

8195. Did you tell the Captain about the Morsing? — Yes.

8196. What did he say? — He saw a light flickering himself, and he passed the remark to me. He said: 'She is answering you'. This was just before I sent the word 'What?'

8197. After that was done, did you have any more conversation with the Captain about the steamer? — When he came up on the bridge he said to me: 'That does not look like a passenger steamer'. I said: 'It is, Sir. When she stopped her lights seemed to go out, and I suppose they have been put out for the night'.

Groves is now telling a different story of how those lights, formerly 'a lot of light', had suddenly become much less. He now says they were 'put out for the night', a very different explanation to his previous agreement with counsel's clever suggestion that they had been obscured by the vessel making a turn. We can see how Groves is being led by counsel. We know that the *Titanic*, unlike some passenger liners, did not put out the lights in her public rooms before midnight. Groves meanwhile is also talking of an alleged incident during his Morsing when Lord was standing beside him on the bridge and both men fancied they saw an answer! Yet Lord does not recount such a dramatic episode. And counsel clearly did not dare ask him…

THE SPEED THAT'S TOO SLOW

Groves says (question 8241) he did not think Lord remained 'up there with me' on the bridge for more than three minutes at the outside. So the captain descended again at 11.48 p.m., by Groves' account, leaving the third officer on the bridge for the short remainder of his watch. Groves added (question 8244): 'After I had tried ineffectually to Morse her I did not pay any particular attention to her'. Second Officer Stone would soon arrive to take over watch, appearing shortly after midnight. Meanwhile the mystery ship wallowed, perfectly stationary. Now that this mystery ship is stopped however, we can take stock of her progress to date.

Lord saw her at 10.30 p.m. and watched for another hour, on and off, until she stopped. The limit of *Californian's* visible horizon from the bridge is estimated at 7.8 miles. This would be increased by the height of the far-off light (on the masthead of the visitor). But her progress, in Lord's hour of observation, is slow.

The *Titanic* was speeding at 22 knots!

The *Titanic's* speed is twice that of the *Californian* (11 knots) for the hours up until the Leyland liner stopped. This other vessel was 'something like ourselves', said Lord. And Lord does not mention the light's extraordinary rate of progress if that light is indeed the *Titanic*.

Yet if the light was the *Titanic*, then she would have been out of sight across the horizon in far less than an hour! Yet Lord saw her first at 10.30 p.m. and could still see her at 11.30 p.m., when he judged that she had stopped.

The light does not make any impressive progress at all. Quite the reverse. In fact, her speed is so 'unremarkable' that neither Groves nor Lord have reason to make remark. Groves believed subsequently that the ship he saw was indeed the *Titanic*. It is not only Lord who indicates that the light did not move significantly; look at Groves' own testimony as to the rate of progress of the ship he saw. He noticed the ship advancing obliquely for half an hour in total. From 11.10 p.m. (question 8135) when he first noticed her, until 11.40 p.m. when he says she stopped. Those are the bookend times in his evidence. At 11.10 p.m., when he noticed the ship first, Groves said it was 'ten to twelve miles away' (question 8160). By the time she stopped however, Groves said she was 'five to seven miles' away from the *Californian*. He revealed this in later examination (question 8385): 'When she came to a stop what was the distance? — Well, I should think about five to seven miles'. In other words, Groves has seen that steamer approach his own vessel by 5 miles in half an hour. From 10 or 12 down to 5 or 7. And 5 miles in half an hour is a speed of 10mph. This is 10 knots. Not 22 knots. This is Groves' own testimony! How can this ship be the *Titanic*? The *Titanic* was charging along at 22 knots before she was stopped. Abruptly.

This is indicated by several members of the *Titanic* crew. Here is Fourth Officer Boxhall's evidence:

> 15643. Can you tell me what speed you assumed as between the 7.30 position and the time you struck? — Twenty-two knots.
> 15644. Twenty-two knots? — Yes.

And here is Second Officer Lightoller (US Inquiry, p.64): 'How fast was the boat going at that time? — About 21½ or 22 [knots]'. Similarly, Quartermaster Robert Hichens, who was at the helm at the time of impact (US Inquiry, p.462) states:

> At 9.45 o'clock p.m., Sunday, the ship was travelling at that rate and going full speed when the log was taken at 10 o'clock.
> Senator Smith: You mean by full speed, 22½ miles per hour?
> Hichens: Yes, sir.

The *Californian* was no Atlantic greyhound. She was a tramp, with a tramp speed of 11 knots, which was actually more than respectable. The ship Captain Lord regarded as 'something like ourselves', a medium steamer, crossed the horizon to stop below them at a rate of 10 knots or slightly less. Groves agreed with this. He inadvertently calculated her as travelling at 10 knots. She looked like a tramp – to Lord, if not Groves – and she *moved* like a tramp.

7

GROVES AND THE SHIP UNSAID

Groves handed over the watch to Second Officer Herbert Stone at some time (question 8250) between 12.10 and 12.15 a.m. This is Groves' evidence regarding what happened next:

> 8255. Did you point out the steamer to Mr Stone? —Yes.
>
> 8256. Did you tell him what you thought she was? —Yes.
>
> 8257. What did you say? — I pointed out the steamer to him and said: 'She has been stopped since 11.40'; and I said: 'She is a passenger steamer. At about the moment she stopped she put her lights out'.

We have already seen that Captain Lord denies being told by Groves that the stranger was a passenger steamer (question 6830): 'Did he say to you [at 11.45 p.m.] that she was evidently a passenger steamer? — No'. In Groves' version, he maintained his position in the teeth of the captain's disbelief, even though there were only some minor deck lights showing to both men at the time. So what does Herbert Stone now say about Groves handing over the watch and telling him about the vessel lying near-to? We see another account contradicting Groves' evidence; Stone never suggests that Groves pointed out a 'passenger steamer', but merely talks of 'the steamer'. Here is Stone being questioned:

> 7822. I suppose you relieved the other officer and took charge? —Yes.
>
> 7823. Did the Third Officer make any communication to you about this steamer when you relieved him? — He told me the steamer had stopped about one bell [11.40] and that he had called her up on the Morse lamp and got no answer.

Just before going on the bridge, Stone had met Lord, who pointed out to him the steamer. It looked to Stone to be about 5 miles away, much the same as both Lord and Groves had judged it to be:

> 7814. He [Lord] pointed out another steamer. What could you see of the other steamer? — One masthead light and a red side light and *two or three small indistinct lights* [author's italics].

Stone next left Lord and went on the bridge and had the same steamer pointed out to him again by Groves. Stone might have been surprised to learn that the steamer with 'two or three small indistinct lights' was in fact a passenger steamer! He gives no indication of ever having been told such astonishing news by the third officer.

> 8088. What kind of steamer did you judge her to be from the appearance of the lights you saw? — [Stone] A smallish steamer.
> 8089. Judging from the appearance of the lights, could she possibly have been the *Titanic* in your opinion? — Not by any means.

Stone was asked at the end of his evidence (question 8108) whether he knew any means by which, on a dark night at sea, he could tell the nature of a light – that is, whether it be 'a very powerful light some way off', or alternatively, 'a less powerful light not so far off'? He replied that he did:

> 8109. How would you do it? — A powerful light generally throws a glow around it, into the surrounding atmosphere. The more moisture there is in the air the greater the glow you will see around this light.
> 8110. How much glow was there round these lights? — Very little.

Groves, meanwhile, the man who says he insisted on a passenger steamer to his captain and colleague, despite both Lord and Stone appearing not to have heard this comment, had now gone off duty. What did he do?

> 8271. You went off the bridge? — Yes.
> 8272. Where did you go? — The Marconi house.
> 8273. Is the Marconi operator, Mr Evans? — Yes.
> 8274. Did you find him there? — I did.
> 8275. Was he asleep? — He was asleep.
> 8276. He had gone to bed? — He had gone to bed, yes.
> 8277. Did you wake him up? — Yes.
> 8278. And have some conversation with him? — Yes.
> 8270. What passed? — The only thing I remember asking him was 'What ships have you got, Sparks?'
> 8280. 'Sparks'? — Yes.
> 8281. Is that his name? — No, it is the name he gets on the ship.
> [The Commissioner] Seeing he is the operator, you know why he is called 'Sparks'.
> 8282. [Mr Rowlatt] You asked him what ships he had got. What did he say? — Only the *Titanic*.
> 8283. Did you take his instruments and put them to your ears? — Yes.
> 8284. Could you read a message if you heard one? — If it is sent slowly – yes.
> 8285. Did you hear anything? — Nothing at all.

8286. How long did you listen? — I do not suppose it would be more than 15 seconds at the outside –well, 15 to 30 seconds. I did it almost mechanically.

8287. Did you do anything more before you turned in? — I may have said a few more words to him, but I have no recollection. When I left his house I went straight to my cabin.

8288. And went to bed? — And went to bed.

8289. [The Commissioner] What time was it you were talking to this man whom you call Sparks? — As near as I can judge it would be between 12.15 and 12.20 a.m.

So Groves was told by the wireless operator that he, Evans, 'had' the *Titanic*. Groves now, incredibly, says nothing about his 'passenger steamer'. Nothing at all – despite in the previous half an hour repeating to both the captain and the second officer that the vessel lying near them was a passenger steamer, which — if he *did* say it — neither apparently believed. Yet Groves was seized with no urge to expound his convictions to Evans, despite the latter's offer of at least one passenger steamer – *Titanic* – to back up his apparently strongly-held deduction. It is the ship unsaid; Groves finds himself saying nothing about a passenger steamer at a crucial moment according to the express testimony of a third crew member, wireless operator on the *Californian*, Cyril Evans:

9037. And he [Groves] came in you say at about a quarter past 12? — He stopped up on the bridge, I think, for 10 minutes until 10 minutes past 12 with the other officer to get his eyes in.

9038. When Mr Groves came into your room, what did he do? — He asked me what ships I had got; if I had got any news.

9039. Yes, what did you tell him? — I told him I had got the *Titanic*. I said: 'You know, the new boat on its maiden voyage. I got it this afternoon'…

9044. Did anything more happen then? — I do not remember Mr Groves picking the 'phones up, but Mr Groves says so.

9045. That he picked them up and put them into his ears? — Yes. Of course, I was half asleep.

9046. Did he tell you, as far as you recollect, then at a quarter-past twelve of anything that he had seen since the ship had stopped? — *No.* [author's italics]

9047. He only came in and asked what ships you had got? — Yes. He generally comes in my room and has a talk.

9048. He generally does that? — Yes. He comes and has a chat.

9049. Just to find out what the news is? — Yes.

9050. And then. I think, you went to sleep? — Then I went to sleep. He [Groves] switched out the light and shut the door.

Groves then went to bed, and thereafter his involvement ends. The summary of his evidence is that he saw a passenger steamer which came up and stopped 5 miles off at 11.40 p.m. He Morsed her, but got no reply.

He certainly did not see any rockets at any time and, by his own evidence (question 8282) did not express a belief immediately after coming off the bridge that the steamer lying off was a passenger steamer, or could have been the *Titanic*. Yet, in the wake of subsequent events, he concluded in testimony that it was indeed the RMS *Titanic* that he saw – despite not entertaining the possibility in the slightest *at the actual time*. Groves is pressed on the issue:

8440. If this vessel which you did see was only some 4 or 5 miles to the southward of you, do you think she could have been the *Titanic*?

8441. [The Commissioner] That is a question I want this witness to answer. (To the Witness) Speaking as an experienced seaman and knowing what you do know now, do you think that steamer that you know was throwing up rockets, and that you say was a passenger steamer, was the *Titanic*? — [Groves] Do I think it? [Does this parrying question from Groves, playing for time, indicate a reluctance to confront the hard choice being pushed upon him?]

8442 Yes? — From what I have heard subsequently?

8443 Yes? —Most decidedly I do, but I do not put myself as being an experienced man

8444 But that is your opinion as far as your experience goes? —Yes it is my Lord.

But Groves, who trusted completely the accuracy of his captain's stop position and said so, was immediately taken to task by Robertson Dunlop, counsel for the owners of the *Californian*, who aptly asked: 'That would indicate that the *Titanic* was only 4 or 5 miles to the southward of the position in which you were when stopped?' – in other words, vastly off course!

If Groves was squirming (and we do not know) the court itself came quickly to his rescue. The Commissioner interrupted: 'If his judgment on the matter is true, it shows that those figures, latitudes and longitudes, that you are referring to, are not accurate. That is all it shows'. *Californian* counsel replied acidly: 'The accuracy we will deal with, my Lord'. But the Commissioner maintained: 'I mean to say, if what he says is right, it follows that the figures must be wrong'. Consider the indulgence shown to Groves in the above remark. Everyone must be out of step but him!

Even though Groves himself has agreed to the accuracy of the *Californian*'s stop position, if the *Titanic* was nearby as the Commissioner appears to want, then the *Californian*'s latitude (her northern position) must be pulled south to accommodate the *Titanic*'s track to New York. It cannot be that the *Titanic* was in the wrong place! And yet the *Californian* was bound for Boston, not New York. So why would she be south?

Counsel for the *Californian*, Mr Robertson Dunlop, obviously chose to interpret the discrepancy differently (question 8445): 'You will appreciate, Mr Groves, that if the latitudes are right it follows that your opinion must be wrong? — If the latitudes are right, then of course I am wrong'. And in the following question, further clarification: 'If the latitude of your ship and that of the *Titanic* are anything approximately right, it follows that the vessel which you saw could not have been the *Titanic*? — Certainly not'.

Bear these late concessions by Groves very much in mind. For there are many other problems with his evidence, as we are about to see.

GETTING TO GRIPS WITH GROVES

We know the thrust of Groves' evidence, but it is the detail that is troubling. For instance, he suggested various points of origin for his strange steamer. The *Californian* was pointing her head north-east, with her starboard beam (or midpoint) offering a 90 degree angle to the south-east. Groves said so in response to questions 8150 and 8157. Therefore her stern, the limit of her starboard side, was backing south-west. Groves said the visitor first appeared 'a little abaft our starboard beam' (8135 and 8149), or a little more to the south of southeast. He then changed her origin to three points and then 'three and a half points abaft the beam' (8156 and 8157), which puts her from south-by-east to virtually due south. There are eight points in a quadrant, such as that between *Californian's* starboard beam and stern. Three and a half points is nearly halfway from amidships to the bottom of the stern. If the *Californian* is heading north-east and stern south-west, then three and a half points abaft the beam indicates south.

But Groves amended further! He next said the visitor was 'south by west' (8159), then 'coming up on the starboard quarter' (anywhere from south-east to south-west), finally telling his captain she was 'coming up astern'. He even confused himself; in response to question 8166 Groves agreed the ship was coming round 'more on our beam, yes, more to the south and west, but very little', which would give that ship both south-east and south-west at the same time – a junk statement.

The above are real compass bearings. North is the North Pole, South the South Pole, East is Europe and West is America. The ship coming up, if we attempt to marry Groves' positions with his later statement of never having seen the vessel's green side light, then appears to be travelling roughly parallel to the *Californian's* heading on a course essentially north-easterly in nature. There is an obvious problem here. *Titanic* was travelling almost due west when she struck her iceberg. She was also showing her green light (starboard side) to any northern observer. Fourth Officer Boxhall claims, in response to question 15316, 'I remember the true course was S. 86 W'. And Second Officer Lightoller states (question 13498): '... we were making S. 86 true... [question 13500] Within four degrees of due West true? — Yes'. It has nothing to do with perceptions. These are real compass points, let it be said again. Groves emphatically does not agree with Lord, who saw a steamer coming from the east, heading west, and showing a green light.

> 8179. Could you see much of her length? — [Groves] No, not a great deal; because as I could judge she was coming up obliquely to us. [question 8180] – perhaps an angle of 45 degrees to us (demonstrating).

So far, so impossible; at least if that vessel is to be the *Titanic* and Groves' description accurate. A 45 degree line, relating to starboard midpoint, would have that vessel coming from the south, heading north. Either he is accurate and that ship is thus not the *Titanic* – or else he is wrong in his eyewitness testimony. A lose-lose situation for the third officer. Groves said he could not see much of her length (question 8179). But to the previous question (8178) – 'Had she much light?' – Groves had answered: 'Yes, a lot of light. There was absolutely no doubt her being a passenger steamer, at least in my mind'. Yet he could only see her obliquely…

Then she stopped. Groves, it should be stated, does not say he saw the mystery ship turn. But he now notices that her light was not as brilliant as before, but had been substantially doused – at a time that coincides with the captain coming up to see an ill-lit stranger. We will recall Groves claiming, in reponse to question 8197, that Lord said 'That does not look like a passenger steamer', to which he replied 'It is, Sir. When she stopped her lights seemed to go out, and I suppose they have been put out for the night'. But later Groves accepted a leading question:

> 8223. I want to ask you a question. Supposing the steamer, whose lights you saw, turned two points to port at 11.40, would that account to you for her lights ceasing to be visible to you? — [Groves] I quite think it would.

This is a question that links Groves' ship directly with the *Titanic*, which turned two points to port to avoid her iceberg. But *Titanic* was heading west. A turn of two points to port would have *Titanic* facing west-southwest, showing her starboard side – and green light – to a viewer to the north.

Groves did not say he *saw* his visitor turn, but agreed with a *Titanic* hypothesis that was in fact contradictory to what he himself described. If Groves' ship was coming from a generally south or south-by-west position towards *Californian*, then a turn to port of two points by her (in imitation of the *Titanic*) would cause her to point north-by-west or north-north-west. That is a whole quarter of the compass – 90 degrees in a 360 degree horizon – away from the heading the *Titanic* was described as taking by those aboard when she turned two points to port from a westward heading to avoid her iceberg. When she stopped, Groves said he continued to see the vessel's masthead lights, but for the first time could also see the visitor's *red* light of her port side. The Commissioner asks about this in question 8229: 'When did you see that? — As soon as her deck lights disappeared from my view'. Groves still does not mention a turn. He never says he saw any turn. Did he miss it, if the decklights disappeared from his view? And if his obliquely-seen ship did turn to port, shouldn't she be shutting in her red port light, not suddenly showing it? There is now an impression of suggestibility in Groves, because he continues to agree with suggestions.

The Commissioner (question 8224) asks whether 'a change of two points to port would conceal the lights in the ship?' Groves replies: 'In my own private opinion it would'. Groves is thus agreeing that a turn or course alteration, which he didn't see, must have changed the lighting of the ship he was looking at. He has agreed to something in court, after the fact, which is at odds with what he told Captain Lord at the time. He told his skipper that when the lights seemed to go out (question 8197) 'I suppose they have been put out for the night'.

Here he squirms on the hook of trying to have it both ways:

8258. [The Commissioner] Wait a moment: 'I pointed the steamer out to Stone and said: "She is a passenger steamer. She put her light out"'. Do you mean by that she shut her light out? — She shut her lights out, my Lord [suggestion is that she shut them out by *turning*].

8259. [Mr Rowlatt] To get it quite clear, at that time was it your impression she had put her lights out or shut them out? — At that time it was my impression she had shut them out, but I remember distinctly remarking to him that she had put them out [why conclude one thing and say another?].

8260. [The Commissioner] That means that she had shut them out? — Yes.

8261. That is what you intended to convey? — Yes.

8262. That she had shut them out? — Yes.

8263. By changing her position? — By changing her position.

[The Commissioner] Is that right, Mr Rowlatt; is that the answer you expected?

[Mr Rowlatt] I was asking for information, my Lord, because I thought he had said before that he thought she had put her lights out because of the time of night.

[The Commissioner] I think he did say something of that sort.

[Mr Rowlatt] I thought he did, and I asked for information to get it clear.

8264. [The Commissioner – to the Witness] Did you say that you thought she had put her lights out because of the time of night? — I did say that, I think, my Lord.

8265. Then which is it to be, that she shut them out because she was changing her position, or that she had put them out because, in your opinion it was bed-time on board the ship? — [Groves] Well, at the time the lights disappeared I thought in my own mind she had put them out because in the ships I was accustomed to before I joined this company it was the custom to put all the deck lights out, some at 11, some at 11.30, and some at midnight – all the deck lights except those absolutely necessary to show the way along the different decks. But when I saw the ice, I came to the conclusion that she had starboarded to escape some ice.

He is extra 'helpful' to the obvious theory at the end, above, to compensate for his contradictions. Now we have the altogether new suggestion of ice as the cause of a turn which Groves never says he saw. Yet he told both his captain and Stone that the nearby ship had merely extinguished her lights. He told Lord the lights went out 'for the night'. Put out or shut out? Groves does not know quite how to help. Clearly he wants there to have been a turn, but he has a problem. If it was the ice-escaping 'turn' that shut in that vessel's lights, making her appear a smaller ship, then the lights – such as they are – are still burning. They have not been physically doused. But Groves says specifically (questions 8228 and 8229, above) that he only saw the red light when the deck lights had 'disappeared' from his view!

He has thus created yet another possibility – that the ship first turned and *then* doused her lights, such that the red became visible. Groves now agrees with, firstly, a turn, secondly, a dousing and, thirdly, both, as a kind of belt-and-braces insurance. It is difficult not to conclude that Groves, seeking to explain why his captain should see only a tramp where he sees a passenger steamer, is being led or has led himself into ever increasing convolutions. Did he really see anything coherent? If so, why can he not explain it?

One is tempted to the view that he saw no turn as suggested by counsel, but indeed saw her red side light. If she was showing only her red light, then she was also showing a substantial portion of broadside to him and the reality is that she must have been displaying little light overall.

Groves now sees but 'a few minor lights' and 'a few deck lights' (8484-8485) even if he will not subsequently be able to tell how this undazzling turnaround took place. He is asked in question 8487: 'What were those deck lights that you saw when the Captain came on the bridge? — [Groves] I do not think that then I could see more than three or four'. Three or four! From a brilliant passenger steamer!

Lord was never in any doubt regarding the vessel's lack of any impressive light:

> 6866. Did you see that the deck lights of this vessel appeared to go out? — Not to me.
> 6867. Did the Third Officer make any observation to you about that? — No.
> 6868. Did he say to you that her deck lights seemed to go out? — No.
> 6869. Or that nearly all her deck lights seemed to go out? — No.
> 6870. [The Commissioner] Was nothing said to you about her deck lights? — Not to me.

Meanwhile, more important clashes in Groves' own evidence soon begin to emerge. Groves agrees (question 8224) that a change of just two points to port would, in Lord Mersey's words, 'conceal the lights in the ship'. But, forty-two questions later, he states that he would have difficulty in perceiving light changes in such a move – at least in the case of masthead lights:

> 8268. [The Commissioner] Would a change of two points, such as we know took place on the *Titanic*, cause the two white masthead lights to alter their relative positions? — [Groves] Yes, it would, but I do not think at that distance the difference would be perceptible.

So we have perceptible and imperceptible in the exact same scenario, both out of Groves' mouth. And next he agrees to more imperceptibility:

> 8447. Were the two mast-head lights which you saw wide apart, indicating a long ship? — They did not look particularly wide apart.
> 8448. Did they indicate to you a long ship? — Well, I can form no judgement as to her length. She was coming up obliquely to us.
> 8449. And at that distance at which you saw her, it would be difficult to estimate the height of those lights? — Oh, quite difficult.

Yet these difficulties do not prevent him from agreeing readily with an off-the-peg hypothesis, nor from believing that he had been watching the largest moving object ever wrought by the hand of man. Remember, also, that the ship Groves believes he saw was on a radically different course to the White Star liner, which would have been bizarrely off course if *Californian's* own stop position (which Groves agreed with) was correct. And all this alongside Groves' obvious handicap of an admitted inability to form any judgement at all about his visitor's length or height. It is not very satisfactory, is it, this identification of a turning *Titanic*?

The indications are mounting that Groves simply did not know what he saw. His evidence certainly provides no basis at all for his own belated conclusion that the ship he viewed was indeed the *Titanic*. It could be argued that Groves was latterly anxious to put himself at the centre of the drama and to reclaim a lost opportunity. Because one of the undoubted ironies of the tragedy is that when he went down to the wireless operator's room after midnight and listened for traffic, the *Titanic* may have been desperately transmitting emergency messages – which Groves failed to hear because the instrument had been wound down. He could have been a hero…

In a clumsily-worded account called *The Middle Watch*, which he composed in later years, Groves pitifully wrote:

> Probably it would not be far from the mark if it is stated that the fate of those fifteen hundred lost souls hinged on the fact that Mr Groves failed to notice that the magnetic detector was not functioning when he placed the 'phones on his head in the wireless office at which time the ether was being rent by calls of distress which he would not have failed to recognize.

Groves could have saved them all. On him alone hinged 1,500 lives. Or so he says. Returning to his garbled evidence of 1912, Groves does not depart without a final flourish of outright floundering. He becomes hopelessly confused and litters his evidence with mistakes when examined by Robertson Dunlop for the Leyland Line about the nearby ship:

8467. Was she making to the westward or to the eastward? — She would be bound to be going to the westward [this is a contradiction of his earlier descriptions].

8468. Was she? — She was bound to.

8469. Did you see her going to westward? — Well, I saw her red light.

8470. If she was going to the westward and was to the southward of you, you ought to have seen her green light? — Not necessarily [yes, necessarily!].

8471. Just follow me for a moment. She is coming up on your starboard quarter, you told us? — On our starboard quarter.

8472. Heading to the westward? — I did not say she was heading to the westward.

8473. Proceeding to the westward? — Yes.

8474. And she is to the southward of you? — She is to the southward of us.

8475. Then the side nearest to you must have been her starboard side, must it not? — Not necessarily. If she is going anything from N to W you would see her port side [not correct. He has previously claimed his vessel was swinging to port, before correcting it to starboard]. At the time I left the bridge we were heading ENE by compass.

8476. Never mind about your heading I am only dealing with her bearings. She is bearing SSE of you – south-easterly? — About south.

8477. She is south of you and apparently proceeding to the westward? — Yes, some course to the westward.

8478. Does it follow from that, that the side which she was showing to you at that time must have been her starboard side [with green light]? — [Groves] No, it does not follow at all. If she is steering a direct west course, yes [as the RMS *Titanic* was...].

8479. Did you see her green light at all? — Never.

So Groves, by his own account, did not see the RMS *Titanic*, which was heading virtually due west and showing her green light to any observer ship located to the northward. He clashes completely with his captain, as he will later clash with his other colleagues. Is Groves any kind of reliable witness? Or is he a man who can see a steamer approach from the south and stop, only to later confirm she is the largest passenger steamer ever built, heading west, which then steams a sustained change of course to the north – and this, *before* 11.40 p.m. *Californian* time, when Groves agrees she suddenly turns to port 'to escape ice' and shuts in all her 'brilliant' deck lights to him, thereafter presenting just a handful of lights to all other witnesses?

His first evidence has been:

8455. How did those deck lights communicate to you that this was a large passenger steamer? —Well, as I said before, by the number of her lights, there was such a glare from them.

8456. You mean from the brilliance of the lights? — Yes, from the brilliance of the lights...

It is perhaps appropriate that, with that steamer now stopped, showing only a few minor lights, a very un-*Titanic* 'three or four', Groves goes off duty and leaves the stage.

8

FORCING A RED LIGHT

Second Officer Herbert Stone, taking over just after midnight, along with apprentice officer James Gibson, would now stand the *Californian*'s middle watch (midnight until 4 a.m.) when drama unfolded elsewhere. Stone and Gibson saw a small or tramp steamer in their vicinity. Both say so. And like Groves, they could see her red side light, meaning she was presenting her port side. Captain Lord had pointed out the other steamer to Second Officer Stone. Stone described her (in response to question 8088) as 'a smallish steamer'. Judging from the appearance of the lights, it could 'not by any means' have been the *Titanic* (question 8089). Stone could see only one masthead light, a red side light and 'two or three small indistinct lights'. Apprentice Officer James Gibson thought she was a tramp steamer (question 7545). He is questioned further:

> 7706. Why did you think so? — She had no appearance at all of a passenger boat.
> 7707. What time did it first dawn on you that this was a tramp steamer? — As soon as I looked at her.
> 7728. [The Commissioner] What was it made you think it was a tramp steamer? You saw nothing but the lights? — Well, I have seen nearly all the large passenger boats out at sea, and there was nothing at all about it to resemble a passenger boat.

Pressed that she must have 'seemed a big steamer', Gibson would only adjust to 'a medium size steamer' (question 7733).

So Captain Lord, Second Officer Stone, and Apprentice Officer Gibson all agree that they could not have been looking at the *Titanic*. Only Groves is out of step. Gibson said he first saw the other ship's light at about twenty minutes past twelve (question 7424 and 7425). He saw a white masthead light and a red side light: 'I could see the red light with the glasses' (question 7426). Ships carry a red light on their port side. The other side light is green (starboard). This, then, is the contention of those who suggest the *Californian*'s stranger was the *Titanic*: that the *Titanic* had turned or voyaged conveniently to the north, showing her red light to a northern observer (being the *Californian*).

It's a nice theory, isn't it? A *Titanic* turn would go some distance to cancel the troubling fact of the red light witnessed by Groves, Stone and Gibson. Because if the *Titanic* was heading west – to New York – and was south of the *Californian*, as all agree, then she would have been showing her green starboard light to any northern vessel.

She must therefore not just turn to starboard, to the north, in order to show her red light (along with the green), but make another half-turn to starboard again to shut out her green light. It would mean moving her bows from facing 9 o'clock on a clock dial to point not just at 12 o'clock, but to at least 1 o'clock.

Obviously, one would hope for evidence to back up this theory, because otherwise, in forcing the *Titanic* to fit the *Californian* facts, there must be a grave danger of wish-fulfilment. What we do know, however, is that the *Titanic*, rather than turning to starboard, in fact first turned sharply to *port* in an effort to avoid her iceberg. In other words, she went to the south of west:

Not an encouraging start for the theory-builders… And in fact there is no solid evidence for the direction in which the *Titanic*'s head was pointing when she came to rest. No less a luminary than the Attorney General himself admitted as much at the British Inquiry (6851):'Of course… it is rather difficult to know, after she struck the iceberg, how she was heading. We have not any very definite or clear evidence how the *Titanic* was heading. We cannot tell'.

Let's look at some alternatives. Could *Titanic* have been pointing west after impact? This is indicated in an exchange between Boxhall and Senator Fletcher (US Inquiry, p.914):

[Fletcher] Apparently that ship came within 4 or 5 miles of the *Titanic*, and then turned and went away; in what direction, westward or southward? — [Boxhall] I do not know whether it was southwestward. I should say it was westerly.

The mystery ship had first approached almost straight on to the *Titanic*'s bow, Boxhall described.

Perhaps the *Titanic* was pointing to the east? Senator Fletcher questioned Major Arthur Peuchen, a passenger in First Class (US Inquiry, p.346):

[Fletcher] …you proceeded to row in the direction in which the ship had been moving, westward? — [Peuchen] No; we started right off from the port side of the boat, directly straight off from her about amidships on the port side, right directly north, I think it would be, because the northern lights appeared where this light we had been looking at in that direction appeared shortly afterwards.

We will leave it with the Attorney General: we cannot tell how the *Titanic*'s bow finished up. A turn that leaves her facing north may be necessary for the theory to work, but there is no clear evidence that this happened. But let us further examine the validity of the theory, for the sake of argument, because it has a fatal flaw.

Here it is: the ship seen two points off the *Titanic*'s bow is argued to be the *Californian*. The *Californian*, then, displays her starboard sidelight, which is *green*. Because the *Californian* is heading north-east, the *Titanic*, no matter which way she herself is facing, will always see *Californian*'s green sidelight. Groves is questioned about this:

8387. In the position to which you had swung round, just at the time you were leaving the bridge, if any person from that ship or from a boat lower down saw you, would they have seen the light you were showing then, your red starboard light? — It is a green light.

8388. I beg your pardon – your green light? —Yes.

But immediately we have a problem. This is simply the wrong colour, according to the evidence of Lowe, Boxhall and others. The *Titanic* observers saw a red sidelight throughout on their mystery ship. This is a massive problem if *Californian* is to be the mystery ship. How can she be?

So, was there then an intervening ship?

The 'ship in-between' theory has long been popular. But it completely dissolves upon examination of its credentials. The *Californian* observers saw a *red* port light on their mystery ship. And the *Titanic* observers also saw a *red* port light from *their* mystery ship. So if there is just an intervening ship, visible to both *Californian* and *Titanic*, she either has two red lights or is pointing in two directions at once. This is clearly impossible. A *single* stranger, the so-called 'third ship', will just not fit the evidence.

Nor will she fit it if she was to move towards *Californian*, turn to starboard, move away, approach *Titanic*, turn to starboard once more, and head away to the south-west. Because the timings show that *Titanic* and *Californian* witnesses are seeing red lights simultaneously.

It is tempting to offer the 'ship in-between' theory. But the evidence is clear-cut. This did not happen. The only alternative, on establishing that the *Californian* was not the mystery ship, is that she and the *Titanic* were each seeing separate unidentified ships, making a grand total of four vessels altogether.

This may seem too many at first, too big an idea – but it may not be so extraordinary. The area was a busy Atlantic highway of different tracks to and from various destinations. The theory would suggest that there are two pairs of ships in operation. Each pair involves ships close to each other, but the pairs are distant from one another over the visible horizon. It is, at minimum, another theory. Yet it is one that cannot be accepted by those who want *Californian* to be *the* mystery ship, the *sole* mystery ship – *Titanic's* nearby stranger.

Therefore, the proponents of a scenario involving *Titanic* and *Californian* alone, sighting each other, must somehow force the *Californian* to show her *red* light to the *Titanic* when she is actually showing *green* to any vessel close by and to the south. We know the *Californian* is showing green all the while. And yet it is beyond contradiction that *Titanic* witnesses saw only red. Therefore the direct clash, on the facts, has to be fudged. Once more the theory is king. And a theory there was. A book written in 1993 seemed to offer an explanation to wedge the stubborn *Californian* with the 'wrong light' into the unanimous *Titanic* evidence. Leslie Reade, author of *The Ship That Stood Still*, argued that, because the *Californian* was swinging in a clockwise fashion, she would *eventually* present her red light to the *Titanic* witnesses.

This is true. Even Captain Lord stated: 'After midnight we slowly blew around and showed him our red light' (US Inquiry, p.732). But the key words are 'slowly' and 'eventually'. And the evidence is that *Titanic* witnesses saw their red light very early in the night. While *Californian* was indeed swinging clockwise, she was doing so very slowly, and would not have presented her red light to the *Titanic* until panic and chaos ruled on the maiden voyager and no-one was interested any more in patient observations of a mystery ship.

Lord claimed his vessel was pointing north-east when it came to rest at 10.21 p.m. that night. But Apprentice Officer Gibson went on duty two hours later and found, at 12.20 a.m., that she was pointing 'east-northeast' (question 7437). So the *Californian* had drifted precisely two points in two hours, or one point of the compass per hour. She was east-north-east, and would have to drift fully another ten points to place her bow due south. So *how* slowly was the *Californian* swinging? Captain Lord said 'slowly', but consider the view of Charles Groves, the dissenter, who became convinced the vessel he saw to southward was the *Titanic*: 'At that time we would be heading NE when I saw that steamer first, but we were swinging all the time… swinging, but very, very slowly' (question 8150). Secondly, the *Titanic* evidence is that the red light of their stranger was there from the first until the sinking and even thereafter, and there is no credible evidence of a green light ever being seen, except when she initially steamed close shortly after 12.30 a.m., presenting *both* side lights in her head-on approach. By 1 a.m., that oncoming vessel had turned to starboard and was presenting her red light to all *Titanic* observers. Boxhall thought the reason she did so was because she had 'probably gotten into the ice'. Thirdly, for the swinging *Californian* to work according to the theory, the *Titanic* must paradoxically stay still in the same current – the current somehow *not* working on the *Titanic* but on the *Californian* alone, even though both ships are supposedly so close to each other. Yet if the same current *had* been in operation, *Titanic* might have been swinging anti-clockwise. This could have shown the *Californian* the *Titanic's* green starboard light. But the *Californian* never saw a green light on the ship near to her. Fourthly, and the reader will have to take this on trust for the time being, the swinging theory requires Officer Boxhall of the *Titanic* to fire a large number of distress rockets in quick succession – before waiting, without firing *any* for at least fifteen minutes, until he fires his last rocket at a time supposedly coincidental with the appearance of *Californian's* red light. This scenario is obviously unlikely and will be shown to be a complete travesty of the evidence. Fifthly, and finally, detailed evidence as to the *Californian's* rate of drift makes it problematical that she could have shown her red light to her nearby stranger in the time required by the 'swing theory'.

All of the five points above will now have to be supported by evidence to finally demolish this notion, which has taken a firm grip among those needful of a plausibly 'scientific' basis for their insistence that the *Californian* must be *Titanic's* mystery ship.

Regarding swinging slowly: Groves says 'We were swinging, but very, very slowly' (question 8150), while Stone says 'We were slowly swinging' (question 7969).

The *Titanic* saw a red light all night, and not just later in the night, as the swing theory requires. This has all been dealt with earlier. The repeated evidence is that the *Titanic's* stranger showed her red light from the moment of arrival when she turned side-on and stopped. Both Fleet and Lowe specifically refer to seeing the red light at 1 a.m., quite apart from Boxhall, who saw it 'most of the time': 'And then, as she got closer, she showed her side light, her red light' (US Inquiry, p.236).

Was the *Californian's* other ship affected by the current? She *should* have been if they were in the same locality. But there is no evidence she was.

Stone claimed 'She [the stranger] was not swinging so far as I could tell, she was steaming away' (question 8046). Gibson, on the other hand, said he could not see whether she was steaming away (7741). Neither did he suggest at any time that she was 'swinging,' but said she was 'disappearing'.

Neither of the two post-midnight *Californian* witnesses saw a green light on the vessel they had under observation. Here is Gibson:

7771. Did you ever see her green? — No.

7779. You told us you never saw the green light of this vessel? — No.

Stone is in agreement: 'Did you ever see this vessel's green light? — No' (question 8056). And what do the *Titanic* witnesses say of any current swing by their vessel after the collision? Boxhall is asked (question 15419) 'Do you know at all whether the *Titanic* was swinging at this time?', to which he answers 'No, I do not see how it was possible for the *Titanic* to be swinging after the engines were stopped. I forget when it was I noticed the engines were stopped, but I did notice it; and there was absolutely nothing to cause the *Titanic* to swing'. So, if *Titanic* was not swinging, she was not in the *Californian's* current. So if the *Titanic* was *Californian's* nearby ship, then the *Californian* was in a current as localised as a tiny river eddy, rather than the centre of the North Atlantic…

Quartermaster George Rowe, meanwhile, on board the *Titanic*, saw the mystery ship move from almost ahead to further along the *Titanic's* port bow and concluded that this was an effect caused by the *Titanic* swinging clockwise. Other *Titanic* witnesses, as we know, knew the mystery ship to be moving. Rowe himself later acknowledged that 'toward daylight… she sort of hauled off from us' (US Inquiry, p.524). Here is what he says:

17669. Was your vessel's head swinging at the time you saw this light of this other vessel? — I put it down that her [*Titanic's*] stern was swinging.

17670. Which way was her stern swinging? — Practically dead south, I believe, then.

17671. Do you mean her head was facing south? — No, her head was facing north. She was coming round to starboard.

17672. The stern was swung to the south? — Yes.

17673. And at that time you saw this white light? — Yes.

17674. How was it bearing from you? — When I first saw it, it was half a point on the port bow, and roughly about two points when I left the bridge.

This evidence from Rowe clashes with Boxhall's 'no swing for *Titanic*' testimony. But Rowe's swing appears at odds with that of the *Californian*. This may illustrate how ill-founded any theory is that relies on a current to somehow get it out of a hole.

The logical conclusion is that if the *Titanic* was within 5 miles of a swinging *Californian*, then the *Titanic* should have followed the same pattern. This is what was indeed concluded by those in the British Government's Marine Accident Investigation Branch (MAIB) in their 1992 re-appraisal of the evidence relating to the *Californian*, when they assumed that the same current would apply over 20 miles: 'Between the collision and sinking, both ships will in all probability have drifted similarly' (MAIB final report, p.11).

As shall be demonstrated later, it is the contention of Second Officer Stone that the *Californian*'s unknown ship did not drift, but actually and actively steamed away. Gibson would state that she 'disappeared' or went 'out of sight'.

So, to recap, the swing theory requires the *Californian* to be actively affected by a vigorous localised current (far more vigorous than the 'slow' drift apparently felt by those on the ship) and the *Titanic* not to be affected by any current whatsoever – even though it is clear from the wreck site location, being south of the streamer track, that a current *was* acting on the *Titanic* after she stopped, slowly pushing her south-west and off her former course. One current for the *Californian* and none for the *Titanic*? It may be possible, but it seems unlikely.

The swing theory also requires an unlikely pattern of distress rocket firing by the *Titanic*. The book advocating the *Californian* swing theory claims that *Titanic* Fourth Officer Boxhall fired 'altogether seven rockets while he could see the green light of the other ship' (*The Ship That Stood Still*, p.148). It asserts: 'Boxhall later saw the other ship's red sidelight alone. He fired off one more rocket, his last. The last went off about 1.30 a.m.'

But here are the facts: Boxhall *didn't* see the red sidelight only very late on, having previously seen a green light as he fired all but one of his entire stock of rockets. The theory conflicts directly with what Boxhall (who should know what he did and did not do) said in his testimony at the US Inquiry (p.933): 'I saw the masthead lights first, the two steaming lights; and then, as she drew up closer, I saw her side lights through my glasses, and eventually I saw the red light. I had seen the green, but I saw the red most of the time. I saw the red light with my naked eye'. An instant's consideration is the end of this book's nonsense. The theory stretches Boxhall's 'eventually' in the above quotation to breaking point and far beyond.

Furthermore, Boxhall never refers to jealously guarding his last rocket for the supposedly long time required to see a slowly-swinging stranger's red sidelight. He can see that red light from the earliest time after the stranger has approached *Titanic*, turned, and lain off, showing her red. And Boxhall is crucially backed up by *Titanic* lookout Fred Fleet and by Fifth Officer Harold Lowe, both of whom notice that red light at 1 a.m. – testifying thus – and not as late as 1.30 a.m., as the book suggests.

Boxhall is questioned about rockets:

15398. Did you send them [rockets] up at intervals one at a time? — One at a time, yes.
15399. At about what kind of intervals? — Well, probably five minutes: I did not take any times.

Note that there is no suggestion of keeping one last rocket, long after the others, until the end of the night.

A convention has grown up that the first *Titanic* rocket went off at 12.45 a.m. *Titanic* time. Testimony certainly suggests one fired contemporaneous with the launch of boat No.7. Boxhall suggests firing even a little earlier. But take 12.45 a.m. as a starting point for the sake of argument in addressing this book's theory. Firing seven rockets at five-minute intervals will bring Boxhall to 1.15 a.m. The theory would suggest that the *Titanic's* stranger was showing *green* all this time (in order to fit the *Californian*), but the evidence of *Titanic* witnesses massively disputes this. No witness on the *Titanic* boat deck sees a green light on the stranger.

No matter. Boxhall is now seven rockets down while the stranger was showing her green light – which she wasn't, but we are indulging the book's theory for a moment. It is now 1.15 a.m. by Boxhall's account of intervals. The book now suggests that he now waited for *fifteen minutes* before firing his last rocket at 1.30 a.m. This runs directly counter to Boxhall's own evidence. The theory suggests Boxhall fired his last rocket when suddenly seeing the stranger's red light at 1.30 a.m. But he did not suddenly see the red for the first time then. Nor was his last rocket fired at that time: 'I was sending the rockets up right to the very last minute when I was sent away in the boat' (question 15420). Boxhall was in boat No.2. This boat had a reported departure time of 1.45 a.m., which has never been disputed. So Boxhall's last rocket is fired close to 1.45 a.m., and not at 1.30 a.m. as specified by the swing theory book, *The Ship That Stood Still*.

Furthermore, Gibson of the *Californian* will see a last rocket close to 2 a.m. by his ship's clock, which hardly seems in-keeping with the time the book would like to have the *Titanic's* last rocket fired. Meanwhile, to cap it all off, Boxhall actually says that the stranger he was observing was turning very slowly from red to the stern light (white), and *not* from green to red (question 15409): 'I judged her to be between 5 and 6 miles when I Morsed to her, and then she turned round – she was turning very, very slowly – until at last I only saw her [white] stern light, and that was just before I went away in the boat [at 1.45 a.m.]'. By now it should be clear that forcing the *Californian* to fit the facts cannot be achieved, no matter how vaunted or superficially attractive this swing theory might be.

Fifthly, and lastly, the *Californian's* swing can be calculated from the evidence, although there appear to be various rates of swing during different stages of the night, according to the testimony. Gibson said:

7467. You came up at five minutes to one… —Yes.
7469. Was she still in the same position? — No, Sir. She was about two and a half points before the starboard beam.

7473. When you say it was 2-and-a-half points upon the starboard beam, do you mean forward of the starboard beam? — Before the beam.

7474. Five and a-half from the bows? — Yes.

There are thirty-two points of the compass, with eight in each quadrant. There are thus eight points between the *Californian's* bow and her starboard beam. Gibson confirms these eight points (five and a half plus two and a half) between the bow and the starboard beam, which is the midpoint on the starboard side. But, at twenty minutes past twelve, when he first saw the lights, Gibson said: 'Where did the lights of this steamer you have spoken of bear from you? — Right on the starboard beam' (question 7438). So, as the *Californian* swung slowly clockwise, the puzzling stranger's bearing had advanced two and a half points from the beam towards the *Californian's* bow. This happened between 12.20 a.m. and 12.55 a.m., according to Gibson's evidence. Two and a half points travelled in thirty-five minutes.

Remember that the stranger's light still needed to 'advance' five and a half points to the *Californian's* bow before the *Californian* – under observation by the other – would begin to show the stranger her port light, the red one. As the *Californian* drifts, it would appear the other light is advancing along the *Californian's* starboard side towards the bow...

Two and a half points in thirty-five minutes. If the current is now unvarying (and it would seem from Gibson's evidence to have picked up since the *Californian* first came to a standstill) then to swing through the next five points will take seventy minutes. Adding one hour and ten minutes to Gibson's time of 12.55 a.m., gives 2.05 a.m. *Californian* time. Yet the ship below her – argued to be the *Titanic* – *still* will not see a red light because this southern vessel (even *if* she remains stationary in the same current) will find herself remaining half a point on the *green* side of the *Californian's* bow.

So Boxhall, contrary to the swing theory book's claims, is not seeing a change of the mystery ship's side light from green to red at 1.30 a.m. He actually saw a change from red to white, around 1.45 a.m.

Look at it another way. According to Gibson, thirty-five minutes of swing have left the strange ship, at 12.55 a.m., with five and a half points still to 'travel' before she can discern the *Californian's* red light. Another thirty-five minutes will bring the time from 12.55 to 1.30 – the point at which the book claims *Titanic* first sees a red light. Even if there is a major difference between 1.30 a.m. on the *Californian* and 1.30 a.m. on the *Titanic*, the swing-rate can hardly suddenly jump from two and a half points in thirty-five minutes to several points in the following thirty-five minutes!

The swinging *Californian* theory should now be dead and buried. But there are further considerations about the rate of swing. Lord and Groves both testified that the *Californian* was heading north-east when she stopped. Stone wrote in his original statement for his captain that a couple of hours later, at 1.50 a.m., the *Californian* was heading west-south-west. Gibson verifies that at 2 a.m. Stone told him to tell the captain 'we are heading WSW'. This would make it appear that the current has speeded up after midnight – and that it did so again from the rate of swing indicated by Gibson's observations!

To illustrate this, consider that from east-north-east to west-south-west is sixteen points (half the compass) or exactly 180 degrees. The *Californian* was pointing east-north-east at the beginning of their watch, according to both Stone (question 8061) and Gibson (question 7437). Thus there is the impression that the *Californian* began to swing more quickly. In the 110 minutes from 12.10 a.m. to 2 a.m., a uniform rate of drift would average 6.87 minutes per point – much faster than the speed from 10.21 p.m. to 12.10 a.m. (one point per hour). This overall rate is also much faster than the fourteen minutes per point suggested by Gibson's observations in the period from 12.20 a.m. to 12.55 a.m. Yet the 'speeding up' contrasts with the common testimony that *Californian* was swinging slowly (in actual fact, the current speed may have stayed the same, with only the 'rate of swing' increasing due to the changing orientation of the *Californian* to the current).

It looks like the *Californian* swung slowly from 10.21 p.m. until almost 1 a.m., then much faster from 1 a.m. to 2 a.m., then slowly again thereafter. With a current flowing to the south-west, this would make sense. As the *Californian* changed her heading from north-east to south-east, the vessel would gradually become more broadside to the current. At south-east it would be broadside to a south-west current (south-east to south-west is 90 degrees), thus swinging much faster as the whole length of the ship would be exposed to the force of the current. Once she got around to west-south-west at 1.50 a.m., the vessel would be end-on to the current and we would expect the swing rate to slow down. This is exactly what the testimony of Stone and Gibson describes. Once again we find the testimony of *Californian* witnesses matching up with expected physical conditions that night. Of course the current could appear to speed up if there was some motive force on the part of at least one of the ships at some stage of the night!

Officer Stone on the *Californian* made it clear (question 7922) that the ship under observation altered her bearing. Stone said that she began altering her bearing from his vessel 'from the time I saw the first rocket' (question 7938). He reported this at the time to Captain Lord, who corroborates. Here is more of Stone's evidence:

> 7940. You say you saw the steamer altering her bearing with regard to you? — She bore first SSE and she was altering her bearing towards the south towards west.
> 7941. Under way apparently? — Yes.

Stone added: 'Two ships remaining stationary could not possibly alter their bearings' (question 7968). If the other ship is indeed moving of her own volition, as described above, then she is not the *Titanic*. The rate of swing, rather than the current, may have speeded up – but since this other ship was moving from south-south-east to south to south-west, the swinging *Californian* would also have to *catch up* with her in order to show her a red light!

An accelerated clockwise swing of the *Californian* moves her head more swiftly toward the south and ultimately to the west-south-west. But the other ship's relative bearing to the *Californian's* starboard side does not move as swiftly – because that ship is steaming toward the south-west!

This takes away the apparent contradiction between Gibson and Stone's swing-speed. In fact they now support one another, because Stone is describing the *Californian*'s absolute heading (by giving compass points for the bow), while Gibson describes the bearing of the other ship by reference to the *Californian* herself.

Gibson's is a relative bearing, and depends in part on what the other ship is doing. If the other ship is moving away as the men describe, then the rate of change in her bearing to the *Californian* will slow down in comparison to the rate of change in the *Californian*'s heading. Stone and Gibson's separate descriptions are thus independently corroborative of the other ship moving. In the final analysis, therefore, anyone trying to prove a point by relying on a simplistic view of the *Californian*'s swing (while ignoring complex testimony on the issue) is on very shaky ground indeed. Not only was the red light on the *Titanic*'s mystery ship seen far earlier in the night (at 1 a.m. by Officer Boxhall and Officer Lowe) than was 'swingable', but the claims of Stone (implicitly backed by Gibson) are that the *Californian*'s nearby steamer actively 'steamed away' or went 'out of sight'.

The evidence will soon point us to a telling conclusion – that *Californian*'s stranger did indeed have locomotive power at the end of the night. And she used it! Because she was not the *Titanic*.

We shall hear later from Gibson and Stone on this point. But now it is time to consider some hard facts, particularly the main breakthrough in the case and its ramifications for the entire debate. That breakthrough was achieved in September 1985 with the discovery of the wreck of the RMS *Titanic*.

9

LOCATION, LOCATION AND LOCATION

The actual *Titanic* wreck site gives us an indisputable and wonderful anchoring point for analysis of the conflicting claims – yet is often completely overlooked in the mystery ship analysis of heading, drift, bearing, course, light effects, and so on. With the wreck site, discovered in 1985, we *know* where the *Titanic* actually was when she sank and can infer where she was when she fired her rockets. This must be a central plank. One can build further, but for now let us enunciate clearly that the *Titanic* sank at:

41° 43' N, 49° 56' W.

The centre of the boiler field, to be absolutely precise, was a further thirty-two seconds north and an extra forty-nine seconds W, but we don't need to be told to the exact second when we ask someone the time.

Knowing this indisputable fact, one can celebrate the famous real-estate maxim: location, location and location.

So, we know where the *Titanic* sank. But where was the Leyland liner *Californian*? The pointers are in the evidence: 'To Captain *Antillian*... Three large bergs five miles to southward of us, regards Lord' (Evans 8941 and 8943; British Report, p.43). This wireless message was broadcast by *Californian* at 7.30 p.m. her time. It related to a sighting an hour earlier at 6.30 p.m. on the *Californian*. This transmission came practically four hours before the *Titanic* hit the berg. The ice warning included the *Californian*'s position at the time. This is useful, as the *Californian* could not have had any reason to mislead as to location at this point, the *Titanic* collision not having happened yet. *Californian* reported seeing those 'three large bergs' at 6.30 p.m. in 42° 03' N, 49° 09' W.

This transmission was a slight error. Captain Lord was adamant (questions 6694/5) that the latitude he had asked his wireless operator to send was 42° 05' N, not 42° 03' N. It appears that Evans misread the scrap of paper he was handed, since 42° 03' N is what he sent (Lord's handwriting could be difficult to decipher, see p.302). But the 2-mile difference (each minute of latitude represents 1 nautical mile on the North–South axis) is not staggeringly important.

Dear Sir:-

We have received your letter and telegram of the 15th
instant, and under separate cover we send you Mate's & Engineer's
Logbooks of steamship "ANTILLIAN", covering the 15th April last.
We think in justice to the Captain of the "CALIFORNIAN" we should
draw your attention to the recorded Marconigram received by the
"ANTILLIAN" which gives the "CALIFORNIAN's position at 6.30.p.m
on the 14th, and this is consistent with the position at 10.30.p.m.
when the engines were stopped for the night.

Yours truly,

For FREDERICK LEYLAND & COMPANY, LIMITED,

Manager.

A letter from the Leyland Line to Sir Walter Howell, secretary of the Marine Department of the Board of Trade, dated 17 June 1912. Captain Lord's employers effectively pointed out that the Californian *could not have prefabricated an alibi as to her position by anticipating an accident that hadn't happened yet. The Leyland vessel's course had been clearly indicated in a series of wireless transmissions before the* Titanic *struck.*

What counts is the general latitude and the time. It is long before the impact and the *Californian* is westbound for Boston just as *Titanic* is westbound for New York. *Californian* stayed heading west on that northern track, Lord later said. She had been in latitude 42° 05' N, and she stopped in latitude 42° 05' N, he testified. Heading due west therefore.

Latitude (northerly axis) is important. There is a twenty-two minute vertical separation between the *Californian's* reported stop position in 1912 and the *Titanic's* actual wreck site, discovered in 1985. That's 42° 05' N (*Californian* reported stop) minus 41° 43' N (*Titanic* wreck) equals twenty-two minutes, there being sixty minutes in a full degree. One minute in all latitudes is 2,026 yards, or 1 nautical mile. Only minutes of longitude change their measurement. Twenty-two minutes of latitude difference between the two positions makes them 22 nautical miles apart. That was the 'height gap' between the ships. So, 22 miles is the gulf on the North–South axis between the *Titanic* wreck and Lord's 1912 reported overnight stopping place.

Naturally the course of the *Californian* is central to the reckoning. From the British Inquiry report: 'The *Californian* proceeded on her course S 89 deg, *West true* [author's italics], until 10.20 p.m. when she was obliged to stop and reverse engines because she was running into field ice' (p.43).

Californian was steaming at just one degree off true West to counter an effect of current. She stopped at 42° 05' N, just as Lord had intended to report her in 42° 05' N nearly three hours earlier. The latitude is exactly the same. That is consistent with her heading due west, as intended. Her line is still 22 miles *north* of the *Titanic's* line. That is the gap between the upper and lower lines in an 'equals sign', or '=', which represents their separate courses to the west.

Californian *Marconigram sent on the early evening of 14 April 1912, which establishes the Leyland liner's course as being north of latitude 42 degrees. It reads: 'To Captain, Antillian, 6.30 p.m. ATS [apparent time ship] Lat 42 3 N, Long 49 9 W, three large bergs five miles to southward of us, regards, Lord'. These are believed to be the same bergs seen earlier by the* Parisian, *far to the north of the* Titanic's *New York course.*

Lord says he stopped at 10.21 p.m. in 42° 05' N, 50° 07' W. This is a crucial assertion. Lord Mersey, Commissioner of the British Inquiry, noted that this position was 19 miles north by east from the *Titanic*'s SOS position. He then went on to declare: 'I am satisfied that this position [*Californian*'s reported stopping place] is not accurate' (p. 43 of the Final Report). Mersey knew there was *something* wrong because of the *direction* in which the *Californian* witnesses had seen the faint rockets, which were certainly those of the *Titanic*. But in fact it was the *Titanic*'s position that was 'not accurate', not that of the *Californian*, as we now know.

An explanation is forthcoming. *Titanic*'s wreckage was found in 1985 in a position 13 nautical miles short of the position she reported by CQD (the old distress sign) and SOS in 1912! This next bit is a little complex and demands careful concentration. If *Titanic*'s SOS position was correct (and it was wrong, as we know from the wreck site) then the *Titanic* would have outstripped the stopped *Californian*. *Titanic* would have gone further west, to reach the SOS position, which was to the west of the ice barrier that had forced the *Californian* to stop. Of course the *Titanic* never reached the SOS position. But the court in 1912 believed she did.

Had she done so, she would have gone further west than the *Californian*, which was to the north. The lower line of the '=' would have run on, to the left of the parallel, *Californian* being stopped to the north (bound for Boston), and *Titanic* (to the south of her) streaking further west (bound for New York).

Yet if the *Titanic*'s SOS position were correct, it would have meant the *Californian* witnesses *should not* have seen *Titanic*'s rockets in the way they did. That's what was wrong! The *Californian* saw the rockets to the south and east. In other words, behind their own limit of westward progress. But if the *Titanic* had been in the SOS position, then they should have seen them to the south and *west*. Because the *Titanic* would have gone on further west.

The fact that *Californian* witnesses did not see rockets where they 'should' have seen them means that the relative positions reported by the *Titanic* and *Californian* (represented by the symbol '_–'), indicating where each finally stopped, could not *both* be correct!

Californian saw rockets that indicated the progress of the two ships was akin to '–_', the *Titanic* being to the south and east of themselves, in other words not at the SOS position at all. Commissioner Mersey was thus presented with a choice. He chose to believe the *Californian* position false. It is sadly true that he should have believed the opposite.

The *Titanic*'s SOS position was simply wrong, and this is now put beyond all dispute by the wreck lying on the sea bed. The *Californian*'s 1912 reported stop position and the *Titanic*'s actual stop position (as determined in 1985 from the discovery of the wreckage) place the *Californian* to the north and west of the *Titanic*. The crew of the *Californian* would have seen the *Titanic* rockets to the south and east, just as they did indeed report in 1912. The 1985 discovery of the wreck site has validated their testimony. They are not telling lies.

This means that not only is there no automatic suggestion that the *Californian* must be lying about her stop position, but that her 1912 reported overnight stop location seems rather more likely to be true. It is surely not reasonable to expect the *Californian* to have been anticipating the fortuitous discovery of the *Titanic* wreck, 2 miles down, when they needed it. It was only found by an exploration team some three-quarters of a century later. So the *Californian* could not have been, and was not, 'tailoring' her position in 1912 to avoid blame! The stop position she reported for herself caused her own case considerable difficulties in 1912 – whereas the purpose of an invention by any accused person is always to get out of, not into, difficulty.

The hard bit is over.

Now we shall have to try to establish the actual distance as the crow flies between the *Californian* and *Titanic* at the time the latter hit the berg, making allowances for the drift of both before the RMS *Titanic* slumped in two pieces to her final resting place. One can hear the objection already: 'Alright, we know the location of the *Titanic* wreck, but why should we trust the *Californian*'s claimed stop location? She could have been anywhere! She could have been close to the *Titanic*! The *Californian* could still be lying!'

We shall first have to deal with this objection. It is an obstacle to further progress.

SHE COULD HAVE BEEN ANYWHERE

Those convinced that the *Californian* had to be the *Titanic*'s mystery ship do not really require a position for her at all. Although stationary all night, it is preferred if she could be a 'movable feast', popping up in a series of alternative locations if others can be shown to be impossible. We must hold firm to the certainty that *Californian* did not move. The evidence has been patiently adduced earlier in this book. Furthermore, if she did move – to come closer to the *Titanic* and go away again – then it requires a mass conspiracy of denial by the *Californian*'s complement. Such a conspiracy might have extended to mass denial of seeing any rockets, or at least not giving the 'wrong' position for those rockets (so that the *Californian*'s claimed stop position should not be thrown into doubt). Indeed, a 'standard' version of events would have prevented *Californian* witnesses saying, as they did, a bewildering variety of very different things.

The conclusion must be that the *Californian* witnesses were attempting to tell the truth as best they could, which is the courtesy extended to *Titanic* witnesses. Meanwhile all are agreed that their vessel did not move. But let us not rely merely on their word…

What can we tell independently about the *Californian*'s stop position, without relying on anything that those aboard her might say? We know the rockets were seen to the south and east. That means the *Californian* must be located somewhere on the curve of a quadrant between the positions of 9 and 12 o'clock on a clock-face, where the lower right-hand corner of the quadrant (the 'centre of the clock') is the location of the firing vessel – *Titanic*. The ultimate question is how far the *Californian* was from the rocket-firing *Titanic*. The challenge then, is to tell her longitude (how far west she was) and her latitude (how far north she was), since longitude plus latitude is position.

Let us deal with longitude (westing). We know, roughly, how far west *Californian* got. At 11 p.m., having stopped, the *Californian* sent a message to the *Titanic*: 'Say Old Man, we are stopped and surrounded by ice', before the *Titanic* told her to keep out as they were transmitting private cables to a land station at Cape Race (8992/3).

Stopped. And surrounded by ice. This is true, because it was transmitted a very substantial time before the *Titanic* collided with her iceberg. But the *Titanic* hit a stray. She did not find herself to have impacted field ice. She was not 'surrounded by ice'. The *Californian* was.

Here is the evidence of Captain Stanley Lord:

6701. Later on did you have to stop on account of ice? — I had to stop and reverse engines.

6702. Would you tell us what time that was? — 10.21 p.m.

6703. That also was ship's time? —Yes, ship's time for that same longitude.

6704. Where were you then? — Forty-two deg, five min N, and 50 deg, 7 min W.

[The Attorney General] … We make it the spot is just under the fringe marked as 'the FIELD OF ICE between March and July'.

That's the British Attorney General telling the court that Commissioner Mersey's *own assessors* have marked *Californian*'s testified stop position on a chart they have prepared themselves, showing the location of the ice barrier reported by a variety of ships at the relevant time that year. In other words the field ice location is independently known and verified. And the ice barrier is where Lord said it was. His ship is stopped on the fringe. So Lord is telling the truth about the location of the field ice. He might have got it wrong if he had invented the stop position! But it is not wrong – the icefield is entirely consistent with where he said he stopped.

6706. Where was it? — [Lord] Right ahead of me.

6707. Did it stretch far? — As far as I could see to the northward and southward.

6712. Did you then stop? — We stopped.

6713. Until? — 6 o'clock next morning...

6773. Did the ice extend at all to the eastward or westward of you? — It seemed to me to be running more north and south, but whilst we were stopped we were surrounded by loose ice.

6774. From north to south was the field? —Yes.

All the *Californian* witnesses who commented on that ship's surroundings spoke of the field ice. Chief Officer Stewart: 'It was thick field ice' (8875); Second Officer Stone: 'Did you find the ship stopped and surrounded by ice? —Yes' (7809), and 'She was in a sea covered with ice? —Yes' (7964); Third Officer Groves: 'What did you find when you got there? — Ice all round us, and icebergs' (8314), and 'Your Captain stopped because of the ice field? —Yes' (8390).

The *Titanic's* SOS position – her claimed location at the height of emergency – was to the south and west of the *Californian's* claimed stopping place, as we have seen. This would put the *Titanic* just to the west of the ice barrier – an ice barrier the *Titanic* could not possibly have penetrated, since it was solid. And of course her SOS position was wrong.

There was independent evidence, even in 1912, for the *Titanic's* SOS position being incorrect. *Californian* in the morning pushed through field ice to get from the eastern edge of the field to the western edge and clear water, then went south to where the *Titanic* had said (by SOS) she was sinking. There was no wreckage there. The Canadian Pacific vessel *Mount Temple* had also arrived at the SOS location, and her Captain, James Moore, could see the ice barrier ahead. He *knew* in 1912 that the *Titanic* had not made it through (US Inquiry, p.777):

> Of course, I reckoned I was somewhere near, if not at, the *Titanic's* position that he gave me, which afterwards proved correct, when I got observations in the morning, sir. I searched for a passage to get through this pack, because I realized that the *Titanic* could not have been through that pack of ice, sir... I had not seen anything of the *Titanic* and did not know exactly where she was; because I think, after all, the *Titanic* was farther east than she gave her position, or, in fact, I am certain she was.
>
> Senator Smith: How much farther away?
>
> Moore: I should think at least 8 miles, sir, of longitude... the *Titanic* must have been on the other side of that field of ice, and then her position was not right which she gave.

Moore was right. So too was Captain Ludwig Stulping of the Russian–Amerika Co.'s SS *Birma*, who wrote in an official report to his owners in April that:

> At 7.30 a.m. we arrived on the scene of the wreck. There we saw some immense icebergs to the east, beginning from NE to S, and as far as the eye could reach there lay pack ice with icebergs, so that it was out of the question to proceed through the ice, and it was quite clear that the *Titanic* could not have been at that spot.

Birma's report was received in translation by the Board of Trade of 4 June 1912. The Inquiry sat for another month until 3 July, but this statement was never read into the record or otherwise entered at all. Yet the *Daily Telegraph* and *Daily Sketch*, on successive days as early as 25 and 26 April 1912, had both printed the *Birma's* account, together with a rude chart or map of the icefield as she had seen it. The captain, his first officer, purser, and two wireless operators all put their names to the assertion that it was 'obvious that the [SOS] position given must be wrong'. *Titanic* could not have got through a dense icefield 69 miles long and 3 to 12 miles wide, they said. The chart – the only drawing of the icefield made by independent witnesses on the scene – was likewise received by the Board of Trade. But it was never considered by the British Inquiry. Thus the *Birma* joined the *Mount Temple* in disputing the claims of where the *Titanic* had gone down. And it was not until the closing years of the twentieth century that this truth was finally established. The vaunted *Titanic* of the White Star Line had got her sinking position wrong when transmitting her distress messages.

A sketch made by the SS *Birma* of the SOS position and icefield location was published in the *Daily Sketch* on 26 April 1912. The sketch showed the *Birma's* original course to the East, from 53° W towards 49° W. It also showed 'the course taken after distress signal was heard', sharply north-east towards the given SOS position, which turned out to be to the west of an icefield said to be 69 miles long and from 3 to 12 miles wide. But the British Inquiry ignored this evidence and decided that the *Titanic* sank at the incorrect SOS location that she had been transmitting to all shipping in her distress messages.

The same newspaper issue quoted an American journalist, Charles Edward Walters, who happened to be on board the *Birma* at the time. Walters was reported as stating: 'the ice-floe lay between [the *Birma*] and the course of the *Titanic*. He added: 'Hence it is obvious that one of the bergs photographed on the easterly side must have caused the disaster'. He was right.

The rescue ship *Carpathia* provided further independent evidence that the *Titanic* had got it wrong. The *Carpathia's* arrival at lifeboats dotted across the ocean to the *east* of the ice barrier further proves that the *Titanic's* SOS position was wrong. The Cunarder picked up the distress signal at 12.35 a.m. (ship's time), her captain telling the US Inquiry: 'I was dressing, and I picked up our position on my chart, and set a course to pick up the *Titanic*. The course was north 52 degrees, west true, 58 miles from my position' (US Inquiry, p.20). At 58 miles, her skipper, Captain Arthur Rostron, expected it to take fully four hours to reach the SOS site. He expected only a 4.35 a.m. arrival at best, and told his wireless operator to tell this to the *Titanic*. Rostron said (US Inquiry, p.25): 'From the very first I sent a message to the *Titanic* – telling them: 'Coming immediately to your assistance. Expect to arrive half past four'. No; it was: 'Expect to arrive in four hours', because I had not then got up full speed'. Four hours at *full speed*. But it turned out he could not maintain full speed throughout. Despite this, he later testified (US Inquiry, p.21): '…it was 58 miles, and it took us three and a half hours… I stopped my engines at 4 o'clock, and I was then close to the first boat'. So Rostron encountered lifeboats more than half an hour earlier than expected. And he had first seen a lifeboat flare after just *two hours* of steaming: 'At 20 minutes to three, I saw the green flare, which is the White Star Company's night signal, and naturally, knowing I must be at least 20 miles away, I thought it was the ship herself still. It was showing just for a few seconds and I passed the remark that she [*Titanic*] must still be afloat' (25394).

The green flare was in Boxhall's No.2 boat, launched around 1.45 a.m. Put very simply, this lifeboat from the *Titanic* could not have pulled 'at least twenty miles away' from the transmitted SOS position in roughly one hour (launch of Boxhall's lifeboat from the *Titanic* at 1.45 a.m. and flare seen by *Carpathia* 2.40 a.m. This holds good despite a difference between *Titanic* and *Carpathia* ship times).

Rostron *knew* at this time that he was at least 20 miles from the SOS position given! Rostron's answer to question 25394 should have given the British Inquiry pause for serious thought as to whether the *Titanic's* SOS position was reliable. But it was simply another missed clue.

Captain Lord of the *Californian*, like these others, asserted strongly in 1912 that the *Titanic's* SOS position was wrong. But Lord was not believed because he was a suspect. He had a 'motive' for casting doubt on the *Titanic's* transmitted location. Here is Lord:

> 6821. [Referring to the SOS position] That particular spot? The spot mentioned here as 19 miles away is not, in my opinion, where the *Titanic* hit the berg.
>
> 6822. Within a radius of 20 miles of you? — No, 30 miles.
>
> 6823. Do you mean she was further from you? — She was 32 miles from where I left the wreckage.

The wreckage had drifted west and a little south since the *Titanic* sank, over more than six hours prior to *Californian's* arrival at the wreckage in its *new* position – not the position where it was originally generated by the sinking.

Let us say again: the *Titanic* never met the field ice. She was felled by a lone iceberg in open sea. Far to the east. How far east? The wreck location on the sea bed is over 13 nautical miles from the SOS position. The SOS position is just to the west of the ice barrier that *Titanic* could not have passed through. Lord's ice barrier was 3 miles thick at its narrow point, as he saw it. All things being equal, *Titanic* would have hit the ice barrier itself at least 3½ miles short of the SOS position. That is if she had not been felled by a stray berg many miles further east. By subtracting the rough width of the icefield from the distance east and west between the known wreck site on the sea bed and the *Titanic's* SOS position, we are left with an indication – an indication merely – that the *Titanic* was 10 miles short of the *Californian* in westerly progress. In other words, the *Californian* was 10 miles further west than the *Titanic*. Let us test the longitude (Westing) of both ships another way. Lord gave a stop longitude without benefit of knowing where the wreck would eventually be found. His stop position is eleven minutes of longitude further west than the *Titanic* on her sea bed wreck site (50° 07' W, Lord's claimed stop longitude, minus 49° 56' W, *Titanic* wreck longitude, equals eleven minutes, there being sixty minutes in a full degree). There are 1,500 yards in a minute of longitude at this location (longitude varies, latitude remains the same), meaning that the westerly separation between Lord's reported stop for the *Californian* and the *Titanic* wreck is just over 8¼ nautical miles (one nautical mile being 2026.66 yards). Now we need the northerly axis to give us an 'L' shape, where the baseline horizon is longitude and the vertical represents latitude. Drawing the diagonal line to complete the 'triangle' will thereafter give us the distance between the *Californian* and the *Titanic* as the crow flies.

As for latitude (Northing), we know the *Californian* reported being in latitude 42° 03' N (intending 42° 05' N) at 6.30 p.m., which was some five hours before the *Titanic* collided (questions 8941-3). An hour later, at 7.30 p.m., Chief Officer Stewart took a new observation, using the Pole Star. It confirmed they were in latitude 42° 05' N. Stewart would later state (question 8706) that he again got the Pole Star at half-past ten just after his vessel stopped. Stewart's reference to getting the Pole Star at 10.30 p.m. must be one of the most overlooked answers in the whole of the British Inquiry:

> 8706. [The Solicitor General] What I want to know is how they arrived at the latitude, which is put down, I presume by dead reckoning, at 10.20 p.m. If I am right, it would be by dead reckoning you would get it? — [Stewart] Not only that. I had the Pole Star at half-past ten.

The Pole Star is the brightest star of the Little Bear constellation and is also known as Ursa Minor, Polaris, Stella Maris, and the Seaman's Star. Its importance has been known to mariners since at least Phoenician times, since it gives effectively exact latitude. As it says in the *Oxford Companion to Ships and the Sea* (edited by Peter Kemp, OUP, 1976): 'By describing a circle of only two degrees 25 minutes daily about the North pole, it is of great service to navigators since it points, within a degree or two, to the true north. The altitude of Polaris is also virtually equal to the latitude of the observer'. Thus Stewart's 10.30 p.m. sighting that night – it is often wrongly suggested he only checked the location the next morning, but he could not have got the Pole Star in daylight! – in addition to ordinary dead reckoning, verified the *Californian's* stop position that night.

There is always the possibility that 'ten' is a misprint. But Evans mentions Captain Lord talking to the 'Chief Officer' close to 11 p.m. that night. And Stewart is talking in the context of 'not only' taking dead reckoning to 10.20 p.m. to get his ship's position. This time – 10.20 p.m. – helps to verify the phrase 'half past ten,' rather than a misheard 'half past seven,' which was the earlier time he had taken an observation of the Pole Star.

The *Californian* position therefore can only be wrong if both Lord and Stewart, with the assent of Groves, and by extension the agreement of others, are lying. A mass lie, and one persisted in – perversely – by Groves, the man who had decided to help the British Inquiry. Yet there is independent support for the *Californian's* claim to have been above latitude 42° N. The veracity of her account is strengthened by the fact that she reported by wireless to other ships the location of three large icebergs seen at 6.30 p.m. These icebergs were in a position entirely consistent with their having been seen a few hours earlier by the *Parisian*. That ship had reported what were likely the same three bergs in very much the same position in a prior wireless message. Be it understood – the *Californian* could not at that stage manufacture an alibi for her latitude in respect of an event – *Titanic's* collision – that would not happen for several hours. Essentially, *Californian* says instead she stayed on that line above the 42nd parallel and stopped in 42° 05' N also. That is twenty-two miles above the 41° 43' latitude of the *Titanic* wreck site. To turn the *Californian* into a mystery ship, it would be necessary to show that she steamed south of her line for a very considerable period.

So, did the *Californian* go south? The *Californian* was bound for Boston. Boston lies above the 42nd parallel. If Lord were to stay on 42 degrees N, West true, it would carry him all the way to the upper arm of Cape Cod. He has no reason in the world to go below the line of 42 degrees North. Meanwhile it should be remembered that Charles Victor Groves was the officer of the watch on duty prior to the *Californian* stopping. This means he had to control her course, and to maintain the heading of due west. If the ship had been on any other heading, surely Groves, the man who co-operated too much with the British Inquiry, would have told them of the secret plan to head south (towards *Titanic*)? But he did not do that, even though the inquiry regarded him as something of a 'whistleblower'. While Groves does not specifically mention the course prior to stopping, he explicitly does not disagree with the captain's stop position. In fact he declares (question 8425) that it was 'bound to be accurate if the Captain put it in'. This is an answer which seems to imply an admiration of the captain's skills in general.

Meanwhile, if the *Californian* does go any way south, she has to correct by going north again at some stage in the voyage. Yet the fact is that Lord's vessel was stopped for more than an hour before the *Titanic* hit her berg. The ice barrier to the west gives us a landmark of longitude. There is no benchmark equivalent for the *Californian*'s latitude – except for the minor point that Lord was correct that the ice extended that far north. The *Mount Temple*, stopped in the *Titanic*'s SOS position the next morning, saw *Californian* coming down towards her – from the north. We know *Californian* was to the north, but it is difficult to establish independently how far north.

This will be done later in this book, when we will consider the *Californian*'s course more closely. And it will be shown that the latitude of Lord's vessel is once again consistent with where he said he stopped. Meanwhile it can be suggested that longitude, plus course, plus speed, gives us an *implied* latitude. When these are weighed together, likely inferences can be drawn about Lord's claimed stop position. We have seen longitude and course. What of speed?

The difference in longitude between the *Californian*'s unimpeachable 6.30 p.m. position, 49° 09'W (unimpeachable in the sense that it was given long before the *Titanic* struck the iceberg and there can be no possibility of fabrication. However the position was a dead reckoning from the ship's noon position) and her 10.21 p.m. stop position (50° 07'W) is fifty-eight minutes west.

A stop position of 50° 07'W, minus 49° 09'W (earlier position) equals fifty-eight minutes, since there are sixty minutes in a degree. In this longitude there are 1,500 yards in one minute. We need to find the mileage travelled to the west in this period, and will first have to find the yardage travelled in total between 6.30 p.m. and 10.20 p.m. Fifty-eight minutes multiplied by 1,500 yards per minute gives 87,000 yards travelled. This distance, divided by the 2,026 yards in one nautical mile, comes to 43 nautical miles. The *Californian* travelled this distance between 6.30 p.m. and 10.21 p.m., when she stopped. It was roughly four hours of travel, which would give a speed of eleven knots (four multiplied by eleven is forty-four). In fact, to be precise, it is three hours and fifty minutes in time elapsed, so the speed was a little faster. To be absolutely exact, it is forty-three divided by 230 minutes of time, multiplied by sixty (minutes in an hour) to establish knots, or nautical miles per hour. So, forty-three divided by 230 gives 0.187. This figure multiplied by sixty gives 11.22

knots (the extra one-fifth of a knot is accounted for by Captain Lord's belief that there was a westward component to the current). That was the *Californian's* speed that evening – eleven and one-fifth knots. What did Captain Lord say about *Californian's* speed?

> 7115. At what speed were you going? — [Lord] 11 knots.

And elsewhere:

> 7137. I understand when you saw ice[bergs] first this evening it was before 6? — [Lord] It must have been about 5.
> 7138. So that it was pretty clear daylight then? — It was perfectly clear, a beautiful day.
> 7139. So that, it being clear at that time, you did not consider at that moment that it was necessary to slacken speed? — No.
> 7140. But assuming that you had first heard of ice at 11.30 that night, wouldn't you have considered it necessary? Did you, as a matter of fact, that night later on slacken speed? — Not until 20 minutes past 10.
> 7141. You were only going 11 knots an hour? — That was my full speed.
> 7142. Thirteen, I thought you said? — Driving on my consumption then, 11 knots.

The *Californian* is going top speed to the west from her 6.30 position. Just as one would expect. She's not dawdling, after the fact, hoping to be 'overtaken' by the SOS position. In other words, the *Californian's* captain did not construct a stop position that would indicate a 'slow' *Californian* and that would allow her to see rockets in the 'right' place and show beyond doubt that it must indeed be some other vessel that *Titanic* is seeing to the north-west after she stops, 'because we were too far behind her'. That is not an argument Lord relied on, even though he could have claimed to have been going slowly 'on account of the ice' seen from about 5 p.m. Instead he did what we expect, what every captain did – top speed – until it was suddenly prudent to stop completely. Despite the very fact that his full speed would inevitably put him 'closer' to the *Titanic's* SOS position!

Let us gather all this evidence together. Is Lord lying about his final stop position? If he is, his lie in 1912 placed him in incredible danger of what eventually happened – his being saddled with the blame for 1,500 deaths. His claimed speed did him no favours, and nor did his longitude, which rather stupidly showed that his crew were seeing rockets in a place where the *Titanic* was not firing them… at least by the 1912 consensus that the *Titanic* was where she said she was. These would be two clumsy mistakes for a man supposedly lying to extricate himself from a problem. But instead he hangs himself twice. And then, spectacularly, a third time, when he argued that the *Titanic* position must be wrong. Yet why should he cast doubt on the *Titanic's* SOS position by suggesting the sinking is further east, when this is *closer* to his own claimed position? What sort of suicidal 'defendant' would do such a thing? Only one who is in fact honest. And one who trusts rather touchingly in judicial fairness.

Why should a captain, after all, be such an enemy to himself when some of his own crew are hanging him too? Third Officer Groves did a lot of damage to Captain

Lord. He was the man who believed he had seen a 'passenger steamer' and who, despite not seeing any rockets at all himself, agreed when asked by counsel that he believed now, after the sinking, that this vessel he saw was 'most assuredly' the *Titanic*. Yet we remember what the same Groves said about his captain's stop position and its credibility:

> 8425. In the log book it is stated that when you stopped your ship in the ice, the position
> of the ship was 42° 5' N and longitude 50° 7' W. Is that accurate?
> Groves: Well, it is bound to be accurate if the Captain put it in.

Remarkable confidence. But an indication of official unhappiness with this opinion, and the Court's innate suspicion, is indicated by an immediate sour objection by the Solicitor General: 'This witness wouldn't know, would he?'

There is another consideration to the notion that Lord was lying. At 11 p.m. on April 14, having stopped, he told *Californian* wireless operator Cyril Evans to send out a transmission that the *Californian* was stopped and surrounded by ice.

It is likely Evans had the *Californian's* exact position at that time – which was a substantial time before *Titanic* hit the berg. Whether Evans would have gone on to offer it is an open question, since he was cut short by the luxury maiden voyager with the rebuff: 'Keep out! I am working Cape Race':

> 9123. When you gave the final message to the *Titanic* did you commence that message by
> giving your address, so to speak – your position then? — [Evans] No.

But Evans never testified about what stop position it was that he might have possessed. If he, an independent Marconi employee, was 'got at' by Lord and told to stitch a fraudulent position into the record, one would expect him to do that. But he did not mention at all in evidence any ship's position he might have been given at that time. And he was only asked about it fleetingly (US Inquiry, p.740):

> Evans: I called him [*Titanic*] up first. I said MGY three times, and gave him my own call
> signal once, which is MWL. I said: 'Say, Old Man, we are surrounded by ice, and stopped'.
> Senator Bourne: You gave your location, did you not?
> Evans: No, sir; I was just giving that as a matter of courtesy, because the Captain requested
> me to.
> Sen. Bourne: You expected a reply from him, or an inquiry as to what your location was,
> where the ice was, did you not?
> Evans: No, sir. I thought he was very much south of me, because we were bound for
> Boston, and we were north of the track. We were following the track of the *Parisian*.

It may be that Evans actually had his vessel's stop position – where ice was – for transmission if it was wanted. Otherwise the communication is meaningless. For Captain Lord it would be akin to sending someone to the shops to make purchases without any money. The report and the position go together. Evans may not have expected the *Titanic* to want the location of the ice, because he thought that vessel was too far away for it to be relevant to her, but it is hardly for him to judge. Evans said in his British evidence (question 9193): 'The Captain told me to expect the *Titanic* to be away to the southward of us'. But in a continuation of his US evidence, cited above, Evans suggests that he indeed had his own ship's position, at least at the time when he was finally finding out about the sinking and the *Titanic*'s SOS position (US Inquiry, p.740):

> Evans: I can only work on that we were about 20 miles away.
> Senator Fletcher: From what?
> Evans: From the *Titanic*, and therefore he would be 20 miles away from us.

It is now time for common sense to tell us some reasonable conclusions.

Firstly, Lord is not going to stop until he meets the ice. Secondly, he has no motive for going south at all. Groves would anyway have told if that happened. Thirdly, his stop position to the west reflects *Californian*'s top speed since the 6.30 p.m. sighting. Fourthly, top speed is what all captains did, but in Lord's case it doesn't aid him in avoiding *Titanic* but arguably puts him closer to that ship as the *Titanic* eats up the gap. In addition, Evans, Groves and others support Lord's time for stoppage and make no suggestion of altered speed or course. And Lord's claimed stop position does him no advantage and actually hurts his case in 1912. His suggestion that *Titanic*'s position was wrong – and he was correct, we know today – made him appear deceitful. But he knew it was wrong in part because he was certain of his own position. In other words, he ironically could have appeared to be a liar because of his innocent devotion to honesty! This leads ultimately to the probability that *Californian*'s stop position is *true*.

Taking this finding, we still must find out the exact distance between the *Californian* and the sinking *Titanic*. By Lord's account, the *Californian* at 10.21 p.m. was stopped only 8¼ miles west of the known *Titanic* wreck, but *crucially* 22 miles to the north. That's the 'L'. The diagonal line completing the triangle gives the exact distance. A child can do it with a ruler. Draw out 22mm of vertical separation on a sheet of paper with 8.25mm along the east–west meridian. Now join the two points to close the right-angle triangle and meas-ure that line. It should come to 23.5mm. That would be a general indicator of mileage. Plotted on computer by the Irish Marine Emergency Service, the exact distance between the *Californian* (reported stop position) and the *Titanic* wreck site (centre of the boilers in the debris field) is 23½ nautical miles. It seems probable therefore that the *Californian*'s position in 1912 when she stopped was 23½ nautical miles from the *Titanic*'s sinking posi-tion. Of course there was some slippage because the *Californian* was drifting slightly south for somewhere around an hour and twenty minutes before *Titanic* stopped abruptly, hav-ing hit the berg. The *Californian* was stopped, and drifting, much earlier.

After the *Titanic* came to rest, both ships thereafter drifted at the same rate until the *Titanic* sank, there being no difference in their respective positions when both were stopped. After the *Titanic* sank, *Californian* drifted further still. The 1992 reappraisal of the evidence conducted by the British Government's Marine Accident Investigation Branch rates the southward drift between the times of *Californian*-stop (10.21p.m., her time) and *Titanic*-stop (11.40 p.m., *Titanic* time) to have been 'some two miles' (p.11). This seems to be excessive. It would imply an estimated rate of current at between 1.33 and 1.74 knots, depending on how *Californian* and *Titanic* times related to each other.

If the times aboard the two ships are taken as the same, (so that 11.40 p.m. *Titanic* time was also 11.40p.m. *Californian* time, for the sake of argument) this British Government calculation produces 1.33 knots of drift per hour. It is almost certainly an excessive estimation, judging from all the evidence of drift available to the 1912 inquiries. Captain Moore of the *Mount Temple* claims: 'From the time I got there, from about 12.30 – the time I received the call – until half past 4, there would be a drift there of perhaps, say, half a knot an hour' (US Inquiry, p.780). Sir Robert Finlay suggests: 'As regards the *Caronia*'s ice, even allowing for a drift of only half a knot, that ice must have got to the Southward of the track which the vessel was pursuing' (British, p.769). US hydrographer John Knapp: 'The Labrador Current, which brings both berg and field ice down past Newfoundland, sweeps across the banks in a generally south to southwest direction…with a set [direction of drift] of about 12 miles a day' (US Inquiry, p.1121). That's another estimate of half a knot per hour.

These are the *only* testified rates of drift at both the US Senatorial and British Inquiries. Half a knot drift by the *Californian* while she alone was stopped would put her at just under 23 miles from the *Titanic* when the latter struck, at least as an interim step. The British reappraisal in 1992 also noted (p.11): 'Between the collision and sinking, both ships will in all probability have drifted similarly so that their position relative to each other would not appreciably change'. But we must also factor in the southerly drift in the *Titanic*'s position between her striking the berg and sinking. The wreck site is not the *Titanic*'s collision point – and two hours and forty minutes (between collision and sinking) of southward drift must be corrected to place the *Titanic* back at the collision point at 11.40 p.m. her time. When this is done, *Titanic* is back on her exact track to New York. The *Californian* position, drifting until the same time (*Titanic* time 11.40 p.m.), is now at a separation of 21½ nautical miles from that vessel. This calculation employs the testified standard drift of half a knot for both ships. Thereafter the two stopped vessels effectively remained at this distance without varying (since both are drifting similarly) until 2.20 a.m., when the White Star Liner left the surface of the ocean. So – 21½ miles. Not the mystery ship's 5 miles from *Titanic*.

Evans, the *Californian*'s wireless operator, a man employed by the Marconi Co. and on only his third trip on that vessel, mentions a distance of some 20 miles when he began trying to find out what had happened the next morning. As the most independent man aboard the Leyland liner, he has no reason to lie, but of course had no real idea of the *Titanic*'s position, except that she was probably on her official track to southward, which he knew to be substantially south of the *Californian*'s more northern Boston track (US Inquiry, p.740): 'I can only work on that we were about 20 miles away… from the *Titanic*…' And the *Titanic* wreck today lies to the south of her track, there since her slow drift while sinking. A total of 21½ miles is rather a considerable distance for *Californian* to be the mystery ship. Especially a mystery ship generally estimated by *Titanic* observers to be at a distance of only 5 miles. And it is an entirely impossible distance for *any* vessel that was showing its red light, or any visible side light.

10

A FLICKER OF DOUBT

We have already seen how Groves said he and Lord thought briefly they were being answered when they attempted to Morse the nearby vessel with their powerful lamp. Groves said:

> 8189. I saw what I took to be a light answering… When I sent 'What?' his light was flickering. I took up the glasses again and I came to the conclusion it could not have been a Morse lamp…
> 8195. Did you tell the Captain about the Morsing? —Yes…
> 8196. What did he say? — He saw a light flickering himself, and he passed the remark to me. He said, 'She is answering you'. This was just before I sent the word 'What?'

Groves says both he and Lord saw a 'flickering' light on the steamer (although Lord, it must be pointed out, makes no reference to any such conversation in his evidence, and never made any mention of such an incident for the rest of his life). Groves says he came to believe it was not a Morse lamp responding to him after studying the light through binoculars. He may indeed have seen a flicker, and if so, who else saw a flickering light on the stranger? Gibson did:

> 7441. Did you notice anything about her masthead light, her white light? —Yes.
> 7442. What was it? — It was flickering.
> 7443. Did you form an opinion about it; what did you think she was doing? — I thought it was a Morse light calling us up…
> 7451. When you tried to call up this steamer with your Morse signals, could you get into communication with her? — No, Sir; the lights were still flickering…
> 7455. Could you read it if it was clear? — I could have done if it was a Morse light, but I looked at her through the glasses afterwards, and found it was a masthead light.
> 7456. Then the light went on flickering, did it? —Yes.
> 7457. And did you look at it then through glasses? —Yes.
> 7458. And when you did that, you say you made out that it was a masthead light? —Yes.

So both Groves and Gibson, on either side of midnight, say they experienced the same thing. Both saw a flickering light but conclude that it is not a signalling Morse lamp after looking carefully through glasses. Gibson goes further – he says the flickering is from the masthead light. He says it three times. Stone agreed about the flickering, according to Gibson:

> 7792. Had you a discussion with the Second Officer as to whether this vessel was a tramp or not? —Yes.
>
> 7793. And did he [Stone] agree with you? —Yes.
>
> 7794. [The Commissioner] Did he give his reason? —That she was probably burning oil lights; that was the cause of the white masthead light flickering.

And Stone himself talks of the stranger's masthead light flickering, when questioned by the Commissioner: 'What do you mean by all her lights? — The deck lights, which were in view. The masthead light would be shut in except for a slight flickering…' (question 7958). Now here we have at least three *Californian* witnesses (Gibson, Stone, and Groves) in a rare degree of unanimity. All directly or reportedly saw flickering. A reasonable person would conclude there was some actual flickering. Gibson and Stone both referred to flickering coming directly from the masthead light. Steamers commonly carried two such lights. Some carried only one masthead light, although they might have had two masts or more masts. There is an unresolved dispute as to whether the *Titanic* carried one or two masthead lights. Blueprints for the *Titanic* do not show provision for a light on the after-mast, although one could, arguably, have been added at the building stage, and there was certainly equipment to hoist an arc light there by halliard. She certainly had one light, on her foremast. How many masthead lights did the *Californian* witnesses see on their nearby stranger? Here is Groves:

> 8396. You did see two masthead lights? —Yes, I did see two masthead lights…
>
> 8484. What lights was she then showing? —Two masthead lights…

Lord says:

> 6733. …I saw one masthead light.
>
> 6805. Can you tell us whether you saw one or two masthead lights? — I only saw one.
>
> 6806. You only saw one? —The Third Officer [Groves] said he saw two.
>
> [The Commissioner] That is very important, because the *Titanic* would have two.
>
> 6807. [The Attorney General] Yes, that is it – two masthead lights. [To the Witness] You only saw one, but the Third Officer said he saw two? — [Lord] And the Second Officer [Stone] said he saw one.

Here is Stone:

> 7814. What could you see of the other steamer? — One masthead light…
>
> 8098-9. If she had had a second masthead light could you have failed to see it? — I think not; I was bound to have seen it.

Gibson similarly saw only one:

> 7787. Had you a good opportunity of seeing whether she had two masthead lights or not
> – I understand you only saw one? — I only saw one.
> 7788. How long had you the one masthead light under observation? — From the time I
> first saw her to the time she disappeared.
> 7789. How long would that be? — A quarter past twelve to five past two.
> 7790. And during that time were you using glasses? —Yes.
> 7791. Do you think you could have missed the second masthead light had it been there?
> — No.

The Board of Trade Inquiry certainly expected the *Titanic* to have two masthead lights
– whether she had or not. Groves obligingly sees two masthead lights, whereas each of
his three shipmates sees only one. This perhaps says more about Groves and his 'passenger
steamer' than anything else.

Steward Leo Hyland, in an eyewitness drawing of the sinking, shows the *Titanic* with
two masthead lights. Robertson Dunlop, counsel for the Leyland Line, stated confidently
to the British Inquiry: 'Witnesses from the *Californian* saw... only saw one masthead light;
the *Titanic* had two' (p.835). *Californian* herself had two.

If Dunlop, Lord Mersey and the Attorney General are right about the *Titanic* having
two masthead lights, and Stone, Gibson and Lord, the *Californian* observers, similarly right
about their own nearby ship having only one, then the steamer seen by the *Californian*
was not the *Titanic*. It therefore follows that the mystery ship seen by the *Titanic* was not
the *Californian*. But if the *Titanic* in fact had only one masthead light, it is noteworthy
that the widespread and authoritatively-stated impression of there being two was never
corrected at the inquiry by any of the many naval architects and representatives of the
builders who attended. Nonetheless, the *Titanic* certainly *did* have a light on her foremast,
the mast containing the crow's nest where the lookouts kept watch. The *Titanic* had a total
of 10,000 electric lights, according to the 'Description of the Ship' in the British Inquiry
Report (p.20). She did not burn oil lights. The same section of the report again refers
only to a light on the foremast: 'A look-out cage was fitted on the foremast... An iron
ladder was fitted... [leading] to the masthead light' (p. 18). The light on *Titanic's* foremast
was electric, as befitted a state-of-the-art brand new steamer. Yet Stone said, in Gibson's
original statement for his captain: 'I then went over to the Second Officer and remarked
that she looked like a tramp steamer. He said that most probably she was, and was burning
oil lights'. And there is no doubt that Gibson is talking about the foremast of his mystery
ship in this extract:

> 7780. Was the glare of light which you saw on the after-part of this vessel forward or aft
> of the mast head light? — Abaft the masthead light [behind the mast].
> 7782. The glare of light which you say was aft, was aft of the masthead lights?
> —Yes.

If it is flickering at close quarters, it almost certainly is not electric. *Titanic*'s foremast light was electric. The *Californian*'s nearby ship had a flickering light – 'she was probably burning oil', as Stone put it. Therefore, on the sole question of her flickering masthead light, she was more likely to be a tramp than the largest modern vessel ever constructed.

In other words, she was likely a small to medium tramp steamer, as Lord, Stone and Gibson all surmised. Only Groves would later declare her to have been a 'passenger steamer'.

WHAT STONE SAW – ROCKETS

Second Officer Herbert Stone was now alone on the bridge. It was after 12.25 a.m. *Californian* time, and apprentice officer James Gibson had gone below to stream a new patent log (the distance-meter trailed behind a ship), the original log having been cut by ice when the *Californian* swerved sharply to avoid the ice floe she had spotted ahead of her some two hours earlier. Presumably this severed patent log is still on the sea floor. If ever discovered, it would establish exactly and beyond all reasonable doubt as to where the *Californian* came to rest that fateful night in far-off 1912.

Creating a new log was Gibson's job. Stone's job had been spelt out to him by the captain just before he went on watch:

> 7815. Did he [Captain Lord] say anything to you when he pointed her out (the steamer lying nearby)? — He asked me to tell him if the bearing of the steamer altered or if she got any closer to us.

In other words, Stone's sole watchword that night was to tell his captain whether the strange steamer, which Stone thought to be 'approximately five miles' away (question 7819), should ever move. Stone himself tells what happened next:

> 7832. …First of all, I was walking up and down the bridge and I saw one white flash in the sky, immediately above this other steamer. I did not know what it was; I thought it might be a shooting star.
> 7833. What was the nature of the flash? — A white flash.
> 7834. You did not know what it was? — No.
> 7835. How long have you been at sea? — Eight years.
> 7836. You know distress signals? — I know what they are, yes.
> 7837. Was it like a distress signal? — It was just a white flash in the sky; it might have been anything.
> 7838. I know, but what did it suggest to your mind? What did you say to yourself? What did you think it was? — I thought nothing until I brought the ship under observation with the binoculars and saw the others.
> 7839. Then you took up your glasses, apparently, and looked? — Yes.

7840. And how many more did you see? — I saw four more then.

7841. What were they, rockets? — They had the appearance of white rockets bursting in the sky.

7842. Did they come in quick succession? — At intervals of about three or four minutes.

7843. Now what did you think they were? — White rockets.

7844. What do you think they meant? — I thought that perhaps the ship was in communication with some other ship, or possibly she was signalling to us to tell us she had big icebergs around her.

This then, is Stone's impression: the steamer is in communication by rocket signal with some other ship. He cannot be sure the rockets, whatever their purpose, are intended to contact his vessel. If read carefully, his testimony does not automatically link the *origin* of the rockets to his near ship, at least until the latter part of his response to question 7844. It may be that Stone did not think the first rockets were from that close steamer because he goes on to say: 'Possibly, what else? — Possibly she [it is not clear whether Stone is referring to the nearby ship or the rocket-origin ship] was communicating with some other steamer at a greater distance than ourselves' (7845). There are two interpretations here – that the intended recipient was a greater distance to the northward than the *Californian*, or at a greater distance to the southward, over the horizon and unseen by the *Californian*. But the *Californian* saw no lights to her northward at all, and they should have been visible to Stone if they were visible to the stranger. Stone likely suspected that the rockets were communication with *Californian* by the near ship, or communication by her with another vessel, unseen by *Californian*, even further to the southward. In other words, Stone is already conveying at least the possibility that an *unseen* steamer to his southward might separately have been firing rockets, while also saying clearly that he believed rockets were being fired by the nearby ship. The Commissioner continues to question Stone:

7846. [The Commissioner] What was she communicating? — I do not know.

7847. Is that the way in which steamers communicate with each other? — No, not usually. [The Commissioner] Then you cannot have thought that. Just attend to the question.

The Commissioner's interruption is hardly helpful here. Stone merely states that he does not know what the stranger was trying to say. He says it is not usual, but the Commissioner reacts as if it is not possible!

7850. Now, what did you think at the time? — I knew they were signals of some sort.

7851. [Commissioner] I know of course – signals of what sort did you think? — I did not know at the time.

7852. [The Commissioner] Now try to be frank? — I am.

7853. If you try, you will succeed. What did you think these rockets were going up at intervals of three or four minutes for? — I just took them as white rockets, and informed the Master and left him to judge.

7854. Do you mean to say you did not think for yourself? I thought you told us just now that you did think? — [No answer].

7855. [Mr Butler Aspinall] You know they were not being sent up for fun, were they? — No.

7856. [The Commissioner] You know, you do not make a good impression upon me at present.

7856a. [Mr Butler Aspinall] Did you think that they were distress signals? — No.

7857. Didn't that occur to you? — It did not occur to me at the time.

7858. When did it occur to you? Did it occur at some later time to you? — Yes.

7859. When? — After I had heard about the *Titanic* going down.

Stone has been legally 'monstered' in this excerpt. But he reiterates what he thought at the time – that these were rockets of communication, signals of some sort. It simply did not occur to him that they were distress signals. But Stone's state of mind that night is of less importance to the court than establishing that they could have been distress rockets:

7860. So throwing your mind back [the next morning] after that information [that *Titanic* had sunk] then you thought they were distress signals? — I thought they possibly might have been distress signals.

7861. [The Commissioner] From the *Titanic*? — No, not necessarily.

7862. After you had heard that the *Titanic* went down, then it occurred to you that those might have been distress signals? — Yes.

7863. From the *Titanic*? — Not necessarily. They may have been from some other steamer. I did not think that vessel was the *Titanic*.

Of course, what Stone thinks the next morning is entirely irrelevant. What is important is what he thought at the time because this necessarily informed his communication to the master, Captain Stanley Lord, which shall be examined in a moment. For now, however, just absorb the confusion in Stone's mind, even *after* learning of the *Titanic* sinking. He says that the nearby steamer was firing rockets, but that the nearby steamer was not the *Titanic*! It still does not seem to him that the nearby steamer was in distress, but if not in distress, was communicating with another ship. But it may be that the other party to such communication was not in distress either… So, possibly, a yet different ship, not the nearby vessel and not her unseen partner, was in distress. If another ship was firing distress rockets, how would Stone know it was the *Titanic*? But it might have been…

When we look at it, Stone's puzzlement the next morning and thereafter is consistent with two certainties in his own mind: that the 'smallish' steamer that he saw (question 8088) simply could not have been the *Titanic* and that he didn't think at the time that any vessel was firing distress rockets. Let us proceed:

7664. [Mr Butler Aspinall] Your vessel had stopped, had she not? — Yes.

7865. That was on account of the danger from ice? — Yes.

7866. Did that fact help you at the time to come to some conclusion as to what these signals meant – danger from ice you know, I suggest, followed by distress signals? — I kept the ship under close observation, and I did not see any reason to suppose they were sent as distress signals from this ship.

7867. You communicated the fact to the Captain? — Yes.

7868. Through the speaking tube? — Yes.

7869. I think you said you left it to him to judge. Did he answer back? — Yes.

We are now at a crucial conversation. It is right that it should be examined in great detail. What we know, however, is that Stone did not communicate to his captain that a nearby ship was firing *distress rockets*. That was emphatically not Stone's own impression, and his voice would therefore have conveyed no sense of urgency – because there was none. In Stone's mind, let us reiterate, he was only seeing unusual signals. But what prompted him to make that report? The puzzle itself, or some other motive? And when did he report it?

WHAT WAS REPORTED – AND WHEN?

There is an enormous issue, all too often overlooked, about the exact time when Stone reported by speaking tube to Captain Lord, and what he could have told him.

At 12.40 a.m. *Californian* time we know there was a preliminary conversation between Stone and Lord, half an hour after the second officer had taken up the watch. This was initiated by Lord. Nothing had been seen by this time. Lord is asked about this first conversation with Stone:

6785. Then did you speak to him through the speaking tube? — [Lord] At 20 minutes to 1.

6786. …I asked him if the steamer was the same. He said it was the same; he had called her up once [by Morse lamp], but she would not reply to him.

6787. Then you went to lie down in the chartroom? — Yes, I told him I was going to lie down in the chart room then.

Captain Lord also stated clearly that he first spoke to the second officer at 12.40am during his US Inquiry evidence (p.729): 'At 20 minutes to 1, I whistled up the speaking tube and asked him if she was getting any nearer. He said, "No; she is not taking any notice of us". So, I said "I will go and lie down a bit"'. Stone does not mention this earlier discussion in his direct evidence. It is hardly surprising. He was being energetically taken to task on other issues. But he did mention it in a statement prepared at Captain Lord's request on 18 April 1912, while the *Californian* was still at sea: 'At 12.35 you [captain] whistled up the speaking tube and asked if the other steamer had moved. I replied "No" and that she was on the same bearing and also reported I had called him up and the result'. The result had been no answer. Stone makes no reference to anything further Lord said. But he must now be keenly aware that Lord wants to know every move the steamer makes.

There are grounds for believing that Stone acted more quickly in reporting the unusual activity than appears from his evidence to the British Inquiry, and indeed from his personal statement for the captain. By 12.35 or 12.40 a.m., Stone has been twice warned, directly and by tube, that Lord wanted to be told about any change in that nearby vessel's position. Stone next sees his first flash in the sky. He does not know what it is. He waits four or five minutes until he sees another. He concludes they may be rockets. What is Stone going to do? Is he going to wait until he sees a substantial number of rockets before reporting them to the captain, or is he going to report them straight away? Common sense would tell us that he is going to report immediately. But Stone in his evidence *gave the impression* of reporting five rockets to Lord – although it is important to emphasise that Stone never actually specified the number of rockets he reported to his skipper. He merely said 'rockets', suggesting that he sighted more than one. This matter deserves the closest attention, because Captain Lord maintained he was told about only *one* rocket in the conversation with Stone. There is an obvious gulf between Lord being told of one rocket and being told of several. Yet an early report by Stone – of perhaps 'one flash and one rocket' – seems more in keeping with Lord's eagerness to be kept informed. Let us see what Stone says about the rockets in his very first account, composed without legal 'interaction' on board the *Californian* within three days of the disaster as the vessel was bound for Boston. Lord had called up the tube at 12.35, Stone said. Ten minutes went by and then:

> At about 12.45 I observed a flash of light in the sky just above that steamer. I thought nothing of it as there were several shooting stars about, the night being fine and clear with light airs and calms.
>
> Shortly after, I observed another distinctly over the steamer which I made out to be a white rocket though I observed no flash on the deck or any indication that it had come from that steamer; in fact, it appeared to come from a good distance beyond her.
>
> Between then and about 1.15, I observed three more the same as before, and all white in colour. I, at once, whistled down the speaking tube and you came from the chartroom into your own room and answered. I reported seeing these lights in the sky in the direction of the other steamer which appeared to me to be white rockets.

This account is taken from Stone's original written statement for Lord on the incidents of the watch (see appendices). Looking at this account, we can understand that Stone naturally thinks nothing of the first flash. The second he 'made out to be a white rocket', but one which appeared to come from a distance beyond the nearby vessel. Yet Stone's account makes it appear that he waited to see three more rockets before he whistles down the tube 'at once' to report. Waiting for five rockets to go by is not reporting 'at once'. If he reported at once, it ought to have been after the second rocket – the first flash he positively identified as a rocket. Here is what Captain Lord told the British Inquiry:

6788. A little later did he whistle down the tube and tell you she was altering her bearings?

—A quarter-past one [accepts the timing cited by Stone in his original statement].

6789. Did he say how she was altering her bearings? — Towards the SW.

6790. Did he tell you whether he had seen any signal? — He said he saw a white rocket.

6791. From her? — From her.

6792. A white rocket? — Yes.

6793. [The Commissioner] She did not change until what time? — A quarter-past 1 it was reported to me first.

6794. And then what was her bearing? — She was altering it slightly towards the SW.

6795. It was then that you saw the rocket? — It was then that we saw the rocket.

6796. Did you see it? — No.

6797. The Second Officer saw it? — The Second Officer saw it.

It is noteworthy that Lord, despite the apparent numerical clash with Stone (which could have done Lord no good and which must have suggested Lord was lying and attempting to minimise the number of rockets he was told about), had not changed his evidence in London from that which he gave at the earlier US Inquiry: 'At a quarter past 1, he [Stone] said, "I think she has fired a rocket. She did not answer the Morse lamp and she has commenced to go away from us". I said, "Call her up and let me know at once what her name is". So, he put the whistle back, and, apparently, he was calling. I could hear him ticking over my head. Then I went to sleep' (US Inquiry, p.729).

Stone, however, in his British Inquiry evidence (he did not give evidence in America), changes the time he spoke to the captain from the 1.15 a.m. cited in his original written account to 'about 1.10 a.m.':

7827. After a time did you make any communication to the Captain? — Yes.

7828. How? — By means of the speaking tube.

7829. What did you communicate to him? — I communicated that I had seen white lights in the sky in the direction of this other steamer, which I took to be white rockets.

7830. What time was it you gave him that information? — Just about 1.10 a.m.

Whether Lord had any independent means of knowing the time, apart from Stone's original statement, is not known. However there is an intriguing line in Lord's testimony which appears for a moment and is gone, unprobed and untested, but intriguing nonetheless: 'And when did she [*Californian's* near ship] begin to go on again? 'From the Second Officer's report she commenced about 1 o'clock — Ten minutes to 1' (question 7070). Ten minutes *to* one!

Meanwhile there is a third party who *does* specify a time. Apprentice Officer James Gibson says he returned to the bridge at 12.55 a.m.; five minutes to one, and his testimony is very different to Stone's:

7463. A little later than that, did the Second Officer, Mr Stone, say anything to you about this ship? — At five minutes to one.

7464. What was it he told you? — That she had fired five rockets.

7465. That was at five minutes to one? — Yes.

7466. Had you not been on the bridge all the time? — No, Sir. I went down at twenty-five minutes to, and came up at five minutes to one.

7467. You went down at twenty-five minutes to one and came up at five minutes to one, and it is when you come up that this message is given? — Yes.

So we have Stone saying that five rockets were seen close to the unidentified ship up to 1.15 a.m. or perhaps 1.10 a.m. And we have Gibson saying he was told of five rockets fired by the time he came back as early as 12.55 a.m. Which is it? Gibson was with Stone from 'five minutes to one' onwards. He does *not* report Stone whistling down the speaking tube to Lord to report rockets in his presence. Here is Gibson:

7476. Now, I just want to get what happened after that. You have told me that the Second Officer said to you that the ship had fired five rockets? — Yes.

7477. Did he tell you anything else about what he had been doing while you had not been there? — He told me that he had reported it to the Captain.

7478. Did he tell you what the Captain had instructed him to do? — Yes.

7479. What was it? — To call her up on the Morse light.

7480. Did he tell you whether he had tried to call her up on the Morse light? — Yes.

7481. Had he? — Yes.

7482. What had been the result? — She had not answered him, but fired more rockets.

Gibson is told by Stone of five rockets fired. Stone had reported to the captain, who instructed him to Morse the steamer. But look carefully at question 7482. This clearly suggests Stone called the captain after the second sighting confirmed that the lights were indeed rockets. The ship had then fired more rockets, and Stone had not taken further action. So far Gibson's account entirely bears out that of Lord, and rather contradicts Stone in certain salient features. Importantly, Gibson's own original statement, composed for the captain while the *Californian* was still at sea, says *explicitly* that Stone contacted the captain after the *second* rocket, not the fifth. It is all we would expect from what common sense would tell us. Here is Gibson's original statement, 18 April 1912:

Arriving on the bridge again at that time, the Second Officer told me that the other ship, which was then about three and a half points on the starboard bow, had fired five rockets and he also remarked that after seeing the second one, to make sure he was not mistaken, he had told the Captain, through the speaking tube and that the Captain had told him to watch her and keep calling her up on the Morse light.

Stone himself will now provide direct evidence to suggest that he saw rockets number three, four and five only *after* he told his captain about white lights in the sky (these lights being the first two rockets). In his first account, written for Lord while at sea on 18 April, Stone makes no mention of Morsing the stranger in the time between Lord's call up to the bridge to ask if the visitor had moved (12.40 a.m.) and his own report of rockets in a call down to Lord. Stone in his earliest version of events did not mention carrying out any Morsing in the interval between these two conversations with Lord. But, in his British evidence, Stone suggests differently: 'When did you call her up on the Morse lamp – after the five rockets were seen? — Previously, and during the time that they were being sent up' (7875). It is known that he had called her up previously, before Lord rang up with his question, but it now appears that Stone, with no further Morsing, rang down to his captain to report only one certain rocket, possibly two. It was at this point that he was told to 'go on Morsing'. This would mean he was then Morsing 'during the time that they were being sent up' – meaning the three further rockets to make five in total. This further serves to confirm that the call to Lord to report lights, as Gibson indicated, was made after only *two* rockets were fired.

There is another reason why both Gibson and Lord could be correct in asserting that Stone reported only one 'definite' rocket following the initial flash in the sky that 'might have been anything'. And that compelling reason was provided by Stone himself:

7938. Was the steamer altering her bearing to your vessel during that period of time? —Yes, from the time I saw the first rocket.
7939. The first of the eight that you have told us of? — The second – excepting the first flash, which I was not sure about.
7940. You say you saw the steamer altering her bearing with regard to you? — She bore first SSE and she was altering her bearing towards the south towards west.

Stone is saying that the steamer was *moving* from the time of what is effectively the second rocket. This is an absolute trigger moment for Stone. He has been asked to report to his captain if the nearby steamer should move or alter her bearing. One can imagine the conversation at this point, and the following is this author's guess at what could have been said: 'Sir, that steamer is going away now. She has definitely fired one rocket. There was another flash earlier, which I wasn't sure about. I Morsed her before all this and got no reply'. Such a possibility is testified to by both Gibson and Lord, although they do disagree on times. Stone, on the other hand, never specifies in any of his direct evidence the actual number of rockets he first told Lord about. Here again is Stone stating categorically when he first saw the steamer move – the very action he was told to report instantly – in yet more pieces of testimony:

8037. Then you had seen them [rockets] from this steamer? — A steamer that is in distress does not steam away from you, my Lord.
8038. You saw these [rockets] before this steamer steamed away from you? — I saw them at the same time the ship started to alter her bearings.

And again:

8042. I said that the ship was altering her bearing from the time she showed her first rocket, she commenced altering her bearing by the compass.

8043. Is not this accurate? When you came on to your watch at twelve o'clock this ship was stationary? —Yes.

8044. And except for a change in her position towards 2.40 she was stationary all the time? — No, she was not stationary.

8045. Was she moving? — She started to move as soon as I saw the first rocket. She was stationary up to that time. She was stationary by our compass, at least so far as I could tell.

8048/9. When did you send word to the Captain that you noticed her steaming away? — At 10 minutes past 1. I reported to the Master that she was altering her bearings, which was the same thing.

Here, at question 8049, we have Stone calling the master because the steamer is beginning to steam away, altering her bearings. This is exactly what the master wanted to know about. The rocket is unusual but almost incidental; in Stone's mind the main news to impart is that the steamer is leaving! There is no urgency to the report, because the steamer is leaving and has merely fired a rocket or two rockets, perhaps in farewell? As Stone says (question 8037): 'A steamer that is in distress does not steam away from you, my Lord'. The stricken *Titanic*, firing rockets, never steamed away…

We can see from the evidence of Lord, Gibson and Stone himself that it is a real possibility that the first the captain knows about a change to the nearby steamer is that she has begun to steam. She has fired only one definite rocket. That is Lord's level of knowledge around 1 a.m. *Californian* time. In Lord's mind, the steamer is going away. The rocket or rockets are confusing. He wants to know more and has instructed Stone to find out more by Morse lamp. But his initial impression is this:

6917. What did you think he was sending up a rocket for? — I thought it was acknowledging our signals, our Morse lamp. A good many steamers do not use the Morse lamp.

Whether this conversation happened before 12.55, or at 1.10, or at 1.15, hardly matters. Captain Stanley Lord has no reason in the world to imagine that *any* steamer is firing distress rockets. This is the only conversation that matters, because it is only at 2.05 a.m. Lord is next told about further rockets. By that stage those left aboard the *Titanic* by her departed lifeboats were beyond all hope. If Lord is told about a vessel steaming away, and if he is told about her firing only one definite rocket (a version of events that Gibson appears to support), then Captain Lord has no possible way of discerning that anything remotely resembling a disaster is unfolding. And Lord sticks to his story throughout – no matter how much it might make him appear to be a barefaced liar about being told of only one rocket. Stone, on the other hand, maintains throughout that he saw the nearby steamer begin to move after she had fired her 'first' real rocket: yet another indication that she was not the *Titanic*. He also maintains (question 8049) that he told the captain about the ship's movement for the very first time at 1.10 a.m. Yet, in his original statement, composed on his own within three days of the disaster, Stone writes – in total contradiction – that he had seen fully *five* rockets by this time:

Between then and about 1.15 I observed three more the same as before, and all white in colour. I, at once, whistled down the speaking tube and you came from the chartroom into your own room and answered. I reported seeing these lights in the sky…

By the time of the British Inquiry, it is Stone who has changed his story. It is Stone who creates uncertainty as to when he first noticed that the steamer nearby was beginning to move, about the exact time that he communicated this fact to the master, and as to how many rockets he told the captain about.

Now, as a sworn witness, he mentions *no* specific number of rockets in his account of the first communication initiated with his captain. Lord and Gibson, on the other hand, are consistent in their separate accounts, apart from the issue of the time at which Stone rang down, which is certainly far less important than what Stone actually said. On this basis, Lord's 'one rocket' evidence is fully worthy of credulity. It is corroborated by Gibson, who came onto the bridge to find Stone having failed in his Morse conversation attempts by seeing only rockets for reply. Yet Stone's account of that crucial first conversation with the master is contradicted – not only by the other two principals – but also, as seen above, by himself.

LORD'S RESPONSE

It is difficult to piece together the crucial conversation between Lord and Stone, largely because Stone is repeatedly vague about it:

> 7827. After a time did you make any communication to the Captain? — Yes.
> 7828. How? — By means of the speaking tube.
> 7829. What did you communicate to him? — I communicated that I had seen white lights in the sky in the direction of this other steamer, which I took to be white rockets.
> 7830. What time was it you gave him that information? — Just about 1.10.
> 7831. Had you seen white lights? — Yes.

As we have seen in the last section, Gibson and Lord suggest Stone may have reported those 'white lights' after seeing just two of them, and only one that he concluded was a rocket. It is noticeable that Stone repeatedly avoids saying in evidence how many rockets or white lights he reported, as in his monosyllabic reply to question 7831. There is no doubt, however, that he creates the strong impression that he reported five. Such a scenario would immediately transfer a lot of responsibility to Lord. But if this is what Stone is seeking to do, even perhaps unconsciously, there is an obvious question to be asked: why did a responsible Officer of the Watch allow five rockets to go by before informing the master? This question is all the more pertinent when set against Stone's own insistence that he noticed the other ship *moving* from the 'first rocket', yet waited for more rockets before communicating to Lord the very news which the captain had asked to be informed about. Finally, on this point, it should be noted that nowhere in his evidence does Captain Lord himself seek to blame his underlings or express any belief that he was let down by his crew. Lord is loyal to those serving with him, and does not insist that any are wrong or mistaken, being content simply to state his own case. Yet he must have seen that the evidence of Stone, with its inconsistencies, was deflecting all the responsibility onto him as master. Stone does not leave this conclusion up to the inference of the reader; it is quite clear that he believes the situation was in Lord's hands: 'I just took them as white rockets, and informed the Master and left him to judge' (7853). This is Stone abrogating responsibility, particularly in light of what it appears he actually conveyed to Lord, who is only as good as the information he receives from the officer up top. Stone's evasions are in stark contrast with Captain Lord's own evaluation of Stone:

> 7094. ...Well, I was waiting for further information. I had a responsible officer on the bridge who was finding things out for me.
> 7304. Have you any reason to doubt that Mr Stone, the officer, is speaking the truth? — I do not see why he should not tell me the truth.
> 7305. [The Commissioner] Is he a reliable, trustworthy man? — As far as I know of him he is.

Such confidence now appears somewhat misplaced. Here is what Stone went on to say in evidence:

> 7869. I think you said you left it to him to judge. Did he answer back? — Yes.
> 7870. What was his answer? — He asked me, 'Are they Company's signals?'
> 7871. What was your answer? — I said, 'I do not know, but they appear to me to be white rockets'.
> 7872. Is that all you told him? — Yes; that I had called her up on the Morse lamp.
> 7874. That you had called them up on the Morse lamp? — Yes, and received no answer whatsoever.
> 7875. When did you call her up on the Morse lamp – after the five rockets were seen? — Previously, and during the time that they were being sent up.
> 7876. Did that suggest anything to you – a ship showing five rockets, you signalling with your Morse lamp, and getting no answer? Did that suggest anything to you? — No, because I have often signalled ships before, and got no answer from them.
> 7877. Now, having given this communication to the Master, and having got his reply, did you continue to keep this vessel under observation? — Yes.
> 7878. Did the Master, when you had this communication through the tube, tell you to go on Morsing this vessel? — Yes.
> 7879. And did he tell you that you were to send him any news and give him any information that you had got? — When I received any information to send the apprentice down to him with it.
> 7880. That is Gibson? — Yes.
> 7881. Was Gibson on the bridge at the time? — No, he did not see the first of the rockets.
> 7882. He came later, did he? — Yes.

Here, Stone again gives the impression that he called the master after five white rockets were seen. But the answer to question 7875 could also mean that he called Lord during the firings, and therefore could not have told the captain of a full five. We know that Gibson, who was on deck at 12.55 a.m., says he was told by Stone that he had contacted the master after seeing the 'second rocket' and that more rockets had then been fired. If five rockets had been reported fired, the captain's reaction may well have been different. Here is Gibson again:

> 7476. Now, I just want to get what happened after that. You have told me that the Second Officer said to you that the ship had fired five rockets? —Yes.
> 7477. Did he tell you anything else about what he had been doing while you had not been there? — He told me that he had reported it to the Captain.
> 7478. Did he tell you what the Captain had instructed him to do? —Yes.
> 7479. What was it? — To call her up on the Morse light.
> 7480. Did he tell you whether he had tried to call her up on the Morse light? —Yes.
> 7481. Had he? —Yes.
> 7482. What had been the result? — She had not answered him, but fired more rockets.

Lord's sworn evidence of being told of only one rocket has already been cited. He remained unequivocal throughout:

> 6880. [The Attorney General] Did you know she had fired a number of rockets? — I did not.
> 6881. According to you did she fire only one rocket? — Only one rocket.

And again:

> 6898. But you saw one rocket fired? — I heard of one rocket. I did not see it fired.
> 6899. You heard of one? —Yes.
> 6900. That was before you went to the chart room? — No, at a quarter past 1.
> 6901. Were you on deck then? — No.
> 6902. Did you remain in the chart room when you were told that a vessel was firing a rocket? — I remained in the chart room when he told me this vessel had fired a rocket.

This, it will surely be seen, was a difficult position for Lord to adopt. He maintained this account long before Gibson gave corroborative evidence, which would be studiously overlooked. Lord was duly attacked:

> 6910. What did you think this vessel was firing rockets for? — [Lord] I asked the Second Officer. I said, 'Is that a company's signal?' and he said he did not know.
> 6911. Then that did not satisfy you? — No, it did not.
> 6912. I mean, whatever it was, it did not satisfy you that it was a company's signal? — It did not, but I had no reason to think it was anything else.

6913. [The Commissioner] That seems odd. You knew that the vessel that was sending up this rocket was in a position of danger? — No, my Lord, I did not.

6914. Well, danger if she moved? — If she moved, yes.

6915. What did you think the rocket was sent up for? — Well, we had been trying to communicate with this steamer by Morse lamp from half-past 11, and she would not reply.

6916. This was a quarter past one? — Yes, we had tried at intervals from half-past eleven.

6917. What did you think he was sending up a rocket for? — I thought it was acknowledging our signals, our Morse lamp. A good many steamers do not use the Morse lamp.

6918. Have you ever said that before? — That has been my story right through – my impression right along.

Given the fact that Stone did not think there was anything alarming about the steamer firing rockets that might have been 'communicating with us', there can be little reason to doubt Lord's own first impression.

6919. [The Attorney General] Just let me put this to you. When you asked him whether it was a company's signal he said he did not know. That would not satisfy you? — [Lord] No.

6920. Was it then you told him to Morse her and find out what ship it was? — Yes.

6921. After the white rocket had been sent up? — After the white rocket had been sent up.

6922. And did you tell him to send Gibson the apprentice, down to let you know his reply? — Yes.

6923. You did? — I did.

6924. What was the message that Gibson brought down to you then? — That morning? I did not get it, not to my knowledge. I never got it.

6825. You had seen the rocket or you had heard of the rocket? — Yes.

6926. You want to know what the rocket is? — Yes.

6927. You have been trying to find out by Morsing him? — Yes.

6928. And you have failed? — Yes.

6929. Then you say to him that Gibson was to come down and tell you what the result of the Morse signalling was? — Yes.

6930. And then, I suppose, you remained in the chart-room? — I remained in the chart-room.

6931. Then, so far as you were concerned, you did not know at all what the rocket was for? — No.

6932. And you remained in the chart room? — Yes, I remained in the chart room.

6933. And you did nothing further? — I did nothing further myself.

6934-5. If it was not a company's signal, must it not have been a distress signal? — If it had been a distress signal the officer on watch would have told me.

6936. I say, if it was not a company's signal must it not have been a distress signal? — Well, I do not know of any other signals but distress signals that are used at sea.

6937. You do not expect at sea, where you were, to see a rocket unless it is a distress signal, do you? — We sometimes get these company's signals which resemble rockets; they do not shoot as high and they do not explode [Stone would testify that the rockets were 'low-lying' and 'half the height of the masthead light'].

6938. You have already told us that you were not satisfied that was a company's signal. You have told us that? — I asked the officer, was it a company's signal?

6939. [The Commissioner] And he did not know? — He did not know.

6913. Very well, that did not satisfy you? — It did not satisfy me.

6944. Then if it was not that, it might have been a distress signal? — It might have been [agreeing now that it might have been, after the fact, in light of what was subsequently known about the *Titanic* sinking].

6945. And you remained in the chart-room? — I remained in the chart room.

6948. Expecting Gibson, the apprentice, to come down and report to you? — Yes.

Lord is more succinct in his American evidence when he tells his version to the Senators (p.729):

> At a quarter past [one], he said, 'I think she has fired a rocket'. He [Stone] said: 'She did not answer the Morse lamp and she has commenced to go away from us'. I said, 'Call her up and let me know at once what her name is'. So, he put the whistle back, and, apparently, he was calling. I could hear him ticking over my head. Then I went to sleep…

Lord is now in the arms of Morpheus, and in the hands of the two crewmen above. No further attempt would be made by them to get in contact with their captain until 2 a.m. – horribly late.

This question is for the reader: is Lord credible about being placed in what would turn out to be a false sense of security?

OPTIONS AND TIMES

All hope for *Titanic* has now disappeared. There was but one single conversation about lights in the sky with the *Californian*'s skipper before 2 a.m. Nothing thereafter can save lives on the *Titanic*. It is important to stress that this was one conversation – one opportunity alone – because those with a determination to saddle Captain Lord with blame are apt to repeat a ridiculous mantra that he was called 'three times' about rockets. The implication of that is obvious, but the reality of what happened very different. There was, perhaps, just one opportunity to grasp the significance of the initial rocket or rockets. And it has passed by. No other instance could have afforded the remotest possibility of saving life. The next information transmitted to Lord came at 2 a.m., *Californian* time. *Titanic* sank at 2.20 a.m., her time.

Since 1912, there has been much sifting of the options available to Captain Lord on receipt of the original rocket-firing message. Yet this overlooks the fact than neither Stone, the message-imparter, nor Lord, its recipient, invested this first communication with much importance. Stone thought the firing could have been an acknowledgement of his own Morsing attempts. Lord received that impression as well, as we have seen. In fact the conversation between the two men – Stone reporting white lights, not knowing if it was a company signal – seems to have had what might be called a 'shrug factor' about it. At the same time, a resting Captain Lord was still awake to at least monitoring the situation.

Yet even if the enormity of what was unfolding on board the *Titanic*, wherever she was, had somehow got through – first to Stone, and through him to Lord – the prospects of effecting any rescue were bleak. Even if Lord had started engines at 12.45 a.m., the moment Stone first saw a rocket (although Stone, understandably, having seen 'shooting stars about', took no initial action), it is clear from our earlier study of *Californian*'s location that she could not have reached the *Titanic*'s position until half an hour or more after she sank (US Inquiry, p.722):

> Senator Smith: If you had received the CQD call of distress from the *Titanic* Sunday evening… how long, under the conditions which surrounded you, would it have taken you to have reached the scene of the catastrophe?
>
> Lord: At the very least, two hours.
>
> Sen. Smith: Two hours?
>
> Lord: At the very least, the way the ice was packed around us, and it being night-time.

This was at Lord's estimated distance of 19½ to 20 miles to the position cited in the SOS. A wrong location! The *Titanic*'s actual collision point, backtracked from the wreck site, was over 20 miles away, and in a *different direction* to the SOS transmitted. Think of *Californian* at the apex of a pyramid – the SOS location and *Titanic*'s actual sinking position were 13 nautical miles distant from each other at opposite ends of the baseline below the 'cap' of the pyramid, where the *Californian* sat with engines idle.

WHY DIDN'T THEY WAKE THE WIRELESS MAN?

This common question is, sadly, easily disposed of. But first of all, let it be borne in mind that this was only the *Californian*'s third voyage with a wireless operator aboard. Her Marconi man, Cyril Evans, first joined the vessel as recently as 29 November 1911, and stated 'I have had three trips on the *Californian*' (US Inquiry, p.733). The *Californian* had been using wireless for only four and a half months! The full possibilities of the new medium were hardly second nature to her captain. And on this night, Lord in his own mind had no reason at all to wake the wireless operator aboard *Californian*. As far as he knew, a nearby steamer was departing, and in apparent acknowledgement of several Morsing attempts by the *Californian*, had fired a rocket. As Lord said: 'I thought it was acknowledging our signals, our Morse lamp. A good many steamers do not use the Morse lamp' (6917). Stone's impression, even after seeing five rockets, was of other ordinary causes:

7844. What do you think they meant? — I thought that perhaps the ship was in communication with some other ship, or possibly she was signalling to us to tell us she had big icebergs around her.

7845. Possibly, what else? — Possibly she was communicating with some other steamer at a greater distance than ourselves.

Stone did not offer any thoughts to Lord, but his initial report cannot have carried any urgency.

If Lord thought an acknowledgement was the reason why the steamer had fired a rocket, meanwhile, then he does not have to find out why it was fired. Because he has already made a humdrum assumption, linked to the fact that the steamer is now underway, moving off by Stone's report. And if the nearby steamer did not even have a Morse lamp – and it appears she did not – then she was hardly likely to have a fully-equipped wireless room and a night operator standing by! Lord is questioned about this:

7082. When you were in doubt as to the name of this ship and as to the meaning of her sending up a rocket, could you not have ascertained definitely by calling in the assistance of your Marconi operator? — When? At 1 o'clock in the morning? [Clearly it was an entirely new idea – wireless operators slept at night]

7083. Yes? — This steamer had been in sight, the one that fired the rocket, when we sent the last message to the *Titanic*, and I was certain that the steamer was not the *Titanic*, and the operator said he had not any other steamers, so I drew my conclusion that she had not got any wireless.

The same logic must have applied to Stone and Gibson, neither of whom thought the steamer they saw at the time of the rockets was in any distress. If they had thought so, then clearly it was open to Stone to act independently and to rouse the wireless man! The fact that he was not roused may simply be a proof that nothing was thought to be amiss. Certainly, Stone would have had no anxieties about the extent of his powers. He was the officer of the watch, and his brother officer, Groves, who ranked below Stone, had had no difficulty in going into Wireless Operator Evans' cabin after midnight 'for a chat' when the latter was in bed!

Elsewhere in evidence Lord continues to explain why the Marconi man was not summoned:

7090. Would not it have been quite a simple thing for you at that time when you were in doubt as to what was the name of the ship, and as to what was the reason of her sending up rockets, to have wakened up your Marconi operator and asked him to speak to this ship? — It would if it had worried me a great deal, but it did not worry me. I was still thinking of the company's signal.

Even if Lord *had* somehow divined that waking the wireless operator could have thrown light on the subject, he would have received *Titanic's* SOS and wrong position:

7091. At all events, now in the light of your experience would it not have been a prudent thing to do? — Well, we would have got the *Titanic's* signals if we had done.
7092. If you had done you would, in all probability, have got the message from this vessel? — No. I do not think so. In my opinion that steamer had not got wireless at all.
7098. What reason have you for thinking that this steamer, a steamer which you say was, at all events, as big as your own, had not got wireless? — At 11 o'clock when I saw her, the operator told me he had not got anything, only the *Titanic*. I remarked then, 'That is not the *Titanic*,' judging from its size and the number of lights about it, and if he only had one ship, then it was not the *Titanic*.

If the wireless operator – who was attached to the Marconi Co. although nominally under the captain's charge – had been at his set, he would have got the *Titanic's* signals, as Lord acknowledges. Yet we know today that the *Titanic* sank 13 nautical miles east (and a little south) of the location cited in the distress messages. Lord would have gone there, as he did the next morning, and found nothing! As *Mount Temple* and *Birma* did, and found nothing. Because of serious *Titanic* error, *Californian*, even with the best will in the world, could not actually have saved any extra lives.

DIFFERING TIMES

Another note about times: after midnight the difference in relative times of *Californian* and *Titanic* may have changed. It appears that on *Titanic* time ran on for most people without going back the twenty-three minutes at midnight that had been planned. They had other things to worry about. On *Californian* however, ship's time may have been put back ten minutes. There are some factors which support such a contention. At 11.40 p.m. *Californian* time, Groves said one bell was struck to signal next watch, due to take over in half an hour. This would have put the changeover at 12.10 a.m. This odd start time would only have been instituted in order to put the clocks back ten minutes, similar to the *Titanic* plan. Groves separately backs up this theory by saying he stayed on the bridge after 12.10 a.m., when Stone came up to relieve, remaining for five minutes until 12.15 while Stone got his eyes accustomed to the dark. Stone would have no reason to be ten minutes late for his shift. Lord confirms the time:

6843. It was he [Stone] who relieved Mr Groves? — Yes, at 10 minutes past 12.

Meanwhile Stone and Gibson give different times for Stone's crucial call to Captain Lord, as we have seen. Stone said it happened at 1.10 or 1.15 a.m. Gibson said it had happened by the time he returned at 12.55 a.m. It may simply be that Gibson put his watch back as planned, but Stone did not. If *Californian* time was retarded at midnight, but the *Titanic's* own retardation was overlooked in the confusion, then *Californian* and *Titanic* times thereafter vary again for those who engage in the huge task of trying to reconcile the timings of both ships. Amending the 'twelve-minute theory' would change *Californian* time after midnight to a giant twenty-two minutes behind run-on *Titanic* time, putting the 2.20 a.m. sinking at 1.58 a.m. *Californian* time. If seventeen minutes ahead is true, *Californian* would be only seven minutes ahead after midnight. This would closely agree with *Titanic* rocket timings.

The apprentice officer of the *Californian*, James Gibson, was sent down to his master to report that their puzzling visitor had disappeared to the south-west. It was 2.05 a.m. by the *Californian's* wheelhouse clock. No matter where she was, therefore, she could hardly have saved any lives in the time it would have taken to start engines and get underway to the supposed point of origin of the rockets. Both official inquiries chose to regard *Californian* and *Titanic* times after midnight as interchangeable. This is a very doubtful proposition. Lifeboat departure times were expressed by the British Inquiry as if *Titanic's* clocks did not go back as planned. Yet if there *is* a substantial difference in times, then it could be all against the *Californian's* room for manoeuvre.

MORE ROCKETS

Stone and Gibson are on the bridge of *Californian*, with Gibson learning for the first time that the stranger has fired five rockets. Here he takes up the story:

7488. [Stone] told you of five before you came back at five minutes to one? —Yes.

7489. And after that you saw three more yourself? —Yes.

7490. How soon was that after you had come back at five minutes to one? — As soon as I went on the bridge at five minutes to one. I called her up as soon as the Second Officer told me.

7491. You called her up on the Morse [lamp]? —Yes.

7492. You mean the Second Officer gave you orders to do that? —Yes.

7493. And she did not respond to you? — No.

There is an important difference here. *Titanic* witnesses said their vessel was sending out Morse signals at the same time that she was firing rockets! If we suppose for a moment that the *Californian's* near vessel was the *Titanic*, then the *Titanic's* Morse signals ought to have been seen at the time described by Gibson. But he could not see any such thing...

Boxhall claims: 'My attention until the time I left the ship was mostly taken up with firing off distress rockets and trying to signal [by Morse lamp] a steamer that was almost ahead of us' (US Inquiry, p.235). And he later states: 'I even got the Quartermaster who was working around with me – I do not know who he was – to fire off the distress signal, and I got him to also signal with the Morse lamp' (US Inquiry, p.934). And here is AB Symons:

> 11468. …That steamer's light was in sight about a point and a half on the port bow, roughly between five and ten miles away when they fired the rockets, and they were also working the starboard and port Morse lights…
> 11472. Working the port and starboard Morse lights? — Yes.

Symons saw this dual signalling happening after 1 a.m. He mentions personally seeing it up to half past, but is generally thought to have left in lifeboat No.1 a little earlier. Gibson is working the Morse lamp, as Stone did, and cannot see any Morse in reply. She does not respond. Captain Lord, as we have seen, may already have formed the view that this stranger did not even possess a Morse lamp. Yet we know that the *Titanic* was frantically working her Morse lamp – in fact *both* Morse lamps on either side of the bridge – flashing towards the steamer at which she was looking. Gibson now sees more rockets instead of a reply to his Morse:

> 7494. And then you saw these rockets? — Yes.
> 7495. Give me an idea of the time – would that take long, or was it at once? — Well, I called her up [by lamp] for about three minutes, and I had just got the glasses on to her when I saw her fire the rocket. That was the first one.
> 7496. The first of the three? — Yes.
> 7497. You say you had just got the glasses on to her. Did you see it through the glasses? — Yes.
> 498. How did you see the second one? — With the eye.
> 7499. With the naked eye? — Yes, without the glasses.
> 7500. And the third one? — With the eye.
> 7501. What colour rockets were they? — White ones.
> 7502. When you got your glasses on the vessel and saw the first rocket going up through them, could you make out the vessel at all? — No, Sir, just her lights.
> 7503. [The Commissioner] Still this glare of light? — Yes.
> 7504. Did that indicate, that glare of light, that this was a passenger steamer? — No, Sir.

Let us now examine this question of 'glare' that was offered up to Gibson.

A GLARING DECEPTION

It is important to note Gibson's answer to question 7504. It is often suggested that because he saw a 'glare' of light in the after-part of the vessel under observation that this is corroboration of Groves' 'brilliant' light from a 'passenger steamer'. But of course

Gibson denies that the 'glare' gives any suggestion whatsoever of a passenger steamer. And we know that Groves said the steamer had put out (or shut out) her brilliant lights before midnight, *Californian* time – more than an hour before Gibson's sightings! Thus Gibson's acceptance of Lord Mersey's word 'glare' in the previous extract cannot be indicative of a passenger steamer, despite efforts to deploy both Groves and Gibson simultaneously, one in corroboration of the other, in support of the theory that this puzzling stranger is the *Titanic*. Gibson also uses the word 'glare' quite loosely it appears. In his original statement for the captain, he said: 'I also observed her port side light and a faint glare of lights on her after deck'. Here is what Gibson says in further evidence about the 'glare':

> 7328. Could you see more than one white light? — I saw a glare of lights on her after-deck.
>
> 7429. You mean the porthole lights? — A glare of white lights on her after-deck.

It doesn't sound very important, does it? Look again at the answer to 7502. These were 'just her lights'. He later clarifies again:

> 7545. What did you think? — I thought she was a tramp steamer, and I told him so.
>
> 7546. You thought she was a tramp steamer, and you had seen her side light at what you thought was between four and seven miles away? — Yes.
>
> 7547. And you had seen a blaze of light in the after part? — A glare of light [note that Gibson resists accepting the word 'blaze'. He is using nautical parlance with 'glare', rather than the 'man in the street's' equation of glare with brightness].
>
> 7548. Four to seven miles away? — Yes.
>
> 7549. And you thought she was a tramp steamer? — Yes.
>
> 7550. (The Commissioner) Did you expect to see a glare of light on the after part of a tramp steamer? — Yes, Sir, on some of them.

Gibson's 'glare' is clearly not counsel's 'blaze' of lights. As if to illustrate this, he next talks about 'glare' from only a masthead light!

> 7626. And after her red light, disappeared could you still see her masthead light or her white light? — Just a glare of it;
>
> 7632. Now, tell me, when you first saw that glare of lights in the after-part, could you see a line of lights? — No.
>
> 7633. It was more than a single light, was it not? — Yes.

Not much of a glare, then. And here's more:

> 7719. And when you looked through the glasses what could you see beyond the mast-head light? — Her red side-light and a faint glare of light on her after deck [see original statement].

But the Commissioner, Lord Mersey, is determined to magnify that 'glare' from Gibson's meaning of the word. Just look at this:

> 7728. [The Commissioner] What was it made you think it was a tramp steamer? You saw nothing but the lights? — Well, I have seen nearly all the large passenger boats out at sea, and there was nothing at all about it to resemble a passenger boat [A categorical answer!]
> 7720. What is it you expected to see? — A passenger boat is generally lit up from the water's edge.
> 7730. This boat was apparently lit up, you know; there was all this glare of light. However, that is all you can say? — Yes.
> 7733. She seemed to be a big steamer? — Well, a medium size steamer.

Such was the pressure on Gibson to say something entirely at odds with what he knew to be the truth. And the Commissioner will later cynically use Gibson's 'glare' in his final report, damning the *Californian*, without mentioning that Gibson in fact thought he was looking at a tramp steamer, with 'nothing at all about her to resemble a passenger boat'. This is from from Lord Mersey's Final Report of the British Inquiry (p.44):

> Mr Stone had with him during the middle watch an apprentice named Gibson, whose attention was first drawn to the steamer's lights at about 12.20 a.m. He could see a masthead light, her red light (with glasses) and a 'glare of white lights on her after deck'.

This is a complete traducement and an utter misrepresentation of Gibson's evidence.
We return to his testimony:

> 7505. [The Solicitor General] When you saw the first of these three rockets through your glasses did you report what you saw to the officer? — Yes.
> 7506. Did he tell you whether he saw the second or the third rocket? — Yes, Sir.
> 7507. Did he? — Yes Sir.
> 7508. He said he did? — Yes.
> 7509. Was he using glasses, too? — No.
> 7510. He saw it with his naked eye? — Yes.
> 7511. What happened after that? — About twenty minutes past one the Second Officer remarked to me that she was slowly steaming away towards the south-west.
> 7512. Had you remained on the bridge from the time that you saw these three rockets until then? — Yes.
> 7513. Had you been keeping her under observation? — Yes.
> 7514. Looking at her with your glasses from time to time? — Yes.

Here is a comparison summary from Gibson's original statement, composed for his captain on the *Californian*:

I then watched her for some time and then went over to the keyboard and called her up continuously for about three minutes. I then got the binoculars and had just got them focussed on the vessel when I observed a white flash apparently on her deck, followed by a faint streak towards the sky which then burst into white stars.

If Gibson can see the flash of a rocket discharging from the deck of the steamer he is looking at, then he surely knows the exact size of the steamer. There can be no two ways about it. But if Stone says the rockets were low-lying, then it is possible Gibson's flash may be one rocket actually detonating (having been fired from over the visible horizon), followed quickly by another that goes rather higher. It shall be seen in another section that just as the *Titanic* was working both the port and starboard Morse lamps, there are good grounds for believing she was firing rockets from two positions also. Symons will say that rockets were going up 'simultaneously'.

But put the deck-flash to one side for the moment. Gibson goes on in this original account:

Nothing then happened until the other ship was about two points on the starboard bow when she fired another rocket. Shortly after that I observed that her side light had disappeared but her masthead light was just visible, and the Second Officer remarked after taking another bearing of her, that she was slowly steering away towards the SW. Between one point on the starboard bow and one point on the port bow I called her up on the Morse lamp but received no answer. When at about one point on the port bow she fired a rocket which like the other burst into white stars.

Think about the above for a moment. Gibson is not saying he saw three rockets in rapid succession with a few minutes between them. But it is a requirement of signalling distress by rockets at night that they should be fired at 'short' intervals. Gibson is saying that he saw those three rockets fired with long intervals between them.

There is a lead-in period to the first rocket seen by Gibson (rocket No.6), since he comes back on the bridge at 12.55 a.m. and Stone tells him that five rockets have been fired. Even if this lapse is only a minute or two, Gibson says he now 'watched her for some time' before calling her up for 'about three minutes'. Only when he gets his binoculars back on the vessel does she fire the first rocket he sees. This interval, then, is 'some time' plus 'some time', plus three minutes. It would appear a relatively long lapse. The second rocket for Gibson (No.7 overall) then arrives after 'nothing then happened until she was about two points on the starboard bow', which again implies a relatively long lapse. The third (No.8) is finally fired after another long lapse, as Gibson says the ship in whose direction the rockets were seen has moved three points of the compass in the time between these rockets. His second was seen when she was 'two points on the starboard bow' and his third 'when at about one point on the port bow'. Such long-delay firings for all three rockets hardly chime with our impression of desperate men on the *Titanic* sending up rocket after rocket! The Board of Trade regulations said that distress could be indicated at night by a range of options, of which the third method was to fire rockets at 'short' intervals. But if the intervals were not short, how was the observer to deduce distress?

> The following signals, numbered 1, 2 and 3 when used or displayed together or separately shall be deemed to be signals of distress at night: 1) A gun fired at intervals of about a minute; 2) Flames on the ship as from a burning tar barrel, oil barrel, etc.; 3) Rockets or shells of any colour or description fired one at a time at short intervals.

How short is 'short'? Is there an implication in the regulations that the rockets should substitute for the gun, making the intended intervals the same – of 'about a minute'? The Board of Trade certified the *Titanic* as carrying socket signals (noise-making rockets) 'in lieu of guns'.

It can meanwhile be seen that, in question 7511 above, Gibson is asked 'what happened after that?' when he has just described Stone also seeing three rockets during their time together. Gibson replies: 'About twenty minutes past one...' This leads to a possible inference that the three rockets had all been seen by 1.20 a.m., which would mean relatively short firing intervals. But in fact it is a matter of how one reads evidence. The author is satisfied that counsel is dragging Gibson back to the period after the first rocket – following a detour as to whether Stone had equally seen the second and third that Gibson later observed. In fact, both Stone and Gibson elsewhere put the last rocket very late. Gibson says it came 'when at about one point on the port bow', and in his original statement for his captain writes: 'just after two o'clock she was then about two points on the port bow'. It can be seen that the last rocket was therefore fired close to 2 a.m. rather than 1.20 a.m. Unfortunately we cannot draw any definite conclusions as to *Californian* clock time for rockets despite Gibson's detailed comments on the bearing of the other ship at the time his second and third rockets were fired.

When Gibson arrived on the bridge (12.55 a.m. by Gibson's evidence), Stone told him that the vessel had fired five rockets. The ship was 'then about 3½ points on the starboard bow', according to Gibson in his original statement. He then discusses the movement of the observed ship to 'two points on the starboard bow' for the second rocket and his third 'when at about one point on the port bow'. So the interval between his three rockets by compass bearings is 1½ points between Stone telling him of rocket No.5 and the firing of rocket No.7 (Gibson does not offer a bearing at the time of rocket No.6, his first). There is then an interval of three points between rocket No.7 and rocket No.8, the last.

The problem is that the evidence is contradictory as to the rate of drift. Here are our markers: from 10.21 p.m. to 12.10 a.m. there is a swing by the *Californian* of only two points (from north-east to east-north-east), according to the evidence. Groves (8150) and Lord testified as to their vessel's heading (the direction in which the bows are pointing) at the time the *Californian* stopped, which was at 10.21 p.m. This heading was north-east. Nearly two hours later, both Stone (8061) and Gibson (7437) said she was east-north-east at the time they started their watch (12.10 a.m.). This is a swing of barely one point per hour.

But the evidence also shows that, from 12.10 a.m. to 2 a.m., the *Californian* experienced a swing of sixteen points (from east-north-east to west-south-west). This is an average of about seven minutes per point. It would appear that the swing was faster at some points and slower at others, depending on the orientation of the *Californian* in relation to the current. And just to confuse things further, there is a third marker. Stone in his original statement discloses a swing between 2 a.m. and 4 a.m. of four points, from west-south-west to west-north-west. This is thirty minutes per point! Thus it is unsafe to rely on Gibson's bearings for exact times as to the rockets he saw. But what we can say from his other language is that the intervals certainly do not appear to be as short as cited by Officer Boxhall of the *Titanic* of 'probably five minutes' (question 15399) for those he personally fired from the White Star vessel.

Most likely there are substantial gaps between all rockets seen, since only three were seen between 1 a.m. and an hour later when the decision was taken to report to the captain. It is now after 2 a.m. At this point, Gibson goes below, tells the captain the ship has disappeared, having fired a total of eight rockets. Lord asks the time and Gibson says (question 7565): 'Five minutes past two by the wheelhouse clock'.

The disparity in the apparent rate of drift, incidentally, may suggest that the ship under observation had moved quicker along the horizon than current could bring her – and was therefore steaming. But the consideration of the rocket intervals has served its purpose, since there are two broad possibilities for the ship seen by the *Californian*. Either she *is* the *Titanic*, in which case she is firing distress rockets highly irregularly, with large gaps between some, contrary to what the distress signal regulations provide, or alternatively, she *is not* the *Titanic*, as she is not drifting in a uniform way, as we know the *Titanic* did, the White Star liner being undeniably stopped while firing her rockets. It is submitted therefore that Gibson's observations mean that the ship he saw was not drifting uniformly, as she should have done in a normal current. Currents cannot easily change their speed! Instead it seems that Gibson's ship bearings (at the time the various rockets were fired) suggest that the speed, initially slow, picked up during the material period, only to slow down again. The observed vessel could have contributed to this apparent anomaly if she was herself moving, thereby going through compass points comparatively rapidly. As Stone says:

> 7962. Cannot you express any opinion? — I should say that at different times she [the ship under observation] was going at different speeds.

This scenario fits in, not with an immobile ship drifting in a current, but with a steamer steaming under her own motive power – 'steaming away', as Stone saw it. And if she is moving under her own power, then she cannot be the *Titanic*.

STONE'S TIMING OF ROCKETS

Be warned! There are irreconcilable differences between Stone and Gibson as to the frequency of the three rockets they saw in their time together before their stranger 'disappeared' or steamed away. Stone says: 'I saw the last of the rockets as near as I can say about 1.40' (7935). Let us go back to the start. Stone testified to initially reporting rockets to the captain by speaking tube at 1.10 a.m. He does not say in the witness box how many he reported, but tells Gibson when the latter returns to the bridge that five have been fired. Stone said he saw these first five rockets 'at intervals of about three or four minutes' (7842). After Gibson arrives, more rockets are seen. Stone states:

7891. How many? — Three, in the direction of this steamer.
7892. In quick succession? — About the same period as the others.

But this 'same period' is clearly impossible, because there is half an hour between 1.10 (initial report to captain) and 1.40 (last rocket seen, according to Stone). The separations here are ten minutes, at a crude average, not 'intervals of three or four minutes'. If all rockets he saw had 'the same period as the others', then all rockets would be concluded by 1.15 – not at 1.40. That is because the four-minute gap would have run as follows: 1) 12.45; 2) 12.49; 3) 12.53; 4) 12.57; 5) 1.01 (Gibson arrives); 6) 1.05; 7) 1.09; 8) 1.13. Stone is clearly too casual in his answers and all rockets were simply not fired in such rapid succession. Otherwise they could not have stretched to the 1.40 a.m. finish time that he himself specifies! In his first report for the captain, written at sea, he said: 'At about 12.45 I observed a flash of light in the sky', which is the starting-point illustrated above. In this written statement, he said five rockets were fired between 12.45 and 'about 1.15'. But Gibson says he arrived on the bridge at 12.55, when five had already been fired! Stone's evidence of 'three or four minutes' would have *all* eight rockets finishing by 1.13 a.m. But this is just after the time Stone says he first rang down to advise the captain (1.10 a.m.), which by common agreement was in Gibson's absence. So once again, Stone's timings cannot be correct.

Stone's account is of seeing eight rockets between 12.45 and 1.40 – or nearly one hour of firings. The mean rocket gap here is nearly every eight minutes, since the clock starts at zero from 12.45 (rocket No.1) and there are another seven rockets to go in fifty-five minutes. Seven multiplied by eight is fifty-six. These lapses are not short: 1) 12.45; 2) 12.53; 3) 1.01; 4) 1.09; 5) 1.17; 6) 1.25; 7) 1.33; 8) 1.41. Of course Stone's timings are also wrong because they would have condemned Gibson to seeing six rockets instead of the three he did see – if Gibson's return time of 12.55 a.m. is not in error…

Relying on plain old common sense, what we can assuredly say is that there does not appear to have been any rapidity between the latter three rockets that these two men saw together because they did not comment on it (and frequency of signalling, in any context, tends to suggest urgency, if not desperation). Put another way, the reverse proof is that the rockets they saw together did not lead them to any action. This in itself is a strong indicator of infrequency.

It might also appear strange that Stone waited for a full twenty minutes after seeing the last rocket – at 1.40 a.m. by his own account – before sending Gibson down at 2 a.m. to tell the captain that she had fired altogether eight rockets and steamed away. Gibson says he saw three rockets between 12.55 and a time that we have seen appears to be *close* to 2 a.m., based on his account of drift in his original statement: 'When at about one point on the port bow she fired a rocket [the last they saw]... Just after two o'clock she was then about two points on the port bow'.

On the other hand, Stone and Gibson do not know the rockets have stopped until some time after they have stopped. If they are seen at intervals of seven to eight minutes, they might wait ten minutes or more before concluding they have stopped. This brings us to 1.50 a.m. or later if Stone's 1.40 a.m. for the last rocket is correct. Stone might then wait a few more minutes before definitely concluding that they have stopped and sending down Gibson. Neither man can know in advance which one is the last rocket.

Captain Lord wanted to know about changes in the other ship's position and bearing. By 2 a.m. the other ship, judged to have been steaming away to the south-west, is almost out of sight. It is now logical to make that second report to the captain. It appears from Gibson's account that the steamer, towards the latter part of their observation, was moving away more rapidly. If point-to-point gaps were indeed seven minutes by now, it would mean that, as Gibson was sent down to tell Lord just after 2 a.m., the last rocket had been fired at 1.54 a.m., *Californian* time. This clashes with Stone's 1.40 estimate, but would tie in with his account, not of a drifting ship, but of one actively moving ('I should say that at different times she was going at different speeds' (7962)). And as he wrote in his original statement: 'I observed the steamer to be steaming away to the south-west, and altering her bearing fast'. It also seems arguable that the last rocket would be fired shortly before the observed vessel finally seemed to be disappearing, so that the combination of both should lead to Gibson being sent down to the captain – while Stone watched in case of more rockets. The truth might thus lie somewhere in between 1.40 and 1.54, *Californian* time. The timings offered by both men are inconsistent – but at least Gibson has been down below on a few occasions and has seen the wheelhouse clock at least once, at 2.05 a.m. There was no clock on the upper bridge.

It is important to point out that *nowhere* does Gibson say that the rockets he saw were fired in close succession (if Stone is right about three or four minute intervals, then Gibson must inescapably know, and know very soon, that several rockets have been fired within a very brief period; in these circumstances, would Gibson himself not want to tell the captain of the rapid-fire developments?)

All the above examination of timings and intervals must be compared to what the 1912 distress regulations specifically say, as previously seen:

1199. [The Attorney General] Article 31, dealing with distress signals: 'When a vessel is in distress and requires assistance from other vessels, or from the shore, the following shall be the signals to be used or displayed by her, either together or separately'; and then, as your Lordship pointed out, 'At night' number three is 'Rockets or shells, throwing stars of any colour or description, fired one at a time, at short intervals'.

Stone's suggestion of short intervals in one part of his evidence can be disproved, while

Gibson's intervals are not short. And Stone meanwhile gave this reply in another part of his evidence:

> 8039. But for a long time while this ship was stationary like your own, you noticed at frequent intervals that she was sending up rocket after rocket? — No.

All of which goes to suggest that either the *Titanic* was paying no respect to what the distress regulations actually required, and fired only eight rockets over a long period –almost as a chore – or else the *Californian* missed some, or many, of *Titanic's* distress rockets.

Could this have been because the *Titanic* was over the horizon and a great distance away? We shall return to this important point when we examine various claims by *Titanic* witnesses as to the number of rockets fired in total.

11

APPEARANCES

Captain Lord, we remember, asked whether the rocket he was first told about was a company signal. Stone replied he did not know. Lord prescribed more Morsing, ordered the apprentice to be sent down 'at once' as soon as her name became known, and fell asleep. We have just seen that rockets at night do not automatically mean distress. The regulations, dictated by the Attorney General in the British Inquiry (question 1199), say distress signals at night could be, as one option, not the exclusive option, 'rockets or shells, throwing stars of any colour or description, fired one at a time, at short intervals'. Different regulations were in force for daytime distress! The regulations were vague. And the truth is that rockets were fired at night for all kinds of reasons. It may be hard for the modern reader to grasp this fact, but Fourth Officer Boxhall of the *Titanic* makes it quite clear (US Inquiry p.910):

> Senator Fletcher: It seems that an officer on the *Californian* reported to the commander of the *Californian* that he had seen signals; but he said they were not distress signals. Do you know whether or not under the regulations in vogue, and according to the custom at sea, rockets fired, such as the *Titanic* sent up, would be regarded as anything but distress signals?
> Boxhall: I am hardly in a position to state that, because it is the first time I have seen distress rockets sent off, and I could not very well judge what they would be like, standing as I was underneath them firing them myself. I do not know what they would look like in the distance.
> Sen. Fletcher: Have you ever seen any rockets sent off such as you say are private signals?
> Boxhall: Yes, sir.
> Sen. Fletcher: Under what circumstances?
> Boxhall: Ships passing in the night, signalling to one another.

So Boxhall has seen rockets fired by ships at night and interpreted them as signalling, not as distress. Stone interprets the rockets as signals, and so does Lord, asking if the rockets are company signals. Indeed, Lord himself, ironically, had fired distress signals as a handy identification custom among ships of the West India Co. in which he previously served. In an incident recounted in Leslie Harrison's 1986 book *A Titanic Myth*, Lord was instructed by his captain to fire a distress rocket as a greeting from the SS *Darien* to the SS *Atlantian* – which in return fired one back.

Meanwhile Apprentice Officer James Gibson will also see rockets from the deck of the *Californian* in 1912 – and he will also conclude that they are *signals*, not indications of distress:

> 7696. Did you know when the rockets were being sent up that they were being sent up as danger signals? — No.
>
> 7697. What did you think they were sent up for? — I thought they were some private signals.
>
> 7698. Who told you they were private signals? — Nobody told me.
>
> 7699. Had you ever seen private signals of that kind? — No.
>
> 7700. And never heard of private signals of that kind? — I have heard of private rockets, private signal rockets.

Both men watching did not know what those rockets meant and were hardly in a position to tell their captain. There is nothing to distinguish distress rockets from any other rockets at night except the 'short intervals'. Otherwise they can be of 'any colour or description'. A recipe for confusion. And confusion is what resulted.

COMPANY SIGNALS

Ships used rockets for signalling at night during *Titanic's* time. Almost all liners – including the *Titanic* herself – carried 'company signal' rockets showing different colours for identification purposes. This, after all, is why Captain Lord took an interest in rocket *colour*. He hoped to identify the shipping line to which the stranger belonged. After all, there was no point in asking about colour in the case of distress rockets, which could be 'of any colour or description'. Lord said: 'We sometimes get these company's signals which resemble rockets; they do not shoot as high and they do not explode' (6937). Stone saw the rockets as 'low-lying' and 'half the height of the masthead light'. The first white flash in the sky had been 'immediately above this other steamer' (7832). And here is Lord:

> 7290. Do just think? — Company signals usually have some colours in them.
>
> 7291. So that if they were white it would make it quite plain to you they were distress signals? — No, I understand some companies have white.

There was no colour for distress. Mayday rockets could be of any colour. Here are further questions about company signals (British Inquiry, questions 8006 and 8007):

> The Commissioner: What sort of signal is it [a company signal]?
>
> Mr Laing: It is a made-up signal to show what particular line the ship belongs to.

The Commissioner: But how is the signal different from distress signals?

Mr Laing: I think they burn different coloured flares or candles, or something of that sort. Sometimes they throw rockets. They throw balls, I know, sometimes – Roman candles. [Mr Laing seems personal proof of the confusion. He 'thinks' that 'something of the sort' sometimes happens…]

The Commissioner: But Roman candles do not go up in the air. [But they did…]

Mr Laing: No, but they throw up balls. It is dealt with by section 733 of the Merchant Shipping Act.

More confusion. The only one who expressed certainty was Charles Lightoller, second officer of the *Titanic*, who was understandably aggrieved at the *Titanic*'s nearby ship not coming to the rescue:

14169. Are there signals of a definite kind and appearance that are known as distress signals? — Yes, there is no ship allowed on the high seas to fire a rocket or anything resembling a rocket unless she requires assistance [this statement does not accord with the reality, nor with the experience of his brother officer, Mr Boxhall, who has seen rockets fired at night, for signalling purposes].

14170. If you had seen signals like those sent up from another ship would you have known, for certain what they were? — I have seen them and known immediately.

14171. We have heard something about companies' signals. Do they resemble these at all? — In no way, to my knowledge.

14172. Would you have any difficulty in distinguishing one from the other? — I never have had.

But Second Officer Lightoller also said of distress rockets, such as those fired from the *Titanic*:

14153. What sort of light do they show? — A shell bursts at a great height in the air [several hundred feet], throwing out a great number of stars.

Yet the strange signals seen by the *Californian* simply did not burst at a 'great height' over their nearby steamer. And this is another feature of company signals – Cunard had Roman candles fired 'in quick succession' to a height 'not exceeding 150ft'; Hamburg–Amerika had the same, to a height 'not exceeding 50ft'; Manchester Liners again 'not exceeding 50ft'… And all three used them on the high seas, contrary to what Lightoller asserted. And incidentally, it might be asked why Cunard fired company rockets in 'quick succession' when they were operating within a system that equated 'short intervals' with distress!

It is a reasonable assumption from the evidence above that Lord might also have initially thought of company signals because of something said about a lack of height in Stone's first report. Here is Lord talking on this subject:

6937. ...We sometimes get these company's signals which resemble rockets; they do not shoot as high... [That is exactly what Stone had seen; Stone who told the master about the lights and 'left it for him to judge.']

Gibson now continues the story of what was seen between 1 a.m. and 2 a.m., while Lord slept, and discloses the conversations that took place between himself and Stone:

7515. What had you noticed between one o'clock and twenty minutes past one, looking at her through your glasses? —The Second Officer remarked to me, 'Look at her now; she looks very queer out of the water; her lights look queer'.

7516. You are sure that is what he said – 'She looks very queer out of the water?' —Yes.

7517. Did he say what he meant? — I looked at her through the glasses after that, and her lights did not seem to be natural.

7518. [The Commissioner] What do you mean by that? —When a vessel rolls at sea her lights do not look the same.

7519. But there was no water to cause her to roll, was there? You were not rolling? — No.

7520. There was no sea to cause her to roll? — No, Sir.

7521. [The Solicitor General] He made this observation to you. Did you look at her then through your glasses? —Yes.

7522. What did you see? — She seemed as if she had a heavy list to starboard.

7523. She seemed to have a list, and you thought a list to starboard? —Yes.

Gibson has described a ship with a queer, unnatural appearance, furthermore with a list to starboard. What did Stone say, on the other hand?

7988. Did you say this to Gibson, 'Have a look at her now; it looks queer; she looks to have a big side out of the water?' — No, I did not say she had a big side out of the water; he remarked it to me.

7989. He remarked that to you? —Yes.

7990. Did you say, 'Have a look at her now; it looks queer?' —That is at the time when I told him the lights appeared to be altering their position with regard to one another. Yes.

7991. Did you think it looked queer? — I merely thought it was a funny change of her lights, that was all. That was before I had looked at her through the binoculars.

7992. In view of the fact that this vessel had been sending up rockets, and in view of the fact that you said it looks queer, did not you think at the time that that ship was in distress? — No.

7993. Are you sure? — I did not think the ship was in distress at the time.

7994. It never occurred to you? — It did not occur to me because if there had been any grounds for supposing the ship would have been in distress the Captain would have expressed it to me.

7995. [The Commissioner] Never mind about the Captain. You are being asked about what you thought yourself. Do you mean to tell us that neither you nor Gibson expressed an opinion that there was something wrong with that ship? — No, not wrong with the ship, but merely with this changing of her lights.

7996. Well, about this changing of her lights? — That is when I remarked that the lights looked queer. The lights, I said, not the ship.

7997. [still Commissioner] The lights are what I call part of the ship. The whole thing, lights and all, make up the ship. You want me to believe, do you, that, notwithstanding these rockets, neither you nor Gibson thought there was anything wrong on board that ship; you want me to understand that? — Yes.

Stone clarifies that it was Gibson alone who claimed to have detected the ship having 'a big side out of the water'. Gibson indeed made the shocking claim that the ship seemed to have 'a heavy list to starboard' (question 7522). Gibson in evidence first said he did not know why she appeared to have a list, but was very clear what led him to that conclusion:

7636. You thought she had a list...what was there about her lights to make you think that? — Her side lights seemed to be higher out of the water.

7637. The side lights seemed to be higher out of the water? — Yes.

7639. And you say that watching her, you thought that her red side light did not stay at the same level, but got higher? — Yes.

7640. That was your impression was it? — Yes.

[The Commissioner] That would make a list to starboard?

7641. [The Solicitor General] Is that why you thought she had got a list to starboard? — Yes.

7642. You thought her red light was rising out of the water, and so you assumed that the other side was dropping? — Yes.

A credible explanation, were it not for one thing. Gibson, in his original statement, composed on board the *Californian* in his own hand, stated: 'She fired another rocket [Gibson's second of three]. Shortly after that I observed that her side light had disappeared...' This is the port (red) side light, the light that he had previously said he was able to see. He and Stone only ever saw one side light. Both say they never saw green. Now Gibson is telling the court that not only has the red one not disappeared, but is rising steadily upwards!

7515. What had you noticed between one o'clock and twenty minutes past one, looking at her through your glasses? — The Second Officer remarked to me, 'Look at her now; she looks very queer out of the water'.

This is when Gibson says she seemed to have 'a heavy list to starboard'. But Gibson wrote in his earliest account of this red side light disappearing shortly afterwards. It cannot just 'disappear' if it has been rising high because of a list to starboard. A list to *port*, not starboard, would cause the red light to disappear quickly, as Gibson describes, but in such a case it is the green light that should go higher. And it is no defence to imagine that it depends on which side one is looking at, because the red and green side lights were introduced for this purpose. Red will always be the port side of a ship under observation, no matter if it appears on the right hand side of the observer. So Gibson is very close to appearing to see both a red light 'rising' and 'disappearing' simultaneously! Such doublethink is perplexing in a witness, and the twenty-year-old soon becomes even more accommodating to his questioners:

> 7687. You have told us about this red light, that you thought it was higher out of the water? — Yes.
>
> 7688. Did you look to see whether these after-lights seemed higher up out of the water, or lower in the water? — I noticed them all at the same time.
>
> 7689. What, the red light and the others too? — Yes.
>
> 7690. And do you mean that the white light seemed higher out of the water as well as the red light? — Yes.

So Gibson sees the ship tilting significantly to starboard (raising her red port side light), but *also* tilting not just from left to right, but from stern to bows – raising the after-lights higher too, and presumably going lower at the bows. This double-effect, 'all at the same time' in Gibson's words, seems an extremely unlikely proposition, like an elephant tipping forward with three legs off the ground.

Particularly when one considers what AB Edward Buley of the *Titanic* said in his evidence about the White Star vessel's red light being *submerged* when he left in lifeboat No. 10, whose departure has been timed at 1.10 a.m.: 'Her [*Titanic*'s] port bow light was under water when we were lowered' (US Inquiry, p.606). And Buley is an extremely accurate eyewitness, as we learned earlier.

There is also something deeply worrying about the alacrity with which Gibson agreed with a suggestion from counsel (questions 7636-9) that it was a red light that had been rising. Gibson previously spoke only of side *lights* (in the plural) getting higher. Anyway, enough of Gibson. What did Stone, the senior officer on duty, think? His version of events certainly casts doubt on Gibson's account, as he did not believe there was any 'list to starboard'; indeed, he did not perceive any list *at all*:

> 8051. Did you notice this ship had a list? — No, I did not.
>
> 8052. Are you sure? — Yes.
>
> 8053. Did you tell Gibson to look through his glasses, and that the ship had a list? — No. He remarked to me that it looked as if she had a list to starboard.
>
> 8054. Did you look? — I looked.
>
> 8055. [The Commissioner] Did you notice it? — I did not. I remarked to him that it was owing very probably to her bearing, and her lights were changing possibly. She had no list as far as I could see.

Stone was seeing a *moving* ship. That is what was causing the vessel under observation to change her lights, he said. Slightly earlier, Stone is questioned about rockets and bearings:

8037. Then you had seen [rockets] from this steamer? — A steamer that is in distress does not steam away from you, my Lord. [A perfectly reasonable presumption]

8038. You saw these before this steamer steamed away from you? — I saw them at the same time the ship started to alter her bearings.

8039. [Mr Scanlan] But for a long time while this ship was stationary like your own, you noticed at frequent intervals that she was sending up rocket after rocket? — No.

8042. What do you mean by saying that you did not see them coming in quick succession one after another? — I said that the ship was altering her bearing from the time she showed her first rocket. She commenced altering her bearing by the compass.

8045. Was she moving? — She started to move as soon as I saw the first rocket. She was stationary up to that time. She was stationary by our compass, at least so far as I could tell.

8046. Do you mean to say she was swinging about? — She was not swinging so far as I could tell, she was steaming away.

8048. When did you send word to the Captain that you noticed her steaming away?

8049. [The Commissioner] It is 2 o'clock? — At 10 minutes past 1. I reported to the Master that she was altering her bearings, which was the same thing.

8050. [Mr Butler Aspinall] Altering her bearings did not mean steaming away? — I do not see how two ships can alter their bearings when stopped. [A landlubber, becoming the third questioner to assault Stone, has his lack of maritime understanding exposed]

[The Commissioner] You need not press this any further. [They give up the unequal fight in attempting to get Stone to agree that his steaming-away ship was instead stationary]

Here, finally, is Stone's clear impression once more stitched into the record:

7938. Was the steamer altering her bearing to your vessel during that period of time? — Yes, from the time I saw the first rocket.

7939. The first of the eight that you have told us of? — The second – excepting the first flash, which I was not sure about.

7940. You say you saw the steamer altering her bearing with regard to you? — She bore first SSE and she was altering her bearing towards the south towards west. [She may have adjusted her course in steaming away, but not necessarily]

7941. Under way apparently? — Yes.

7942. During that 20 minutes did you notice anything which you would call funny or odd about her lights? — Yes.

7943. What did you notice? — On one occasion I noticed the lights looked rather unnatural, as if some were being shut in and others being opened out; the lights appeared to be changing their position – the deck lights.

7944. Her deck lights? — Yes, and I lost sight of her red side light.

7944A. That would be consistent with her altering her heading? — Yes.

7945. What was there funny about it? — Merely that some lights were being shut in and others exposed and I remarked to Gibson that the lights looked peculiar, unnatural, but when I took the glasses and brought her under close observation I took it to be due to the fact that very likely she was porting for some iceberg close at hand and was coming back on her course again, showing her other lights, the original lights.

Again, in Stone's view the 'unnatural' or 'peculiar' changes of lights are consistent with the steamer steaming away. At question 7995 above, he states that neither he nor Gibson thought there was something 'wrong with the ship, but merely with this changing of her lights'. He repeats (question 7996): 'The lights, I said, not the ship'. And Stone confirms Gibson's disappearing red side light, saying he lost sight of it — because the vessel had *turned* (altered her heading). This certainly seems a more logical account than Gibson's red light rising and rising into the air, only to disappear suddenly. Stone, on this sole point, lacks Gibson's many contradictions. Thus Stone is not particularly concerned, merely puzzled, about the unfolding oddities. No alarm bells ring at any time for him, even when he later concedes that 'a ship is not going to fire rockets at sea for nothing'.

7934. Did anything of that sort pass? Did you say something of this sort to Gibson: 'A ship is not going to fire rockets at sea for nothing?' — Yes, I may possibly have passed that expression to him.

Stone was not even concerned enough to keep the steamer constantly at the forefront of their watch:

7986. And were you talking about the ship all the time until she disappeared? — No.
7987. Are you sure? — Yes.

Stone had already told Lord the steamer was beginning to move off. He may have felt he had little to add. We return to Gibson in the witness box:

7525. What was there to show you [that she appeared to have a list to starboard]? — Her lights did not seem to look like as they did do before when I first saw them.
[The Commissioner] What was the difference?
7526. [The Solicitor General] Could you describe them at all, Gibson? — No, Sir.
7527. You have told us what the officer said to you. Did you think yourself when you looked at her through the glasses that something was wrong? — We had been talking about it together.
7529. I should like you to tell me what were you saying to each other? — He remarked to me that a ship was not going to fire rockets at sea for nothing.
7530. Who said that? — The Second Officer.
7532. I daresay you agreed with him? — Yes.

7533. What took place after that between you and him? — We were talking about it all the time, Sir, [contradicts Stone at 7986] till five minutes past two, when she disappeared.

7535. [The Commissioner] Then do I understand from you that the Second Officer came to the conclusion that this was a ship in distress? — No, Sir, not exactly.

7536. What do you mean by 'not exactly'? The Second Officer said to you, 'A ship does not fire up rockets for nothing?' — Yes, Sir.

7537. Did not that convey to you that the ship was, in his opinion, in distress? — Not exactly in distress, Sir.

7538. What then? — That everything was not all right with her.

7539. [The Solicitor General] In trouble of some sort? — Yes, Sir.

We have already seen how Stone denies noticing anything about the vessel's red side light being higher out of the water, or drawing Gibson's attention to it. Stone denied it twice, and here is the other reference:

7946. Is this right, that during this 20 minutes Gibson said this to you: 'Look at her red light; is not there something funny about it?' Did anything of that sort happen? — Not her red light that I remember.

7947. Gibson has been here, and he told us that he directed your attention to the red light. If you do not remember it, say so? — I do not remember his saying anything about her red side light at all.

Gibson had said:

7642. You thought her red light was rising out of the water…? — Yes.

7643. Did you call the Second Officer's attention to that? — Yes; he remarked it at the time; he told me to look through the glasses at it.

7644. He told you to look through the glasses at that very thing? — Yes.

But Gibson later flatly contradicts himself on this issue: 'Did he [Stone] speak to you about her port light? — No' (7653). So once more Stone's account stands out clearly, such as it is, whereas Gibson's is riven with his own contradictions. It would appear Gibson has gone on something of a 'solo run' in relation to his higher red light and the list to starboard. It should be noted that Gibson does not mention *anything* about a list to starboard in his original statement composed on board the *Californian*. With his mind so fresh, would he have left out such dynamite detail? There is no evidence that Gibson on the night in question voiced any meaningful misgivings to his senior officer, Stone. Of course, the twenty year-old apprentice had little experience, and Stone would likely give his opinions little value in any case. Gibson instead appeared to have confined himself to musings about the stranger's odd changes of lights, perhaps suggesting (question 7538) that everything was not all right with her. Things were very different on the *Titanic* when Gibson was seeing his 'tramp steamer' possibly listing to starboard…

A LIST TO PORT

The *Titanic* consensus is that there was a noticeable list to port:

> [Mr Cotter] Before she sank, my Lord; we have evidence that there was a list to port.
> [The Attorney General] There is no doubt there is some [such evidence] already, and
> there is a good deal more to come.

Such as…

> Second Officer Charles Lightoller (question 13852):'she had a pretty heavy list to port'.
> Harold Bride (question 16551):'There was a heavy list to port'.
> Thomas Ranger (question 4056):'A slight list to port'.
> Frank Morris (question 5475):'A list to port'.
> Frederick Scott (question 5651):'The port side was where she had listed over'.
> Charles Joughin (question 5989):'Yes, a list to port'.
> Samuel Rule (question 6502):'A list to which side? — To port'.
> Edward Brown (question 10530):'The ship took a list to port'.
> Alfred Crawford (question 17945):'A list to port? —Yes'.
> John Hardy (US Inquiry, p.589):'A heavy list to port'.
> Bruce Ismay (US Inquiry, p.965):'The ship had quite a list to port'.
> AB Edward Buley (US Inquiry, p.606): 'Her port bow light was under water when we
> were lowered'.

Even the Commissioner (question 11443) at one point interjected:'I suppose you will have
some theory to explain the great list to port that there was, according to the evidence, on
this ship before she went down?'

Yet even Gibson, with his frankly astonishing 'list to starboard', did not feel the need to rouse
the captain about a listing nearby ship, nor now think that the rockets he saw indicated distress:

> 7696. Did you know when the rockets were being sent up that they were being sent up
> as danger signals? — No.
> 7697.What did you think they were sent up for? — I thought they were some private signals.

Gibson appears to be suspecting two contradictory things at once – that is, if he is to be
believed about his list. He thought he was witnessing private signals (company signals)
from a ship that he also thought was sliding heavily to starboard! A most unfortunate state
of affairs, but perhaps the truth is that he only saw puzzling lights.

Gibson, in evidence, has already mentioned the starboard list (contradicted by the evidence
of those on the *Titanic*) when he tells the court of his belief that the steamer was sending only
private signals. And he was certainly well satisfied with Stone's explanation that the ship under
view was manoeuvring to avoid obstructions before coming back on her course again. We can

assume this, since the captain was not notified again (according to Gibson's timings), until more than an *hour* had elapsed from the time when Gibson walked on to the bridge at 12.55 a.m.

A FLASH AND A FAINT STREAK

We return to the matter of the 'deck flash'.

In Gibson's original written statement for Captain Stanley Lord of the *Californian*, composed on board that ship within a few days of the tragedy while still at sea, he wrote that he had been told by Stone on arriving on the bridge that the nearby tramp steamer had fired rockets. And this is what he says happened next:

> I then watched her for some time and then went over to the keyboard and called her up continuously for about three minutes. I then got the binoculars and had just got them focused on the vessel when I observed a white flash apparently on her deck, followed by a faint streak towards the sky which then burst into white stars.

It has been said that because Gibson saw this flash on her deck, the steamer they were looking at must have been the one firing all the rockets. The counter-argument, of course, is that if Gibson really can see a flash on her deck – and if the sole vessel firing rockets is the *Titanic* – then Gibson has no excuse for not immediately identifying this vessel as a gigantic passenger steamer, the largest ship ever to go down the ways. And if he can see a flash on her deck, then he must be extraordinarily close to this monster of the seas, whose deck was 70ft above the water. But Gibson does not perceive any height to that deck – at least, he does not mention it.

Gibson can also see a 'faint streak' towards the sky, which then bursts into stars. But this is what Lightoller, second officer of the *Titanic*, had to say about the rockets his ship fired:

> 14150. Now then, about signals from your boat. You have rockets on board, have you not? Were they fired? — You quite understand they are termed rockets, but they are actually distress signals; they do not leave a trail of fire.
> 14151. Distress signals? — Yes. I just mention that, not to confuse them with the old rockets, which leave a trail of fire.

It is not disputed that the *Californian* saw the *Titanic*'s distress rockets. But Second Officer Stone, who was on watch throughout, did not see any trail nor any 'faint streak'. And one should not expect him to by Lightoller's evidence (although Boxhall did say (question 15397): 'you see a luminous tail behind them').

In fact, *Californian* Chief Officer George Stewart stated that Stone was emphatic that the rockets he saw did not leave a trail:

> 8863. Did you ask him [Stone] what kind of rockets they were – whether they made any report or anything of that kind? — [Stewart] Yes Sir.

8864. What did he say? — He said, No, they did not make any report, and they did not leave any trail in the sky, and they did not seem to go any higher than the masthead lights.

Indeed, in Stone's earliest written account, composed at sea on 18 April 1912, the direct equivalent of Gibson's statement, he had this to say:

Shortly after I observed another distinctly over the steamer which I made out to be a white rocket though I observed no flash on the deck or any indication that it had come from that steamer, in fact, it appeared to come from a good distance beyond her.

Two things are perhaps instructive about Gibson's early flash-on-deck account:

1) Captain Lord retained it and later made it publicly available, when on the face of it his position would be stronger if this reference simply did not exist;
2) Gibson, when called to give evidence, no longer mentioned seeing a flash on deck or a streak skywards (he never saw Morsing from the stranger, involving a multiplicity of flashes, as sent by *Titanic*). Instead he abandoned those contentions.

This is what Gibson said to the British Inquiry of the first rocket he saw:

7495. …Well, I called her up for about three minutes, and I had just got the glasses on to her when I saw her fire the rocket. That was the first one.
7497. You say you had just got the glasses on to her. Did you see it through the glasses? —Yes… [No mention of a flash on deck, or a streak skywards. And Gibson soon gets another opportunity to comment again on this first rocket he saw]
7502. When you got your glasses on the vessel and saw the first rocket going up through them, could you make out the vessel at all? — No, Sir, just her lights. [He does not mention seeing the 'flash on the deck'. Now he can only see the lights of the vessel]
7503. [The Commissioner] Still this glare of light? —Yes.
7504. Did that indicate, that glare of light, that this was a passenger steamer? — No, Sir.

Gibson still maintains that he was looking at a tramp steamer, 4 to 7 miles away (questions 7548–9). He will repeatedly maintain (7706, 7728) that there was nothing at all about her to resemble a passenger steamer. He could not see how many funnels she had. In this overall context, one is tempted to the conclusion that Gibson saw no such flash on deck and no streak to the sky and was initially over-imaginative about what he saw.

Alternatively, he *did* see a single rocket fired by a tramp steamer, purpose unknown (possibly to respond to *Californian*'s signals, as Lord thought, or to acknowledge other rockets being fired by a ship further to the southward, as Stone suggested).

But the *Titanic* saw no answering rocket – although some claim to have seen lights elsewhere than off the port bow.

Perhaps the nearby stranger to the *Californian* did indeed fire one rocket, because this is what Stone declares all of a sudden in his British evidence:

7923. That pointed to this, that the rockets did come from this steamer? — It does, although I saw no actual evidence of their being fired from the deck of the steamer except in one case.

7924. [Mr Butler Aspinall] Which is the one case? — One rocket that I saw that appeared to be much brighter than the others.

7925. Was that one of the five or one of the three? — One of the three. [Seen by Stone and Gibson together]

7926. That, you felt confident, came from the vessel that was showing you these navigation lights? — I am sure of it.

7927. That you were sure of? — Yes.

7928. And you had further confirmation in the fact as you have told my Lord, that when the navigation lights altered their bearing, the rockets altered their bearings in a corresponding manner? — Yes.

7929. That would tell you as a sailor that it was almost certain that those rockets were being fired from that steamer which was showing you those navigation lights? — Almost certain, yes.

7930. I suppose, at any rate, now you have not any doubt but that that ship which was showing you the navigation lights was the ship which was showing you these series of rockets? — Except, as I say, that they were very low; they did not appear to go high enough to me.

It is sometimes said that Stone, as some kind of 'co-defendant', had a motive for claiming the rockets were 'low-lying' and seeming to come from a greater distance beyond the near ship. This reference gives the lie to his lying – because he himself suggests he is close to a vessel firing a rocket or rockets.

It is impossible to know what Gibson actually saw with his first rocket that night in 1912. Because it was his first sighting, it might have become more dramatic in his mind. The streak skywards is entirely out-of-keeping with Stone's low-lying rockets reaching only halfway to the height of the nearby ship's masthead light. And it defies not only Stone's evidence, but some from the RMS *Titanic*.

Stone, on the other hand, described no qualitative difference *at the time it happened* between any of the rockets, but later, in court, cites one brighter than the rest. He now seems to 'remember' the flash that Gibson in court will 'forget'.

Again, these inconsistencies are evidence of testimony given in good faith – the two men have no agreed script. One omits an inconsistency and the other brings it up, unhelpful and all as it is to their case.

Meanwhile, were it not for Stone's later remarks, we could argue that, because Gibson himself has discarded his purple description of the first rocket, the appropriate course is for us to discard it too.

The reader will have to make up his or her own mind as to what is happening here.

12

A STEAMER STEAMING

This is Stone's original statement, 18 April 1912:

> The other steamer meanwhile had shut in her red side light and showed us her stern light, and her masthead's glow was just visible.
>
> I observed the steamer to be steaming away to the SW and altering her bearing fast. We were also swinging slowly all the time through S and at 1.50 were heading about WSW and the other steamer bearing SW by W.
>
> At 2 a.m. the vessel was steaming away fast and only just her stern light was visible and bearing SW a half W.

There is an important distinction here that was not grasped by counsel at the British Inquiry. *Heading* means the direction a ship's head is pointing, and does not necessarily indicate that she is going that way – it has nothing to do with her position from the observer. *Bearing* has everything to do with an object's position from the observer.

Apprentice officer Gibson's account (his original statement, from around 18 April 1912) does not conflict with Stone's analysis, except that he suggests Stone thought the nearby stranger was steering away slowly instead of altering her bearing fast:

> Shortly after that I observed that her side light had disappeared but her masthead light was just visible, and the Second Officer remarked after taking another bearing of her, that she was slowly steering away towards the SW. Between one point on the starboard bow and one point on the port bow I called her up on the Morse lamp but received no answer.

The British Inquiry expected Stone and Gibson to be able to see a green light – the departing steamer's starboard light as she moved to the south-west. They did not see it, and instead saw only the stern light. Here is Gibson:

> 7769. Did you continue to see her red light? —Yes, it was about 2 points on the starboard bow.

7770. When the officer told you she was going away to the SW were you still seeing her red light? — No, it had disappeared then.

7771. Did you ever see her green? — No.

7777. I understand you to say you got to WSW? — Yes.

7778. What was causing that? — We were swinging round.

7779. You told us you never saw the green light of this vessel? — No.

7786. Did you see her turn round? — No.

And this is Stone:

8056. Did you ever see this vessel's green light? — No.

8057. If she was going away SW she must have gone under your stern? — No, she went across our bow.

8058. Were you turned round? — We were slowly swinging.

8059. She could not cross your bow showing you a red light? — Why not?

8060. Well, I do not think so; I may be wrong? — That is the light she would show, her red light.

8061. If you turn round – heading WSW. I think you said? — We were heading ENE at the beginning of the watch and slowly turned round to WSW. When I lost sight of this steamer we would be heading then about WSW and she would be about 2 points on our port bow. I saw then her stern light, not her red light. She shut in her red light.

8062. You must have seen her green light if it was showing, before she shut in her stern light? — If she shut in her *red* light [Stone corrects counsel, who seems hopelessly confused]. I did not say she shut in her stern light. She did not shut her stern light in at all the whole period…

8069. And she goes away to the SW? — Yes as near as I could judge. That was approximate.

8070. She must open her green light to you? — No.

8071. [The Commissioner] Is not that so? She must have opened her green light to you? — To steam away to the SW?

8072. Yes? — No.

Stone does not entertain the landlubber's notions, even though they are those of the president of the Court of Inquiry. Nonetheless, just consider the lamentable lack of understanding displayed in what is an Admiralty case, with Lord Mersey assisted by no fewer than five nautical assessors. Why is Stone's entirely reasonable exposition of what happened being so powerfully resisted?

Is it, perhaps, because the *Titanic*, which the court would like to have facing north while sinking (towards the *Californian* – to accommodate Groves and little light) cannot next turn 180 degrees to show her stern light to Stone?

Stone had to demonstrate his concept by using two little model ships in court!

He would have held the model *Californian* bows stationary for effect (we can represent the bows here with the symbol '△') while passing the departing ship from right to left in front of them ('<' across at right angles). This means the other vessel is showing the red light on her port side all the while. As this vessel then turns to starboard (represented by '\') she closes in her red and exposes the white stern light instead.

It will be seen at once that if this other vessel were to be the sinking and immobile *Titanic,* then she cannot possibly change her bearing (her direction from the observer) as dramatically as Stone describes.

There then follows this exchange:

8079. How far did you get? — To WSW.

8080. That is about it? — Yes.

8081. Now where does she go to? — To the SW.

8083. [The Commissioner] She went across your bows? — It was merely our swinging that brought her across our bows.

8085. [The Commissioner] How did she do it without showing her green light? — I did not see her green light at all. She ported. She shut in her red side light and showed her stern light.

Stone says she 'ported'. He means 'ported her helm', or turned to starboard, which was the effect in 1912 of porting one's helm (to go to port, one would starboard the helm). What he should have said for the layman was that she turned right as she went away – not turning around left to go away, as Lord Mersey and his counsel seem to think, in which case she would indeed show her green light to the *Californian* to the northward.

Still Mersey cannot grasp it. And Stone displays further patience in his explanation:

8087. [The Commissioner] She must have shown her green light, you know? — We are heading WSW and the steamer's stern was SW ahead of us. All we would see is her stern light. I did not see any side light at all after she started to steam away.

This lack of understanding by the court in 1912 was seized upon by the author of a book published in 1993. In *The Ship That Stood Still,* which seeks to implicate the *Californian* as *Titanic's* mystery ship, it is claimed that for the departing steamer not to have shown her green light, she must have *reversed* to the south-west. This attempt to make a nonsense of Stone and Gibson's concurring evidence – and thereby liars of them both – is a transparent deceit.

A VISIT TO THE SKIPPER

Here again is Stone's original statement:

I sent Gibson down to you and told him to wake you and tell you we had seen altogether eight white rockets and that the steamer had gone out of sight to the SW. Also that we were heading WSW.

When he came back he reported he had told you we had called him [the steamer] up repeatedly and got no answer, and you replied: 'All right, are you sure there were no colours in them,' and Gibson replied 'No, they were all white'.

And here is Stone in evidence:

7948. At the end… did you then send Gibson to report to the Captain? —Yes.
7949. What report did you tell Gibson to give to the Captain? — I told Gibson to go down to the Master and be sure and wake him up and tell him that altogether we had seen eight of these white lights, like white rockets, in the direction of this other steamer; that this steamer was disappearing in the SW; and that we had called her up repeatedly on the Morse lamp and received no information whatsoever…
7952. When Gibson returned did he tell you what had passed between him and the Captain? — He told me he had woken the Captain up and given him my report; the Captain asked him the time and asked him if he were sure there were no colours in them, red or green.
7953. You mean the rockets? — Gibson assured him they were white rockets.

Compare Stone with Gibson. Here is Gibson's original statement:

Just after two o'clock she was then about two points on the port bow, she disappeared from sight and nothing was seen of her again.

The Second Officer then said, 'Call the Captain and tell him that that ship has disappeared in the SW, that we are heading WSW, and that altogether she has fired eight rockets.' I then went down below to the chartroom and called the Captain and told him, and he asked me if there were any colours in the rockets. I told him that they were all white. He then asked me what time it was, and I went on the bridge and told the Second Officer what the Captain had said.

And this is Gibson in evidence:

7552. What were the orders which the Second Officer gave you when she disappeared? — 'Call the Captain and tell him that that ship has disappeared in the south-west; that we are heading west-south-west, and that she has fired altogether eight rockets'.
7553. Did you report that to the Captain? —Yes.
7554. Where did you go? — Into the chart-room.
7555. Was the chart-room door shut? —Yes.
7556. Did you open the door and go in? —Yes
7559. Did you give him the report you were ordered to give him? —Yes.
7560. What did the Captain say? — He asked me were they all white?
7561. The rockets? —Yes, 'Were there any colours in the rockets at all?'
7562. What did you tell him? — I told him that they were all white.

7563. Did he give any instructions? — No.

7564. Did he say anything further? — He asked me the time.

7565. What was the time? — Five minutes past two by the wheelhouse clock…

7570. [The Commissioner] Was he awake? — Yes, Sir.

7571. [The Solicitor General] Did you return to the bridge? — Yes.

7572. Did you report that you had done what you were told to do? — Yes.

The above is a rather ordinary summation. But Gibson will later be heavily pressurised to agree with an apparent desire on the court's part to believe that the word 'disappeared' must mean 'sank' rather than 'went out of sight', which was Stone's original phrase.

It now seems as if counsel and the Commissioner are anxious to fit the evidence to the theory that the *Californian*'s nearby ship was the *Titanic*, rather than allowing the evidence to speak for itself.

7610. When the ship disappeared she had got a little on to your port bow? — [Gibson] Yes.
[The Commissioner] Will you ask him what he understood by the word 'disappeared'?

7611. [The Solicitor General] Yes, my Lord. [To the Witness] You say you were told to report that the ship had disappeared. What did you understand by [the word] 'disappeared'? — We could not see anything more of her.

7612. [The Commissioner] Did it convey to you, and did the man who was speaking to you, in your opinion, intend to convey that the ship had gone down? That is what I understand by disappearing. Did you understand him to mean that? — No, my Lord.

7613. What did you understand him to mean – that she had steamed away through the ice? — That she had gone out of sight.

7614. [The Commissioner] Oh, yes. A ship goes out of sight when she goes down to the bottom. What did you understand by the word 'disappeared'? — That is all I could understand about it.

7615. [The Commissioner] A ship that had been sending up rockets; then you are told to go to the Captain and say: 'That ship which has been sending up rockets has disappeared'. What did you understand the Second Officer to mean? Did not you understand him to mean that she had gone to the bottom? — No.

7616. Then what did you understand, that she had steamed away through the ice? — [No answer]

Perhaps Gibson gives no answer because the question appears rhetorical, or maybe he is just tired of denying the Commissioner's preconceived notion. We do not know if he nodded his head or made any other non-verbal reply, but we know that he has already denied the proposition repeatedly.

Some have used Gibson's 'no answer' to suggest that he is tongue-tied, but it is impossible to know whether he simply shrugged, or made a face, or whether the Commissioner's tone of voice suggested he no longer wanted an answer. Perhaps the next question, from the Solicitor General, which changed the subject, came in quickly on top, since the court had exhausted this line of enquiry. Gibson has already clearly denied that the word 'disappeared' could have meant 'gone to the bottom'.

We shall return to other elements in the above passages, but it is clear that Stone continued to see the disappearing steamer for twenty minutes more after Gibson had returned at 2.05 a.m. This would bring the *Californian* time to 2.25 a.m. And if the *Californian* and *Titanic* had the same times, as the British Inquiry liked to think (the court equating Groves' ship stopping at 11.40 *Californian* time with the *Titanic* hitting an iceberg at 11.40 her time) then, by 2.25 a.m. (for both), *Titanic's* lights were *not* visible because she had quite simply gone to the bottom. So Stone could not be seeing her at 2.25 a.m. as she had foundered (by common agreement of those who survived the disaster) by 2.20 a.m. And despite the persistence of the twelve-minute theory, it would mean an even worse outcome for the case against Captain Lord. Now Stone would be seeing his departing steamer at 2.37 a.m. *Titanic* time (2.25 plus twelve) – some seventeen minutes after the *Titanic* had foundered.

But we know instead that *Titanic* officer Boxhall (US Inquiry, p.918): 'At 11.46 p.m., ship's time, it was 10.13... New York time'. Officer Lightoller testified to the same during Pitman's US testimony. We know *Californian* was separately one hour fifty minutes ahead of New York time (although Wireless Operator Cyril Evans claimed one hour fifty-five minutes ahead). The direct 1912 evidence that *Titanic* was one hour thirty-three minutes ahead of New York (as against latter-day guessing) thus suggests *Californian* was at least seventeen minutes ahead of Titanic time, not behind her. If this is the case, then Stone seeing his stern light at 2.25 a.m. equates to the more reasonable time (for those implacably set against the *Californian*) of 2.08 a.m. *Titanic* time – she has not yet sunk.

All this would be very well, were it not for the *stern* light that Stone should not be seeing! Here is Stone:

7971. Did you make any report to the Captain about this disappearance? — When I sent Gibson down at two o'clock I told him she was disappearing in the SW.
7972. [The Commissioner] Did you say to Gibson 'Tell the Captain she is disappearing', or did you say 'Tell the Captain she has disappeared', which did you say? — I could not have said that she had disappeared, because I could still see her stern light. I saw this light for 20 minutes after that.

Let us pause here to ponder the enormity of Stone's statement. Gibson saw the wheelhouse clock showing 2.05 a.m. He comes back and reports to Stone. Then Stone sees the steamer for twenty minutes thereafter. Stone's account of continued viewing appears to disagree with Gibson's original statement leading up to the visit down below to the captain: 'Just after two o'clock she was then about two points on the port bow, she disappeared from sight and nothing was seen of her again'. Yet Stone's own original statement goes on to say: 'At 2.45 I again whistled down again and told you we had seen no more lights and that the steamer had steamed away to the SW and was now out of sight...'

This agrees completely with his sworn evidence. Gibson's phrasing – 'nothing was seen of her again' – may suggest no more rockets, or may simply be a way of leading into his next action, telling the captain that she has 'disappeared' (Stone: 'steamed away') to the south-west.

Gibson, significantly, was not questioned about whether he saw any light after he came back from visiting the captain and made his report to the second officer. What comes next ends his evidence, and the repeated verbal pummelling by counsel has its effect after a prolonged grilling:

7741. Could you see whether she was steaming away? — No. The Second Officer was taking bearings of her all the time.

7742. [The Commissioner] The message he sent you with was that she disappeared? —Yes.

7743. [Mr Harbinson] Not that she steamed away, but disappeared? —Yes.

7744. The Captain made no reply? — He asked me if there were any colours in the lights, or were they all white.

7745. You saw no coloured rockets? — No.

7746. As a matter of fact isn't there a code of rockets for use at sea? Do you know as a matter of fact whether there is or isn't? — I know now there are only distress rockets used at sea and private signals used near the shore. [Not true in 1912]

7747. And what colour are distress rockets? — White – any colour at all.

7748. Did you say anything to the Second Officer, Mr. Stone, or did he say anything to you, with reference to these rockets that were repeatedly sent up? —Yes.

7749. Did not you think it very curious that so many rockets should be sent up so close to one another? —Yes. [A leading question – Gibson testified to seeing three rockets in up to an hour]

7750. Did you say anything to him about going to see the Captain and saying this seemed to be a serious matter? — No, he told me he had reported it to the Captain and the Captain had told him to keep calling her up.

7751. Did Mr Stone say this vessel seemed to be in distress? — No; he said there must be something the matter with her.

7752. Did he make any remarks to you as to the Captain taking no action? Did he say anything to you at the time? — No.

7753. Are you sure? —Yes.

7754. [The Commissioner] Did you say anything to yourself about it? — I only thought the same that he thought.

7755. What was that? — That a ship is not going to fire rockets at sea for nothing, and there must be something the matter with her.

7756. Then you thought it was a case of some kind of distress? —Yes.

[The Commissioner] We are anxious to get the other witnesses from this steamer into the box, and unless you have something really important, I suggest you should finish.

[Mr Harbinson] I have finished, my Lord.

Gibson at the end thus agrees to 'some kind of distress', a phrase that is not his own. But 219 questions earlier he had testified that the rockets had conveyed to him that the ship was 'Not exactly in distress Sir' (questions 7537 and 7538), but that 'everything was not all right with her'. Crucially, of course, Gibson offered no opinion of distress in his report to the captain – he merely reported that the ship had fired rockets and disappeared in another direction. He certainly did not mention any 'list to starboard'. And at no time did Gibson, whatever might have been 'not all right' with the departing steamer, consider that she may have been anything other than a tramp steamer, an opinion he voiced repeatedly.

> 7546. You thought she was a tramp steamer, and you had seen her side light at what you thought was between four and seven miles away? — Yes.
>
> 7795. [Mr Robertson Dunlop] How long have you been at sea? — Three and a half years.
>
> 7796. And have you seen passenger steamers? — Yes.
>
> 7797. Large passenger steamers? — Yes.
>
> 7798. And medium-size steamers? — Yes.
>
> 7799. Seen them at night? — Yes.
>
> 7800. And have you been able to tell the difference between a large liner like the *Titanic* and a tramp? — Yes.
>
> 7801. From the appearance of her lights? — Yes.
>
> 7802. From the height of her lights? — No, from the quantity.

CAPTAIN'S VERSION OF THE VISIT

A brief recap of what Gibson said – he claimed that he reported to the captain that the steamer had disappeared to the south-west and had fired altogether eight rockets. Lord replied: 'Alright, are you sure there were no colours in them?' Gibson said they were all white. Lord then asked the time and was told it was 2.05 by the wheelhouse clock. After this perfunctory conversation, Gibson returned to the bridge.

Lord's first description of this conversation was equally perfunctory (US Inquiry, p.729):

> I have a faint recollection of the apprentice opening the room door; opening it and shutting it. I said, 'What is it?' He did not answer and I went to sleep again. I believe the boy came down to deliver me the message that this steamer had steamed away from us to the southwest, showing several of these flashes or white rockets; steamed away to the southwest.

There is an obvious difference here, insofar as Lord says he heard nothing. At the British Inquiry, Lord's failure of recollection was put sorely to the test. But he held to his version of events eight times, as listed below:

Questions 6859–62

'I have a recollection of Gibson opening and closing the chart-room door some time between half-past 1 and half past 4. I said, "What is it?" and he did not reply; he closed the door'.

Questions 6893–96

Lord said he learned the next morning from the second officer that Gibson was sent down for the purpose of telling him the vessel had fired 'several rockets' and had 'steamed away'. Lord said this was the message he understood was given to Gibson by Stone.

Question 6896

'I am putting to you, you know, that what was said was the vessel had disappeared? — No, it was never mentioned, "disappeared", to me'.

Question 6924

'What was the message that Gibson brought down to you then? — That morning? I did not get it, not to my knowledge. I never got it'.

Questions 6950–54

'I heard Gibson open and close the door and said, "What is it?" He did not say anything. I had been asleep. I was wakened up by the opening of the door – the banging of the door'.

Questions 7075–79

'I do not recollect Gibson coming into the room. I said, "What is it?" I cannot tell what time it was'.

Question 7179–7285

7179. …I have no recollection of Gibson saying anything. I do not remember him saying anything. He did not say anything to me as far as I know.

7280. I want to put this to you: Did not the boy deliver the message to you, and did not you enquire whether they were all white rockets? — I do not know; I was asleep.

7281. Think. This is a very important matter. — It is a very important matter. I recognise that.

7282. It is much better to tell us what happened, Captain? — He came to the door, I understand. I have spoken to him very closely since. He said I opened my eyes and said, 'What is it?' and he gave the message, and I said, 'What time is it?' and he told me, and then I think he said I asked him whether there were any colours in the light [sic – singular].

7283. That is what the boy has said to you. You have questioned him a good many times since? — Yes, I have questioned him since.

The Commissioner: Is he telling the truth? — Is the boy telling the truth?

7285. Yes. — I do not know. I do not doubt it for a moment.

Questions 7287–88

> 'I was asleep. I very likely was half-awake. I have no recollection of this apprentice saying anything to me at all that morning'.

At this next point, Captain Lord appears to agree with the proposition that he could have asked questions, even though he has no recollection of it:

> 7289. Why did you ask whether they were white rockets? — I suppose this was on account of the first question they asked, whether they were company signals.
> 7290. Do just think? — Company signals usually have some colours in them.
> 7291. So that if they were white it would make it quite plain to you they were distress signals? — No, I understand some companies have white.
> 7292. Do really try and do yourself justice? — I am trying to do my best.

And finally, for an eighth time:

> 7368. Did you sleep soundly? — I must have done.
> 7369. If the apprentice came to your room subsequently, are you conscious of anything that he said to you or what you said to him? — All I recollect saying is, 'What is it?'
> 7370. Did you remain asleep until 4.30? — Until 4.30.

The next morning, subsequent to finding out about the *Titanic* sinking, Lord questioned Second Officer Stone.

> 7374. What was his [Stone's] explanation to you? — He said that he had sent down and called me; he had sent Gibson down, and Gibson had told him I was awake and I had said, 'All right, let me know if anything is wanted'. I was surprised at him not getting me out, considering rockets had been fired. He said if they had been distress rockets he would most certainly have come down and called me himself, but he was not a little bit worried about it at all.
> 7375. If they had been distress rockets he would have called you? — He would have come down and insisted upon my getting up.
> 7376. And was it his view that they were not distress rockets? — That was apparently his view.

And here is the essence of Gibson's visit at 2.05 a.m. It undoubtedly happened, but it was simply an informative mission. Gibson was to tell Lord the ship had fired eight rockets and steamed away. Nothing in particular was sought from the captain, but any instructions he might choose to give would be followed. Stone was giving final news of the steamer Lord had been interested in from the start, specifying that he should be told if 'she moved or came closer'. The captain was certainly not being roused to the point of getting up. He was not being asked to come to the bridge. Captain Lord had been awake since 7 a.m. the previous morning – 'When did you go on duty on the Sunday morning? — I got up the usual time – 7 o'clock in the morning' (7346) – and had completed a seventeen-hour day.

And Gibson did not lay a hand on Lord to shake him awake – unlike Chief Officer Stewart, who hours later would jostle the shoulder of Wireless Operator Cyril Evans in a similar bed-side visit, to make sure of waking him up and getting him to function. Gibson's account of the conversation, when he returned to Stone, meanwhile also indicates that the exchange ended puzzlingly, in a rather open-ended way, with no decision being taken. Yet there is one curious piece of evidence which suggests that Captain Lord may indeed not have been in much posi-tion to take in what he was being told. It comes from the evidence of Herbert Stone:

> 7954. Is that all? — Then he [Gibson] told me that as he shut the door he heard the Captain say something – what, he was not quite certain about.
> 7955. Did Gibson then remain on the bridge with you? —Yes.

This fragment is very telling. Here is the apprentice officer leaving the captain's room, and he hears the captain say something. He cannot decipher it, being outside the door. But Gibson does not re-enter and ask the captain what it was he said. This is very curious. The master is potentially issuing an order or asking a question – Gibson does not know – but he does not feel the need to ascertain exactly what it is the captain is saying. Why not?

Gibson said in evidence that the last he heard was his captain asking the time, which he gave:

> 7567. Did he ask you anything further? — No.
> 7568. Or tell you anything further? — No.
> 7569. And did you go away? —Yes.
> 7570. [The Commissioner] Was he awake? —Yes, Sir.

But if the captain was awake, why did Gibson not re-enter? Would he really walk away while something further was being said, casually ignoring the imparting of a potential order? Why would Gibson, being merely an apprentice officer, turn on his heel and risk the wrath of the Old Man? Was it perhaps because Gibson actually knew the exhausted captain was not alive to what he was being told? Did he know the captain, half-roused, was talking rubbish and that therefore there was no point in attempting to decipher the latest rambling? Was that why he walked away?

If we allow the possibility of this being the case, then some of Lord's evidence begins to make sense. He asks 'what is it?' because he hears the door banging. The door banged closed after Gibson said his piece, and Lord rambled. Lord only begins to come out of his subcon-scious when the door bangs shut: 'I heard Gibson open and close the door and said, "What is it?" He did not say anything. I had been asleep. I was wakened up by the opening of the door – the banging of the door' (composite of responses to British Inquiry questions 6950–54). Lord's somnolence, backed by Stone's evidence, would explain in a very ordinary way the Commissioner's earlier acid opinion of matters. Lord Mersey observed tartly (7180–81):

> The boy came in and shut the door, [and Captain Lord] then said to the boy, 'What is it?' and the boy behaved in a most extraordinary manner by shutting the door and going away.

CREDIBILITY

Lord's failure to recollect anything said to him by the apprentice is hardly calculated to impress a court. Yet it is easy to suggest he must be lying, as the Attorney General of the British Inquiry did, with remarks such as: 'Do really try and do yourself justice?' (7292). Yet why would Lord lie in this way? What possible benefit is there? On the other hand, to simply accept the apprentice officer's evidence and assert that one was fully awake and cognisant would be a much better approach for any determined liar. Lord could have said he was indeed told the ship which was firing rockets had disappeared, just as he had previously been told she was steaming away.

So what? The steamer has departed. That is the only impression he need form. It is also an impression that, apart from argument about what the number of rockets might have meant, is entirely blame-free. But Captain Lord, as on most issues in the case, took a route in evidence that was very difficult for himself.

He may have innocently believed that a court could easily accept that a man spoken to, but not shaken awake, and in the bottom of the trough of his mere four-hour slumber, could respond with inanities and thereafter in the morning forget having uttered anything (it is also a curious fact, as we shall see, that, on the very same night, an officer of the *Titanic* did not hear a colleague come into his room to tell him his ship had struck an iceberg!).

At the end of the day, there has been a failure of communication. Yet Lord was the one who was 'dead to the world'. Where, exactly, is the fault here? And if there is any, whose is it?

ROCKETS UNSEEN

We are now beyond the time of the sinking of the *Titanic*. The *Californian* has seen eight rockets by this time. But how many rockets were fired by the *Titanic*? Eight! At least, this is one of the received wisdoms of *Titanic* lore. But the notion of just eight rockets being fired from the White Star vessel begins to crumble upon closer investigation. It is a tribute to the British Inquiry that the idea of eight rockets and eight alone was so assiduously implanted into public consciousness, where it has remained in the decades since. Lord Mersey first espoused this dogma in his final report, published at the end of July 1912 (British Report, p.45):

> In all, Mr Boxhall fired about eight rockets. There appears to be no doubt that the vessel whose lights he saw was the *Californian*. The evidence from the *Californian* speaks of eight rockets having been seen between 12.30 and 1.40. The number sent up by the *Titanic* was about eight. The *Californian* saw eight.

Thus we have eight. And eight has been ingrained ever since. The *Californian* certainly saw only eight rockets. But did the *Titanic* really only fire eight? Just eight? Why would they limit their distress rockets to such a small number? The *Titanic* had no fewer than forty-eight rockets aboard, not to mention a variety of other flares and signals, as listed in the 'Description of the Ship' in the British Report (p. 19):

> Distress signals: These were supplied of a number and pattern approved by the Board of Trade – i.e., 36 socket signals in lieu of guns, 12 ordinary rockets, 2 [boxes] Manwell Holmes deck flares, 12 blue lights, and 6 lifebuoy lights.

Why then fire such a sparse amount? Why economise so much on rockets when a $10 million vessel is sinking? If we ignore Lord Mersey and examine what the *Titanic* witnesses who gave evidence actually said, it is suddenly revealed that there was no agreement that eight and only eight were fired. Third Officer Herbert Pitman says: 'It may have been a dozen or it may have been more, sir'. (US Inquiry, p.293). Second Officer Charles Lightoller, in response to question 14160, states: 'I should roughly estimate somewhere about eight' (but he is referring to the starboard side only). Quartermaster Arthur Bright claims (US Inquiry, p.832): 'Six were fired in all, I think' (but he refers only to those fired by himself and Quartermaster Rowe). Fourth Officer Joseph Groves Boxhall (question 15395) states: 'How many rockets did you send up, about? — I could not say, between half a dozen and a dozen, I should say, as near as I could tell'. And Steward Alfred Crawford states (question 17973): 'I should say I saw about a dozen go up – probably more'.

The only agreement above is between Crawford and Pitman, who both believe it could have been the case that more than a dozen rockets were fired. If we imagine this means a minimum of thirteen, then it is at least five more than Lord Mersey would have us believe. The average number from the crew accounts given above is ten rockets. And even this does not allow for 'more' rockets over a dozen, nor add any rockets to the totals of those who speak about only one side. From the evidence, it looks more like a dozen rockets fired. Lord Mersey is hardly entitled to state as a found fact that 'the number sent up by the *Titanic* was about eight'. And despite Mersey's pronouncements, Joseph Boxhall did not say that he fired eight rockets. He says instead that he *personally* could have fired up to twelve. And it is crucial to state clearly that Boxhall was not the only one firing! The indications we have are that there were two firing positions on either side of the bridge. This is an important concept, bearing in mind the evidence from Apprentice Officer James Gibson aboard the *Californian* that he saw only *three* rockets in the hour from 1 a.m. to 2 a.m. *Californian* time.

Yet the evidence from the *Titanic* is of Boxhall firing alone for a time, followed by forty minutes of extra firings from the time when Quartermaster George Rowe was called up from the stern to assist, lasting until 1.45 a.m. Surely the *Titanic* could not have fired only three rockets in that latter period?

When we compare the experiences of the *Titanic* and *Californian*, we do not see Mersey's 'coincidence' of only eight rockets fired and seen. Instead we see the possibility that the *Californian* did not see all of *Titanic*'s rockets but instead saw only some. This in turn suggests that the *Californian*'s own nearby ship – stubbornly unresponsive some 5 miles away – was not the one firing rockets, but that the rockets were being fired by a distant and unseen vessel over the horizon, as Second Officer Herbert Stone suspected at the time may have been the case.

In the original statement for his captain, Stone had this to say: 'I observed no flash on the deck or any indication that it [a rocket] had come from that steamer, in fact, it appeared to come from a good distance beyond her'.

It is now worth looking at the *Titanic* evidence in a little more detail. Here is Third Officer Pitman (US Inquiry, p.293):

> ...I should say about a dozen rockets were fired.
> Senator Smith: What did you see? What did they do?
> Pitman: They were fired from the rail. They make a report while leaving the rail, and also an explosion in the air, and they throw stars, of course, in the air.
> Senator Smith: And you saw about a dozen or so of them?
> Pitman: It may have been a dozen or it may have been more, sir.

And George Symons gives the following evidence:

> 11468. Before you left the boat deck had you noticed any rockets being fired from the bridge? —Yes, the rockets were going up simultaneously, every minute, minute intervals, and that steamer's light was in sight about a point and a half on the port bow, roughly between five and ten miles away when they fired the rockets, and they were also working the starboard and port Morse lights.

Symons' use of the word 'simultaneously' strongly implies two firing positions. Rockets were going up *simultaneously*, he says. It appears that that there were two firing sockets either side of the bridge, as indicated by Pitman (and elsewhere by Boxhall). Indeed, the *Titanic* was designed so that rockets could be fired from a rail socket on both the starboard and port sides (if they *were* sent up 'simultaneously', it broke the distress regulations of 'one at a time').

In a moment we shall see that Quartermasters Rowe and Bright were indeed firing separately to actions carried out by their senior officer, Boxhall. The evidence is that rockets were fired on the port side (where the mystery ship was seen) and also on the starboard side, where *Titanic* witnesses saw the flash of rockets going off and where Officer Lowe was 'nearly deafened' by the detonations taking place beside him at boat No.1. Symons says above that they were 'also' working the starboard and port lights, which suggests that other work was being done on the starboard and port sides, perhaps involving the firing of those simultaneous rockets.

Meanwhile his description of rockets going up – sometimes together, or 'every minute, at minute intervals' (11468) – is totally at odds with Boxhall's telling the British Inquiry that he himself was firing rockets at intervals of 'probably five minutes' (15399). If Symons is right and Boxhall is equally right, then only having two firing parties can explain the contradiction. And two firing parties are also suggested in a remark by John Hardy: 'He [Captain Smith] was superintending the rockets, calling out to the Quartermaster about the rockets' (US Inquiry, p.601). The quartermaster is either QM Rowe or QM Bright. Captain Smith was giving orders to a quartermaster because no officer was present in charge of rockets at that location – it will be argued that this was on the port side, since officer Boxhall was operating to starboard.

Second Officer Lightoller, meanwhile, says that eight rockets were fired from the starboard side:

14160: Did you notice at all how many were sent up, or at what intervals? — I should roughly estimate somewhere about eight [rockets] at intervals of a few minutes, five or six minutes, or something like that. [This agrees with Boxhall's intervals]

14161. One at a time? —Yes, all fired from the starboard side, as far as I know.

Below is further evidence of two separate firing stations, operating independently on both the port side and the starboard side. Here is Rowe (US Inquiry, p. 525):

Senator Burton: When did you first see her [the mystery ship]?

Rowe: When I was on the bridge firing the rockets. I saw it myself, and I worked the Morse lamp at the port side of the ship to draw her attention.

This evidence of Rowe suggests he was on the port side of the bridge, firing the rockets. Obviously he could not fire rockets in the middle of the bridge area, because it was covered. If he was firing on the starboard side, where there was both a firing socket and a Morse lamp (located on top of the wing cab), why go all the way to port to work the lamp there? Either lamp could be seen by the mystery ship, since they were deliberately located high on the *Titanic* superstructure. Rowe's evidence also agrees with Hardy's remark about the captain speaking to a quartermaster about the rockets.

Rowe said in his American evidence that he was firing rockets until 1.25 a.m. But it is interesting that he remarked in the course of his British testimony (questions 17694–5) that he was *not* present on the starboard side when the emergency boat was lowered at 1.10 a.m. Since he was still firing rockets at 1.10 a.m., it surely follows that he was on the port side. Rowe said in his US evidence (p. 519):

...I assisted the Officer to fire them, and was firing the distress signals until about five and twenty minutes after 1. At that time they were getting out the starboard collapsible boats. The Chief Officer, Wilde, wanted a sailor. I asked Captain Smith if I should fire any more, and he said, 'No, get into that boat [collapsible 'C'].'

This may support Hardy in relation to the captain supervising Quartermaster Rowe's rocket firings on the port side. If he heard a request from the chief officer to the captain on the 'middle' bridge and took his opportunity, who can blame him?

The following extract from Boxhall would seem to confirm that Rowe (named only as a quartermaster) was firing rockets and then Morsing on the port side (US Inquiry, p. 934):

Senator Burton: And you kept firing up those rockets?

Boxhall: Then leaving off and firing rockets. There were a lot of stewards and men standing around the bridge and around the boat deck. Of course, there were quite a lot of them quite interested in this ship, looking from the bridge, and some said she had shown a light in reply, but I never saw it. I even got the Quartermaster who was working around with me – I do not know who he was – to fire off the distress signal, and I got him to also signal with the Morse lamp, that is just a series of dots with short intervals of light, whilst I watched with a pair of glasses to see whether this man did answer, as some people said he had replied.

And that steamer was off the port bow. It would be a natural human inclination to fire rockets on the side of the ship closest to the mystery vessel, even though rockets fired from any point on the *Titanic* would be seen just as well.

We know Lightoller says (question 14160) that his 'rough estimate' is that eight rockets were fired, 'all on the starboard side as far as I know'. This is what Fourth Officer Boxhall adds:

15434. I know the starboard emergency boat had gone some time, and that they were working on the collapsible boats when I went, because I fired the distress signals from the socket in the rail just close to the bows of the emergency boat on the starboard side.

We have just seen Quartermaster Rowe deny that he was present on the starboard side at the lowering of the 'emergency' boat (boat No.1), even though he was firing rockets at the time. Now we see that Boxhall was firing rockets close to boat No.1 on the starboard side. This is very strongly indicative of two firing positions. Boxhall goes on (question 15434):

Every time I fired a signal I had to clear everybody away from the vicinity of this (starboard) socket, and then I remember the last one or two distress signals I sent off the boat had gone, and they were then working on the collapsible boat which was on the deck.

Boxhall suggests he is alone here at starboard all night, since he does the clearing away as well as the firing. The absence on the starboard side of Rowe and Bright (who were called up by Boxhall to help fire rockets) becomes an argument that they were instead busy on the port side. Yet another proof of this contention arises if we reduce the contrary argument to absurdity. It does not take three men to fire rockets from one socket position; Boxhall had been successfully firing rockets alone before the other two arrived (these rockets were sent off with a lanyard; but any rockets are simple for one man to fire – see photo section). Conversely, if the other two were there with Boxhall, why then did he have to shoo everyone away on his own when he wanted to fire? The indications in Boxhall's evidence are that he personally fired six to twelve rockets:

15395. How many rockets did you send up about? — I could not say, between half a dozen and a dozen, I should say, as near as I could tell.

Now we shall see that Boxhall was already busy with firing rockets on his own when he unexpectedly got the opportunity to call up assistance. His evidence specifically states

1. '*A ship like the* Titanic *at sea is an utter impossibility for anyone to mistake…*' Titanic *at Southampton, Good Friday, 5 April 1912. The funnels to the left belong to three other liners. They are (from left): the* Majestic *(9,950 tons), the* Philadelphia *(10,650 tons), and the* St Louis *(10,250 tons). The cargo steamer* Californian *was 6,223 tons. Her captain described the vessel lying nearby as 'something like ourselves'. What would the world's largest passenger ship look like within 'easy distance'? (Southampton City Collection)*

2. The RMS Titanic *at Queenstown, midday, Thursday 11 April 1912. (William W.L. McLean)*

Vessel Five Miles Away Ignored Distress Signal, Says Titanic Officer

Joseph G. Boxhall, Fourth in Command, Tells Senate Investigating Committee He Flashed in Morse Code "We Are Sinking," but Steamship Continued on Her Way Without Answering.

IDENTITY OF SHIP IS NOT KNOWN,
BUT HE SAYS HE SAW HER LIGHTS

Mr. Franklin Swears He Never Tried to Withhold True Facts of Disaster and Says He Prevailed Upon Mr. Ismay Not to Return at Once to England with Crew and Lifeboats.

3. *The presence of a mystery ship within 5 miles of the sinking* Titanic *made for sensational headlines. That this vessel 'continued on her way' remains shocking a century later. (New York Herald, 23 April 1912)*

4. *White Star Line managing director J. Bruce Ismay. (*The Sphere*)*

5. *Journalists and photographers outside the White Star Line offices at Bowling Green, New York, before the full extent of the disaster became known. The offices also served the Leyland Line. (Library of Congress)*

A TRIP ABROAD

BY THE
LEYLAND LINE
BOSTON TO
LIVERPOOL

6. A Leyland Line leaflet
showing the boat deck
of one of their steamers,
around 1918. Apprentice
James Gibson saw a
tramp 4–7 miles from the
Californian. Meanwhile,
Officer Pitman of the
Titanic believed his ship's
blowing off steam ought to
have been heard
10 miles away. The Titanic
also fired rockets 'in lieu
of guns' – but although
Gibson saw rockets,
he could not hear their
detonations. Lawrence
Beesley, in a lifeboat, was
able to hear Carpathia
rockets at least 7 miles
away.

7. *Captain Stanley Lord in 1908, aboard the Leyland Liner SS* Louisianian. *The port companionway to the steamer's flying-bridge is in the background. He had previously seen the* Olympic, Titanic's *sister ship, at a distance of 5 miles. Lord made clear the steamer close to his own vessel was 'something like ourselves'. (Estate of Stanley Tutton Lord decd)*

8. *The* Boston Herald *of Friday 26 April pictured the 'steamship* Californian *of [the] Leyland Line lying at her dock at East Boston'. A pejorative headline – 'Liner Charged with Deserting* Titanic' *– accompanied the photograph.*

9. The Californian *at 8.30 on the morning of 15 April 1912. Photographed from the* Carpathia *by honeymooning couple James and Mabel Fenwick. The vessel clearly still has some way on her, indicating Captain Lord's anxiety to reach the scene. The* Carpathia, *laden with* Titanic *lifeboats, is reflected on the hull of the* Californian. *(Courtesy George Fenwick)*

10. The Californian *under construction at the Robb Caledon yard. She cost £105,000, compared to the* Titanic's *£1.5 million ten years later. When this picture was taken, in November 1901, her later captain, Stanley Lord, had already been awarded his Extra Master's certificate – at the extraordinarily young age of twenty-three. (Dundee City Archives)*

11. The Californian *photographed from the* Carpathia *by passenger Louis Ogden on the morning of the rescue. She is flying the 'J' signal flag, indicating that she wishes to communicate by semaphore with the Cunarder. The* Californian *was sunk by U-35 off Cape Matapan, Greece, on 9 November 1915. (National Archive and Records Administration)*

12. Californian *crew members, put out of court on the morning of Tuesday 14 May as their captain was giving evidence. From left: George Glenn, fireman; William Thomas, greaser; Cyril Evans, wireless operator (holding his messages log); James Gibson, apprentice; Herbert Stone, second officer; William Ross, A.B.; Charles Groves, third officer; George Stewart, chief officer. (*Illustrated London News*)*

13. The Titanic's surviving officers. Back row, from left: Fifth Officer Harold Lowe, Second Officer Charles Lightoller, Fourth Officer Joseph Groves Boxhall. Front, seated: Third Officer Herbert Pitman. All these men clung to low estimates of distance to the mystery ship, despite Inquiry findings. (Southampton City Council collection)

14. Above left: *Captain Stanley Lord. (Estate of Stanley Tutton Lord decd)*

15. Above right: Californian *Second Officer Herbert Stone. (Public Record Office)*

16. Above left:
Californian *Third Officer Charles Victor Groves.* (Public Record Office)

17. Above right:
Californian *apprentice officer James Gibson. He was sure the vessel he was looking at had only one masthead light, and thought she 'looked like a tramp steamer'.*

18. Right: Titanic *Able Seaman Thomas Jones and Quartermaster George Rowe. Rowe fired rockets and worked a port-side Morse lamp in a bid to summon the mystery ship. Thomas Jones was sent away in boat No. 8, charged by Captain Smith with landing his passengers on the near steamer and returning with her to rescue all aboard* Titanic. *(Courtesy Chris Dohany)*

19. Above left: Californian *Donkeyman and deserter Ernest Gill.* (Boston American)

20. Above right: Californian *lookout Benjamin Kirk. He was told to 'look out for the Titanic' when hoisted up the* Californian *mainmast on the morning after the sinking.*

21. Left: Californian *Chief Officer George Frederick Stewart. The British Inquiry indicates he took a Pole Star observation at 10.30 p.m. which neatly verified the* Californian's *latitude. It had already been estimated by means of traditional 'dead reckoning'. (Public Record Office)*

22. *Captain Edward John 'E.J.' Smith of the RMS* Titanic. *The White Star Line's most experienced commander thought a previously unseen vessel was eventually close enough to read a detailed message sent through flashes of a Morse lamp. He ordered the signal sent: 'Come at once, we are sinking'. He also believed a lifeboat could reach the vessel and land passengers. (J.&C. McCutcheon collection)*

23. Above left: *Fifth Officer Harold Lowe. He saw a red light on the mystery ship at 1 a.m. The* Californian *at this time could only have been showing her green light to any vessel to the southward. (Public Record Office)*

24. Above right: *RMS* Titanic *Fourth Officer Joseph Groves Boxhall. He swore to seeing the mystery ship come ever closer to* Titanic *until it turned and stopped. (Public Record Office)*

25. Left: Titanic *Second Officer Charles Herbert Lightoller, pictured aboard the* Oceanic *in 1908. A leader in the port side evacuation, he was 'perfectly sure' he saw a light attached to a vessel 'about two points on the port bow'. It was 'not over five miles away'. He reassured passengers that a rescue ship was coming. (Author Collection)*

26. Above left: *Jack Phillips*, Titanic *wireless operator. He told the* Californian *to keep out when she tried to warn of ice a short time before the* Titanic *struck.*

27. Above right: *Harold Bride, surviving* Titanic *wireless operator. He endured a freezing night's exposure on an overturned collapsible lifeboat. Bride said Phillips clung to the same raft, but succumbed to the cold.*

28. Right: Californian *Wireless Operator Cyril Furmstone Evans. Third Officer Groves entered his room as he lay in bed after midnight, but could not read any transmissions. Evans was roused the next morning by Chief Officer Stewart and asked to investigate what happened in the night. (Photo © courtesy Günter Bäbler and Claes-Göran Wetterholm)*

29. Top left: *Able Seaman Edward Buley claimed to be able to see a distance of 21 miles. He said he was 'very positive' that the steamer 'off the port [side]' was stationary for about three hours, and then 'made tracks'.*

30. Top right: *Quartermaster Robert Hichens was at the ship's wheel when the* Titanic *struck. He later took control of lifeboat No.6, which left the port side under instructions to pull towards the tantalising light. 'The light was moving, gradually disappearing', Hichens testified, 'we did not seem to get no nearer to it'. (Public Record Office)*

31. Above left: *Thomas Dillon testified to extra* Titanic *movement after she had struck her berg. There is evidence she temporarily 'resumed her course' to the west before stopping. (Southampton City Archives)*

32. Above centre: *The man who spotted the fatal iceberg,* Titanic *lookout Frederick Fleet. He told the Inquiries that he could see 'no lights at all' of other ships when he and colleague Reg Lee were in the crow's nest, where they remained for some time after impact. He later saw the mystery ship from the deck, on the port bow at 'about 1 o'clock'. (Public Record Office)*

33. Above right: *First class passenger Archibald Gracie thought the ship was 'coming to our rescue'. (Houghton Mifflin)*

34. Left, above: *Lady Lucile Duff Gordon wrote: 'Just beside us there was a man setting off rockets and the ear-splitting noise added to the horror'. She looked back at the* Titanic *from her ill-filled lifeboat and described the liner as like 'a giant hotel, with light streaming from every porthole'. The Californian witnesses did not see a floating hotel, but a tramp steamer nearby. Nor did they hear rockets or see high displays. (Library of Congress)*

35. Left, below: *The Countess of Rothes, who steered lifeboat No.8 ahead of all others toward the mystery ship, declared: 'For three hours we pulled steadily for the lights seen three miles away; then we saw a port light [red] vanish and the masthead lights grow dimmer until they disappeared'. (Illustrated London News)*

36. Right: *Lord Mersey, the seventy-one-year-old chairman of the British Inquiry. Suspicious of the Californian from the start, he would declare himself satisfied that her declared stop position was 'not accurate'. Before retiring to write his report, he also wondered aloud about what powers he had to sanction a captain who would fail to come to the aid of a vessel in distress. (Southampton City Collections)*

37. *Lord Mersey sitting at the later* Empress of Ireland *Inquiry. He rejected the entire testimony of* Titanic *witnesses as to the distance away of the mystery ship, preferring to take 'advice' from others. Despite his findings of an 8–10 mile separation,* Titanic *officers maintained their much shorter claims during a 1913 court case on the legal liability of the White Star Line. (Author collection)*

38. Above left: *A younger Lord Mersey. Born and brought up in Liverpool, the former Mr Justice John Charles Bigham represented the city in parliament and acted at the bar for big shipping companies. He allowed a legal ambush, knowing Captain Lord had no chance to answer it. His 1929* Times *obituary was unusually sour, accusing him of 'premature expression of opinion or bias'. (*Daily Sketch*)*

39. Above right: *Lord Mersey, President of the British Inquiry, was brought out of retirement to sit over an investigation deemed a 'whitewash' by* Titanic *Second Officer Lightoller. A former MP, he was intimately attuned to Government needs and would later preside over the* Empress of Ireland, Falaba *and* Lusitania *inquiries. His conclusions in each case suited the state, but later fell suspect. (Author collection)*

40. *Attorney General of the United Kingdom, Sir Rufus Isaacs. He appeared for the Board of Trade at the* Titanic *Inquiry and was later elevated Lord Justice of Appeal and ennobled as Lord Reading. (Incorporated Law Society)*

41. British Solicitor General Sir John Simon appeared on behalf of the Board of Trade, which both licensed the Titanic to go to sea and administered the later Inquiry. Sir John examined many of the Californian witnesses and, on the twenty-fourth day, after they had been heard, connived in the Attorney General's application to amend the terms of reference whereby a finding might be made about the conduct of the Californian. (Author collection)

42. Senator William Alden Smith of Michigan, chairman of the US Senate Subcommittee Inquiry. (Library of Congress)

43. *Captain John J. Knapp, US hydrographer. He claimed the* Titanic's *sidelight could be seen at a range of 16 miles when it was required to be visible for 2 miles. Not content with this stretch of the imagination, he would also invent a hypothetical location for the* Californian. *(US Navy)*

44. *The US Senate Subcommittee on Commerce* Titanic *investigation in session. Taken in Washington DC on Tuesday 23 April 1912 during the evidence of* Titanic *Third Officer Herbert Pitman (not visible in this photograph). Chairman William Alden Smith is pictured, centre. Pitman said he saw a white light on the horizon 'to the westward, right ahead' while in lifeboat No. 5. It 'may have been three miles'. To the right of centre, bearded with arms folded, is passenger Arthur Peuchen, saved in boat No. 6. (Library of Congress)*

45. *The* Titanic *is shown here with two masthead lights in an eyewitness drawing of the sinking by Steward Leo Hyland. Californian witnesses said their nearby vessel had one masthead light. (Collection of the late Walter Lord, National Maritime Museum)*

46. *The* Titanic *boat deck, port side, at Queenstown, Thursday 11 April 1912. An arrow indicates a trawler a few points by compass off the port bow – close to where the mystery ship would be seen three nights later. The near lifeboat is No. 8. Its crew members were told by Captain Smith to row to the stranger, which Boxhall said was showing 'beautiful lights'. He left in boat No. 2, hanging over side, while the visiting steamer was showing a stern light. To the top-right of the picture is the crow's nest, with a perfect view of all in front. Yet the lookouts saw* no *other ship, either before or immediately after* Titanic *struck ice – indicating the mystery ship drew close under power, whereas the* Californian *was stationary throughout. Note: author has airbrushed the mast of a tender from lower left of picture for purposes of clarity. (Fr Browne Collection)*

47. *Captain Smith at the* Olympic's *starboard wing-cab, with the starboard Morse lamp above. The sidelight of the* Titanic's *sister ship (green for starboard, red for port), is shown in the lower left hand corner.* Titanic *evidence shows she was Morsing even as she sent up her rockets. The US Inquiry accepted the patently absurd suggestion that a* Titanic *sidelight could be seen at 16 miles. (Southampton Pictorial)*

48. Lightoller saw eight rockets fired from starboard (seen to left, above), where Boxhall fired from six to twelve rockets. But the mystery ship was seen to port (right of picture)... and firing here also would mean many more rockets! (20th Century Fox)

49. Above: Captain Maurice Clarke, Marine Surveyor of the Board of Trade, watches a rocket being fired at a pre-sailing inspection on the American liner New York at Southampton in 1907. Five years later Captain Clarke inspected the Titanic immediately prior to her maiden voyage, while the New York nearly collided with the White Star liner as the latter left her berth. (The Graphic)

50. Opposite below: German star shells, left, and Belgian reply rockets, right, photographed by camera-plate on the Western Front in 1916, four years after the sinking of the Titanic. In reality the human eye sees not the whole journey (as shown here over the flooded defences of Ypres), but a travelling ball of light. Rockets further away are distinguishable by a lower trajectory, smaller points and less glow. Gibson used binoculars to look at a vessel short miles away which he concluded was only a tramp steamer. (The Sphere)

51. Right: *A contemporary artist's rendition of a pyrotechnic burst at sea. Most depictions, including on film, show rockets ridiculously low (in order to fit the frame). Officer Lightoller confirmed the* Titanic *rockets went 'several hundred feet' in the air, and other witnesses corroborated their extreme height – this itself is a fundamental property of distress rockets so that they might be seen over the horizon.*

52. *A rowboat with a dying 'Holmes light' on the water, left, during the search for the lost submarine A–1 in 1904. The* Titanic *was equipped with flares made by Manwell Holmes and other firms.* (The Graphic)

53. *Looking forward on the shelter deck of the* SS Californian. *When daylight began to break after 4 a.m., Chief Officer Stewart could make out a new steamer to the south – a ship Stone insisted was not the one he and Gibson had been viewing, and which had instead steamed away.* (Dundee City Archives)

54. *The cable ship* Minia *demonstrates how the* Californian *might have looked when stopped in ice, facing north-east, on the night of 14 April 1912. The* Minia *was chartered by the White Star Line to search the vicinity of the* Titanic *sinking for bodies, and recovered seventeen. (Author collection)*

55. *The SS Birma, photographed from the* Carpathia *on the morning of 15 April 1912. Her experiences proved the* Titanic *could not have reached the transmitted distress position. (Courtesy of George Fenwick)*

56. *The* Carpathia *steamed west to New York with survivors. (Southampton City Collection)*

57. Left: *Captain Sir Arthur Rostron of the rescue ship* Carpathia. *He could see 'all around the horizon' as he rescued* Titanic *lifeboats at 5 a.m. 'The first I saw of the* Californian *was at about eight o'clock.'* (Library of Congress)

58. Below: *The Almerian was half the size of her sister,* Californian. *(Author collection)*

59. The Antillian. *A wireless message to her reporting three icebergs confirmed* Californian's *northerly position several hours in advance of* Titanic's *collision and was overheard by the White Star vessel. When she stopped at the edge of an icefield, the* Californian *attempted to warn* Titanic. *(Mariners' Museum, Newport News)*

60. The oil tanker Paula. *Like a modern bulk carrier, her housing – arguably her 'glare' – was all the way aft. (Mariners' Museum, Newport News)*

61. The 5,595-ton SS Parisian. *She passed over the spot where the* Titanic *sank. (Contemporary postcard)*

Dampfer Präsident Lincoln (Hapag)
Länge 183 m
Breite 21 m
Tiefe 16,90 m
Raumgehalt 18 000 Tons.
Passagiere und Besatzung 4100

62. Above: President Lincoln. *(1910 postcard)*

63. Left: *The Hansa Line oil tanker* Lindenfels. *Like her sister ship, the* Trautenfels, *also in the North Atlantic that night, she had a black funnel containing a white band with the heraldic device of a Maltese cross. (Peabody Museum of Salem)*

64. Below: *The SS* Saturnia. *She heard the* Titanic *SOS and turned back, but was supposedly stopped by heavy ice 6 miles from the scene. (Contemporary postcard)*

D. „Frankfurt"

65. *The Norddeutscher Lloyd liner,* Frankfurt. *She responded to the* Titanic's *distress messages, asking questions, until she was told by* Titanic *Wireless Operator Jack Phillips that she was a fool and to shut up. His dismissal of her remains controversial to this day. (Contemporary postcard)*

66. *Advertising for the sister ships RMS* Virginian *and RMS* Victorian. *(1912 poster)*

67. *The* Samson, *later the* City of New York, *at the edge of the ice in the Bay of Whales, Antarctica, in 1930.*

68. *The Canadian Pacific liner* Mount Temple *grounded off Nova Scotia in December 1907. She had a yellow funnel in common with other CPR liners, but was to the* west *of the icefield when finally met by the* Californian. *Chief Officer Stewart saw a yellow-masted vessel to the east of the field at 4 a.m. on the morning of 15 April. Stone and Lord both also saw that steamer to the south, but never learned her name. (Mariners' Museum, Newport News)*

69. Right: *Captain James Henry Moore of the* Mount Temple. *His sighting of the* Carpathia *supports Lord's evidence. (Courtesy Edward P. DeGroot)*

70. Below left: *Stanley Lord as an old man. He was eighty-two when he made his final deposition on the critical events of nearly half a century before. (Estate of Stanley Tutton Lord decd)*

71. Below right: *Captain James DeCoverly. His report, endorsed by the Chief Inspector of Marine Accidents, Captain P.B. Marriott, formed the basis for the official reappraisal conclusion that it was 'probable' the* Californian *had been 18 nautical miles away and seen some other vessel. (PA)*

72. *Grave of Captain Stanley Lord, New Brighton, Liverpool. (Author collection)*

that he had already sent up rockets in the early part of the night when he got the sudden chance to order that even more rockets be brought up from the stern of the ship:

> 15593. I knew one of the boats had gone away, because I happened to be putting the firing lanyard inside the wheel house after sending off a rocket, and the telephone bell rang. Somebody telephoned to say that one of the starboard boats had left the ship, and I was rather surprised.

Quartermaster George Rowe told the US Inquiry that it was *he* who had rung the bridge. He was ringing, remember, after Boxhall has already begun firing off rockets (US Inquiry, p. 519):

> I telephoned to the fore bridge to know if they knew there was a boat lowered. They replied, asking me if I was the Third Officer. I replied, 'No; I am the Quartermaster.' They told me to bring over detonators, which are used in firing distress signals.

So Boxhall already had at least one box of rockets at his disposal and already in use, and he wanted more. Rockets were kept in two places on the *Titanic*, being stowed both on the bridge and in a locker all the way aft, as Rowe testified in America (US Inquiry, p. 522):

> Senator Burton: Were there any detonators or other signals kept aft?
> Rowe: The detonators, such as the distress signal rockets, green lights, and blue lights.
> Sen. Burton: Were there any kept forward?
> Rowe: Yes; on the fore bridge.

Two places. And now there are at least three boxes of rockets brought to the bridge, because this is what Quartermaster Arthur Bright has to say (US Inquiry, p. 832):

> I went out to the after end of the ship to relieve the man I should have relieved at 12 o'clock, a man by the name of Rowe. We stood there for some moments and did not know exactly what to do, and rang the telephone up to the bridge and asked them what we should do. They told us to bring a box of detonators for them – signals. Each of us took a box to the bridge. When we got up there we were told to fire them – distress signals.

Rowe separately says: 'I took them to the forebridge and turned them over to the Fourth Officer. I assisted the officer to fire them…' (p. 519). Bright was asked who fired the rockets, and replied: 'Rowe and I, and Mr Boxhall, the Fourth Officer' (p. 832). This reply in itself seems to suggest two firing parties. On the one hand, Rowe and Bright, on the other, Boxhall. That telling comma between the two quartermasters and mention of Boxhall appears in the transcript, the stenographer indicating Bright's pause. And Boxhall's tale of lone firings and shepherding people away by himself serves to confirm what Bright is saying. Bright then says, when asked how many 'you' fired: 'Six were fired in all, I think' (US Inquiry, p. 832). It would seem that he is speaking only for his firing party. Because if 'six in all' means everybody aboard the *Titanic*, then Bright cannot be right. *Californian* undoubtedly saw eight rockets. And of course when Bright answers as to how many 'you' fired, he is not answering in a context that includes Boxhall's use of rockets before Bright and Rowe came up from the stern.

So here we are – Boxhall had previously been able to fire rockets alone, and now there are at least three designated men and three separate boxes of rockets on the bridge, which has available firing sites to port and starboard. And yet we are asked to believe that *Titanic* fired only eight rockets!

Let us return to boat No.1 (an 'emergency' boat, in that she and her companion on the port side, boat No.2, were kept permanently swung out, ready for lowering in case of a man overboard or other incident). It was located all the way forward on the starboard side. Symons is in charge of this boat (lowered at 1.10 a.m., according to the findings of the British Report), and says rockets were fired 'simultaneously', while they were 'also working the port and starboard Morse lamps'. Fifth Officer Lowe was helping to fill and lower boat No.1. He says of rockets fired in this location: 'Yes; they were incessantly going off...' (US Inquiry, p.401). When Symons' phrase – 'simultaneously, minute intervals' – is compared with Lowe's phrase – 'incessantly' – it vouches for Symons' concept of great rapidity of firing. Eight rockets would be quickly expended in such a scenario!

Lightoller, in his 1935 book *Titanic and Other Ships*, meanwhile, said rockets went up 'every minute or two' (p.161). We remember that he spoke in evidence of 'about eight' rockets, all from the starboard side. Minimalists who prefer only eight rockets would have to deal with a maximum firing time of sixteen minutes by this account, compared to Rowe's forty minutes of firing after they got their boxes of rockets to the bridge.

Perhaps the earliest survivor account was composed by a Japanese passenger, Masabumi Hosono. Writing on *Titanic* stationery he had on his person aboard the rescuer *Carpathia*, Hosono told of being up on deck: 'All this while, flares were signalling emergency and were being shot up into the air ceaselessly, and the hideous blue flashes and noises were simply terrifying'. He told how four lifeboats on the port side, aft, were quickly filled. He managed to jump into one when it halted on the way down. Once away from the vessel, he turned back towards the sinking ship and wrote: 'The *Titanic* was still shooting up one emergency flare after another'. Hosono's report, then, is of 'ceaseless' rockets, one after the other, over some period. Even allowing for natural hyperbole, his account clashes with the British Inquiry's preference for a paucity of just eight rockets fired.

Meanwhile, it seems Rowe and Bright are not on the starboard side where boat No.1 was located, but helping with the incessant, simultaneous rockets by separately sending them up from the port bridge wing.

TIMINGS & INTERVALS

It is now worth looking at times and the gaps between *Titanic* rocket firings as cited by different witnesses, to see whether only eight rockets were fired. A single man, if he were firing those eight at the intervals suggested by Boxhall (five minutes) would be done and dusted in forty minutes. So what say the rocket-firers? Here is Quartermaster George Thomas Rowe:

> 17683. Did you take any part in firing distress rockets? —Yes.
> 17684. How long do you think it was from the time you commenced firing the rockets till you finished firing the rockets? — From about a quarter to one to about 1.25.
> 17685. Yes, that is right. You gave evidence in America about it, and I see what you said there was 'I assisted the officer to fire them, that is, rockets, and was firing distress signals until about five and twenty past one'. That is accurate? —Yes.

But Boxhall had been firing rockets before Rowe made his way to the bridge! Boxhall meanwhile indicated that he himself continued firing rockets until 1.45. Rowe's watch may have been put back twenty minutes at midnight. So when Rowe cites 1.25 as a stop time, this is actually 1.45, and agrees with Boxhall. Both parties are firing rockets for forty minutes –'simultaneously', says Symons. And Boxhall specifically states that he began firings before Rowe had even telephoned the bridge. So, just eight fired in all?

Bright says that he and Rowe each brought a box of rockets to the bridge. Presumably those two boxes did not contain just a couple of rockets each. No – the evidence is trying to tell us something very much to the contrary; two firing parties with separate boxes each must have managed far more than eight rockets.

If Bright's six are married to Boxhall's maximum of a dozen, then eighteen rockets seems to be the outer limit sent into the night sky by the drowning *Titanic*. Steward Alfred Crawford says not only a dozen, but probably more:

> 17972. After the boat was launched that you were in, did you see any rockets sent up? —Yes, from the *Titanic*. I also saw the Morse code being used. [This agrees with Symons, earlier]
> 17973. About how many rockets did you see sent up? — I should say I saw about a dozen go up, probably more.
> 17974. A dozen rockets from the *Titanic*? —Yes, they kept going up.
> 17975. And you could see those quite distinctly? —Yes.

And, in the US Inquiry (p.828):

> Senator Smith: Did you see any rockets?
> Crawford: Yes, sir; plenty of them went up from the *Titanic*. [Would eight be plenty?]

Yet the *Californian* saw only eight.

It is not clear when Boxhall began firing the very first rockets of all. But the evidence we have is capable of suggesting that he was busy for some time before that telephone rang on the bridge, allowing him to summon Rowe and Bright.

In parts of his evidence, Boxhall implies that he had been firing rockets early in the night, when the mystery ship was just a pair of masthead lights: 'I had been firing off rockets before I saw her side lights. I fired off the rockets and then she got close...' (US Inquiry, p.910). Was this before Rowe and Bright were summoned up to the bridge? It would appear so. And Boxhall is firing rockets in the plural. In fact, Boxhall had obtained rockets as soon as he saw a light. And think about this – the *Titanic*, as soon as she knew she was sinking (which was very early indeed) was bound to send up distress rockets whether there was a ship in sight or not.

Here is Boxhall:

> 15393. ...I could see the light with the naked eye, but I could not define what it was, but by the aid of a pair of glasses I found it was the two masthead lights of a vessel... but she was too far off then.
>
> 15394. Could you see how far off she was? — No, I could not see, but I had sent in the meantime for some rockets, and told the Captain I had sent for some rockets, and told him I would send them off, and told him when I saw this light. He said, 'Yes, carry on with it'. I was sending rockets off and watching this steamer.

This was early in the night, then. But how early? Quartermaster Rowe indicates in his evidence that the *Titanic's* mystery ship had approached and was close by the time he got to the bridge (US Inquiry, p.525):

> Senator Burton: When did you first see her [the mystery ship]?
> Rowe: When I was on the bridge firing the rockets. I saw it myself, and I worked the Morse lamp at the port side of the ship to draw her attention.

She was close enough to Morse, in Rowe's opinion. But Boxhall had been 'firing off rockets before I saw her side lights. I fired off the rockets and then she got close' (US Inquiry, p.910). A number of rockets had already been fired by Boxhall then, according to his own evidence, before he had the good fortune to be able to summon Bright and Rowe. Can we make further progress and establish when exactly Boxhall began this mysterious number of pre-telephone rocket firings? We return to Boxhall (US Inquiry, p.910):

> Senator Fletcher: I understood you to say that you saw a steamer almost ahead of you... about the time of the collision?
> Boxhall: Shortly afterwards...
> Sen. Fletcher: And how soon after the collision?
> Boxhall: I cannot say about that. It was shortly after the order was given to clear the boats.

Not to lower the boats, or even to man the boats, but simply to take the covers off the boats. So Boxhall strongly implies that he was firing rockets long before any boat had been lowered, and indeed Rowe and Bright only came to the bridge from aft after seeing a boat in the water for the first time. AB George Symons supports this view. He gave a deposition to the British Consul in America on 2 May 1912, which was later read into the record of the British Inquiry. It reads in part (11721):

> Shortly after I had got on the boat deck I noticed rockets being fired at very frequent intervals from the bridge, Morse signals being used, and at about 12.30 I saw about one point on the port bow, distant some five or six miles, a light…

Symons (sent away in boat No.1 at 1.10 a.m.) appears to place 'very frequent' rockets being fired shortly after he got on the boat deck. His arrival was just after midnight because he referenced something else happening (11418) at about 11.55. He said: 'as I was on my way to the deck, they struck eight bells in the crow's nest [meaning midnight]'. So what do Boxhall and Symons mean by their word 'shortly' in this context? How early can Boxhall's first rocket firings be placed? There is no point in exhaustively examining times. What appears to be indicated is that rockets had been fired before Rowe and Bright brought two more boxes of rockets forward, which were used next. If Symons is right about 'very frequent' rockets, then three men would certainly dispose of only eight rockets in a very short time.

Rowe said however (17684) that the second phase of firings (in other words those rockets that he himself took part in firing), lasted forty minutes. Bright says half an hour, but this is a guess, whereas Rowe gives specific times for the beginning and end of his firings. Meanwhile the distress regulations called for rockets at 'short intervals', akin to Symons' 'very frequent'. Even if five-minute intervals (incompatible with distress) are considered, then the parties should have fired six in half an hour, or eight in forty minutes, on top of whatever Boxhall had already sent up before he got the telephone call from the stern docking bridge where Rowe and Bright were standing by with other boxes. So here we are – Boxhall was firing rockets. He is later joined by Rowe and Bright and all three take part in the further firings. A number of *Titanic* witnesses talk of seeing a dozen rockets or more – 'plenty'.

Boxhall only refers to firing on the starboard side, and is there alone. He says he fired six to twelve, a guess very similar to Lightoller's estimated eight, which the latter emphasised were 'all from the starboard side'.

Bright's figure of six is the lowest mentioned by anyone. But this must be wrong as a *Titanic* total, since at least eight were fired because eight were certainly seen. If however, Bright's six refers to all those fired on the port side alone, then the judgment of other witnesses makes sense. Six from port and eight from starboard makes fourteen, and we remember a couple of witnesses mentioning a dozen or more. But the *Californian* saw just eight. She may have missed a number. Perhaps because she was very distant?

WHITE OR COLOURED?

The *Californian* also saw only white rockets. Not that there was anything significant in this, since distress rockets could be 'of any colour or description' and company signals sometimes carried white, although usually with other colours. But the *Titanic* witnesses talk of firing coloured rockets, at least alongside the white. Third Officer Herbert Pitman suggests that they were 'various colours' (US Inquiry, p.293). Quartermaster Robert Hichens states: 'I did not take no particular notice of the colour, Sir. Some were green, some were red, and some were blue – all kinds of colours – and some white, Sir. I think, if I remember rightly, they were blue' (question 1198). Lookout Reginald Lee was asked whether there were coloured rockets, or only white ones? He replied: 'No, coloured rockets' (question 2584). Passenger Major Arthur Peuchen saw 'different colours flying down' (US Inquiry, p.352). Fourth Officer Joseph Boxhall observed: 'Just white stars, bright... not red' (US Inquiry, p.910). Second Officer Charles Lightoller saw rockets that were 'principally white, almost white'. (question 14154). So, Boxhall and Lightoller emphasise the white, yet they are hardly emphatically exclusive. Their brother officer Pitman is in no doubt about various colours. Boxhall says in his US evidence (p.911): 'we did not have time to use any of those things', referring to coloured signals other than distress rockets. But he may be speaking only for himself – it will be remembered that Rowe and Bright had been asked to bring up detonators from aft. Rowe specified 'the detonators, such as the distress signal rockets, green lights, and blue lights' (US Inquiry, p.522). It is a puzzle. The evidence of various colours is there, yet the *Californian* saw only white.

FLARES UNSEEN

Joseph Boxhall, in emergency cutter No.2 of the *Titanic* lifeboats, burned green flares during the night to attract attention. They were not seen by anyone aboard the *Californian*. Boxhall stated (US Inquiry, p.244): 'I had been showing green lights most of the time. I had been showing pyrotechnic lights on the boat'. Boxhall claimed that 'this was a box of green lights' he had deliberately asked a quartermaster to put into boat No.2:

> 15448. In your boat did you also put in some green lights? —Yes, there were some green lights lying in the wheelhouse. I told the Quartermaster or someone who was around there to put them in the boat.

These appear to have been green flares, intended to be used as White Star Line company signals, with which *Titanic* could indicate her identity to other ships. They may have been brought up from aft by Rowe and Bright. The nature of the flares is not indicated in the manifest of pyrotechnic items carried by the *Titanic* (British Report, 'Description of the Ship', p.19), since company signals were not regulated. Captain Arthur Rostron of the rescue ship *Carpathia* knew what they were: 'I saw the green flare, which is the White Star Company's night signal...' (25394). A fireman in emergency boat No.1 also saw them, as related by passenger C.E.H. Stengel: 'One of the stokers said: "The green light is the company's colour"' (US Inquiry, p.973). Passenger Archibald Gracie spoke of a lifeboat 'steering ahead of us, with green lights, and throwing up rockets, I think, or making lights every little while – not rockets, but making a light. I do not know what kind of light they had, but it was a green light that was every little while conspicuous' (US Inquiry, p.996). Boxhall described just how conspicuous his flares were (US Inquiry, p.248):

Senator Smith: Did they make a brilliant light?
Boxhall: Yes; a very brilliant light.
Sen. Smith: You think the *Carpathia* steamed toward these lights?
Boxhall: They did.

Passenger Hugh Woolner could see 'a green light that appeared, not all the time, but most of the time, down to the south' (US Inquiry, p.890–1):

Sen. Smith: That was probably the green light that was on Officer Boxhall's boat?
Woolner: Very likely. I did not identify it.
Sen. Smith: How far away?
Woolner: I could not tell, but I should think about half a mile or a mile.

And it was claimed the green lights could also be seen at an extreme distance by the rescue ship. The *Carpathia*'s captain, Arthur Rostron said: 'At 20 minutes to three, I saw the green flare…' (25394). Rostron repeated his estimations of 2.40 a.m., suggesting the green flare was visible for several miles at least, because it would take him another hour and twenty minutes of steaming to reach the light.

25401. Will you go on and tell us? — At twenty minutes to three I saw a night signal, as I was saying, and it was just about half a point on the port bow, practically right ahead. At a quarter to three I saw what we knew was an iceberg by the light from a star… from then on till four o'clock we were altering our course very often to avoid the bergs.

At four o'clock I considered I was practically up to the position and I stopped, at about five minutes after four. In the meantime I had been firing rockets and the Company's signals every time we saw this green light again.

At five minutes past four I saw the green light again, and I was going to pick the boat up on the port bow, but just as it showed the green light I saw an iceberg right ahead, of me. It was very close, so I had to put my helm hard-a-starboard and put her head round quick and pick up the boat on the starboard side. At 10 minutes past four we got alongside [the lifeboat].

Rostron had given the same evidence in the US Inquiry (p.21):

At 2.40, I saw a flare, about half a point on the port bow, and immediately took it for granted that it was the *Titanic* itself, and I remarked that she must be still afloat, as I knew we were a long way off, and it seemed so high.

Between 2.45 and 4 o'clock, the time I stopped my engines, we were passing icebergs on every side and making them ahead and having to alter our course several times to clear the bergs.

At 4 o'clock I stopped.

At 4.10 I got the first boat alongside.

Passenger C.E.H. Stengel suggested in his evidence that the green flares had indeed been seen at a distance of some miles (US Inquiry, p.973):

After the green lights began to burn I suggested it was better to turn around [our life-boat] and go toward the green lights, because I presumed there was an officer of the ship in that boat, and he evidently knew his business.
Senator Smith: That was evidently from another lifeboat?
Stengel: Yes, sir; it was from another lifeboat... We did not reach its side. It was toward morning that we turned, and by that time another man and myself thought we saw rockets – one rocket; that is, a rocket explode – and I said, 'I think I saw a rocket', and another one said, 'I think I saw a rocket', and one of the stokers, I think it was, said, 'I see two lights. I believe that is a vessel'. Then, after that, when another green light was burned, there was a flash light from a boat, and I said, 'Now, I am pretty positive that is a boat, because that is an answer to the green signal'...

The *Carpathia* had been firing rockets to reassure the *Titanic* survivors that help was on the way. In her affidavit to the US Inquiry, passenger Mrs Mahala Douglas claimed the green flares could be seen from the *Carpathia* from 'ten miles away' (US Inquiry, p.1101):

Mr Boxhall had charge of the signal lights on the *Titanic*, had put in the emergency boat a tin of green lights, like rockets. These he commenced to send off at intervals, and very quickly we saw the lights of the *Carpathia*, the Captain of which stated he saw our green lights 10 miles away, and, of course, steered directly to us, so we were the first boat to arrive at the *Carpathia*.

Meanwhile, it should incidentally be noted that it was also claimed that the ship *Mount Temple* could see 'green lights' appearing to be flares or signals from *Titanic* survivors when she was arriving that night. W.H. Baker, replacement fourth officer in the *Mount Temple* on its next journey, wrote to Captain Lord in August, describing how the ship's officers told him 'they not only saw her deck lights but several green lights between them and what they thought was the *Titanic*'. But her captain, James Moore, had previously testified: 'I simply saw the green light of a sailing vessel... shortly after 3 o'clock':

9250. You saw a green light? —Yes, of a sailing vessel.
9251. Did you see the ship herself? — Not at all; it was dark.

The evidence indicates that the green flares displayed by Officer Boxhall could be seen for some miles. But the *Californian* saw no green flares or green lights whatsoever.

ROCKETS UNHEARD

Here are the International Signals of Distress in force in 1912, prescribed for emergencies at night:

1. A gun or other explosive signal fired at intervals of about a minute.
2. Flames from the vessel as from a burning tar barrel.
3. Rockets or shells, throwing stars, of any colour or description, fired one at a time at short intervals.
4. A continuous sounding with any fog signalling apparatus.

We have already seen the significance of No.3. Clearly, besides visibility, *audibility* was of prime importance (signals No.1 & No.4). Here, again, is what the *Titanic* carried: 'Distress signals. These were supplied of number and pattern approved by the Board of Trade – i.e., 36 socket signals in lieu of guns, 12 ordinary rockets...' (British Report, p.19). The socket signals, or detonators, were in the two boxes carried to the bridge by Rowe and Bright. Boxhall was asked: 'What sort of rockets were they?' and replied 'the socket distress signal' (15396). The socket signals were 'in lieu of guns'. They were intended to make an ear-splitting bang to help attract attention. Second Officer Lightoller described what socket signals were like:

> 14155. How are they discharged; are they discharged from a socket? — In the first place, the charge is no more and no less than what you would use in a 12-pounder [cannon] or something like that.
>
> In the rail is a gunmetal socket. In the base of this [rocket] cartridge, you may call it, is a black powder charge. The pulling of this wire fires... the charge at the base of the cartridge. That exploding throws the shell to a height of several hundred feet, which is nothing more or less than a time shell and explodes by time in the air.

Lightoller in his 1935 book (*Titanic and Other Ships*) said the rockets burst a couple of hundred feet in the air with a 'loud report' (p.161). Fifth Officer Lowe tells what the sound was like of Lightoller's 12lb charge exploding (US Inquiry, p.401):

> Lowe: [Ismay] was there, and I distinctly remember seeing him alongside of me... when the first detonator went off... the flash of the detonator lit up the whole deck...
> Senator Smith: Did you hear any such thing?
> Lowe: Yes; they [the rockets] were incessantly going off; they were nearly deafening me.

Lady Duff Gordon was just getting into boat No.1 at Officer Lowe's location. In her 1932 book *Discretions and Indiscretions*, she wrote:'Just beside us was a man setting off rockets and the ear-splitting noise added to the horror…' (p.171). Third Officer Herbert Pitman also described the noise (US Inquiry, p.294):

> Senator Smith: Did the firing of the rockets make any noise, like the report of a pistol?
> Pitman: Like the report of a gun. [He means like artillery, rather than a handgun]

And indeed they were designed to be 'in lieu of guns' to agree with Section 1 of the International Signals of Distress ('a gun or other explosive signal fired at intervals'). It is noteworthy that counsel at the British Inquiry used a precise phrase from Section 1 – 'explosive signal' – when asking Gibson about the rockets seen by the *Californian*:

> 7757. I should like to ask one question. Did you hear any explosive signal? — No.
> 7758. Were those rockets, which you saw go up, explosives? Did you hear any explosion? — I did not hear any report at all.

Captain Lord stated:

> 6957. At the distance we were away from that steamer, if it had been a distress signal we would have heard the report [explosion].
> 6958. I do not understand. From what you had been telling us just now, you did not know that this rocket which you saw was not a distress signal? — Well, I am under the impression it was not.
> 6959. Why? — Because we did not hear the report, we were close enough to hear the report of any distress signal.
> 6960. How many miles off were you? — About four or five – four to five miles.

Captain Lord did not see any rockets himself. But it must be that he questioned his crew about audibility. The only time in his career that Captain Lord had fired a distress rocket – and then only as a greeting – he described it as 'loud enough to be heard ten miles away'. Second Officer Stone meanwhile did not touch on the subject of audibility in his evidence. It is perhaps safe to presume he also heard nothing, which is implicit in Lord's account. So, should high-charge socket signals be heard at a distance of 5 miles as Lord believes? *Titanic's* Third Officer, Herbert Pitman, might be able to throw some light on the subject. Which is likely to be louder – the *Titanic* blowing off steam, or the *Titanic* firing socket signals in lieu of guns (US Inquiry, p.315)?

> Senator Fletcher: If there had been a vessel that night within five miles of the *Titanic*, could not her [*Titanic's*] whistle have been heard that distance?
> Pitman: No; but you could have heard her blowing off steam at a far greater distance than you could hear the steam whistle. She [*Titanic*] was blowing off steam for

three-quarters of an hour, I think, and you could hear that much farther than you could hear any steam whistle.

Sen. Fletcher: Then it would stand to reason that if there was a ship or vessel of any kind within a distance of five miles it ought to have heard the blowing off of the steam?

Pitman: She could have heard that 10 miles that night.

That's 10 miles. *Steam*. And *Titanic* Fourth Officer Boxhall told the US Inquiry that he could even hear that his lifeboat was in the presence of icebergs during the blackness of the night (US Inquiry, p.256):

> Of course, sound travels quite a long way on the water, and being so close to the water and it being such a calm night, you would hear the water lapping on those bergs for quite a long, long way.

Lapping. Yet there is no estimate of how many miles sockets signals ought to have been audible except Lord's belief that they would have heard it at 4 to 5 miles. And of course the inherent need is for such rockets to be highly audible. The *Carpathia* fired rockets and displayed pyrotechnic 'company signals' that night as she headed for the SOS site specified by the *Titanic*. Boxhall says in his US evidence (p.911): 'I saw rockets on the *Carpathia*'. Senator Fletcher asks: 'What sort of a rocket was that?', to which Boxhall replies: 'An ordinary rocket. I think it was, so far as I could see; a distress rocket in answer to ours'. Whatever type they were, whether socket signals in lieu of guns or 'ordinary rockets', these projectiles were audible from miles away.

Lawrence Beesley (a second class passenger) wrote a book called *The Loss of the SS Titanic* (1912), and he states (p.131):

> About 3.30 a.m., as nearly as I can judge, someone in the bow called our attention to a faint faraway gleam in the southeast. We all turned quickly to look and there it was certainly: streaming up from behind the horizon like a distant flash of a warship's search-light; then a faint boom like guns afar off, and the light died away again. The stoker who had lain all night under the tiller sat up suddenly as if from a dream... I can see him now, staring out across the sea to where the sound had come from, and hear him shout 'That was a cannon!' But it was not. It was the *Carpathia*'s rocket, though we did not know it until later... She stopped at 4 a.m... We rowed up to her about 4.30.

Beesley in lifeboat No.13 could see a 'gleam', probably 8 to 10 miles off, yet he could also hear a 'faint boom'.

The *Carpathia* claimed to have been running at 17½ knots; Rostron claimed that they would usually travel at 'about 14' but that 'We worked up to about 17-and-a-half that night' (25390). The distance to the SOS position was 58 miles when she turned around, but the *Carpathia* met the lifeboats in three and a half hours. The real distance was much shorter, because the SOS position was wrong, and it appears the *Carpathia* actually averaged 14–15 knots. After half an hour's travel therefore – from the faint boom at 3.30 to the stop at 4 a.m. – *Carpathia* would have travelled in any case a minimum of 7 miles. The 'boom' of the rocket was heard over that distance and more, because it still took Beesley half an hour to reach the side of the rescuer. Lifeboat No.13's occupants therefore could hear a rocket boom that night from at least 7 miles away. *Californian* observers, looking at a vessel at an average of 5 miles away (Lord said four to five, Groves said five, Stone said five, Gibson four to seven), heard nothing.

Then there is the non-audibility of other explosions that came from the *Titanic* as she was in her last throes – thought to be boiler explosions, refrigeration blasts, trapped-air implosions, or simply the process of her breaking in two. Most witnesses say they heard up to four explosions or booms.

TITANIC EXPLOSIONS

There are numerous accounts of explosions and other sounds travelling through the night. Third Officer Herbert Pitman states:

> 15240. Did you hear anything in the nature of explosions before she went down? — Yes, I heard four reports.
> 15241. What do you estimate they were? — Boilers leaving the bedplates and crashing through bulkheads.

Fifth Officer Harold Lowe claims (US Inquiry, p.411): 'I heard explosions, yes; I should say about four'. QM George Rowe differs slightly in his description (US Inquiry, p.525): 'Not an explosion; a sort of a rumbling... more like distant thunder'. QM Alfred Olliver says (US Inquiry, p.531): 'I heard several little explosions'. QM Arthur Bright suggests a slightly differing sound (US Inquiry, p.841): 'I would not call it an explosion. It was like a rattling of chain'. Lookout Archie Jewell states: 'We heard some explosions' (175), and goes on to say: 'I heard two or three' (181). AB Joseph Scarrott: 'Then followed four explosions' (426). Fireman George Beauchamp claims:

> 758. I could hear a roaring just like thunder.
> 758A. ...explosions? — Yes.

AB William Lucas states: '[I was at a distance of] about 100 yards before the first explosion went. It was a very loud report' (1549). Lookout Reginald Lee describes 'Underwater explosions, like a gun-cotton explosion under water at a distance off. I suppose it was the boilers' (2563). AB John Poingdexter was asked 'Did you hear any explosions?', and replied: 'A slight one' (3096). Steward Edward Brown describes: 'What I took to be an explosion, Sir – a great noise, a great report' (10551). AB George Symons heard 'two sharp explosions in the ship' (11510). AB Albert Horswill cannot describe what he heard in any detail: 'I only know that I heard explosions' (12447). Steward Alfred Crawford is asked 'What character of explosion?' he heard, and he says it was 'sort of sharp, like as if there were things being blown up' (US Inquiry, p. 116). Major Arthur Peuchen suggests: 'It seemed to be one, two, or three rumbling sounds' (US Inquiry, p. 338). AB Frank Osman is quite precise: 'She exploded, broke in halves... red-hot boilers caused the explosions' (US Inquiry, p. 541). AB George Moore claims he 'can remember two explosions' (US Inquiry, p. 563). Chief Second Class Steward John Hardy agrees: 'There were two reports or explosions' (US Inquiry, p. 595). Steward William Ward similarly recalls hearing 'a couple of reports, more like a volley of musketry than anything else. You would not exactly call them a heavy explosion' (US Inquiry, p. 599).

Steward George Crowe (US p. 620/1):

> ...There were several explosions.
> [Next question] ...loud, like a cannon? — Not so loud as that, sir. A kind of muffled explosion. It seemed to be an explosion at a very great distance, although we were not very far away... about a mile.

Steward Charles Andrews similarly emphasises that the sounds were not especially loud: 'I heard just a small sound, sir; it was not very loud' (US Inquiry, p. 626). AB Fred Clench states: 'I heard two explosions, sir' (US Inquiry, p. 637). AB Ernest Archer is in agreement: 'I heard a couple of explosions. I heard two' (US Inquiry, p. 646). AB Walter Brice states that he 'heard two rumbling noises' (US, p. 653). Passenger Hugh Woolner recalls 'a sort of rumbling roar, it sounded to me, as she slid under' (US Inquiry, p. 889).

Passenger C.E. Henry Stengel heard 'four sharp explosions... quite hard explosions' (US Inquiry, p. 980). Passenger Mrs J. Stuart White states: 'I heard four distinct explosions, which we supposed were the boilers'. When asked how loud the explosions were, she replied: 'They were tremendous' (US Inquiry, p. 1008).

Passenger Olaus Abelseth heard 'A kind of an explosion. We could hear the popping and cracking' (US Inquiry, p. 1038). Barber Gus Weikman 'heard a second explosion. There was a great number of people killed by the explosion' (US Inquiry, p. 1099). Fireman Fred Barrett heard 'a knocking noise, but no explosion' (US Inquiry, p. 1141). Passenger Catherine Crosby states: 'I heard repeated explosions. The cries of the people and the explosions were terrible' (US Inquiry, p. 1145). Mrs Imanita Shelley claims: 'On reaching a distance of about 100 yards from the *Titanic* a loud explosion or noise was heard, followed closely by another' (US p. 1148).

A number of witnesses, including two surviving officers, specifically stated four explosions. It does not seem as if they made as loud a noise as the socket distress detonations. But whatever their strength of sound, these too went unheard by the *Californian*. And what of the cries of the drowning, hundreds of voices in unison, carrying over the freezing water on a calm and starry night?

Steward Alfred Crawford claims that he was 'a mile and a half' from the *Titanic* when he heard cries (18058). Crawford says his boat was the furthest away from the ship, rowing

in the direction of the light. Could the cries have carried 5 miles to the *Titanic*'s mystery
vessel? The answer is almost certainly 'no'. But she should have heard the socket distress
booms! The rockets that went unheard are of a piece with the 'low-lying' flashes seen from
the *Californian* – they indicate many miles of distance between her and the rocket-firer.

A THIRD NOTIFICATION

After Gibson's sleep-disturbing conversation with the captain at 2.05 a.m. when he told
the master the nearby steamer had 'disappeared' to the south-west, Gibson returned to the
bridge. He was not asked, and did not say, whether he saw anything further of the 'disappeared' ship. Stone, however, the officer again joined by the apprentice, continued to see
the departing steamer for twenty minutes more, as we have seen. Here is Stone:

> 7957. What did you see of her, which disappeared? — A gradual disappearing of all her
> lights, which would be perfectly natural with a ship steaming away from us.
>
> 7958. ...The masthead light would be shut in except for a slight flickering, the glare of it,
> and the red side light would be shut in altogether. The lights I would see would be the
> lights at the end of the alleyway or engine-room skylight, and the stern light. [Suggesting
> a small vessel]
>
> 7959. Did the stern light that you speak of as disappearing, suddenly become black [sug-
> gesting a sinking] or gradually fade away as if it was going away? — It gradually faded as
> if the steamer was steaming away from us.
>
> 7960. Did it have the appearance of being a light on a ship which had suddenly foundered?

This last question is bizarre, and smacks of desperation. However, Stone answered it, even
though he had never knowingly seen a ship founder at night in all his years at sea. He said:
'Not by any means'.

> 7961. [The Commissioner] Can you give me an idea of the speed at which she was
> steaming away when these lights gradually disappeared? — No, it would be very difficult
> to express an opinion.
>
> 7962. ...I should say that at different times she was going at different speeds.
>
> 7964. She was in a sea covered with ice? — Yes.
>
> 7966. You thought she was steaming away? — Yes.
>
> 7967. In the same condition of water that you were lying in? — Yes.
>
> 7968. Did you really think so? — I did. The only confirmation I had of it was the
> bearings of the compass. Two ships remaining stationary could not possibly alter their
> bearings.
>
> 7969. You were swinging round? — We were slowly swinging.
>
> 7970. [Mr Butler Aspinall] When you saw her disappear, did you think something had
> happened to her? — No, nothing except that she was steaming away.

Very humdrum and prosaic. And now, Stone says, that vessel finally disappeared, and he decided to convey that fact to the captain. Here is a section of Stone's original statement for the captain, 18 April 1912:

> At 2.45 I again whistled down again and told you we had seen no more lights and that the steamer had steamed away to the SW and was now out of sight, also that the rockets were all white and had no colours whatever.

This would be the captain's third notification. Lord had retired to the chart room at 12.15 a.m., where he rested, fully dressed (7352). He did not fall asleep before twenty minutes to one (7353). The call is supported by Stone's colleague, Gibson, in his separate original written statement of the same vintage: 'At about 2.45 he [Stone] whistled down to the Captain again, but I did not hear what was said'. Stone also described this communication in direct evidence:

> 7976. Twenty minutes later you reported to the Captain. How? — About 2.40 [five minute difference] by means of the whistle tube. I blew down again to, the Master; he came and answered it, and asked what it was. I told him the ship, from the direction of which we had seen the rockets coming, had disappeared; bearing SW to half W, the last I had seen of the light.
> 7977. In view of the fact that when you saw her stern light last you thought nothing had happened to her, why did you make this report to the Captain? — Simply because I had had the steamer under observation all the watch, and that I had made reports to the Captain concerning her, and I thought it my duty when the ship went away from us altogether to tell him.
> 7978. [The Commissioner] But why couldn't you have told him in the morning? Why wake up the poor man? — Because it was my duty to do so, and it was his duty to listen to it.
> 7980. It was of no consequence if the steamer was steaming safely away? — He told me to try and get all the information I could from the steamer. I got none and I thought it my duty to give him all the information I could about the steamer.
> 7981. Were you anxious about her?— No.
> 7982. Was *he* anxious about her? — No, as far as I could judge from his answers and instructions.

It is sometimes contended that Stone must have realised what the rockets meant – but was simply reluctant to confront or challenge his master about what should be done. But look at that reply to question 7978; Stone says he woke up the captain with a call 'because it was my duty to do so, and it was his duty to listen to it'. It hardly bespeaks an officer in dread of his superior!

The questions continue:

7998. [Mr Aspinall] I want now to take you to the later period, when you spoke to the Captain and told him that the steamer had disappeared? —Yes.

7999. Will you tell me whether the Captain made any reply to that, and if so, what? — He again asked me if I was certain there were no colours in those lights whatsoever. I again assured him that they were all white, just white rockets.

8000. Can you explain why it was that the Captain should again ask you if you were sure there were no colours in the lights? — No.

8001. Have you no idea? You are a sailor? —Yes.

8002. You had been taking part in this matter, so to speak? —Yes.

8003. You were an onlooker paying careful attention, keeping those lights under observation, and then this question again comes from the Master. What did you think he meant by such a question? — I did not know, except that he had the thought in his mind that they may have been company signals of some sort.

8004. But do you really mean that? — That thought may have been in his mind; I did not say it was in his mind.

8005. Was it in yours? —That they were company's signals?

8006. Yes? — No, not that they were. They may possibly have been.

The above accounts of a conversation with Captain Lord at 2.40/2.45 a.m., when the steamer had finally disappeared in Stone's view, may appear to clash with another part of Stone's evidence which could lead one to think that the last he saw of the steamer was at 2 a.m., coinciding with Gibson's evidence to that effect. This is Stone:

8100. For how long had you this vessel's stern light under observation? — From just about 1 o'clock to the time I lost her, I should say. The last light I saw must have been her stern light. It may have been the light at the end of an alleyway, or some bright light on deck.

8101. About how long do you think she was showing her stern light? — About an hour.

Add one hour to 1 a.m. and you get 2 a.m. But Stone says the stern light, not all lights on the ship, showed for an hour. The stern light was only displayed when his strange ship turned, shutting in her red side light to display her stern light only. Stone's original statement, written on the *Californian*, 18 April 1912, states:

Gibson and I observed three more [rockets] at intervals and kept calling them up on our Morse lamps but got no reply whatsoever. The other steamer meanwhile had shut in her red side light and showed us her stern light…

Stone makes mention of the stern light for the first time before noting a heading for the *Californian* at 1.50 a.m.

The opening of the stern light seems to have happened just prior to the vessel firing the last rocket that they saw. Stone says this happened at 1.40. If he saw the stern light for the first time at 1.35 and sees it for about an hour thereafter, then he is again seeing the light of his mystery steamer long after the *Titanic* is no longer showing any. But elsewhere Captain Lord suggests that Stone told him that he had seen the last of the steamer at 2 a.m.:

> 7064. [The Commissioner] When did you lose sight, and how, of the ship the lights of which you had seen? — The Second Officer reported to me he last saw her at 2 o'clock, and it was then bearing SW one half W by compass. [Does he mean the hull, rather than the light?]
> 7065. Is that the last so far as you know that was seen of that vessel from your ship? — As far as I know it was, my Lord.
> 7067. How many miles [away]? — I think eight.

This refers to a conversation between Stone and Lord subsequent to the night's events. It may not be important. Yet *Californian*'s chief officer, George Stewart, also testified to being told of a 2 a.m. disappearance by Stone:

> 8638. He [Stone] told me the steamer that had fired rockets had steamed away to the south-west, and he last saw her about two o'clock, just faintly with glasses. She steamed away from him.

Meanwhile Gibson, in evidence, ascribes a wrong time of 3.40 (surely it should be 2.40?) when he recalls Stone's final call to the captain:

> 7574. What was it? — About 3.40 the, Second Officer whistled down to the Captain again.
> 7575. Twenty minutes to four? — Yes.
> 7576. Did you see him doing it? — Yes.
> 7577. Did you hear what he said? — No.

But Gibson admitted he was 'not exactly' sure about the time. In any case, errors, slips of the tongue and minor contradictions are common to all oral evidence. Of much more importance is the fact that Captain Lord testifies that he simply has no recollection at all of this third conversation:

THE THIRD NOTIFICATION – LORD'S VERSION

> 7295. I must ask you something more. Do you remember Mr Stone reporting at twenty minutes to three to you that morning through the tube? — I do not.
> 7296. Is there a tube? — There is a tube.
> 7297. What is the tube? — A speaking-tube.
> 7298. To your chart room? — To my own room. [Captain's room]
> 7299. Were you in your own room? — No, I was in the chart room. [The chart room and Captain's room adjoined one another below deck]

7300. Would you hear if he reported through the tube to you? — At a quarter past one?

7301. He reported through the tube then? — At a quarter past one.

7302. Listen to this – he reported to you at twenty minutes to three through the tube and told you that the steamer had disappeared bearing southwest half west. Do you remember that? — I do not remember it. He has told me that since.

7303. Have you any reason to doubt it? — I do not know anything at all about it.

7304. Have you any reason to doubt that Mr Stone, the Officer, is speaking the truth? — I do not see why he should not tell me the truth.

7305. [The Commissioner] Is he a reliable, trustworthy man? — As far as I know of him he is.

7306. [The Attorney General] Is he still with you? — He is still with me.

7307. Listen to this: 'The Captain again asked me if I was sure there were no colours in the lights that had been seen'. Do you remember that? — I do not.

7308. And that he – Mr Stone – 'assured you that they were white lights'? — He has told me all about this since, but I have not the slightest recollection that anything happened that way.

7309. He has told you of this – what he reported to you that night? — Yes.

7310. And you have no reason to doubt it? — If he is telling the truth I have not.

7311. Do you doubt it at all? — I do not know.

7312. This is what he says: 'I assured him that they were white lights and he' – that is you – 'said "All right". Have you no recollection of that conversation? — I have no recollection of any conversation between half-past one and half-past four that I had with the Second Officer.

If Lord spoke to Stone as Stone says, but cannot remember it, then the captain has a case of somniloquy. He was talking in his sleep. Or else his subsequent sleep has blotted out his entire recollection of a conscious conversation. It seems rather akin to what he said when describing why he could not recall anything said by Gibson, who had called down to his room thirty-five minutes before Stone's tube-call of 2.40:

7287. [Have you] any reason to doubt [Gibson was telling the truth]? — No, I was asleep.

7288. Then do you mean you said this in your sleep to him, that he was to report? — I very likely was half awake. I have no recollection of this apprentice saying anything to me at all that morning.

The speaking tube was to Captain Lord's own room (7298) whereas Gibson had found him in the next-door chartroom, Lord with his eyes closed, thirty-five minutes earlier. Lord would have had to get up to answer the call. If he indeed answered the call. Stone remembers a complete conversation and says that Lord 'came and answered it' (question 7976), implying movement from the chartroom to the captain's own room. Lord has no recollection of walking or talking, whereas Gibson saw a call being made but heard no conversation.

The idea of Lord sleepwalking to the speaking tube – and back again – is obviously open to high ridicule by his modern critics. Yet it is quite common for some people to appear to function normally in this way and then have no recollection of it in the morning. Lord's lack of recollection must have been perceived by the Inquiry as perilously close to evasiveness or denial. He could have used his location in his own defence, like so: 'I ought to remember, because it would have involved me getting up, walking to the tube, walking back again, and going back to sleep'. Lord did not directly pit himself against Stone in that way, even though his evidence at one level seemed to imply a contradiction of the second officer.

Lord thus inhabited the worst of all possible worlds – somewhere between sleep and wakefulness and the two conscious certainties of acceptance or outright denial. He just could not remember. And there is evidence that exactly the same blank forgetfulness happened on the *Titanic* that very night – and with one of her officers! Fifth Officer Harold Lowe actually slept through a man entering his room and telling him that his ship had struck an iceberg! This is much more dramatic news than the matters reported to Captain Lord! Here is Lowe at the US Inquiry (p.388):

Senator Smith: You were not aroused from your slumber by anyone?

Lowe: No, sir. Mr Boxhall, the Fourth Officer, told me that he told me that we had struck an iceberg, but I do not remember it.

Senator Smith: You do not remember his telling you that?

Lowe: I do not remember his telling me that.

Sen. Smith: That is, while you were [asleep]?

Lowe: It must have been while I was asleep. You must remember that we do not have any too much sleep and therefore when we sleep we die.

Officer Lowe slept on, only roused by shouting voices outside his cabin. He was then amazed to see large numbers of passengers roaming the decks in lifebelts! Though Lowe's strange but matter-of-fact story was accepted by the US Inquiry, no such sympathetic treatment was offered to Captain Lord when he offered a similar tale at the British Inquiry.

'When we sleep we die': Captain Lord had been on duty for seventeen consecutive hours that day.

7346. When did you go on duty on the Sunday morning [April 14]? — I got up the usual time, 7 o'clock in the morning.

7347. And were you on duty the whole of that day? — I was on deck practically the whole of that day. [Retiring at fifteen minutes past midnight]

Lord would then have had a very short period of rest that night, remaining asleep only until 4.30 a.m. when he was summoned by his chief officer (question 7370). Crucially, we also know that his slumber, such as it was, became interrupted more than once. The corroborated evidence from Gibson suggests that Stone's 2.40 call – the third notification of the night – was at least initiated. If Stone is correct in saying that his call was answered and that this led to a conversation, then Lord has forgotten movement to the tube in another room, and back again, as well as what was actually said. He does not remember any of it, just as he has no recollection of the message Gibson intended to give him earlier. The evidence suggests the tube was in proximity to Captain Lord throughout. He may not have been actually 'sleep-walking' in order to talk to Stone, but it hardly matters whether he was or not. The simple fact of him attempting to hold fast to his own uncertainty left the captain at the mercy of the Inquiry. The perplexing reality is that Captain Lord had no possible motive to lie about this third notification. A defence-minded man would have freely admitted to a full recall of the conversation. After all, the steamer has disappeared, and Stone, at 2.40 a.m., by his own evidence, is telling the captain almost exactly what Gibson had been sent down to tell him more than half an hour earlier, at 2.05. The steamer has steamed away in Stone's estimation, and there is nothing in his new communication that would require a master intent on evad-ing all blame to 'forget' his receiving of it. It was open to Lord to cheerfully admit receiving both Gibson and Stone's messages and thinking no more about the strange ship, other than what he has been told – that she has by now steamed away. If she is steaming away, then she is not in distress. Yet Lord, by stating frankly that he remembers neither episode in the course of what would be only a four hour sleep, is voluntarily putting his head in the noose. Why would he do that, if it were not the truth?

Meanwhile, the White Star liner *Titanic* has long since sunk with catastrophic loss of life.

MORE ROCKETS!

Lord Mersey, in his final report, wrote that the *Californian* saw eight rockets. She actually saw eleven! It is granted that the first eight seen were from the *Titanic*. But the last three of the eleven were almost certainly those fired by the Cunard Line's *Carpathia*, racing to the SOS position, which Lord estimated to be 19½ to 20 miles from his own stop position. Nonetheless, it is interesting that Lord Mersey should discard three rockets seen by the *Californian* to arrive at a final figure of eight, in order to agree with what we have seen was a spurious conclusion that the *Titanic* must have fired eight. The *Titanic* must have fired many more than eight. Here is what the *Californian* observers said about the further rock-ets they saw late in their watch, long after the *Titanic* had sunk, taken from their original statements, composed while *Californian* was still at sea. This is Gibson on the issue:

> At about 3.20 looking over the weather-cloth, I observed a rocket about two points before the beam [port], which I reported to the Second Officer. About three minutes later I saw another rocket right abeam which was followed later by another one about two points before the beam. I saw nothing else and when one bell went [signalling half an hour to change of watch], I went below to get the log gear ready for the Second Officer at eight bells [4 a.m.].

And here is Stone:

We saw nothing further until about 3.20 when we thought we observed two faint lights in the sky about SSW and a little distance apart. At 3.40 I sent Gibson down to see all was ready for me to prepare the new log at eight bells.

The two men later gave evidence about these 'rockets' or 'lights,' which must have made an unusual night weirder still. This is Gibson's evidence:

> 7586. [The Commissioner] Now, am I to understand you to say that at twenty minutes to four you saw three more rockets? — Yes, Sir. [Gibson and Stone said 3.20, not 3.40, in their original statements, prepared on the *Californian*]
>
> 7587. Were they reported to the Captain? — I reported them to the Second Officer.
>
> 7588. Did he report them to the Captain? — No.
>
> 7589. Why not? — I do not know.
>
> 7590. If they were really there, why were not they reported to the Captain? — I do not know, Sir.
>
> 7591. Are you quite sure that these three rockets were ever seen by you at all? — Yes, Sir. I saw the first one, and I reported it to the Second Officer, and we looked out for more to see if we could see any more — and we saw two more.
>
> 7592. [The Solicitor General] You say you saw the first one? — Yes.
>
> 7593. Do you mean you saw it with your naked eye? — Yes.
>
> [The Commissioner] Did any of the [life]boats of the *Titanic* fire Roman candles?
>
> 7594. [The Solicitor General] Yes, my Lord, Roman candles. [To the Witness] If it was twenty minutes to four it was not very far off the beginning of dawn, was it? — No, dawn was just breaking.
>
> 7595. Had it got any lighter? — Yes.
>
> 7596. Could you see when you saw this flash at all how far away you thought it was? — It was right on the horizon.
>
> 7597. What sort of a light was it? You called it a rocket? Was it a flash; did you see it go up into the sky? — Yes.
>
> 7598. What colour was it? — White.

All this is highly significant. We can see how the Commissioner, who will later create an equation between the number of rockets fired by the *Titanic* and those seen by the *Californian*, initially does not want Gibson to have seen any rockets after the *Titanic* is known to have sunk (see question 7591).

When Gibson persists, the Commissioner gradually realises he could turn the unwanted sightings to his advantage by suggesting the lights came from *Titanic* lifeboats. But only green flares were ever displayed from a lifeboat, and Gibson says these were white.

Gibson says the white flash was right on the horizon, and it must be presumed these were rockets fired by the *Carpathia* that the lifeboats could both see and, crucially, *hear* from at least 7 miles away.

Finally, notice how questioning proceeds with no suggestion that these new white rockets mean a ship in distress, as the court had been strenuously trying to show during the earlier timeframe:

7599. And you called Mr Stone's attention to it, did you, and then there were two more seen? — Yes.

7600. I understand that is after Mr. Stone had spoken on the tube [at 2.40 a.m.] to the Captain? —Yes.

7601. Do you say he did not report these three further lights to the Captain at all? — No.

7602. When you saw these three further lights did you get your glasses on to the place? —Yes.

7603. Could you see any sign of a ship? — No.

7604. No sign of a masthead light? — No.

7605. No sign of a side-light? — No.

7606. Nothing except these flashes? —That is all.

7607. Is that right? —Yes.

7608. Then I think you went off your watch at four o'clock? —A quarter to [four].

We can see that three further rockets play no part in Commissioner Mersey's pre-formed idea of what happened. He suggests to the witness twice that they were not really there. Finally he concludes for himself they were lights displayed by the *Titanic's* lifeboats.

Only one of the *Titanic* lifeboats had flares, boat No.2, commanded by Officer Boxhall. He stated that no other lifeboat showed such lights. And the flares he displayed were green, not white. They were not rockets.

Mersey will simply discard this troubling evidence, even though the explanation is readily to hand. Captain Rostron of the *Carpathia* ordered his company's rockets to be fired at 2.45 a.m. and at every quarter of an hour thereafter to reassure the *Titanic* that help was on the way. Stone and Gibson would see them much the same time as Lawrence Beesley – whose fellow occupants of boat No.13 also heard them – at 3.30 a.m. At what was judged by the British Inquiry to have been 3.15 a.m. *Titanic* time (had she remained on the surface of the ocean), the *Mount Temple* heard the *Carpathia's* wireless operator send a transmission intended for the vanished *Titanic*: 'If you are there we are firing rockets' (9570).

What perhaps deserves some emphasis however is the qualitative difference in distance in Gibson's perception of the early and later rockets. Gibson's nearby ship had previously been very close (he repeatedly estimated 4 to 7 miles) until she steamed away. But these rockets are showing 'right on the horizon' (7596), which is rather in-keeping with Stone's suggestion that the earlier rockets could have been coming from an unknown ship over the horizon from the one at which they were looking. If this was the case, then the *Titanic's* mystery ship could not have been the *Californian* as the White Star liner and its visitor were closely in sight of each other, with side lights showing. Meanwhile the great distance of these later rockets may have been a factor in deciding not to inform the captain. Possibly, also, these new rockets were just too much for Stone and Gibson on a very unusual night. They may have thought their departed steamer was somewhere trying to illuminate her way through the ice. Yet it is noticeable that they were not pressed about these later rockets by counsel, nor repeatedly invited to say they believed they might have signified a post-*Titanic* vessel in distress. Quite the contrary! The British Inquiry, great seekers after truth, simply did not want to know about them.

Nonetheless, the *Carpathia's* attested firing of rockets gives the lie to that other myth – that only *Titanic* fired rockets that night. And if Stone and Gibson finally shrugged their shoulders after all they had been through, it is noteworthy that no other vessels rushed to the rocket-firing *Carpathia's* side, believing *her* to be in distress! This is what Stone had to say in evidence about these last-of-all lights on the horizon:

8007. After this conversation with the Captain through the tube, did you later see anything more? — Yes.

8008. What did you do? — At about 3.20, just, before half-past three, as near as I can approximate, Gibson reported to me he had seen a white light in the sky to the southward of us, just about on the port beam We were heading about west at that time. I crossed over to the port wing of the bridge and watched its direction with my binoculars. Shortly after, I saw a white light in the sky right dead on the beam.

8009. [The Commissioner] How far away? — At a very great distance I should judge.

8010. What do you mean by a very great distance? — Such a distance that if it had been much further I should have seen no light at all, merely a faint flash.

8011. [Mr Butler Aspinall] Was it the same character of light as the rockets, or something quite different? — It was so far away that it was impossible to judge.

8012. Did you think it could have come from the steamer you had been looking at before? — No.

8013. It was something different, you think? — Yes, because it was not on the same bearing, unless the steamer had turned round.

[The Commissioner] And were these lights rockets? — I think not.

8014. [Mr Butler Aspinall] Did anything further happen between that time and the end of your watch? — Nothing further.

The *Carpathia* stopped at 4 a.m. Her rockets from 3.20 a.m. to 3.40 a.m. were tiny points of light 'at a very great distance'. A very great distance 'southward of us'. Stone was not asked to quantify his 'very great distance' separating *Californian* and what we might take to be the *Carpathia*. However it is known that the *Carpathia* stopped south and east of the *Titanic's* SOS position, the SOS position being 19½ to 20 miles as the crow flies from the *Californian's* reported stop position. Captain Lord said (questions 6984–5): 'I thought we might have seen [*Titanic's* distress rockets] at 19 miles'. They certainly did see them, although admittedly very low-lying, as Stone said. But Stone barely saw those of *Carpathia*. If they had been any further away he would have missed them altogether, he suggested. This evidence should further indicate that the *Titanic*, when she hit her berg, was similarly 'a very great distance' from the *Californian*!

13

THE WRONG STEAMER

The Chief Officer, Mr Stewart, came on the bridge at 4am and I gave him a full report of what I had seen and my reports and replies from you [Captain Lord], and pointed out where I thought I had observed these faint lights at 3.20.

He picked up the binoculars and said after a few moments: 'There she is then, she's all right, she is a four-master'. I said: 'Then that isn't the steamer I saw first', took up the glasses and just made out a four-master steamer with two masthead lights a little abaft our port beam, and bearing about S, we were heading about WNW. Mr Stewart then took over the watch and I went off the bridge.

This is from the original statement of Herbert Stone. Chief Officer George Stewart saw a four-masted steamer with his binoculars after dawn. But Stone insists it is not the steamer he had been watching all night, the one that had steamed away. The four masts mentioned by Stewart immediately disqualify her. Yet Boxhall, having separately studied the *Titanic*'s mystery ship – the key vessel in the whole conundrum – had this to say about her: 'The only description of the ship that I could give is that she was, or I judged her to be, a four-masted steamer' (15401). Here then is clear evidence from the prime witnesses from both the *Titanic* and the *Californian* that they were looking at two different strangers that night. Boxhall, on *Titanic*, was looking at a four-masted steamer. Stone, on *Californian*, was certain that he *had not* been looking at a four-mast steamer. He may not have been able to see the number of masts on the previous stranger during the hours of darkness, but Stone could see only one masthead light. This is inconsistent with a grand total of four masts, which would have required the display of two sets of masthead lights. The evidence of Lord, Stone and Gibson all goes to imply a two-masted original stranger, although no witness is specific on the point. The absence of four masts on the ship the *Californian* observers had been studying further weakens the ship-in-between theory, since Boxhall was looking at a four-masted steamer. It thus conversely strengthens the contention that there were two separate pairs of ships involved – *Titanic* plus mystery ship, and *Californian* plus the earlier nearby stranger. Stone further emphasises the masthead-light difference in his testimony:

8017. …Just after 4 o'clock… the Chief Officer… remarked to me, 'There she is, there is that steamer, she is all right'. I looked at the steamer through the glasses, and I remarked to him 'That is not the same steamer, she has two masthead lights'. I saw a steamer then just abaft the port beam showing two masthead lights, apparently heading much in the same direction as ourselves.

8018. Do you know what that steamer was? — No.

8019. That could not have been the steamer you have been telling us about I suppose? — I should say not.

8020. I want you to consider this. You gave a full report, full information to the Chief Officer, and then he looks over the side and he says 'There is that steamer, she is all right'. According to the story you have told us, when you saw this other steamer's stern light disappear you thought she was all right. What was there in your story to the Chief Officer which led him to make this observation 'There is the steamer, she is all right'? — I do not know what led him to make that observation.

8021. Why should he have said it, in view of the evidence you have given us here today? Don't you think you told the Chief Officer that you were fearful the steamer you had seen had gone down? — No I told him the steamer had steamed away from us in a south westerly direction.

We can see from the above extract that counsel for the Board of Trade (Butler Aspinall) was not at all anxious to dwell on the difference in masthead lights – instead he moved with indecent haste to suggest that Stone had secretly confided fears of the nearby ship having gone down. This is completely at odds with Stone and Gibson's position all along.

Yet the earliest vouchsafed reality is that Stone's four-master in the gathering daylight had two masthead lights, whereas his steamer of the darkness had only one.

8097. Had the steamer which you have referred to, whose lights you saw, one masthead light or two? — The first steamer I saw had one masthead light.

8098-9. If she had had a second masthead light could you have failed to see it? — I think not; I was bound to have seen it.

Yet Fourth Officer Boxhall on the *Titanic* saw *two* masthead lights on the mystery ship close by:

15388. What sort of light was it? — It was two masthead lights of a steamer.

15392. And then you saw this light, which you say looked like a masthead light? — Yes, it was two masthead lights of a steamer.

15393. …I found it was the two masthead lights of a vessel.

Boxhall and Stone had not been looking at the same vessel. It is important to state at this point that the four-masted vessel *Californian* now saw in the early dawn was *not* the

Carpathia, which came to the rescue of the *Titanic* lifeboats. The Cunard liner *Carpathia* was a four-masted red-funnel vessel. She had fired rockets as she steamed towards the *Titanic*'s SOS position which were barely distinguished at 'a very great distance' by Stone and Gibson. The only detailed description of this other four-master seen by *Californian* to the southward at 4 a.m. (when Chief Officer George Stewart relieved Second Officer Stone) comes from Chief Officer Stewart himself:

> 8905. Is it in your mind at all that it was the *Carpathia* you saw? — No, I thought it was a yellow funnel boat when the sun was up.

Neither Stone nor Stewart (who had just come on duty) knew where this four-master had come from. Yet despite Stone's insistence that it was not the vessel he had previously seen, Stewart personally considered that the steamer seen during the night could indeed have gone off to the south-west but, finding the ice impassable there, might have steamed back some distance, unnoticed by Stone. In other words, that it might have been the same vessel Stone and Gibson watched earlier. It appears that, wherever she came from, the yellow-funnel four-master was now, at 4 a.m., between the *Californian* to the north and the *Carpathia* to the south, and all three vessels were still to the east of the ice barrier. Meanwhile, the *Mount Temple*, a Canadian Pacific vessel, had arrived at the *Titanic*'s SOS position on the western side of the ice barrier. She was indeed a four-masted yellow-funnel steamer, but her captain testified that he arrived at the SOS position only at 4.30 a.m., having steamed diagonally north-east from far to the south and west of the barrier, closer to North America. By her evidence, the *Mount Temple* was certainly out of sight of the *Californian* at 4 a.m. and could not have been the yellow-funnel steamer seen by Stewart. Ships on the far side of the barrier could not be seen. This new one was to the south, on the eastern side.

There have been persistent, but unsustainable, attempts to suggest that the four-mast steamer was the red-funnel *Carpathia* – and that therefore she and the *Californian* were in sight of each other in the morning. This would mean that they were much closer than the 'very great distance' suggested by Stone. The first sly attempt came at the British Inquiry when Stewart was being examined:

> [Mr Clement Edwards] May I suggest that your Lordship asks this witness this question: How many funnels the *Carpathia* has?
> 8902. [The Commissioner] Can you tell us how many funnels the *Carpathia* has? — One funnel, my Lord.

And when examined by Mr Cotter:

> 8903–4. How many masts has the *Carpathia* got? — Four masts.
> 8905. Is it in your mind at all that it was the *Carpathia* you saw? — No, I thought it was a yellow funnel boat when the sun was up.

Captain Lord in his US Inquiry evidence agreed with his chief officer (p.733):

> Lord: …At daylight we saw a yellow-funnel steamer on the southwest of us, beyond
> where this man had left, about 8 miles away.
> Senator Fletcher: Do you suppose that was the same one?
> Lord: I should not like to say. I don't think so, because this one had only one masthead
> light that we saw at half past eleven [the previous night].

So this four-master with a yellow funnel is only 8 miles away from the stopped *Californian*
at 4.30 a.m. when Lord comes on the bridge. It is further away than where the nearby
stranger had been stopped, and is not the earlier ship. Neither is it the *Carpathia* (*Carpathia's*
captain testified that he did not see the *Californian*, rushing to assist, until 8 a.m.). There
is a difference in the bearing of the yellow-funnel ship, Stewart seeing her to the southward, and Lord mentioning south-west. It may or may not be important. Stewart says
the yellow-funnel vessel was to the southward, and repeats it several times: 'Did you see
anything?—Yes, I saw a steamer to the southward' (8596). He later indicated the direction
to Lord: 'Yes, after he [Captain Lord] had spoken about proceeding on the voyage I asked
him if he was going to the southward to see what that ship was' (8623). And Stewart later
went to rouse Evans, *Californian's* wireless operator:

> 8758. …I told him to get out and see what the ship was to the southward…
> 8766. …I told him to call up and see what that ship was to the southward.

He also declared it in his statement to the Receiver of Wrecks on *Californian's* subsequent
arrival in Liverpool: 'I looked to the southward…' (8612). Stone, of course, says this ship
was 'about south' and 'just abaft the port beam' when the *Californian* was heading west-
north-west (halfway between west and north-west), which is the same thing. Lord further
states the presence of this ship to the British Inquiry:

> 6962. Did you then (4.30am) go on the bridge? — [Lord] Yes.
> 6963. Do you remember just before 5 o'clock a conversation with your Chief Officer
> [Stewart]? — I do.
> 6964. About the steamer? — About this, which he said was a yellow-funnelled steamer.

One could speculate on the identity of this yellow-funnel vessel. But she was certainly not
the vessel previously seen by the *Californian*. It is arguable, however, whether she might,
merely might, have been the four-master seen by the *Titanic*. Four-mast yellow-funnel
steamers are in short supply when it comes to attempting to identify this new vessel seen
by the *Californian*. It is an area that needs further research.

The *Mount Temple* says she was many miles to the other side of the ice barrier at the time, and
in any case Chief Officer Stewart certainly later saw the *Mount Temple*, as he knew the difference. He implies here that in his opinion she was not the yellow-funnel ship he saw at 4 a.m.:

8851. What kind of a steamer was she [at 4 a.m. to southward]? — A four-masted steamer
with one funnel.

8852. Have you been able to ascertain what her name was? — No.

8853. ...Well, we never knew what ship that was that we saw to the southward.

Chief Officer Stewart's use of 'we' seems to imply that others were involved – himself as
well as Lord maybe, or perhaps the entire ship's company? And Lord, who had also studied
the yellow-funnel steamer by 4.30 a.m., using glasses, later saw the *Mount Temple* on the
other side of the icefield and drew no connection between them:

6998. ...I only saw one steamer, passenger steamer, of any size that day, and that was the
Mount Temple.

6999. Is the result of your evidence that you cannot suggest the name of any other passenger steamer that was in the neighbourhood of your vessel at about midnight on the
14th April? — No, I cannot.

Californian later passed the *Mount Temple* at about 7.30 a.m. in the vicinity of the SOS position
(7014–5). She was stopped. Neither Lord nor Stewart equated her with the earlier yellow-
funnel vessel. There is another four-mast yellow-funnel vessel which moved into the vicinity.
She was the *Birma*, which arrived only at 8 a.m., having reported herself by wireless earlier
in the night as 70 miles from the SOS position. The *Frankfurt*, of Norddeutscher Lloyd, had
a yellow funnel, but only two masts instead of the necessary four. We need not be detained
further by speculation, except to rely on this yellow-funnel vessel of 4 a.m.–4.30 a.m. for
what she can tell us: firstly, that there were more vessels in the immediate locality – and at an
early stage – than is commonly imagined; secondly, that she was visible to the *Californian* at
8 miles away at that time, and the *Californian* saw no other ships at this time – certainly not
the *Carpathia*. The *Californian*, therefore, was over the visible horizon from the red-funnel
Carpathia and must have been at a considerable distance from her.

FINDING OUT

Stanley Lord came back on duty at 4.30 a.m. ship's time on 15 April 1912. Stewart
briefed him, just as Stewart had previously been briefed by Stone. Stewart's information from Stone was that Stone had seen a ship 4 or 5 miles off when he first went
on watch, and at 1 o'clock had seen some rockets. Stone did not say how many (question 8578). Stewart asked Stone what he did and was told by Stone that the moment
the ship started firing rockets she had started to steam away. Stewart then formed a
belief, based on what Stone told him, as to why this ship should be firing rockets:

8586. ...I thought what had really happened was she had seen a ship firing rockets to the
southward, and was replying to them.

Stewart repeated his conviction to Commissioner Mersey, who then asked:

> 8588. Replying? Do you reply to another ship by firing rockets? — Well, my Lord, he told
> me he had called him up repeatedly by the Morse lamp and the ship did not answer.
> 8589. But I do not understand this replying by means of rockets. Did you ever hear of
> such a thing? — Well, I never heard of such a thing, but he might have replied [with
> rockets] to let them know he had seen them.

Stone had told Stewart that he did not think these were distress rockets being fired by the
ship to the southward. Stewart said: 'I asked him during our own talk were they distress
signals, and he said he did not think they were. He said he had informed the Captain on
three occasions at intervals'. Stewart added that Stone had given him three reasons for his
belief that the rockets were not distress signals: 'They did not make any noise or report'
(8860); 'They did not leave any trail in the sky' (8864); 'They did not seem to go any higher
than the observed vessel's masthead light' (8864). Stone also reported that he thought
the rockets might have been 'replying to somebody else to the southward' (8862). And
Stewart says:

> 8868. Did he [Stone] state any opinion to you? — He said he thought she was answering
> to somebody else.

And then:

> 8884. When he reported that the vessel had steamed away, what did you gather from the
> way in which he made his report of what he told you that had happened to this steamer?
> – That she had gone down to the other ship.

Stewart then picked up his glasses, spotted the four-master to southward and had the
exchange with Stone in which the latter denied she was the ship he had seen. Stewart
privately concluded that this may have been the same ship – which he believed could have
cruised off but found no way through the ice, and so returned some of the way to her
original place (questions 8641–43):

> I thought she might have come back, or she might have known something about the
> other ship. I thought all the time that that ship [the yellow-funnel four-master] had
> something to do with it or knew something about it.

But on the morning in question Stewart did not mention his hunch or theory to Stone
or to anyone else. Stewart may even have tried to call up the stranger with the Morse
light in the early after-dawn: 'I saw a ship to the southward there, but she would not
answer' (8917). A little later on, Stewart called the captain. It was about 4.30 a.m. when he
did so:

8616. I told him that the Second Mate told me he had seen rockets in the middle watch…

8618. [Lord replied] 'Oh, yes, I know'…

8619. Is that all he said? — He said: 'Yes, I know, he has been telling me'.

Captain Lord told the British Inquiry he was called by the chief officer at 4.30 a.m: 'He [Stewart] told me it was breaking day and the steamer that had fired the rocket was to the southward' (6875–6). The issue was pursued:

6880. Did you know she had fired a number of rockets? — I did not.

6881. According to you did she fire only one rocket? — Only one rocket.

This initial wake-up call by Stewart – a knock at the door, a few words, the chief officer leaving Lord to dress fully – may have involved the two men talking at cross-purposes, Lord still thinking only one rocket had been fired during the night. It is for the reader to judge.

Lord's account states that he slept through Gibson's visit and had no recollection of Stone's 2.40 call by speaking-tube. The captain duly came on the bridge. It was now getting on for 5 a.m. Stewart takes up the story:

8622. You were still stopped. Did you hear from him what his plans were? — He talked about the possibility of going through the ice and proceeding on our voyage.

8623. I asked him if he was going to the southward to see what that ship was.

8625. He said, 'No, I do not think so; she is not making any signals now'.

Lord is still blissfully unaware. The questions continue:

8629. Did you and the Captain look at this other ship together? — Yes.

8630. Did you tell the Captain that Mr Stone, who had been on watch, thought this was not the ship that had thrown up the signals? — No.

8631. You did not? — No. [Perhaps because Stewart had come to a different impression from Stone as to whether she was that original steamer or not]

8632. Did the Captain say this: 'No, she looks all right; she is not making any signals now?' — Yes, I believe those were his exact words.

8633. When the Captain said: 'She looks all right', what was he referring to? — She just looked like an ordinary steamer stopped.

8650. [The Solicitor General] Anyhow, you and the Captain at half-past four in the morning were talking about this steamer as though it was this steamer which had thrown up the signals, although the Officer of the Watch who had seen the signals told you it was not? — Yes.

8651. And you never told the Captain of that mistake? — No.

It appears that Stewart now injects a bit of urgency into the conversation by getting it across to his captain for the first time that a *number* of rockets were fired during the night.

Lord says it was half an hour after he was awoken that he first learnt this important fact: 'The Chief Officer told me, about 5 o'clock, that she had fired several rockets' (6885). This is Lord's account of a casual discussion that suddenly turned deadly serious:

> 6961. Let us go back to the story. At half-past 4 in the morning, when the Chief Officer called you, do you remember saying to him that the Second Officer had said something to you about a rocket? —Yes, I said that.
> 6962. Did you then go on the bridge? —Yes.
> 6963. Do you remember just before 5 o'clock a conversation with your Chief Officer? — I do.
> 6964. About the steamer? — About this, which he said was a yellow-funnelled steamer…
> 6968. I only want the substance of it? — Well, I was conversing with him about the probability of pushing through the ice, to commence with. I was undecided whether to go through it or to turn round and go back, and we decided to go on, so I told him to put the engines on and stand by. He did so. [The *Californian's* engines were started up at 5.15 a.m.]

Lord continues:

> …Then he [Stewart] said, 'Will you go down to look at this steamer to the southward?' I asked him, 'Why, what is the matter with it?' He said, 'He might have lost his rudder.' But I said, 'Why? He has not got any signals up'. 'No', he said, 'but the Second Officer in his watch said he fired several rockets'. I said: 'Go and call the wireless operator.'
> 6967. Did he? — He did.
> 6968. Did he go to the wireless operator? —Yes.

Stewart knew Captain Lord had been under the impression that the steamer they had just been observing was the same one seen by Stone. He knew Lord was also unaware that Stone denied this was the same vessel – because he, Stewart, did not mention this disavowal to the master. But what Stewart did not know was that Lord was under a significant misapprehension – that only one rocket had been fired instead of several. Yet when the decision was being made to continue the voyage to Boston, Stewart was keen (from what he had himself been told by Stone) to ensure that at least a check was made. He then tells Lord that several rockets had been fired. And finally, as the penny drops with the Master, the response is decisive and immediate: 'Go and call the wireless operator'. Stewart is questioned on the issue:

> 8757. You went in to see the Marconi operator, didn't you? —Yes.
> 8758. Try and remember what it was that you told him? — I told him to get out and see what the ship was to the southward.
> 8759. I want you to be as accurate as you can. Do you think that is all you said to him? — I think so.
> 8760. What this ship was to the southward? —Yes.

8762. The ship that Mr Stone had already told you was not the ship that had sent up the rockets? — Yes.

8763. You think that is what you asked him? — Yes.

8764. I must just put it to you. Didn't you go to his [Evans'] room and didn't you say to him that rockets had been seen during the night? — I do not think so, Sir.

8765. You do not think you did? — No.

8766. And didn't you ask him whether he could find out with his Marconi apparatus whether anything was amiss? — I told him to call up and see what that ship was to the southward. I remember that distinctly, Sir.

8767. Didn't you ask him whether he could find out whether anything was amiss? — I do not think so. No, Sir; I do not remember that.

8768. Did you at that time think that anything was amiss? — I thought something had happened, yes.

8769. But you do not think you said that? — I do not think so, Sir.

Cyril Furmstone Evans, *Californian* wireless operator, had this to say to the US Inquiry (p.736):

Evans: He said, 'There is a ship that has been firing rockets in the night. Please see if there is anything the matter.'
Senator Smith: What ship's officer was that?
Evans: The Chief Officer of our ship, Mr Stewart.
Sen. Smith: He said rockets had been fired during the night?
Evans: Yes, sir.
Sen. Smith: And he would like to have you see if there was anything the matter?
Evans: Yes, sir.

Evans said the same thing to the British Inquiry:

9059. Just tell us carefully, if you will, what it was he said? — He said: 'There's a ship been firing rockets. Will you see if you can find out whether there is anything the matter?'
9060. [The Commissioner] Find out what? — If there is anything the matter.

There is a silly controversy over what time the wireless operator was woken. Opponents of Captain Lord would like to believe he delayed as long as he could, perhaps arguing for another option. But this jaundiced view is based on a clumsy misinterpretation of times; we must now examine the subject in order to dismiss the claim. Evans told the British Inquiry he was roused at 5.35 a.m. or 5.40 a.m. *Californian* time. At the US Inquiry he cited times equivalent to 5.20 and 5.30 *Californian* time by Captain Lord's navigation (3.30 & 3.40 NYT). There is a difference of twenty minutes in the spread of times, from first to last.

Yet Evans was also unaware of any clock retardation on the *Californian* overnight. As he said himself (US Inquiry, p.742):

I do not know. I have not worked out the ship's time. I do not know if the ship's clock was changed during that time.

When Evans called other ships seeking information, his first response was from the *Mount Temple*. Her wireless operator, John Durrant, said he received the first message from the *Californian* (9574) at 3.25 a.m. New York time – corresponding to 5.11 a.m. *Mount Temple* time. This would independently tend to show that Evans was summoned much earlier than he specified in his British evidence.

The wireless log of the *Mount Temple* is helpful in that she was one hour forty-six minutes ahead of New York time. *Californian* herself was one hour fifty minutes ahead of New York, according to Captain Lord. This would mean that 5.11 a.m. *Mount Temple* time equated to 5.15 a.m. on the *Californian*. Evans testified, however, that his ship was one hour fifty-five ahead of New York. His basis for this claim is unclear, but it is wrong in relation to longitude (this would make the time he was transmitting 5.20 a.m.).

The *Californian's* engines were first started at 5.15 a.m. ship's time. Lord states: '5.15 we moved the engines for a few minutes' (6713). This is Stewart: 'What time did you start moving? — 5.15' (8778). And Captain Lord said in his US evidence (p.717): 'We moved the engines first at 5.15 on the 15th of April, full ahead'.

The two events – starting engines and rousing Evans – simply must have been very closely related in chronology. Lord said of his conversation with Chief Officer Stewart that he ordered him to put the engines on and stand by. Stewart immediately raised the issue of the steamer to the southward and mentioned 'several rockets'. Lord grasped the point and said: 'Go and call the wireless operator'.

An indication of this is that Evans says the ship was not moving when he was woken: 'When Mr Stewart came to your cabin was your ship moving? — No' (question 9162). Evans' times are self-admittedly approximate, but there does not appear to have been any undue delay in seeking answers through the wireless operator. Stanley Lord now tells what happened after he sent for the Marconi man to be roused:

> 6969 Did the wireless operator come back or did the Chief Officer come back? — The Chief Officer came back some time after.
> 6970 How long after? — I suppose 15 to 20 minutes.
> 6971 And what did he say? — He said: 'There is a ship sunk!'

GETTING GOING

Here is Evans (US Inquiry, p.738):

> ...we never lock a door on the ship. [Chief Officer Stewart] came into my room, and I did not wake up and he caught hold of me. As soon as he touched me I woke up with a start, and he said, 'Wireless, there is a ship that has been firing rockets in the night. Will

you call and see if you can find out what is wrong – what is the matter?' I slipped on my trousers and called at once. Within five minutes I knew what had happened.

During those five minutes, Evans somehow had the idea that a vessel might need to be towed (US Inquiry, p.748):

Two or three days before that I got word from another operator that there was [a] boat wanting to be towed, an oil tank[er]. She was short of coal, and wanted to be towed, and I believe he [Stewart] thought it was her, I would not say. He did not happen to mention it to me; he has not mentioned it to me.

Evans specifically said he was told about rockets when he was woken, contradicting Stewart's account of asking the wireless to find out about the ship to southward:

9164. Did he [Stewart] say anything to you about a ship being to the southward, would you find out what she was? — No, not to my knowledge.

But the news was altogether more grim than a vessel merely needing a tow:

9072. [I heard from] the *Mount Temple* first.
9073. That is a Canadian Pacific vessel, I think? — Yes.
9074. Did you get any information from her? — He said, 'Do you know the *Titanic* has struck an iceberg, and she is sinking', and he gave me her position.

Wireless Operator John Durrant of the *Mount Temple* recalls the following:

9579. *Californian* calls CQ [all stations]. I answer him and tell him the *Titanic* has struck an iceberg and sunk, and give him her position.
9580. That was 5.11 by your time? — Yes.

Incidentally, Durrant later conceded in evidence that he presumed the *Titanic* had indeed sunk by then.
Lord resumes the narrative (US Inquiry, p.730):

The first report I got to the bridge that morning, after I had sent down and had the operator called, the Chief Officer came back and said, 'He reports a ship sunk'. I said, 'Go back and wait until you find out what it is. Get some more about it'. So he went back, and I suppose 10 minutes afterwards he came back and said, 'The *Titanic* is sunk, and hit an iceberg'.

This first confirmed report, according to Lord, was from the *Frankfurt*, received 'between 5 a.m. and half past' (US Inquiry, p.731). Durrant on *Mount Temple*, at 5.26 a.m. ship's time, could now hear the *Californian* working the *Frankfurt* and receiving *Titanic's* SOS position. Evans states (US Inquiry, p.737):

> The Chief Officer was in the room, and I said, 'Wait a moment; I will get an official mes-sage'. I got the official message and the positions were both the same.

> The DFT [*Frankfurt*] answered me. He said, 'Do you know the *Titanic* has sunk during the night, collided with an iceberg?' I said, 'No; please give me the latest position'. He gave me the position. I put the position down on a slip of paper, and then I said, 'Thanks, old man', to the German operator, and then the *Virginian* started to call me, 'MGM'. He started to call me up, and I told him to go. I answered him and told him to go. He said, 'Do you know the *Titanic* has sunk?' I said, 'Yes, the *Frankfurt* has just told me.' [Evans did not need the *Virginian* at this point. But when further confirmation was required, he would have to call her back up again]

Evans continues:

> 9084. The *Frankfurt* told me the same thing [as the *Mount Temple*]. The Chief Officer was in my room at the time.
> 9085. I gave him the position, and he went off to get the Captain.

And here is Lord's account:

> The Chief Officer was delivering the message. I was on the bridge, and he was running backward and forward to the operating room. I said, 'Go back again and find the position as quickly as possible'. So he went back...
> He (Stewart) came back and said 'We have a position here, but it seems a bit doubtful'. [Possibly from the *Mount Temple* mentioning that she had arrived at the transmitted SOS position to find nothing]

He went on to state (US Inquiry, p.730–1):

> I said, 'You must get me a better position. We do not want to go on a wild goose chase'. So in the meantime, I marked off the position from the course given me by the *Frankfurt* in the message just from one operator to another. I marked that off and headed the ship down there.

Lord said in his British evidence that he himself left the bridge for the wireless room:

> 6974. What did you say then? — I left the bridge and went to the wireless room myself...
> 6982. It never occurred to you [that there might have been any connection between the sinking and events of the night before] at all? — Not then.
> 6979. ...I never mentioned a thing to [Stewart] then. I went right to the wireless.

Evans confirms that Lord did indeed arrive:

> 9090. When you gave Mr Stewart the message and the position what did he do? — He
> went off to the Captain and fetched the Captain. Then I got the *Virginian* and asked him
> for an official message.
> 9092. You asked the *Virginian*, did you, for an official message? — Yes, so that I could give
> it to the Captain.

Thus, Evans called up the *Virginian*, the vessel he had minutes earlier asked to stand by
(US Inquiry, p.737):

> I sent them a message of my own, what we call a service message, that an operator can
> always make up if he wants to find out something. I sent a service message, and said,
> 'Please send me official message regarding *Titanic*, giving position'.

Evans at the British Inquiry:

> 9093. What was the message that you got from the *Virginian*? — It gave the position of
> the *Titanic*, and said she was sinking, passengers in boats.
> 9094. [The Solicitor General] I have it here: '*Titanic* struck berg, wants assistance, urgent,
> passengers in boats, ship sinking. His position, 41° 46' North, 50° 14' West – Gambell,
> Commander'. Is that right? — Yes.

Lord says the same in his US evidence (p.731): 'As we were trying to get official news from
the *Frankfurt*, the *Virginian* chipped in, and he gave me this message, which I will read to
you: '*Titanic* struck berg; wants assistance; urgent; ship sinking; passengers in boats...' Evans
says: 'The position I got from the *Virginian* and the position I got from the *Frankfurt* were
both the same. I sent that up to the skipper' (US Inquiry, p.737). Lord now had the best
position obtainable. But it was by no means certain that the *Titanic* had indeed sunk. He
therefore ordered his own lifeboats cleared away and swung out, and the *Californian* was
put on an urgent course to assist.

At 6 a.m. the *Californian* was determinedly underway. Wireless Operator Evans could
hear 'the ship trembling a bit through hitting the ice...' (question 9169).

CALIFORNIAN'S COURSE

Lord recalls the course of the *Californian*:

> 7001. Did you receive a message from the *Virginian* at 6 o'clock that morning? — Yes.
> 7002. That the *Titanic* had struck a berg? — 'Passengers in boats, ship sinking.'
> 7003. And it gave you the position? — Latitude and Longitude 41° 46', 50° 14.'

7004. And did you at once start for that position? — I did.

7005. What course did you make? — I made, from 6 a.m. until half-past, anything between South and Southwest. I was pushing through field ice.

7006. That was of course in order to reach the position of the *Titanic*? —Yes.

For half an hour until 6.30, Lord was pushing his vessel slowly.

At the end of this first half-hour of floe-traversing, Lord had worrisome things on his mind:

6983. Were you quite comfortable in your mind when you heard the *Titanic* had sunk, in reference to your own actions? — Well, I thought we ought to have seen her signals [rockets] at 19 miles, that was the only thing that was worrying me.

And later:

7201. At what time did you think it was possible to have seen her signals? —At half-past six the next morning I was thinking about it.

Stewart had no such doubts:

8653. It was a little later that your wireless people heard that the *Titanic* had sunk? —Yes

8654. When you heard that, did it occur to you that the steamer that had been sending up distress rockets might have been the *Titanic*? — Not the steamer we saw.

8655. That is not what I asked you, I will put my question again, if I may. When you heard that the *Titanic* had sunk that night, did it occur to you that that steamer which you had heard had been sending up rockets, might have been the *Titanic*?

8656. [The Commissioner] Now, come, answer that question? — No I did not think it could have been the *Titanic*.

Lord meanwhile wanted to establish for himself that the *Titanic* had been warned of ice:

7215. When I heard that the *Titanic* had sunk, I sent along and asked [Evans, the wireless operator] whether he delivered the message I sent at 11 o'clock [telling *Titanic* the *Californian* was stopped and surrounded by ice]. He said he had, and they told him to please keep quiet, or shut up.

7216. To shut up? — Something like that; they were busy.

7217. Did you have any conversation with him as to the character of this message? — No.

Evans gave evidence of warning the *Titanic* late on the Sunday night at 11 p.m. ship's time that the *Californian* was stopped and surrounded by ice:

8992. What did you say? — I said, 'We are stopped and surrounded by ice'.

8993. Did you get an answer from the *Titanic*? —They said, 'Keep out'.

To digress for a moment, it is perhaps revealing to hear the attitude of the surviving *Titanic* wireless operator, Harold Bride, to the *Californian's* warning, in his evidence at the US Inquiry (pp.902–3):

Senator Smith: Mr Bride, did you receive, or did Mr Phillips to your knowledge receive, a wireless message from the *Californian* at 11.15 ship's time or about 10 o'clock New York time, Sunday evening, saying, 'Engines stopped. We are surrounded by ice'? Now, think hard on that, because I want to know whether you took that message.

Bride: Mr Phillips was on watch at the time.

Sen. Smith: Do you know whether he received a message of that kind? — He did not say so, sir.

Sen. Smith: And you have no means of knowing?

[The witness did not answer]

Senator Fletcher: What do you mean by saying [earlier] there was no necessity for keeping in communication with the *Californian*?

Bride: If the *Californian* had anything for us he would call us, or if we had anything for the *Californian* we would call him; and there was no necessity for us to call the *Californian* unless we had business with him, or vice versa, because it would then interrupt other traffic.

Sen. Fletcher: The *Californian* said he was endeavouring to communicate with you and you stopped him and said he was jamming. Do you know about that? — No; the chances are he might have been jamming during the evening, when the senior operator was working Cape Race [to receive incoming private messages for passengers, invariably those in First Class].

Sen. Fletcher: But you cannot say that you on the *Titanic* knew of all that he [*Californian*] was endeavouring to communicate? — No, sir.

Senator Smith: Do you know whether… the *Californian* operator was told 'Keep out; am working Cape Race'? — I heard nothing about it at all, sir.

Sen. Smith: Would Mr Phillips have made a memorandum of such a message if he had received it? — He would have if the *Californian* had persisted in sending it.

Bride also said in this evidence (p.903) that Phillips 'had finished working with Cape Race ten minutes before the collision with the iceberg'.

Meanwhile, 3 miles and half an hour have now elapsed since Lord began his attempt to assist, the *Californian* pushing slowly south-west through field ice at half-speed (6 knots, or nautical miles per hour). It is now 6.30 a.m. Stewart states:

8780. What pace did you make for the first three or four miles? — We were going very, very slow.

8781. How slow? — I could not tell you what we were going, I was not very much on the bridge after that time.

8782. Cannot you give us any idea of the pace? — I could not give you any idea.

8783. Just crawling through? — Just crawling through the ice.

For the next hour (6.30–7.30 a.m.) the *Californian* could enjoy a major navigational break-through. She had diagonally penetrated the ice barrier to the west (as represented by '/') during the previous half hour, and could now steer directly south, aiming for the *Titanic*'s SOS position. Since she had reached open water after crawling through the ice barrier, her speed now increased dramatically:

> [Robertson Dunlop to Stanley Lord] Then at 6.30 you steered a southerly course, and passed the *Mount Temple* [where she had stopped] at about 7.30? —Yes.
>
> 7261. What rate were you going at? —We were driving all we possibly could. The Chief Engineer estimated the speed at 13 and-a-half [knots]. I estimate it at 13.

Ninety minutes had now elapsed from 6 a.m. when the *Californian* got going. In that ninety minutes a minimum of 16 miles has been steamed by Lord's vessel. That is 3 nautical miles in the first half an hour, and 13 miles (top speed) in the next hour. Lord is now, at 7.30 a.m. at the position indicated by the *Titanic*'s SOS messages. *Mount Temple* is already in the vicinity. It has taken Lord ninety minutes to get there, but of course the *Titanic* did not sink in this place.

Meanwhile Lord would estimate the distance between the SOS position and his over-night stop position to be some 19½ to 20 miles at the time of the sinking. With overnight drift southward by the *Californian*, it turns out to be a minimum of 16 miles away from her position at 6 a.m., as we have just seen. This is 16 miles of dog-leg separation from *Californian*'s position in the daylight, and not from her position at the time of collision or sinking. With southerly drift factored back in – to account for slippage over the hours from 2.20 a.m. (sinking of the *Titanic*) to positive movement at 6 a.m. (and from 10.21 p.m. to 11.40 p.m. the previous night when *Californian* was drifting slightly south but *Titanic* steaming west) – it is clear that Lord's original estimate is remarkably accurate. So, 10.21 p.m. to 6 a.m. on the *Californian* (both her own times) gives seven hours thirty-nine minutes of drift at half a knot. Half a knot is half of 1 nautical mile per hour. *Californian* will therefore drift south 3½ miles over the seven hours, plus ⅓ mile for the remaining two-thirds of an hour. A grand total of 3.83 nautical miles – plus the 16 miles steamed – gives Lord's estimate to a nicety. He said 19½ to 20... the crude count-back shows 19.83 (it doesn't matter at this point where the *Titanic* actually sank – which actually was to the east and further south – since Lord is only ever assessing his distance from the SOS position). The encounter with the *Mount Temple*, stopped at the *Titanic*'s SOS-declared position, is now described:

> 7257. How far from that point was the *Mount Temple*? — I think she was very close to it [the distress position]. I should think she had been looking for the *Titanic*, boats or wreckage, or something. She was stopped there.
>
> 7258. You went on from that point? —Yes.
>
> 7259. In what direction did you proceed after that point? — I steered, as far as I recollect, about South, or South by East true, from there along the edge of the ice – the Western edge of the ice.

7260. …I passed her somewhere about half-past seven – somewhere in the vicinity of half-past seven.

There was no sign of wreckage in the transmitted SOS position, which Lord now knew must be wrong. He concluded the *Titanic* had sunk the other side of the ice barrier and that he would have to steam across there.

Lord can see the ice extending further to southward. He must now go below the *Titanic*'s SOS position and turn to port to go back through the ice in an 'L' shape:

7401. [Mr Dunlop] After 7.30 had you to navigate through the field ice again? — Yes, I ran along till I got to the *Carpathia* bearing north-east and then I cut straight through the ice at full speed.
7402. From 7.30 to 8.30? — We were not going through ice the whole of that time. We were running 'til it must have been about eight.

'Running' in this context means going south, beside the field. So the *Californian* went south for half an hour after passing the *Mount Temple* at 7.30 a.m. At 8 a.m. she stopped 'running' and 'cut' through the ice towards the *Carpathia*.

7260. How, far did you go till you got to the wreckage? — I passed her [*Mount Temple*] somewhere about half-past seven – somewhere in the vicinity of half-past seven. I got there [to *Carpathia*] at half-past eight.
7261. What rate were you going at? — We were driving all we possibly could. The Chief Engineer estimates the speed at 13½. I estimate it at 13.
7262. You were about an hour? — We were an hour.

They were running at full speed, even through the ice. This was a distance of a further 13 or 13½ miles from the SOS position at 7.30 to the location where the *Carpathia* was picking up boats. *Californian* reached her at 8.30 a.m. A quick bit of calculation – half an hour at full speed south sends the *Californian* 6½ to 6¾ miles south of the *Mount Temple* in the period 7.30–8 a.m.

If Lord now cuts through the ice at full speed at 8 a.m. and reaches the *Carpathia* at 8.30 a.m., then that distance covered, no matter how one cuts it, is also 6½ to 6¾ miles in the half hour. She has thus covered a total of 13 to 13½ miles since she left the SOS position an hour earlier at 7.30.

Of course the actual separation between the SOS position and the rescuing *Carpathia* is less 'as the crow flies' than the 13 or 13½ miles the *Californian* travelled to reach her – but there is a mass of intervening ice that had to be negotiated. Let us now cross-check the *Californian*'s course (which resembled the symbol '/' on top of an 'L') and her elapsed time. We can use other viewpoints. How far away from the SOS position, for instance, was the *Carpathia*?

Firstly we can say that she was unquestionably south-east of the *Titanic*'s transmitted SOS position when she stopped to pick up survivors in the lifeboats.

18089. [The Attorney General] Having followed out where the *Carpathia* was to some extent, we make her a little to the SE [of the SOS position when she stopped].

[The Commissioner] South and east.

18090. [The Attorney General] Yes, almost exactly SE; but we will work it out later, and your Lordship will see from the evidence of the Captain of the *Carpathia* it will be made clear. That is calculating it according to the evidence already given in America. He did not give his position, but he did give a position at one time, and said how many miles he steamed after it, and from that we work out she would have been to the SE [of the SOS position].

Captain James Moore of the *Mount Temple* (at the SOS position) tells us expressly the distance from his vessel to the *Carpathia* as that vessel lay stopped diagonally (as represented by the symbol '\') to the south-east (US Inquiry, p.778):

> Senator Smith: How near the *Carpathia* did you get that morning?
>
> Moore: This pack of ice between us and the *Carpathia*, it was between 5 and 6 miles. She did not communicate with me at all. When we sighted her she must have sighted us.

If the three ships form a triangle of locations (which can be represented by the symbol '▷') with the *Mount Temple* to the north, the *Californian* having journeyed down to a position at the south so that the *Carpathia* bears to the north-east of her (as Lord indicated at question 7401) and the *Carpathia* is to the east of both other vessels (north-east of *Californian* and south-east of *Mount Temple*), then we can make certain observations. We can say, very roughly, that it resembles an equilateral triangle. If the line between the *Mount Temple* and the *Carpathia* is 6 miles, then the *Californian*'s hour-long journey is the sum of the other two sides to close the triangle, making a distance of up to 12 miles travelled.

One can reconstruct the *Californian*'s journey after passing *Mount Temple* through any series of changing lines, but the triangle is the most economical. *Californian* passed *Mount Temple* at 7.30 a.m. and arrived at the *Carpathia* at 8.30 a.m. She travelled 13–13½ miles in that hour, thereby completing a 2½ hour journey since starting off at 6 a.m.

Overall then, she travelled over a minimum distance of 29 miles (3 plus 13 plus 13) to a maximum of 30 miles (3 plus 13½ plus 13½), depending on whether you prefer Lord's estimate of speed or that of his Chief Engineer (question 7261). The Chief Engineer (William Mahon) was not called to give evidence at either the British or US Inquiries, although we can assume he said nothing controversial since all *Californian* crew gave depositions on their return to Liverpool, with the British Inquiry summoning just a few.

COURSE AND LATITUDE

It is possible to use these new considerations of course, time and speed to arrive at a calculation as to the mileage separating the *Californian* from the *Titanic* at 11.40 p.m. (*Titanic* time) when the latter collided. As we have seen, the *Californian* steamed 3 miles south-west through the ice from 6 to 6.30 a.m. at a rough 45 degree angle. The *Californian* has therefore come down 1½ miles in latitude (the north–south axis), because half the time she was going west and half the time south.

From 6.30 to 7.30 a.m., she was steering directly south at top speed, and made a minimum distance of 13 miles south. This is a total of 14½ miles in latitudinal descent since 6 a.m. And we know that the 7.30 SOS point represents the baseline along which the *Titanic* was travelling, because she had been on a straight-line westerly course – until she struck her iceberg a considerable distance further east along that baseline.

To our running total we must add drift by the *Californian* from the time she stopped (10.21 p.m.) until she started moving (6 a.m.). This is seven hours and thirty-nine minutes. But we must also subtract from this the two hours twenty minutes when *Titanic* was similarly drifting south, after coming to a halt, before she sank. This leaves five hours nineteen minutes of southerly drift by *Californian*. The current, as has been seen, is of the order of half a knot, giving 2½ miles in southerly drift over the five hours, and another sixth of a mile for the nineteen minutes. It may be prudent to adopt a deliberately conservative estimate of the *Californian*'s drift southward before she started her engines and say that it amounted to no more than 2 miles in latitude.

It has already been determined that the *Californian* descended 14½ miles on the north–south axis until she reached the SOS position, which was on the *Titanic*'s baseline track. Adding the 2 miles of drift now gives a total of 16½ miles of latitude, representing the vertical upright on an 'L' shape, where the baseline on the 'L' indicates the distance east to be travelled to arrive at the *Titanic*'s actual collision location. We have seen that the *Titanic* was *at least* 8 miles further east than the *Californian* at the time of the crash. Closing this triangle therefore, will give us another check on the mileage separation between the two ships, *Californian* and *Titanic*, when the iceberg was struck. At a 'height' of 16½ miles and a 'length' of 8 miles, the 'width' works out in quick measurement at 18½ nautical miles.

Nothing is ever exact when dealing with estimations, but every time the calculation is re-checked using different parameters in testimony, the result is broadly the same. The *Californian* could not, therefore, have been the *Titanic*'s mystery ship at an average estimated distance of only 5 miles!

The bottom line in all of this is that the *Californian*'s course and speed, and known times at landmarks the following morning, are all entirely consistent with her reported stop position of the night before. This is further evidence that she was where she said she was.

14

POSITIONAL PROOFS

The *Carpathia* eventually came to the rescue of *Titanic* survivors, as the world knows. Less commonly grasped is the importance of the course line that she plotted to the SOS position sent out by the *Titanic*. Captain Rostron gave evidence in America that the *Carpathia's* course was north 52 degrees west (modern 308 degrees). This line is as true today as it was then, and is simply drawn from the distress position to his ship's location an estimated 58 miles away – a nice diagonal. Rostron declared:

> 25394. ...At twenty minutes to three I saw the green flare, which is the White Star Company's night signal, and naturally, knowing I must be at least 20 miles away, I thought it was the ship herself still.

Because we know his course, we can plot 20 miles to the south-east along the diagonal line from the SOS position. The important point to grasp is that the flare incident was directly on the *Carpathia's* course. It is Rostron who says this:

> 25401. ...At twenty minutes to three I saw a night signal, as I was saying, and it was just about half a point on the port bow, practically right ahead.

This establishes that the lifeboat was on the *Carpathia's* course line (the flare being seen on the port bow); in other words, the lifeboat had gone to the south. The *Titanic's* course, established by the wreck site and complying with the latitude of the SOS position, was along the line of 41° 46' N. That is the northern co-ordinate. The lifeboat encounter by the *Carpathia*, 20 miles to the south and east, along the diagonal, thus appears to be several miles south of the line on which the *Titanic* struck her iceberg. The *Carpathia* could not have come across those lifeboats so quickly (or at all) if those lifeboats had gone to the north – where it is claimed the mystery ship lay (by those wanting her to be the *Californian*).

Since the *Titanic* lifeboats did not go to the north, it means they were in fact pursuing the mystery ship in another direction. Which means that vessel was not the *Californian*. The point is independently established by Captain Rostron.

There is yet another proof of this contention, which hardly needs to be made. If Rostron had in fact chased north-going lifeboats as far as the point of impact (latitude 41° 46' N) then his vessel would have been seen by the *Mount Temple*, which reached the SOS position shortly after daylight. *Mount Temple* was thus on the line of 41° 46' N, albeit much further to the west. Her captain had lookouts on high who could not have failed to see the *Carpathia*. We shall see what the evidence from *Mount Temple* is about the *Carpathia* location in a moment. But *Mount Temple's* captain said his vessel did not see flares or 'night signals' from the lifeboats, nor any lights at all, which further indicates the lifeboats did not go north.

Meanwhile it is unfortunately necessary to prove some of the positions and timings cited in the last chapter because of lazy claims that the *Californian* arrived *early* at the *Carpathia's* side and therefore must have been closer to the *Titanic* than Lord's overnight stop position would indicate.

This 'early-arrival' claim is based on timings for the morning-after given by *Californian's* third officer, Charles Victor Groves. The claim also uses the supporting crutch of an account by an officer of the *Carpathia*, James Bisset, that he could see the *Californian* lying stopped at 6 a.m. while the *Carpathia* was working at the rescue scene.

We shall deal with Bisset first, and leave Groves' timings for later. Bisset's account was published (and ghost-written at that) in 1959, nearly half a century after the disaster. It was also coloured by the conventional wisdom of the British and American Inquiries, which both condemned the *Californian* as being the ship nearby which could have helped the *Titanic* but did not. In fact, James Bisset likely saw the *Mount Temple* – as a glance at the locational argument in the previous chapter will demonstrate. Remember that Captain Moore of the *Mount Temple* said: 'This pack of ice between us and the *Carpathia*, it was between 5 and 6 miles. She did not communicate with me at all. When we sighted her, she must have sighted us' (US Inquiry, p.778).

This next extract from Moore establishes that *Mount Temple* was originally north-west of the *Carpathia*, and the *Carpathia* therefore south-east of the SOS position (US Inquiry, p.778):

> Of course, it proved afterwards when, after coming southward and trying to find some place I could get through, on the way back again – I suppose about 6 o'clock in the morning – that I sighted the *Carpathia* on the other side [east] of this great ice pack, and there is where I understand he picked up the boats.

The point here is that the *Mount Temple* saw the *Carpathia* at 6 a.m. But the *Mount Temple* did not see the *Californian* until nearly 7.30 a.m., when they passed, according to Lord. So how could Bisset, aboard the *Carpathia*, many more miles and a whole icefield away, have seen the *Californian* ninety minutes earlier than the *Mount Temple* did? The available evidence of Captain Moore of the *Mount Temple* is sketchy on this point, but essentially agrees with Lord:

> 9244. And I think shortly before 8 a.m. you came in sight of the *Carpathia* and the *Californian*? —Yes.

This is Moore's only timed reference to the *Californian* in the whole of his British evidence. Moore agrees that the *Mount Temple* saw the *Californian* within that timeframe of 'shortly before 8 a.m'. It is obviously open to him to disagree if he had seen the *Californian* earlier – but he does not disagree (US Inquiry, p.778):

> Moore: …I saw the *Californian* myself cruising around there, sir.
> Senator Smith: She was there when you were there?
> Moore: She was there [at the SOS position] shortly after me…

Moore continues (p.779):

> The *Californian* was to the north, sir. She was to the north of the *Carpathia* and steaming to the westward, because, after… giving up my attempt to get through that pack [to the south], I came back again and steered back [north], thinking I might pick up some soft place to the north. As I was going to the north the *Californian* was passing from east to west.

Moore's *Mount Temple* had left the *Carpathia* to the south-east, and had gone back north towards the SOS position. Moore knew from wireless reports – he does not say visuals – that the *Californian* was coming through the ice to the west and then steering down to meet him. He does not say he saw the *Californian* at this point, and the next extract will show he was merely supposing where she might have been. The two vessels had been in wireless contact, as to where they were and what they were doing, ever since Evans first heard from *Mount Temple* Wireless Operator John Durrant about the sinking. Moore recalls more about the situation (US Inquiry, p.779):

> Senator Smith: And you were also cut off from the *Carpathia* by this ice pack?
> Moore: Yes, sir; by this ice pack. He [*Californian*] was then north of the *Carpathia*, and he must have been, I suppose, about the same distance to the north of the *Carpathia* as I was to the westward of her.

The immediately preceding enquiry was: 'On which side of the ice pack was the *Californian*?', and Moore had replied: 'the *Californian* was to the north, sir… north… and steaming to the westward', meaning that the *Californian* was simply not on the same side of the ice pack as the *Carpathia*, as the subsequent reply might suggest. Moore may, at a stretch of the imagination, be suggesting he first saw the *Californian* when she was 6 miles to the north of his vessel (he estimated his distance from the *Carpathia* at his closest to be 5–6 miles and 'at least five miles'). He does not however give a time for this encounter, if this is what he means. The timing of the first visual contact between *Mount Temple* and *Californian* is clearly implied in an entry in the wireless record of Moore's vessel: '5.20 NY time [7.06 a.m. *Mount Temple* time, 7.10 a.m. *Californian* time]: Signal *Californian*. Wants my position. Send it. We are very close' (US Inquiry, p.782). The time is 7.06 a.m. on the

Mount Temple at the time of this message. *Mount Temple* notes that the *Californian* is 'very close' to her. Seen or unseen, the *Californian* has been steaming to meet them for over an hour. Moore explains (US Inquiry, p.782):

> This is my ship and *Californian*, sir. When I get him to confirm my position, I ask him if he can give me his position. I understand he is cruising, because after we go up toward him he goes to the south and misses us, passes about a mile off, and then he gets to where we came from. Then we go over the ground, and we have not seen anything of the ship [*Titanic*], and we think we must cruise on farther.

The net result: *Mount Temple* sees the rescuing *Carpathia* at 'about 6 in the morning', but then does not see the approaching *Californian* until somewhere between 7.06 a.m. and 7.30 a.m. her time. Therefore *Californian* and *Carpathia* could not have been in sight of each other at or before 6 a.m. Bisset, who did not give evidence in 1912, is wrong in his forty-seven-year-old recollections (his account of the *Titanic* sinking is littered with other factual mistakes, but this is by the by). Bisset did not give evidence, yet he did accompany his captain, Arthur Rostron, to the US Inquiry – a relatively open forum at which unsolicited contributions were common during the evidence. He could obviously have intervened at any stage if he really believed he could see the *Californian* from the rescuing *Carpathia* at 6 a.m. He did not do so.

We have seen in a previous chapter how the *Californian* only noticed a yellow-funnel vessel and no other ship to the southward before getting underway at 6 a.m. The *Carpathia* had a red funnel. Bisset does not mention seeing any yellow-funnel ship.

We know *Californian* went south-west at 6 a.m. through the ice. We also know, from Moore of the *Mount Temple*: 'after coming southward… about 6 o'clock… we spotted the *Carpathia*'. This is what Bisset of the *Carpathia* offered in his ghost-written 1959 memoirs, entitled *Tramps and Ladies*:

> While we had been picking up the survivors, in the slowly increasing daylight after 4.30 a.m., we had sighted the smoke of a steamer on the fringe of the pack ice, ten miles away from us to the northwards. She was making no signals, and we paid little attention to her, for we were preoccupied with more urgent matters; but at 6 a.m. we had noticed that she was under way and slowly coming towards us.
>
> When I took over the watch on the bridge of the *Carpathia* at 8 a.m., the stranger was little more than a mile from us, and flying her signals of identification. She was the Leyland Line cargo steamer *Californian*…

It must be that the steamer first seen is the *Mount Temple*. The *Californian* likely did not significantly 'show smoke' at 4.30 a.m. because the engines were not engaged until 5.15 a.m., and she was not underway before 6 a.m.! Yet *Mount Temple was* steaming at this very time. *Mount Temple* was also clearly 'on the fringe of the pack ice' – *Californian* entered that pack ice at 6 a.m. *Mount Temple* also 'came towards us' to the southward, whereas the *Californian* was moving from 6 a.m.–6.30 a.m. at an oblique angle *away* from the *Carpathia*.

There is a further difficulty with Bisset's account – he appears to put his steamer to the east side of the icefield, coming south, whereas the *Mount Temple* was west of the ice and the *Californian* went through that ice to the west at 6 a.m. – not merely moving south along the east side. Bisset's account admits he 'paid little attention' since he was understandably 'preoccupied'. There is a clear hiatus between the time when he sees a far-distant steamer and when he next notices a ship, just 1 mile off, which is indeed the *Californian*, which made her way to the *Carpathia*'s side after finding no wreckage at the SOS position. But it cannot be that the *Californian* is the far-distant steamer seen between 4.30 a.m. and 6 a.m., because she did not behave in the way Bisset describes.

Indeed it is possible that Bisset, if he did see smoke to the north after 4.30 a.m., was seeing Stewart's yellow-funnel steamer on the east side of the icefield (this being the vessel that lay to *Californian*'s southward; and which seemed to come out of nowhere, if Stone is to be believed). It may have been her smoke that Bisset sighted initially, before his next sighting at 6 a.m. The second mention comes an hour and a half later. Who is to say it is the same vessel? If it is not the yellow-funnel, then the smoke could very well be from a two-master, as we shall see in a moment. But to recap – *Mount Temple* could see *Carpathia* about 6 a.m. She could not see *Californian*. *Mount Temple* believed *Carpathia* could see her. It must be most likely that Bisset's casually-noticed 6 a.m. steamer is simply the *Mount Temple*. She was at the SOS position at 4.30 a.m. Rostron, captain of the *Carpathia*, Bisset's commanding officer, told the British Inquiry in 1912 when he first saw the *Californian*:

> 25551. It was daylight at about 4.20 a.m. At 5 o'clock it was light enough to see all round the horizon. We then saw two steamships to the northwards, perhaps seven or eight miles distant. Neither of them was the *Californian*. One of them was a four-masted steamer with one funnel, and the other a two-masted steamer with one funnel. I never saw the *Mount Temple* to identify her.
>
> The first time that I saw the *Californian* was at about eight o'clock on the morning of 15th April. She was then about five to six miles distant, bearing WSW true, and steaming towards the *Carpathia*.

This agrees precisely with Captain Lord, who was then heading towards the *Carpathia*, which bore north-east of him, just as he was south-west or west-south-west of her.

This ought to be game, set and match against those who want to imagine that the *Carpathia* could see the *Californian* at 6 a.m. She simply could not. Her captain's evidence, above, could not be more clear-cut. It is deserving of careful attention.

Meanwhile there is the case of one Mabel Fenwick, a honeymooning bride on the *Carpathia*, who dashed onto that vessel's deck in the early morning light before a single *Titanic* lifeboat had been rescued. She took a remarkable series of photographs, some of which show an empty horizon. Others pick out various lifeboats as they are met by the *Carpathia*. Further pictures of approaching boats – and distant icebergs – were taken by Frank Blackmarr, a doctor on the *Carpathia*. Still more passengers, like Lawrence Stoudenmire, hurried to take snaps of the hungry ocean. One *Carpathia* passenger taking pictures – encouraged by Captain

Rostron himself – was Louis Ogden, who had been on deck from the earliest. The first picture of the *Californian* is one taken from close-up, when that ship arrives at 8.30 a.m. from the south-west, 'below' the recovery site.

Had the *Californian* been approaching from the north, as Bisset claimed, Mrs Fenwick, Dr Blackmarr, Mr Stoudenmire or Mr Ogden might have been expected to photograph her while she was still far off. They did not! Similarly, the *Titanic* lifeboats, instead of coming south, could have been expected to go to Bisset's ship which should have been seen at 4.30 a.m. or 6 a.m., if it was supposedly in sight on the east side of the barrier.

We saw earlier how the *Californian* had drifted at least 2 miles south overnight. If she was the mystery ship seen from the *Titanic* at 5 miles, then she was by now only 3 miles from the sinking. Meanwhile, Crawford, in boat No.8, said he had pulled for over two hours towards the mystery ship, but made no headway – she 'disappeared'.

Clearly *Californian* cannot be Bisset's ship in these circumstances. It is most likely that Bisset's 1959 account is just a garbled tale, unreliable in detail.

THE SMALL STEAMER

Meanwhile, Rostron of the *Carpathia* has mentioned being able to see two ships, somewhere after 5 a.m., one of them a four-master, the other with two masts. This description corroborates what Moore in the *Mount Temple* observes. Moore can see *Carpathia* and also a small steamer, which indicates that the four-master Rostron is seeing is likely the *Mount Temple* and vice versa. If Rostron and Moore can both see the small steamer, then they are also seeing each other. As Moore says: 'This pack of ice between us and the *Carpathia*, it was between 5 and 6 miles. She did not communicate with me at all. When we sighted her she must have sighted us' (US Inquiry, p.778). The captain of the four-masted *Mount Temple* now describes how he saw a smaller steamer close to his own position in the morning – a position far to the south of the *Californian*:

> 9257. …I saw her afterwards in the morning, when it was daylight. She was a foreign vessel – at least, I took her to be a foreign vessel. She had a black funnel with a white band with some [heraldic?] device upon it, but I did not ascertain her name.

Moore states (US Inquiry, p.763):

> Moore: …When I turned [after receiving the SOS] there was a steamer on my port bow.
> Senator Smith: Going in the same direction?
> Moore: Almost in the same direction. As he went ahead, he gradually crossed our bow until he got on the starboard bow, sir.
> Sen. Smith: Did you see that ship yourself?
> Moore: I saw it myself. I was on the bridge all the time.

Sen. Smith: Did you communicate with it by wireless?

Moore: I do not think he had any wireless; I am sure he had no wireless, because in the daylight I was close to him.

Sen. Smith: How large a vessel was it?

Moore: I should say a ship of about 4,000 or 5,000 tons.

This is smaller than both his own 6,661-ton *Mount Temple* and the 6,223-ton *Californian*. Moore speculated that this was a 'foreign ship' (US Inquiry, p.764), that 'she was not English. I do not think she was English, because she did not show her ensign'. Moore continues (p.764):

> Moore: I had no communication with her. We were trying to pick him out in the signal book, and we were trying to signal with him, because I think he was under the impression that I was going to the eastward, that I was bound to the eastward, and I think when I turned back after we both stopped, when we found the ice too heavy, he followed me, because when I turned around, after finding the ice too heavy to the southward, after I went to the southward later on in the morning, when it got daylight, and I went down to where he was, thinking he perhaps had gotten into a thin spot, when I got there he had stopped, he had found the ice too heavy. I went a little farther, and I turned around because it was getting far too heavy to put the ship through. But that would be about 5, or perhaps half past 5, in the morning, sir.

This puts the two ships together, as they would be seen by Rostron, and in the exact time-frame specified by the *Carpathia's* captain. Rostron's two ships therefore, are the *Mount Temple* and an unknown small two-master. Neither ship, as he explicitly states, is the *Californian*. Also from Moore of the *Mount Temple* (US Inquiry, p.767):

> I steered away to the south-southeast true, because I thought the ice appeared thinner down there, sir. When I got down, I got within about a mile or so of this other ship, which had already stopped, finding the ice was too strong for it to go through.

Meanwhile Captain Lord of the *Californian* will declare:

> 7400. Was there another vessel near the *Mount Temple*? — There was, a two-masted steamer, pink funnel, black top, steering north down to the north-west.

This is actually a different vessel to the black funnel one seen by Moore, but the point is still made about there being more vessels around that morning than is commonly imagined. Lord will later cite the *Almerian* as the pink-funnel ship, belonging to the same line as the *Californian*, which also had a pink funnel, in common with all Leyland Line vessels. Moore's black-funnel tramp is much harder to identify, but a black funnel with a white band and a 'device' in it, may suggest either of the German tankers *Trautenfels* or *Lindenfels*.

WHEN DID *CALIFORNIAN* ARRIVE AT THE *CARPATHIA*?

This is the second argument for assuming that the *Californian* must have been close – she supposedly arrived early at the *Carpathia*'s side. This is a kind of 'alternative trap' for Lord's figures, locations and timings, and depends on Third Officer Groves of the *Californian*, even though his account clashes with that of Bisset. Groves is the same man who, uniquely among the ranking officers of that vessel, saw a 'passenger steamer' nearby the previous night (but only for a single hour), and who also saw two masthead lights on her – whereas Lord, Gibson and Stone all saw only a small to medium tramp (Stone says 'smallish') with one masthead light. True to form, Groves the following morning is once more out of step with his colleagues – and also clashing with independent observers like Captain Moore of the *Mount Temple* and Captain Rostron of the *Carpathia*. Here is an abridgement of what Groves has to say, even if he immediately weakens his timings by offering that they are only approximate:

8290. …turned out again in the morning about 6.40, I did not notice the time particularly…

8296. …Stewart, the Chief Officer, told me to come on the bridge.

8297. …'the *Titanic* has sunk, and the passengers are all in the lifeboats in the water ahead of us', or words to that effect.

8313. I went straight up on the bridge as soon as I was dressed.

8314–5. What did you find when you got there? — Ice all round us and icebergs. The ship was under way then, and I could feel her bumping the ice, and I knew she had got a good speed on by that.

8321. Now it is getting on for 7? — I suppose by the time I got on the bridge it would be 6.50, but you understand the time is only approximate.

8322. I quite understand that. Were there any other vessels in sight? — Yes.

8323. What were they? — There was a four-masted steamer abeam on our port side.

8324. What steamer was that? — I did not know at the time, but I knew afterwards she was the *Carpathia*.

8328. How far off was she? — I should think she would be about 5 miles – possibly more, possibly less, but about five.

8331. Did you make out anything about her? — After I had been looking at her I made out she had her house flag half-mast. She had a red funnel with a black top.

8337. What did your vessel do then? — We continued on our course for a little time after I had told the Captain she had a red funnel with a black top and the house flag half-masted, and the next thing that was done we starboarded [the helm, turning to port, turning left].

8338. You made straight for her? — We made practically straight for her.

8339. Did you see any other vessel? — Yes, I saw two other vessels.

8341. At this time? — Yes. I fancy one of them was in sight at the same time as I noticed this four-master. [Supports Rostron seeing only two steamers, neither being the *Californian*, in the early part of the morning]

8341–2. …I know what one of them was; the *Mount Temple*.

8343–4. ...She was ahead, a little on our starboard side when I saw her first, before we headed for the *Carpathia*.

8345. How far off was she, do you think? — Well, when I noticed her first – I had been paying particular attention to this other steamer – I should think she would be perhaps a mile and a half away from us.

8346. Nearer than the *Carpathia*? — Much nearer than the *Carpathia*.

8347. Was she stopped? — Stopped.

8348. In the ice? — In the ice.

8349. Did you see any other vessel? — I saw another vessel a little on our port bow, she was coming down almost end-on.

8350. [The Commissioner] You do not know her name? — I do not, but as far as I remember she had a black funnel. She was a small steamer. [Agrees with Rostron, and with Moore particularly]

8351. [Mr Rowlatt] Did you reach the *Carpathia*? — We did.

8352. What time did you reach the *Carpathia*? — I think it would be about 7.45 a.m. [Everyone else says 8.30 a.m.]

Groves suggests in response to question 8339 that he saw 'two other vessels' besides the *Carpathia* that morning, one being the *Mount Temple*, the other the small steamer. Taken in the round, his evidence suggests both these vessels were to the south of the *Californian* as she herself steamed south – again supporting Rostron's two vessels to the north, neither of which was the *Californian* (there is agreement here in 1912 between Groves, Lord, Rostron and Moore, whereas Bisset has made a lazy assumption in his 1959 memoirs). Meanwhile, Captain Lord said *Californian* reached *Carpathia* at 8.30 a.m. Officer Groves 'thinks' it was 'about' 7.45 a.m. (question 8352). Who is right?

Here is Lord: 'I got there at half-past eight' (7260); 'We arrived at half past eight' (7284). And Bisset, in his 1959 recollections, states: 'When I took over the watch on the bridge of the *Carpathia* at 8 a.m., the stranger was little more than a mile from us'. Evans, wireless operator on the *Californian*, gives the following evidence:

9165. How soon did you get into touch with the *Carpathia*? — I did not get her until I got nearly alongside of her.

9166. What time was that? — About half-past 8, I think.

Here is *Californian* Chief Officer Stewart: 'And you stopped close to the *Carpathia* at 8.30? —Yes' (8826). And Captain Rostron of the *Carpathia* states:

25551. ...The first time that I *saw* the *Californian* was at about eight o'clock on the morning of 15th April. She was then about five to six miles distant, bearing WSW true, and steaming towards the *Carpathia*.

At the US Inquiry, Rostron says (p.22):

We got all the [life]boats alongside and all the people up aboard by 8.30. At 8 o'clock the Leyland Line steamer *Californian* hove up, and we exchanged messages. I gave them the notes by semaphore about the *Titanic* going down, and that I had got all the passengers from the boats…

So Groves' timings, and he 'did not notice the time particularly' are wildly out-of-step with all other witnesses. Meanwhile, the other element of Groves' questioning is this:

8321. I got on the bridge at 6.50, but you understand the time is only approximate.
8322. …other vessels in sight? —Yes.
8323. …four-masted steamer [he says *Carpathia*] abeam on our port side.

Quite apart from it not being explicit that the other vessel was in sight *immediately* he arrived on the bridge (leading to a possible gap between his arrival and noticing other vessels in due course), Groves' evidence clashes with that of Captain Moore of *Mount Temple*:

5.20. [7.06 a.m. *Mount Temple* time] Signal *Californian*. Send my position… 'This is my ship and *Californian*, sir. When I get him to confirm my position, I ask him if he can give me his position…'

Mount Temple cannot see *Californian* even some time after 7.06 a.m. (7.10 a.m. *Californian*). Subsequently *Californian* replies to Moore's message, and the *Mount Temple* signals anew to ask for *Californian*'s position. Allow five minutes for them to see each other after exchanging these messages, meaning 7.15 a.m. *Californian* time.

Can it really be that Groves alone can miraculously see the *Mount Temple* an astonishing twenty-five minutes earlier (see Groves' responses to questions 8321 and 8341 when he appears to claim to be able to see *Mount Temple* at 6.50 a.m.)? It must be remembered that Groves times are 'only approximate', whereas wireless message times are written down religiously the moment they are transmitted.

Moore of the *Mount Temple* continues: 'After we go up toward him [*Californian*] he goes to the south and misses us, passes about a mile off…' And Groves said: 'When I noticed [*Mount Temple*] first, I should think she would be perhaps a mile and a half away from us' (8345). These distances are very similar. Groves does not time the sighting. Nor does Moore mention a time for when the *Californian* passes, but it is certainly substantially after 7 a.m. by his ship's clock. Lord, it will be remembered, specified on a couple of occasions that *Californian* passed the *Mount Temple* at 7.30 a.m. So Moore independently backs Lord, not Groves.

Groves' supporters obviously suggest that his times were correct – meaning in turn that the *Californian* must have been far to the south of her log position of latitude 42° 05' N, and therefore a candidate for the mystery ship seen by the *Titanic*. However American researcher Paul Slish has dismissed Groves' timings by examining drift, steaming time, and *Californian*'s relationship to other ship positions, all factors which strongly argue against such a hypothesis.

To make Groves' times work to meet the *Mount Temple* and the *Carpathia* at the right latitudes, for instance, he points out that the *Californian* would have to have been several miles further south than she believed – clearly impossible at the known rate of drift, and particularly since the *Californian* had got very good celestial observations the previous evening to establish her latitude accurately. Groves at no point implies his ship went south. Indeed, as the last officer of the watch before she stopped, it was his duty to see that the ship remained on a course of due west above the latitude line of 42° N. Groves testified that the overnight stop position was bound to be correct (8425). Yet this is incompatible with his times and the known duration of steaming the next morning. Mr Slish gives this example in relation to the suggestion by Groves that he can see the *Mount Temple* at around 7 a.m., if not before:

> 6 a.m.: Latitude 42° 01'. In the almost eight hours since stopping (at 10.21 p.m.) the *Californian* drifts south about 4 miles at the testified rate of a current of half a knot (stop position 42° 05' N).
> 6–6.30 a.m.: Latitude 41° 59' as the *Californian* steams 3 miles south-west through heavy ice at six knots. She thus goes about 2 miles south. One minute of latitude (the north-south axis) always equates to 1 nautical mile.
> 6.30–7 a.m.: Latitude 41° 52½'. The *Californian* steams south at 13 knots for half an hour and reaches the *Mount Temple* at Groves' implied time.

But Captain Moore of *Mount Temple*, a master with twenty-seven years' experience on the North Atlantic, is thus rendered in gross error; he thinks he is at 41° 46', the *Titanic's* transmitted SOS latitude, but is supposedly 6½ miles further north!

Now try the times by Captain Lord and Stewart's testimony:

> 6 a.m.: Latitude 42° 01', as above.
> 6–6.30 a.m.: Latitude 41° 59', as above.
> 6.30–7.30 a.m.: Latitude 41° 46'. The *Californian* has steamed at 13 knots for an hour and reached the *Mount Temple*. This is exactly where Captain Moore said he was – at the *Titanic's* transmitted SOS latitude.

Mr Slish points out that Lord and Stewart's times perfectly agree with the proper positions and times of not only the *Mount Temple* but also the *Carpathia*, when Groves is once more out of step with all others. Groves also testified, in response to questions 8323–4, that he saw the *Carpathia* abeam on the port side (due east) and then the *Mount Temple* a little ahead (south) on the starboard side (questions 8339–48). This would place the *Carpathia* slightly north of the *Mount Temple*. This contradicts Captains Lord, Moore and Rostron, none of whom suggest the *Carpathia* was picking up survivors north of 41° 46'.

Witnesses agree that the *Californian* arrived just as the last passengers were brought aboard the *Carpathia*. If the *Californian* had indeed arrived at 7.45 a.m. (Groves' time for the rendezvous), she could have taken up a boatload or two of survivors herself!

The *Californian* did not pick up any survivors, because when she arrived at the *Carpathia* it was 8.30 a.m. and all the survivors were already aboard the Cunarder. Rostron said in his US evidence (p.718): 'We gradually got all the boats together. We got all the boats alongside and all the people up aboard by 8.30 a.m.', repeating that time elsewhere. Lord says that when the *Californian* arrived at the *Carpathia* 'she was taking the last of the people out of the boats'.

The entry '8.30. Stopped close to the *Carpathia*' was, furthermore, entered in the *Californian's* official log, maintained by Chief Officer Stewart, and this entry, among others, was read aloud to the US Inquiry by Lord (in his manuscript, *The Middle Watch*, Groves perplexingly goes even further and states that the *Californian* arrived at the *Carpathia* at about 7.30 a.m.!)

Finally, Groves' other timings should be examined:

8367. At about 9 a.m. did the *Carpathia* steam off? —Yes, almost exactly at 9 a.m., because I heard her bell strike.

8368. Did you search longer? —Yes, we searched longer.

8369. Till about 10.40? —Ten-forty exactly. That is when we resumed our course.

A 9 a.m. *Carpathia* departure agrees with Rostron and Lord. Rostron says: 'I left him [*Californian*] when I returned to New York at 8.50, I think it was' (US Inquiry, p.33). And Lord states: 'I talked to the *Carpathia* until 9 o'clock. Then he left' (US Inquiry, p.723). Hearing her bell has helped fix the hour in Groves' mind, but his 10.40 a.m. departure time for the *Californian* is again the subject of contradiction by his shipmates. Lord states:

7267. ...11.20 proceeded on course.

7268. ...[The Commissioner] Is that [by] the ship's log? —This is the ship's log, my Lord.

And Stewart says:

8825. According to your log, you proceeded on your course at 11.20? —Yes.

8826. You stopped close to the *Carpathia* at 8.30? —Yes.

8827. And remained until 11.20? —Yes.

Groves, unsupported by anyone else, is forty minutes behind the departure time. Applying that forty minutes to his 6.50 time would give 7.30 a.m. for being on the bridge and argu-ably seeing the *Mount Temple*. But Groves' times are essentially inexplicable and hopeless. Anyone relying on him for proof of anything is clutching at straws. In Groves' 1957 personal recollections of the affair, entitled *The Middle Watch* (a poorly punctuated account), he does not mention a time for departure, but remains true to his ever-imaginative self:

Scanning the sea with his binoculars the Third Officer [referring to himself] noticed a large icefloe a mile or so distant on which he saw figures moving and drawing Captain Lord's attention to it remarked that they might be human beings was told that they were seals. *Californian* now made one complete turn to starboard followed by one to port and then resumed her passage to Boston...

GAMBELL AND THE *VIRGINIAN*'S TIME

There is one last matter to be cleared up. The book *The Ship That Stood Still*, which purports to set out that the *Californian* was the *Titanic*'s mystery ship, claims that shortly after 6.10 a.m. (according to *Virginian* Captain G.T. Gambell in a press interview) the *Californian* declared: 'can now see *Carpathia* taking passengers on board from small boats…' (p.132). This supposedly damning time is explicable by comparing *Virginian*'s time with New York time, and then with *Californian* time. *Virginian* reported *Titanic* signals ceasing at 1.57 ship's time, equivalent to 12.27 New York (British Inquiry Report). This shows she was one hour thirty minutes ahead of New York, compared to *Californian*'s one hour fifty minutes, so *Californian* time was twenty minutes ahead of *Virginian* time. Captain Lord initially received the *Titanic*'s position from the *Virginian* at 6 a.m. *Californian* time: 'Did you receive a message from the *Virginian* at 6 o'clock that morning? — Yes' (7001). But it was not a mere half an hour later (6.10 a.m. *Virginian* equals 6.30 a.m. *Californian* time, since there is a twenty minute gap between these ships) when Captain Lord next heard from that ship (US Inquiry, p.732):

> Senator Smith: You heard nothing further from the source?
>
> Lord: From the *Virginian*? I had a message about an hour and a half after. He said, 'When you get to the scene of disaster will you please give me particulars of what is happening?'

So Lord was replying to this message and reporting his first visuals of the *Carpathia* rescuing survivors somewhere about 7.30 a.m. *Californian* time. If *Californian* replied to *Virginian* at 7.30 a.m. her time, and we take the twenty minute difference into account, this would be 7.10 a.m., not 6.10 a.m., *Virginian* time. Captain Gambell, talking to reporters at Liverpool, would be out by an hour. The inconsistency is proven to lie with Gambell because he was also quoted in the same report as stating that the *Californian* was '17 miles north of the *Titanic*' at 5.45 a.m. *Virginian* time. This is just twenty-five minutes before *Californian* was supposedly so close as to be able to see the *Carpathia* at about 6.10 a.m. *Virginian* time!

This is the relevant extract from the actual report, in the *Weekly Freeman*, 27 April 1912, p.15:

> At 5.45 a.m. I was in communication with the *Californian*, the Leyland Liner. He was 17 miles north of the *Titanic* and had not heard anything of the disaster. I Marconied her as follows – '*Titanic* struck iceberg. Wants assistance urgently. Ship sinking. Passengers in boats. His position latitude 41.46, longitude 50.14.' Shortly after this I was in communication with the *Carpathia*, the *Frankfurt*, and the *Baltic*, all going to the *Titanic*. At 6.10 a.m. I Marconied the *Californian*: 'Kindly let me know condition of affairs when you get to *Titanic*'. He at once replied – 'Can now see the *Carpathia* taking the passengers on board from small boats'. The *Titanic* foundered about 2 a.m.

The converse proof, of course, is that the *Californian* barely cleared the ice at 6.30 her time (6.10 *Virginian*) to arrive on the western side of the field. The *Mount Temple* was still far over the visible horizon to the south, and she confirms she was invisible to the *Californian* because we have seen there was no reverse sighting. *Californian* could thus see no ship at all at the relevant *Virginian* time.

It may also be, of course, that a passed-on wireless report about '*Carpathia* picking up boats' has led to an assumption that the ship re-transmitting such a report is herself seeing it, which is not necessarily the case. Captain Gambell was not, after all, his own ship's wireless man.

Be reminded: *Californian* achieved 13 knots (2 knots above usual top speed) that morning. She could not, in twenty-five minutes, have come from a position 17 miles north of the SOS position, across an icefield, in order to then be able to see the *Carpathia*, which Captain Moore (who was actually at the SOS position) said was 5-6 miles further to the south-east!

An initial call is agreed by both ships (around 6 a.m. *Californian*), and Lord's evidence of the next conversation with *Virginian* occurring an hour and a half later is consistent with the rest of his evidence. Lord made this statement in evidence in Washington, not knowing what a press report at Liverpool would attribute to Captain Gambell. More importantly, it should also be noted that *none* of the other ships listening to traffic on the morning of 15 April recorded a conversation between *Californian* and *Virginian* at 6.10 a.m. by the latter's time. Instead the logs of both the *Baltic* and the *Mount Temple* record that the *Californian* was speaking to the *Birma* at the time in question – and do not mention the *Virginian!*

The '6.10 a.m. sighting' is an error on someone's part – because there now follows further proof that the *Californian* could not have been talking to the *Virginian* and seeing *Carpathia* shortly after 6.10 a.m. *Virginian* time (6.30 *Californian* time). This is because at some time close to 6.30 a.m. *Virginian* time (supposedly twenty minutes after the *Californian's* report about seeing the *Carpathia*), the *Virginian* herself was talking to the *Birma*. *Virginian* told the *Birma* at 6.30 that the *Californian* was now 'only fifteen miles' from the SOS position – a location that was several miles to the north-west of the *Carpathia!* Why would the *Virginian* give out this information if the *Californian* had reported being able to see the *Carpathia* twenty minutes earlier? It's double *Californian's* visible horizon!

Critics of Captain Lord seize on this one strange time of 6.10 a.m. They act once more as if all times were interchangeable. The time was in a newspaper report, and Gambell and his officers never gave evidence at a sworn inquiry. Obviously, if the 6.10 a.m. allegation is right, it would be extremely relevant. But not only is the claim untested hearsay, it is also demonstrably contradicted not once, but twice, by *Virginian's* own wireless log! It is also contradicted by testified evidence concerning *Californian*, *Birma*, *Baltic* and *Mount Temple*. No-one logs this alleged conversation (at what would be 4.40 a.m. New York time). Captain Gambell was not his ship's wireless operator and never a sworn witness. A so-called 6.10 a.m. sighting flies in the face of a mountain of other evidence, particularly the declaration of *Carpathia* Captain Arthur Rostron that he first saw the *Californian* at 8 a.m. If the *Californian* could see the *Carpathia* at 6.10 a.m., then the *Carpathia* should have been seeing *Californian*… Thus the canard of the *Californian* being within sight of the *Carpathia* in the very early morning of 15 April is totally exploded. If she was, how come *Carpathia* didn't see her? Rostron says he first saw *Californian* 'about 8 a.m.' (25551). Captain Lord is entitled to be judged on the sworn evidence, and not a single newspaper reference. Meanwhile, as we have seen, all the independent evidence heard at the inquiries verifies the *Californian's* account – and does so, literally, time and time again.

15

WRECKAGE

There was no wreckage in the SOS position transmitted by the *Titanic* for the obvious reason that the *Titanic* did not sink there, but further east. Captain Moore of the *Mount Temple*, who brought his vessel to the distress-message spot told this to both inquiries.

Senator Smith: No wreckage?
Moore: Nothing whatever, sir, in the way of wreckage.

And at the British Inquiry, he says the same: 'Did you see any signs of wreckage? — None whatever' (9242). Moore also estimated the *Titanic* to have sunk at least 8 miles to the east. But despite his evidence and that of Captain Lord and Captain Rostron, the inquiries persisted pig-headedly in the belief that the *Titanic* had sunk exactly in the SOS position given – and that the current must have taken the wreckage swiftly to the east. But even in the position where the *Carpathia* finally came to rest, there was little wreckage. Lord describes the scene when the *Californian* got there at 8.30 a.m. (US Inquiry, p.723):

I saw several empty boats, some floating planks, a few deck-chairs, and cushions; but considering the size of the disaster, there was very little wreckage. It seemed more like an old fishing boat had sunk.

Rostron of the *Carpathia* also said the very same (US Inquiry, p.22):

I was then very close to where the *Titanic* must have gone down, as there was a lot of… hardly wreckage, but small pieces of broken-up stuff; nothing in the way of anything large.

And at the British Inquiry:

25496. Did you see any wreckage, at all, of the *Titanic*? — The only wreckage we saw there was very small stuff – a few deck-chairs and pieces of cork from lifebelts, and a few lifebelts knocking about, and things of that description, all very small stuff indeed. There was very little indeed.

This was because the *Titanic* lifeboats had pulled considerably away from the site of the sinking, while the current appears to have been drifting slowly south-west (although Officer Boxhall had an alternative view, see later).

We do not know the exact longitude and latitude of where the last boat was picked up, because *Carpathia* did not log the position, and neither, apparently, did the *Californian* when she joined her. Moore estimated the pack of ice between his ship (*Mount Temple*) and that of Rostron as 'five to six miles' wide. We know however that the meeting of Lord and Rostron's vessels was south-east of the SOS position, while also south-west of the 1985 wreck position.

Location 'X', representing the historic conjunction of the *Californian* and *Carpathia* (see Fenwick photograph), is the bottom point of a 'V', or inverted pyramid, between the SOS position and the place along the same line of latitude, further east, where the *Titanic* collided (Captain Lord appears to have approximated the spot; a sketch map he made in 1912 is reproduced towards the end of this book, showing a position for the *Carpathia* at 8.30 a.m.).

When the two ships met, *Carpathia* informed *Californian* she had taken all of the *Titanic's* lifeboats and survivors on board. *Californian* then offered to search 'down to leeward' and cruised off. The *Californian*, on leaving the *Carpathia*, certainly searched further east and further south. She encountered wreckage and left that debris at a location 13 miles south of the SOS latitude and nearly a similar distance to the east. She left the wreckage at 11.20 p.m. By noon she was several miles further west, travelling slowly, according to Lord's description.

It can be seen that the logged latitude at which the *Californian* left the search at 11.20 (41° 33') was far to the south of the *Californian's* overnight stop position of 42° 05' N. A minute of latitude is 1 nautical mile, so the separation on the north–south axis from the *Californian* stop position to the abandonment of the search was 32 miles (the *Titanic* actually sank over 23 miles from the *Californian's* reported stop position). There is a ten-minutes latitude gap between the *Titanic's* sinking position at 2.20 a.m. (wreck site) and Lord's point of 'leaving the wreckage' exactly nine hours later at 11.20 a.m. It might appear wreckage had thus drifted 10 miles in nine hours, contradicting general drift evidence of half a knot (½mph)...This suggests that Lord's 'leaving the wreckage' is a loose phrase meaning 'abandoning the search', while the wreckage seen at higher latitude was not main *Titanic* wreckage. Yet both Lord and Rostron referred to 'deck-chairs' where they met, which could hardly be from lifeboats. How could they drift there and not lifebelt-supported bodies? Surface items drift more quickly – but the wreckage evidence on the whole is unsatisfactory.

Lord said in a 1959 affidavit that, while carrying out his search, 'we passed about six wooden lifeboats afloat, one capsized in the wreckage...' This then is certainly lifeboat wreckage, and the lifeboats had pulled far from the main wreck. Captain Rostron says: 'Of course lots of gear had been knocked out of the [life]boats and thrown out of the way of the people as they were getting up...' (US Inquiry, p.24). Lord also declared that his position for leaving the wreckage (wreck area?) was an estimate, and not one taken at the wreckage scene itself, but arrived at through backtracking once his officers had taken the noon position forty minutes later, having left the scene at 11.20: 'From this [noon] position, I placed the wreckage in position 41° 33' N, 50° 01'W'. Captain Arthur Rostron of the rescue ship *Carpathia* confirms that abandoned lifeboats had been scattered over a

wide area, essentially meaning to the east – where Lord found them – since the icefield itself
was a barrier to the west:

> 25500. [The Commissioner] I understand you to say those [life]boats were spread over an
> area of five miles? — Four to five miles, yes.

He had also said earlier: 'They were within a range of four or five miles' (25491).

It is a common supposition that the *Carpathia* reached the area, stopped once, and had all
the lifeboats row towards her. But this is a fallacy: she did not.

Instead Rostron says: 'We had been dodging about picking up the other boats. As soon as
we had finished taking the passengers from the boats I cleared off to another boat to pick them
up, and was dodging about all over the place to pick them up…' (25499). And a little earlier:
'We picked them up here and there within a range of four or five miles, as I say' (25494).

When the *Carpathia* finally stopped, Rostron says his ship was 'only two or three miles
from a huge icefield' (25501). So some of the lifeboats were abandoned further east (only
thirteen boats of twenty were brought to New York) in the area where Lord searched,
with Officer Groves saying the search yielded 'only boats and wreckage' (8364–8367). The
point is that this *may not* have been wreckage that had drifted from the main *Titanic* sinking site. From Lord and Rostron's guesstimates, plus the linking of wreckage to lifeboats,
as well as the very little overall wreckage, it would seem that most of the wreckage was
instead elsewhere and had not drifted that far south or west.

It may be assumed that the current was not anything of the order of 1 knot. Otherwise the
Californian could have been expected to see bodies, and she did not see any. Here is Lord:

> 7283. Had you also any observations to enable you to fix the spot where the wreckage
> was found? — I had very good observations at noon and that afternoon.
> 7265. Can you give your noon observations? —Yes, 41° 33' N. and 50° 9' W.
> 7266. That is your noon position? —That is my noon position on the 15th April.

Earlier, Lord has stated:

> 7029 Did you see any wreckage anywhere? — I did.
> 7030. Where? — Near the *Carpathia*.
> 7031. What did you see? — I saw several boats, deck-chairs, cushions, planks.
> 7033. Did you see any bodies? — No.
> 7034. Any lifebelts floating? — No.
> 7035. Any wreckage? —Yes.
> 7036. Much? - Not a great deal.
> 7037. Did you cruise round and search? — I did.
> 7038. To see if you could find any bodies or any living persons? — I did. I did not see
> anything at all.

7039. I should like to understand from you, if you say that the position indicated to you was wrong, what do you say was the position? —The position where I left the wreckage was 41° 33' N, 50° 1' W.

Groves says:

8433. ...How far do you think you had travelled from the time that you got on your way after searching round the wreckage until your noon position? Do you think it would be about five miles? — No, more than that, about 11. That is in distance.

Groves is wrong *again* here. Probably because of his 10.40 departure time. Lord left the wreckage at 11.20 and could not possibly have covered 11 miles in the forty minutes until he took his noon position. His ship had a top speed of 13–13½ knots. Lord also said (in response to question 7270) that when he left the scene of the wreckage he 'went slow… I went back slow'.

Groves continues:

8434. You would be in the same latitude then as the wreckage was found? —That I could not say… [The noon sights and the leaving position of 11.20 are indeed at the same latitude of 41° 33' N, indicating a straight line steered since breaking off the search]
8436. If the *Titanic* was in latitude 41° 33', which is… the position in which the wreckage was found, and your vessel was [stopped overnight], as stated in the log, in latitude 42° 5', the *Titanic* would be some 33 miles to the southward of the position where you were lying stopped? — If she [*Titanic*] stopped in 41° 33' and we were in 42° 5'?
8437. Yes? —Yes, about 30 miles.
8438. And if the *Titanic* was 30 miles to the southward of the position where you were stopped, I do not suppose you could see any navigation lights at that distance? — No, none whatsoever.

Incidentally, *Titanic* struck the iceberg in 41° 46', not 41° 33' as suggested. Wreck site in 41° 43'.

Chief Officer Stewart gives the following evidence:

8823. That is your noon position? —Yes.
8823. Are you able from working back from that noon position to fix accurately the position of the wreckage, which you came up to at 8.30? —Yes.
8824. How many miles had you travelled between the time you proceeded on your course and when you took this position? — About four or five miles… [A much better guess than Groves!]
8830. Is the position stated in your log as the position in which you were searching for

the boats of the *Titanic* accurate or not: latitude 41° 33' north and longitude 50° 01' west? —Yes.

8831.Was that the latitude and longitude in which you found the wreckage? —Yes.

8832. How many miles was the position of the wreckage from the place where you had been stopped from 10.21 the night before until six o'clock that morning? — About thirty miles.

8833. Do you know in what direction, thirty miles? —About south, a little east.

8834.Assuming the *Titanic* struck the iceberg in the position which was reported by the *Virginian* at 6 a.m., according to your log, latitude 41° 46' north and longitude 50° 14' west [SOS transmission], how far was that position from the place where you were stopped? Stewart —About 19 or 20 miles.

8835.And bearing how? — Bearing about south-south-west — south, a little west.

8836. Could the *Titanic*, assuming she was in either of those two positions, or was to the eastward of either of those two positions, by any possibility have been visible to anyone on board your ship while you were lying stopped in the ice? — No.

And this is Lord:

7378. How many miles had you, in fact, to steam to get to the place where the wreckage was found? — I should think 30 miles at the least.

Lord, Stewart and even Groves are in rare harmony as to the distance between their overnight stopping place and the location of wreckage or search. Lord and Stewart put it at about 30 miles, and Groves agreed both the noon position and the overnight stop. Lord also emphasised the difference between the *Titanic's* SOS position and what he believed was the *real* sinking position. He would be vindicated seventy-three years later with the discovery of the *Titanic* wreck:

6821. The spot mentioned here [the SOS position] as 19 miles away is not, in my opinion, where the *Titanic* hit the berg. [Imagine this heresy!]

6822.Within a radius of 20 miles of you? — No, 30 miles.

6823. Do you mean she was further from you? — She was 32 miles from where I left the wreckage.

He emphasised his belief again, but counsel could not, or would not, grasp what he was saying:

7018. And then you eventually saw the *Carpathia*... Did you eventually get to the position of the foundering of the *Titanic*? —The real position or the position given?

7019.The position given? — I passed that position.

7021.That is the position given of 41° 46' and 50° 14'? —Yes.

7023. How did you know what was the position? — I got a good observation at noon that day.

7024. I do not quite understand what you mean. You said just now that you passed the position indicated to you by the wireless messages? —Yes.

7025. Where the *Titanic* had sunk? —Yes.

7026. Did you see anything at all there? — The *Mount Temple* was in the vicinity of that position.

7027. She was near there? —Yes.

7028. Did you see any wreckage? — Not where the *Mount Temple* was.

7029. Did you see any wreckage anywhere? — I did.

7030. Where? — Near the *Carpathia*.

7036. Much? — Not a great deal.

7037. Did you cruise round and search? — I did.

7038. To see if you could find any bodies or any living persons? — I did. I did not see anything at all.

7039. I should like to understand from you, if you say that the position indicated to you was wrong, what do you say was the position? — The position where I left the wreckage was 41° 33' N, 50° 1' W.

Not only Lord, but Captain Moore of the *Mount Temple* and Captain Ludwig Stulping of the *Birma* separately came to the conclusion that the *Titanic* had sunk a good deal further east than the longitude (east–west axis) indicated in the SOS transmissions. Captain Stulping sent in a statement that was ignored. But there was already enough material to allow the British court at least to conclude that the *Titanic's* transmitted SOS position was in error. Instead it concluded the *Californian* was 'not accurate' with her navigation. And this is the moment when Lord Mersey thinks he has finally skewered the *Californian* – using Captain Lord's own carefully-logged 'wreckage' departure position (British Inquiry Final Report, p.45):

> Captain Lord stated that about 7.30 a.m. he passed the... vicinity of the position given him as where the *Titanic* had collided [the SOS position, and later the *Mount Temple* position]... He saw no wreckage there, but did later on near the *Carpathia*, which ship he closed soon afterwards. And he stated that the position where he subsequently left this wreckage was 41° 33' N, 50° 1' W... If it is admitted that these positions were correct, then it follows that the *Titanic's* position as given by that ship when making the [SOS] signal was approximately 19 miles from the *Californian*; and further that the position in which the *Californian* was stopped during the night, was thirty miles away from where the wreckage was seen by her in the morning... [note that Mersey has no doubt about the *Titanic's* position 'when making the SOS'; in fact his certainty on this point sets up the coming *coup de grace*...] or that the wreckage had drifted eleven miles in a little more than five hours.

Mersey is subtracting 19 miles (*Californian's* stop distance from the SOS position) from 'about 30 miles' (distance to the search abandonment position), to arrive at 11 miles. The north–south separation of 41° 46' (SOS position) from 41° 33' ('wreckage' departure latitude) is actually 13 miles, and Mersey is being incredibly imprecise – not least in treating different directions from *Californian*'s stop position as being along the same yardstick.

Californian did not steam directly south to accord with Mersey's crude subtraction. The SOS position was considerably to the west of the wreckage area. Longitude comes into it, besides latitude. *Californian* reached the SOS position, found nothing, and steered an 'L' shape from there to meet the *Carpathia*. The actual separation from the SOS position to *Californian*'s 11.20 position is a south-east diagonal of 16 nautical miles!

Meanwhile Lord Mersey's five-hour time-frame is impossible to understand. The *Californian* position was determined at 11.20 a.m. and the *Titanic* sank at 2.20 a.m. (allowing wreckage to begin drifting), which is nine hours. It seems that Lord Mersey is only allowing the wreckage to drift from 6.20 a.m. or a little before. This is bizarre. It appears to link the *Californian* beginning to get underway in the morning (to steam to the SOS location) with the time the wreckage began drifting. In other words, Mersey seems to think the *Californian* had been in the latitude of wreckage from the beginning. It appears he has allowed his pre-formed conclusion about her being the mystery ship to get in the way of clear thinking.

Alternatively, since Lord Mersey favoured Groves, the difference may be between *Titanic* foundering at 2.20 a.m. (at the SOS position, he believed!) and *Californian* arriving at the *Carpathia*'s side at 7.45 a.m. according to Groves.

Mersey may be equating where *Carpathia* was with the wreckage. From 2.20 to 7.45 a.m. is five hours and twenty-five minutes. Might this be 'little more than five hours'? But according to this concept, once the wreckage drifted to the *Carpathia* position it just stayed there until 11.20 a.m.!

Yet the sting is in the tail, however much Mersey has misconceived the situation. The crucial point is the question of wreckage drifting 'eleven miles in five hours' – from the *Titanic* SOS position to Lord's scene-departing position. Mersey was unable to accept that the wreckage could have drifted 11 miles in 'five hours' when there was evidence that the current was of the order of half a knot. The distance from the SOS position (Mersey accepted the latter unquestioningly) meant the wreckage had speeded at more than *four times* the usual rate of drift, by Lord Mersey's reckonings. Never mind that his distance and time-frame are both horribly misjudged (neither did he appreciate that the wreckage was not bodies and main wreckage, but might have been merely lifeboat flotsam – the lifeboats having pulled away from the wreck site). So, in Mersey's determination, Lord and officers are likely lying about their positions. In Mersey's view, the *Titanic*'s SOS position could never be open to challenge. The *Titanic* would not transmit an incorrect position because it is demonstrably in the *Titanic*'s interest to get her distress position right.

But the *Titanic* did indeed get it wrong. The incontrovertible evidence offered by the discovery of the wreck site in 1985 proved her sinking position (latitude 41° 43' N, longitude 49° 56' W). Mersey did not know this at the time, so he chose to conclude instead that the wreckage could not have moved so quickly from what must be the sinking position (the place specified by SOS). It therefore must follow that Captain Lord and officers were lying about the wreckage and, in addition, are most likely lying about their overnight position!

Thus Lord is finally defeated (in the mind of the court), by impersonal mathematics – a science which does not rely on lights or rockets, cannot make mistakes, cannot enter into disputes or contradictions, and which cannot have ulterior motives in its output. Mersey has got his man, even though his figures are wrong, because he thinks they are irrefutable. He chooses to overlook the independent evidence of Captain Stulping and Captain Moore about the SOS position being a nonsense. The apparent impossibility of 'speeding' wreckage enables him to conclude that the *Californian* position of the night before was inaccurate. Of course, we know today that the *Titanic's* wreck is 13 miles east and a little south of the SOS location. And the drifting of her wreckage can only ever have been consistent with the *Titanic's* sinking position (the wreck site).

Moore, Stulping, and Lord (and Rostron, with his flare encounter 'twenty miles' early) were all correct in their comments. Mersey was toweringly wrong. But it was Lord who paid the price!

NO BODIES, NO WORRIES

Neither the *Carpathia* nor the *Californian* saw any massed bodies. *Carpathia* saw one, wearing a lifejacket, almost certainly pushed overboard by a lifeboat. Here is Rostron: 'Any bodies in the water? — We only saw one body' (25497). Rostron states that the *Californian*, left behind to search for wreckage, later transmitted this message to *Carpathia*: 'Have searched position carefully up to noon and found nothing and seen no bodies' (US Inquiry, p.34). And Lord confirms this: 'Did you see any bodies? — No' (7033). Yet there was a sea of bodies floating in the vicinity of the *Titanic* wreck. Several witnesses confirm this. Scarrott states: 'We were amongst hundreds, I should say, of dead bodies floating in lifebelts' (question 439). Frank Evans says: 'There were plenty of dead bodies about us. You couldn't hardly count them, sir' (US Inquiry, p.678); 'I should think between 150 and 200. We had great difficulty in getting through them to get to the wreck' (US Inquiry, p.751). Archibald Gracie states: 'I saw what seemed to be bodies all around' (US Inquiry, p.994). The chairman of the US Inquiry wrestled manfully with the problem, confident at all times that the *Carpathia* had actually reached the sinking site when in fact she had not (US Inquiry, p.780):

> Senator Smith: I think I may be pardoned for saying that when I found the *Carpathia's* Captain saw no bodies, and then found from the testimony of those in the lifeboats that there were hundreds of bodies all around in the water, I came to the conclusion that they had either been sucked in with the sinking ship or that they were inclosed somewhere in the ship.

Captain Moore of the *Mount Temple* attempted to help out. He speculated to Smith: 'It may be that, as you say, the ice has covered the spot where the *Titanic* sank, and that has kept those bodies under. I think that is a very feasible suggestion that you have made as to that' (US Inquiry, p.785). On 19 April, four days after the disaster, the North German Lloyd vessel *Bremen* passed through the vicinity and saw masses of bodies: 'The officers of the *Bremen* estimated that in one group there were two hundred corpses' (*Daily Sketch*, 25 April 1912). It is clear why the *Californian* did not encounter the mass of bodies: she did not go far enough east and north.

Titanic bodies in fact drifted east and only a little south. The recovery ship *MacKay-Bennett* would report: 'Bodies are numerous in Lat. 41° 35' N, Long. 48° 37' W' (*Daily Sketch*, 26 April 1912). The *Titanic* wreck site is at 41 43' N, 49 56' W. It can thus be seen that the bodies drifted only eight minutes south – but a full seventy-nine minutes east. The Gulf Stream current in later days was pushing the flock of corpses almost ten minutes to the eastward for every minute they slipped to the south. Note also that this ten-day old latitude of 41° 35' for the bodies is still 2 miles to the north of latitude 41° 33', where Captain Lord said he left the 'wreckage' at 11.20 the morning after! Yet, unlike the US Inquiry, the absence of bodies in the SOS position or even further south-east in both *Carpathia*'s position and Lord's scene-departure position did not impinge at all on the British investigation.

Perhaps it ought to have done.

16

ERNEST GILL

Breaking off her fruitless search for bodies or survivors, the *Californian* resumed her course to Boston. Notoriety was not far away. It was at Boston that Ernest Gill, a below-decks member of the *Californian's* crew, turned 'whistleblower'. Gill had been planning on making money from the tragedy, according to the evidence of *Californian* wireless operator Cyril Evans (US Inquiry, p.746–7):

> Senator Burton: Was it said [on the *Californian*] that the rockets [seen] were those which had been sent up by the *Titanic*? Was that the talk on board the ship?
> Evans: Some of them seemed to think so, and some not, sir.
> Sen. Burton: Has anyone told [you] that he was to receive $500 for a story in regard to these rockets – anyone on your boat?
> Evans: I think the donkeyman mentioned it.
> Sen. Burton: What did he say?
> Evans: He said 'I think that I will make about $500 on this'.
> Sen. Burton: He said that he thought he would make $500?
> Evans: Yes.
> Sen. Burton: When was that said?
> Evans: The night before last… I had gone ashore, and I was outside the station, I think. It was after I had landed, yes, sir. He asked if I was not going back anymore [Gill never returned to the ship after making his charges and was marked as a deserter at Boston]. He said he had been up and had told the newspaper about the accident. He said, 'I think we shall make about $500 out of it'.

Gill duly told a sensational story about the *Californian* seeing rockets on the night the *Titanic* went down. It resulted in him being called to give evidence at the US Senate Subcommittee Inquiry into the greatest maritime disaster the Western world had known. This is the statement from donkeyman Gill that was read into the record of those proceedings (p.710–11):

> I am 29 years of age; a native of Yorkshire, single. I was making my first voyage on the *Californian*.

On the night of April 14, I was on duty from 8 p.m. until 12 [midnight] in the engine room. At 11.56 I came on deck. The stars were shining brightly. It was very clear and I could see for a long distance. The ship's engines had been stopped since 10.30 and she was drifting amid floe ice.

I looked over the rail on the starboard side and saw the lights of a very large steamer about 10 miles away. I could see her broadside lights. I watched her for fully a minute. They could not have helped but see her from the bridge and lookout.

It was now 12 o'clock and I went to my cabin. I woke my mate, William Thomas. He heard the ice crunching alongside the ship and asked, 'Are we in the ice?' I replied, 'Yes but it must be clear off to the starboard, for I saw a big vessel going along full speed. She looked as if she might be a big German'.

I turned in but could not sleep. In half an hour I turned out, thinking to smoke a ciga-rette. Because of the cargo I could not smoke 'tween decks, so I went on deck again. I had been on deck about 10 minutes when I saw a white rocket about 10 miles away on the starboard side. I thought it must be a shooting star. In seven or eight minutes I saw distinctly a second rocket in the same place, and I said to myself, 'That must be a vessel in distress'.

It was not my business to notify the bridge or the lookouts; but they could not have helped but see them. I turned in immediately after, supposing that the ship would pay attention to the rockets.

I knew no more until I was awakened at 6.40 by the Chief Engineer, who said, 'Turn out to render assistance. The *Titanic* has gone down'. I exclaimed and leaped from my bunk. I went on deck and found the vessel under way and proceeding full speed. She was clear of the field ice, but there were plenty of bergs about.

I went down on watch and heard the Second and Fourth Engineers in conversation. Mr J. C. Evans is the Second and Mr Wooten [sic – actually 'Hooton'] is the Fourth. The Second was telling the Fourth that the Third Officer had reported rockets had gone up in his watch. I knew then that it must have been the *Titanic* I had seen.

The Second Engineer added that the Captain had been notified by the apprentice officer whose name, I think, is Gibson, of the rockets. The skipper had told him to Morse to the vessel in distress. Mr Stone, the Second Navigating Officer, was on the bridge at the time, said Mr Evans. I overheard Mr Evans say that more lights had been shown and more rockets went up. Then, according to Mr Evans, Mr Gibson went to the Captain again and reported more rockets. The Skipper told him to continue to Morse until he got a reply. No reply was received.

The next remark I heard the Second [Engineer Evans] pass was, 'Why in the devil didn't they wake the wireless man up?' The entire crew of the steamer have been talk-ing among themselves about the disregard of the rockets. I personally urged several to join me in protesting against the conduct of the Captain, but they refused, because they feared to lose their jobs.

I am quite sure that the *Californian* was less than 20 miles from the *Titanic*, which the officers report to have been our position. I could not have seen her if she had been more than 10 miles distant and I saw her very plainly.

I have no ill will toward the Captain or any officer of the ship, and I am losing a profitable berth by making this statement. I am actuated by the desire that no Captain who refuses or neglects to give aid to a vessel in distress should be able to hush up the men. *Signed* Ernest Gill.

There are a large number of difficulties with Gill's self-serving account. The main problems are listed below:

His vessel is moving at full speed before midnight at a time when Groves and Lord had both observed their nearby steamer to be stopped (all three are citing *Californian* time).

She is showing a lot of light whereas Groves said her lights had all gone out 15 minutes earlier.

She's also 'broadside', whereas Groves agreed with a suggestion that his steamer had turned, shutting in her lights.

Gill saw the vessel going along 'full speed' towards an ice barrier, yet it was no concern of his! Lord, Stone, Gibson and Groves' steamer was doing no such thing.

A ship at full speed from a distance of ten miles will look stationary. One minute is not sufficient time to detect speed.

Gill reports hearsay that the 'Third Officer had reported rockets'. The Third Officer was Groves. He neither saw any rockets nor reported them. The Second Officer did.

Gill sees white rockets in the same place as he had seen his large passenger steamer half an hour earlier. The steamer has gone. He concludes this must mean 'a vessel in distress' – not necessarily *the* vessel he had seen, which he implies has departed – yet Stone and Gibson continued to see their vessel long thereafter.

He does not feel the need to respond in any constructive fashion to what he concludes must be a vessel in distress and in fact tells no-one.

Gibson did not notify the captain initially as Gill thinks; Stone did. Gill is again reporting erroneous hearsay.

Gibson was not told by Captain Lord to Morse the stranger. Not once, let alone twice.

The entire crew had been talking among themselves about the disregard of rockets, says Gill. He sees no irony in his own disregard of the rockets.

Unperturbed by this, he urged other members of the crew to protest the captain's alleged conduct based solely on the garbled gossip he had heard.

He is certain the *Titanic* was less than 20 miles from the *Californian* but offers no basis on which to distrust the opinion of his officers except his own linkage of the rockets to the steamer he had seen earlier. Despite the fact that the rockets had appeared in a place left behind half an hour earlier by a passenger steamer going at full speed!

He has no ill will towards the captain, yet attempted to organise something akin to a mutiny.

He says he is losing a profitable berth by making the statement. Yet Gill is not being frank. He made the equivalent of nearly two years' salary in one lump sum with his sensational allegations. His pay had been £5 10s per month, the equivalent in 1912 of $27.50.

He claims that $500 was not what actuated him, but a desire to punish anyone who neglects to give aid to a vessel in distress. Yet Gill himself did not offer even the basic aid to a 'vessel in distress' by checking that the responsible officers of the watch were aware of it.

It is not even true (line one) that he was making his first voyage on the *Californian*. His name appears on the ship's articles for the 29 November 1911 Atlantic crossing, returning to Britain on 15 January 1912. His previous ship on that occasion was cited as the White Star Line's *Cedric*.

Gill's remarkable self-centredness jumps out from every line of his official affidavit, just as it does from Evans' evidence about him. One might find it nauseating that he should dress up such self-interest in the guise of someone motivated solely by concern for his fellow humanity.

He did not interact with the officers of the watch that night, but says he spoke to his cabin mate. Gill swore that he woke his bunkmate William Thomas immediately after midnight and told him that he could see a big vessel, perhaps a German, going along at full speed.

Unfortunately, William Thomas disagrees! A 'highly indignant' Thomas told the *Boston Herald* (26 April) that Gill had only mentioned that his own ship was stopped in the ice. No mention of the speeding big German!

'I don't believe he could see a ship ten miles off if there was one, because the change from the engine room to the deck partly blinds a man', said Thomas, who was called to the British Inquiry but never put into the box to give evidence (unlike Gill). Thomas added, in relation to Gill's other claims: 'I think [he] would have told me if he had seen rockets'. Gill duly followed up on his US Inquiry outing by telling his story to the British Inquiry. It is summarised here: 'Just before midnight I saw a large steamer. She was too large. Several groups of lights. A passenger boat. She was a good distance off...' (questions 18136–18137). But in his US affidavit he said the steamer was 'about ten miles away'. He now says: 'not more than ten miles and probably less' (question 18137). Why is he bringing her closer? He adds: 'I supposed she would be moving' (question 18138). He *supposed* she would be moving? In America he said she was going full speed. Now he cannot tell?

> 18138. Did you notice whether she appeared to be moving? — I did not stand to look at the ship [interesting... in his American affidavit he says: 'I watched her for fully a minute'] but I supposed she would be moving.

Gill squirms when tested on the movement question again:

> 18208. Was the vessel that carried these lights moving? — Well, I did not stay long enough to see whether she was moving or in what direction she was going. She was there, she was a ship passing, and I had no interest in her...
> 18209. You could not make out whether she was moving or not? — No.

Remember, in America, Gill had said the vessel was at 'full speed'. The summary of his British evidence continues: 'I called my mate [to take over engine room duty]. Talked to him. Went back on deck and smoked a cigarette. Then couldn't see anything of the steamer at all… She had steamed away. She had either steamed away or I do not know what she had done' (18150–18155). This was between 12.40 and 1 a.m. Then he was 'looking around' and saw a falling star. He paid no attention. Five full minutes went by. And then: 'I could see… what was unmistakably a rocket' (18157). At question 18162, he was asked: 'Did you watch for any more?'. Gill replied: 'I stayed for about 3 or 4 minutes after that, but it was extremely cold, and I was just dressed in a thin flannel suit and I did not care to stay any longer on deck. I went below'. Gill said in his US evidence: 'I had been on deck about 10 minutes', having a smoke when the first rocket appeared. Ten minutes in a 'thin flannel suit' in the perishing cold? He took that rocket to be a falling star and thought nothing of it. Five minutes then went by (making a total of fifteen minutes on deck) before he saw an unmistakable rocket, followed by another '3 or 4 minutes', for which time he stays on deck. So he spends a minimum of eighteen minutes on deck having his smoke – an eighteen-minute after-midnight smoke in his thin threads on a freezing deck. Is this likely?

Remember, he says: 'I had pretty nearly finished my smoke and was looking around and I saw what I took to be a falling star [rocket No.1]. I did not pay any attention. A few minutes after, probably five minutes, I threw my cigarette away' (18157). So he has stayed on deck, in the cold, in his thin flannels, after throwing away his smoke, to see a second rocket which he could not have expected, having previously noticed only a falling star! Why did he stay out in that weather if his smoke was finished? He offers no explanation.

He says he then stayed a further three or four minutes on deck in sub-zero temperatures, ill-clad, even though he did not care to do so because of the cold. Why? He could not reasonably have been expecting anything to happen. Remember Second Officer Lightoller aboard *Titanic* had been worried that the plunging temperatures would freeze that vessel's fresh water supply. It was indeed extremely cold.

Gill's story is odd. He does not seek out the company of others on deck (who presumably have a degree of shelter from the cold) when he is having his everlasting smoke on an open deck. He does not talk to anyone or see anyone who might verify his presence. No *Californian* witness on watch that night sees Gill, who had 'turned in', but goes from his bedclothes to a thin flannel suit for virtually one-third of an hour on deck. No-one sees the red glow of the cigarette.

Gill is so interested in a falling star that he waits to see more, but is not interested enough when he sees 'distress rockets' to tell any officer or lookout, nor even to wake any pals below. He did not even seek out any crew member on duty to tell them this astonishing news, not even the one he alleges he had previously roused and chatted with about the minor matter of 'a big German' ship passing. By the time of the British Inquiry, Gill's US evidence – that he immediately realised these rockets meant a vessel in distress – had noticeably changed. He said: 'Whether it was a distress signal or a signal rocket I could not say, but it was a rocket'. But counsel for the Leyland Line would not let him get away with such a fudging of his own responsibilities:

18193. Did it occur to you that what you saw was something which you ought to report to the officer who was in charge of your ship? — No, I had no business to report it…

18195. You did not attach much importance at the time apparently to what you say you had seen? — No, not any importance [a direct contradiction of his US evidence; having immediately meant 'a vessel in distress', his sighting now had 'no importance']. It was a signal, and other people on the ship, the proper people, would attend to that. It was nothing to do with me.

18196. And it was not 'til after you had heard of the loss of the *Titanic* that it occurred to you that this signal that you had seen might have been of some importance? — Yes. [His US evidence: 'I saw distinctly a second rocket in the same place, and I said to myself, 'That must be a vessel in distress']

The same counsel extracted this wriggle:

18212. Have you ever stated that the vessel you saw was heading in the same direction as the *Californian*? — Yes, I have made that remark. [Heading meaning the direction in which the ship's bows are pointing – *Californian* was stopped]

18213. Is that right or wrong? Do you want to correct it? — Well, I am not sure whether she was going in that direction or not. On second thoughts I cannot be sure.

18214. On second thoughts you appreciate now that if that other vessel was heading in the same direction as you were, she was heading towards Europe? — Well, I do not know.

If he saw it, it should be easy for Gill to say what direction the 'very large steamer' was going in. Gill's evidence particularly fell apart in London, although this was not in the interests of the British Inquiry, which had proclaimed the absolute trustworthiness of this witness before he had even opened his mouth (see the Attorney General's quote, later in this narrative). Gill's problem was that he had said in his American affidavit that he had seen a passenger ship proceeding quickly in the first place, and it had *not* been there when he noticed rockets. For it not to be there, the ship has to go away – except that every other witness on every ship testified that the ice barrier extended vastly to the south of the *Californian*, blocking the route west to the *Titanic* and other shipping. The magical solution for Gill, to allow his passenger ship to leave the scene, was for the icefield itself to disappear! It extended to the south, to be sure, but by his account only for a few miles, then dissolving to allow the big passenger liner he saw steam at full speed through open water – departing conveniently in order that he could later see rockets, but no ship.

This artful device also absolved Gill of any conceivable responsibility for seeing a vessel rushing headlong at a blockade that would spell her doom, while himself doing nothing about her obvious danger. In his American affidavit, Gill mentions a conversation with his bunkmate which the bunkmate denies. Gill says he was asked by Thomas 'Are we in the ice?', replying 'Yes, but it must be clear off to the starboard, for I saw a big vessel going along full speed'. Thomas said later he did not believe Gill saw any ship, and that he had only mentioned their being in the ice. Not that the sea was clear and ice-free elsewhere. The ice simply was not clear to the south, as we know from the *Mount Temple*, the *Carpathia*, the *Birma, Frankfurt, Virginian*, and *Californian* herself, in their accounts of the icefield that night and next morning.

At question 18138 in the British Inquiry, Gill repeats that there was 'nothing to stop her':

> I did not expect a ship to be lit up like she was and stationary, and nothing to stop her, because I could see the edge of the ice floe, the edge of the field of ice; it appeared to be 4 or 5 miles away.

So the limit of the field is 4 or 5 miles away. And Gill had meanwhile said in reply to the previous question that the ship he saw was 'a good distance off, I should say not more than 10 miles, and probably less'. A simple way around the problem; the ice only goes 5 miles, but the moving steamer is close to 10 miles away, allowing her to pass unobstructed. And he will spell out this *deus ex machina* again:

> 18148. So that the ice that you were in extended for about five miles on your starboard side [to the south]? — About that.

This clearly allows a few miles clear water for the vessel he saw to surge onward and far away, out of sight. As he will happily confirm: 'I did not think the ship would be standing still with nothing to stop her' (18211). Donkeyman Gill then, by his own words, could see where the icefield ended – yet Captain Lord and his officers could not. Those idiots on his ship could not see their way (even with binoculars) around an obvious corner – obvious to a donkeyman from below deck – and these holders of various Board of Trade certificates of competency, up to and including Captain Lord's Extra Master's certificate, had to wait until morning! The amazing shrinking icefield may, in Gill's mind, protect his evidence on all sides. In reality, however, it sounds its death knell.

One option is that Gill is right in his claim that the steamer rushed away unimpeded and disappeared. If so, it cannot be the *Titanic*! Do not forget that Gill says he saw his vessel rushing away fully forty minutes before he claims to see his rockets (according to his US affidavit). Where then is the eminently-desired corroboration of the theory that Gill's vessel, being supposedly the *Titanic*, was the *Californian*'s near ship and vice versa?

The other alternative, of course, is that Gill is wrong – the icefield was there, and it proved impenetrable, as it was to all shipping that night. In which case he ought to be able to see that stopped vessel when he later sees rockets. But now he cannot see a ship!

This is what he says in London about when he went up on deck for a smoke, prior to seeing rockets:

> 18155 Did you see the steamer then? — No, I could not see anything of the steamer at all. She had disappeared. She had either steamed away, or I do not know what she had done. She was not there.
>
> 18156. [The Commissioner] What time was this? — After one bell.

[Mr Rowlatt] Between half-past 12 and 1.

[The Commissioner] I do not understand that.

Lord Mersey is right not to understand it, because the *Titanic* has not sunk by this time. If Gill's ship is the *Titanic*, a liner undoubtedly stopped by ice – whether iceberg or icefield – then she must still be visible at this time. She is just beginning to lower lifeboats. Let us not put a tooth in it: Gill did not see any ship at all. The widely-testified extent of the ice barrier proves him a liar. He has invented the story of a big passenger liner to add to his own newsworthiness, to thrill readers who will help fund his sensational story of the garishly-lit leviathan impelled to her doom. Merely seeing rockets is not worth $500 – for that kind of money, the Lady herself must make an appearance.

Gill, in evidence, does not appear to have the heart to conclusively put the big ship and the rocket-source together as one and the same. His bunkmate would say that he cannot join the two because Gill did not see a big ship at all. Gill says the rockets he saw came 'from the water's edge – what appeared to be the water's edge – a great distance away' (18157), which is a description that has no ship blocking the view all the way to the horizon. But it is also unquestionably a different distance to that at which he saw the steamer, which was at a 'good' distance, not a 'great' distance:

> 18137 How far off do you judge she [the previously visible steamer] was? — She was a good distance off, I should say not more than 10 miles, and probably less.

This is also a change from his US position, when both his big steamer and his rockets were each about 10 miles away.

Elsewhere in his evidence Gill expresses doubts that his ship was a British vessel, as he knew the *Titanic* was: 'She was a big ship, I could see that at a glance, in fact, I did not think she was a British ship, I thought probably she would be a German boat' (18208). This is hardly important, but the real significance is that Gill's big ship is irrelevant from any viewpoint from which his evidence is assessed.

If he indeed saw the *Titanic*'s rockets, then they were from 'a great distance' and after this other vessel had gone away. The substance of his evidence is then simply to place the *Californian* at a great distance from the *Titanic*, over the 'water's edge' (horizon) and invisible to that vessel just as she was invisible to Gill – in which case the *Californian* is not the *Titanic*'s mystery ship, which came not just within sight, but to a distance of only about 5 miles. And if Gill sees rockets 'a great distance away', he is only echoing Stone who thinks at times that the rockets are coming not from the ship he can indeed see in the foreground, but 'possibly from a greater distance past the ship' (7908). There is an obvious similarity here.

The only other alternative left open is that the big steamer Gill had seen was the *Titanic*. This would mean that she was, at the time he saw her (close to midnight) more than 5 miles away from the *Californian* but less than 10 miles away. Why then is this vessel moving when the *Titanic*, by commonest reckoning, has long been stopped? And more importantly perhaps, why does she disappear so suddenly when the *Titanic* did not? Why also are the rockets seen in a place that must be far in the wake of (behind) this 'full speed' moving vessel that Gill first saw no less than forty minutes earlier? How can the *Titanic* fire rockets to her rear?

If the ship he saw was the *Titanic*, going along at full speed of 22 knots, then she will be more than 14½ miles away by the time of the rockets, if indeed she was able to steam unmolested for forty minutes. But if she stopped, then she should be visible.

Why are we even debating Gill? This big steamer simply cannot be the *Titanic*. She cannot be because she is moving aggressively when the *Titanic* is sinking, but she cannot be, more plainly, because Gill has simply invented her! Gill's rushing ship must be discarded. Because as Lord Mersey knows ('I cannot understand that'), the argument can be distilled this simply – if the *Californian* is seeing the *Titanic* at a short distance at midnight, then the *Titanic* must still be there and visible when the rockets are fired at a time some forty minutes later. Gill's evidence is in trouble. It conflicts with Gibson and Stone who see both a ship *and* rockets. Gill sees only rockets and the empty water's edge. Gill has a disappearing ship, followed by shipless rockets.

Stone and Gibson's ship had not disappeared. She was very much present, within short miles, as rockets went up. They could see her plainly and Gill could not. And these two deck officers also saw rockets not only while another ship was present, but when an extensive icefield had caused that nearby 'tramp steamer' to stop, prudently.

But perhaps that vessel too was incompetently navigated and could not see the 'break in the ice' within yards of her that Gill had so effortlessly espied from miles to her north! The more one tests Gill's story, the more it resembles his account of the shrinking field ice – with features that speedily resolve themselves into water. Can we trust anything Gill says? Consider these twists and turns from his brief US examination (p.712):

> …What colour was the rocket?
> Gill: It would be apt to be a very clear blue; I would catch it when it was dying. I did not catch the exact tint, but I reckon it was white.
> Senator Fletcher: Did it look as if the rocket had been sent up and the explosion had taken place in the air and the stars spangled out?
> Gill: Yes, sir; the stars spangled out. I could not say about the stars. I say I caught the tail end of the rocket.

He has come a long way from a 'shooting star'. Now he can see thrown stars from an individual rocket. Yet, terrified of being caught out, he immediately retracts this claim. 'I could not say about the stars'. At the end of the day, his evidence can only be boiled down to a claim that rockets were seen 'at a great distance' from the deck of the *Californian*. And we know that already, just as Gill knew it already from gossip he had heard below decks after the tragedy.

Gill testified towards the end of the British Inquiry when all the other *Californian* witnesses had long since been heard and were gone. Why, one wonders? Yet this is how the Attorney General chose to introduce this witness (p.407; 18128–9):

Your Lordship will remember this was the assistant donkeyman of the *Californian*, with regard to whom some statement was made by the other witnesses of the *Californian*. The only point was he was referred to as a deserter at Boston. The suggestion at one time was that he had made a statement which was not true in America about the distress signals having been sent up, and there was a suggestion at one time made that in consequence of a story which he had put forward, which would not bear examination, he had deserted the vessel at Boston. It is no longer necessary to clear that up, because Mr Gill's story, as told in America, has – I do not want to say more than this – been very much confirmed by the evidence which we have put before the Court of the various officers – your Lordship will remember we called a number of them – and also of Gibson, the apprentice, so that it is not necessary now to go into his story, whatever it may be, as your Lordship will see the substance of it is no longer in dispute, and he was fully justified in what he said in America. The officers have now borne out the substance of his statement.

This was said before Gill had uttered a word in London. It is, on the face of it, quite an extraordinary preface to his appearance. It is entirely untrue to say that Gill's story had been 'very much confirmed by the evidence' when Gill alone would completely contradict himself. It is also not true that 'the various officers' confirmed Gill's account – quite the reverse. They do nothing to back it up. Only Groves with his passenger steamer is superficially supportive of Gill's big ship, yet Gill will go on to clash with most of Groves' evidence. If the substance means that rockets were fired, then it is a poor remnant of Gill's elaborate tale. And it is, on the evidence, thoroughly shocking for a British Attorney General to say Gill was 'fully justified in what he said in America'. Gill, in reality, is completely untrustworthy.

We know one person to desert a ship in trouble: Ernest Gill. He absented himself from the *Californian* after selling his fable to the newspapers. She nonetheless sailed home with her full crew, apart from fireman William Kennerdale, who died of heart trouble during the stay at Boston. Captain Lord saw to Kennerdale's burial, sorted out paperwork with the British Consul, and brought home the dead fireman's wages, clothing and effects. Captain Lord reported the death in a letter to the Marine Superintendent at Liverpool, and expressed apologies for leaving out some details earlier, promising to 'guard against omissions in the future'. Kennerdale was buried on Friday 26 April 1912 – the day Lord testified in Washington and the day the *Boston Herald* branded his ship the 'Liner charged with deserting *Titanic*' in a headline over a picture of the *Californian* at her dock.

17

BOSTON

The *Californian* duly made landfall in Boston on 19 April and was greeted by a number of reporters because of an erroneous report that she could be bringing back bodies from the disaster area. Lord first had a meeting with the local agent of his line, Leyland's John Thomas, at which he may have outlined what the *Californian* had seen, and certainly gave his overnight position. Lord later met reporters and described the morning dash to the scene, not mentioning rockets, and when asked by one reporter for his latitude and longitude, remarked that he was 'asking for a state secret', adding that it would 'have to be answered by those in the office', perhaps pointing to the local agent's premises. Later in the company's office, with agent Thomas in attendance, Lord did indeed give out to the press his overnight stop position.

Next a carpenter from the *Californian* named McGregor went on shore leave to visit a cousin in the small town of Clinton, west of Boston. After the visit, the cousin – not the carpenter himself – told the local newspaper of Gill-like gossip that his ship (reported throughout as the '*California*') had seen rockets and been 'within ten miles of the *Titanic*'. This erroneous, and now at least third-hand, story had the *Californian* steaming all through the night, never having stopped, as her crew universally later testified she did. It also claimed 'those on board the *California* could see the lights of the *Titanic* very plainly'.

Captain Lord rejected this the next day to the *Boston Post*, denying his vessel had seen or ignored any distress signals. The *Californian* had sighted no rockets or other signals of distress, the newspaper reported. Lord did not mention the *Californian* had seen someone's rockets – and seemed to rely on his crew's assertions that the rockets they saw were not distress signals since, as Stone would say, 'a vessel in distress does not steam away from you'.

The *Boston Globe* followed up their rival's story and spoke to agent Thomas, who described the claims in the Clinton newspaper as perfectly absurd, adding that the vessels were 20 miles apart and 'no signals could possibly be seen at this distance'. The *Globe* noted that Captain Lord 'simply ignored the story yesterday'. It added: 'None of the crew would say they had seen any signals of distress or any lights on the night of Sunday April 14'. Prompted by press interest however, Ernest Gill now told his yarn to the *Boston American*. Controversy was inflamed again.

The reporters returned to the dock and demanded answers of Captain Lord. He told his inquisitors that they could judge Gill for themselves: the *Titanic* had struck a berg at twenty minutes to midnight 'and here this man says he saw the vessel proceeding at full speed about midnight, some twenty minutes after the accident'.

Lord also pointed out that Gill had been paid $500 for his affidavit and added that he did not expect any difficulty in explaining to US investigators his entire innocence of 'ignoring any signals from the *Titanic*'. He also said he did not see why Gill's story should be given credence 'especially when such obviously unsailorlike deeds were admitted in the affidavit', continuing:

> Do you suppose any man of any race would see signals of distress and fail to report them either to the bridge or to the lookout? Can you imagine a man, realising that fellow sailors were in dire straits, failing to notify someone that he had seen such signals?

The *Boston Herald*, a 'yellower' newspaper than the *Globe*, said Captain Lord's story was corroborated by First Officer Stewart, by Second Officer Stone, and by a quartermaster on duty that night. It added that Stone 'emphatically denied that he had notified Captain Lord of any rockets, as he had seen none, nor had any been reported to him'. This was the first outright falsehood, and it is attributed to Stone. It will be seen elsewhere that Lord's comments have been defensive and economical, as one might expect in the case of a man thrown into a difficult position by the hyperbole of a crewman's 'confession', but he has not resorted thus far to outright lies.

Lord was already on his way to Washington to give evidence when a story appeared in the *Boston Journal*, a newspaper catching up with its fellows. It said one of its reporters had spoken to Captain Lord the night before and quoted the master thus:

> Mr Stewart, the First Officer, was on the bridge during the times that the signals were supposed to have been seen, and he can tell you himself that nothing of the kind was seen by him or any of the men who were on watch with him.

This would appear to make Lord a direct liar. But the story is quite evidently wrong – Stewart was not on the bridge at the time the signals were 'supposed to have been seen'. The article continued to quote Lord, now saying he received news that the *Titanic* was sinking 'from the *Virginia*' (the ship was the *Virginian*) at 'about 3.30 a.m.' – when in fact Lord first heard the confirmation shortly before 6 a.m. and was not even woken before 4.30 a.m.

The 'about 3.30 a.m.' may be a misunderstanding for the New York time kept by the wireless operator (who gave 3.30 a.m. NYT, as one of the times he was woken up!), but such a failure of comprehension suggests the newspaper imported this time from elsewhere. Lord kept apparent ship's time throughout and had no truck with New York time. This is demonstrated as the same newspaper quotes Lord further, as follows, leading him into what would appear to be blithe and stupid contradiction of the earlier attributed remark about the time of finding out:

Everything had been quiet during the night and no signals of distress or anything else had been seen, and about 5 o'clock in the morning, which is my regular time for getting up, I told Mr Stewart to wake up Wireless and have him get in touch with some ship and get an idea of what kind of an ice field we had gotten into.

These 'quotes' then, and the other statements in quotation marks, are entirely at odds with the actual events of that night as testified to by Lord and others at the American and British Inquiries.

Opponents of Captain Lord regularly charge that he 'lied' and told 'falsehoods' to the newspapers in Boston. Yet any fair-minded assessor may conclude that, in the face of obdurate silence from the crew and denials of Gill's story by Lord, the *Boston Journal* at least may have felt it could put all manner of words into Captain Lord's mouth, denying everything. Failing that, the glaring mistakes in a version of events supposedly acquired from the horse's mouth hardly inspire confidence that what Captain Lord actually said was faithfully transcribed and accurately reproduced. And why would Lord lie in such crass, contradictory terms to only one newspaper? No, the fairest assessment of Lord's press statements in Boston is that they were defensive and deflective. He was warding off controversy. And this at least is a perfectly understandable human reaction.

Both the press and the captain knew at this time that he had been called to the US Inquiry. It would be not only irresponsible, but downright silly, for Lord to comment in such circumstances. Instead Lord was already in Washington DC when the *Boston Journal* tried to put one over on its rivals. We do not know if Lord was exasperated at these misrepresentations. And yet the suggestion that he himself descended into outright mendacity would mean behaviour totally out-of-keeping with his conduct during the inquiries – when his plain and non-excusatory testimony created greater difficulties for himself.

The reader must decide what, if anything, these press reports mean. Certainly they were ignored by both the US and British Inquiries, which asked their own questions and recorded the answers verbatim in open court. Finally, it should also be pointed out that whatever view is taken of Lord's character – and he would see it as his sole asset in commanding the respect of his men – the impugning of Lord the man is essentially irrelevant to the overall question as to whether his vessel, the *Californian*, could have been the *Titanic*'s mystery ship.

18

THE US INQUIRY

The US Inquiry heard evidence from only three *Californian* witnesses. The first was Gill, whose affidavit was read into the record, and who was briefly questioned by senators. Also called was Wireless Operator Cyril Evans. And between these men was Captain Stanley Lord, the first two-thirds of whose evidence was largely pedestrian, leading up to his account of the night itself (US Inquiry, p.728):

> Senator Smith: Captain, did you see any distress signals on Sunday night, either rockets or the Morse signals?
> Lord: No sir; I did not. The officer on watch saw some signals, but he said they were not distress signals.
> Sen. Smith: They were not distress signals?
> Lord: Not distress signals.

One can conceivably see that the above resembles Lord's conversations with Boston newsmen. He denies distress signals were seen, but waits until the Inquiry to describe exactly what was seen from the *Californian* that night. At this point, Lord describes at some length his account of what happened (US Inquiry, p.728–9).

> Lord: Not distress signals.
> Sen. Smith: But he reported them?
> Lord: To me. I think you had better let me tell you that story.
> Sen. Smith: I wish you would.
> Lord: When I came off the bridge, at half past 10, I pointed out to the officer that I thought I saw a light coming along, and it was a most peculiar night, and we had been making mistakes all along with the stars, thinking they were signals. We could not distinguish where the sky ended and where the water commenced. You understand, it was a flat calm. He said he thought it was a star, and I did not say anything more. I went down below. I was talking with the engineer about keeping the steam ready, and we saw these signals coming along, and I said: 'There is a steamer passing. Let us go to the wireless and see what the news is'. But on our way down I met the operator coming, and I said, 'Do

you know anything?' He said, 'The *Titanic*'. So, then, I gave him instructions to let the *Titanic* know. I said, 'This is not the *Titanic*; there is no doubt about it'. She came and lay at half past 11 alongside of us until, I suppose, a quarter past, within 4 miles of us. We could see everything on her quite distinctly, see her lights. We signalled her, at half past 11, with the Morse lamp. She did not take the slightest notice of it. That was between half past 11 and 20 minutes to 12. We signalled her again at 10 minutes past 12, half past 12, a quarter to 1 o'clock. We have a very powerful Morse lamp. I suppose you can see that about 10 miles, and she was about 4 miles off, and she did not take the slightest notice of it. When the Second Officer came on the bridge, at 12 o'clock, or 10 minutes past 12, I told him to watch that steamer, which was stopped, and I pointed out the ice to him; told him we were surrounded by ice; to watch the steamer that she did not get any closer to [us]. At 20 minutes to 1, I whistled up the speaking tube and asked him if she was getting any nearer. He said, 'No; she is not taking any notice of us'. So, I said 'I will go and lie down for a bit'. At a quarter past he said, 'I think she has fired a rocket'. He said, 'She did not answer the Morse lamp and she has commenced to go away from us'. I said, 'Call her up and let me know at once what her name is. So, he put the whistle back, and, apparently, he was calling. I could hear him ticking over my head. Then I went to sleep.

Succinct. And rather ordinary. It is interesting that Captain Lord spoke to the chief engineer about keeping steam ready. He wanted to be able to move quickly in any eventuality. This point had come into play just before Lord's thumbnail sketch of events (US Inquiry, p.728):

Senator Fletcher: You were asked by Senator Smith a moment ago whether, if the wireless operator on the *Californian* had been on duty, he would have picked up this message from the *Titanic* giving the alarm?

Lord: Yes.

Sen. Fletcher: Could you have gone to the relief of the *Titanic* at that time?

Lord: Most certainly.

Sen. Fletcher: You could have gone?

Lord: We could have gone; yes.

Sen. Fletcher: The engines were not running then.

Lord: The engines were stopped; perfectly stopped.

Sen. Fletcher: But you could have gone to the *Titanic*?

Lord: The engines were ready. I gave instructions to the chief engineer and told him I had decided to stay there all night. I did not think it safe to go ahead. I said, 'We will keep handy in case some of those big fellows come crunching along and get into it'.

So Lord's self-described attitude was to be ready at all times to help anyone else who might get into difficulties. Very different from Gill's affidavit about a 'Captain who refuses or neglects to give aid to a vessel in distress'.

Remarkably, Captain Lord was almost uniquely equipped to render just the type of assistance the *Titanic*'s people needed. He had taken part in one of the first seaborne military landings of the twentieth century. In 1904, Lord was a chief officer when 4,000 men were put ashore by ship's boats from a flotilla that lay off the Essex coast in a major exercise, the first such joint operation between the British Army and the Royal Navy since the Crimean War. Lord had also picked up troops in small boats during the withdrawal. An interesting piece of trivia, perhaps.

However, returning to 1912, by far the most extraordinary thing about Lord's US testimony, in this writer's experience, is that Gill's allegations were simply never put to Captain Lord for his comments. Lord was never given an opportunity to comment on Gill's statement in an official setting. An Inquiry may indeed be different to a criminal trial, but this Inquiry chairman would nonetheless produce a report that went beyond its remit of establishing facts, and instead made a finding tantamount to the guilt of the *Californian* and the vindication of Gill. Quite how Smith was able to level such an accusation on so little evidence, with no testing of Gill, may puzzle the dispassionate student of the US Inquiry. Yet there was to be one rabbit pulled from a hat at the conclusion of the Senate Subcommittee's hearings which did much to establish the climate for a distinctly adverse verdict on Lord and the *Californian*. It came from one who should have known better.

Captain John J. Knapp, US Navy hydrographer at the Hydrographic Office in Washington DC, was in charge of a surveying and charting body, one primarily concerned with gathering and disseminating information on hazards to navigation. He plotted the iceberg reports for the US Inquiry, showing the ice barrier and its estimated extent. And he illustrated where the *Titanic* had gone down – using the incorrect SOS position. But then Knapp went further. He ventured into an area of supposition that would never have been allowed in a criminal trial. For not only did he mark on his chart the reported overnight position of the *Californian* as given by her captain, officers and logbook, but he also marked her hypothetical position if she were to have been the vessel seen by the *Titanic*. His hypothetical position was doubly ridiculous and utterly invalid because the *Titanic* was not ever in the SOS location. And it was *triple* idiocy because Knapp placed his *Californian* to the north-east of the SOS position, whereas a cursory glance at the available facts would have prompted him to impose her to the north-north-west. *Californian* saw rockets to the south-south-east, not to the south-west, as Knapp would have it.

Knapp, deskbound, with no credentials to offer an opinion on where any vessels were that night, was not only venturing a flawed opinion, but presenting it as if it were scientific fact. He might as well have drawn a 'hypothetical position' for the *Flying Dutchman*.

It is noteworthy that he did not plot 'notional' positions for any of the other vessels in the locality that night, in which Senator Smith had previously shown interest and asked questions about – the *Hellig Olav*, the *Frankfurt*, and the *Amerika*, for instance. Knapp had simply taken it upon himself to directly equate the *Titanic*'s mystery ship with the *Californian*. The audacity of such a construct beggars belief, quite apart from its grotesque unfairness and cast-iron certain inadmissibility in any legal setting because of its glaringly prejudicial nature. This is what Knapp had to say (US Inquiry, p. 1118–9):

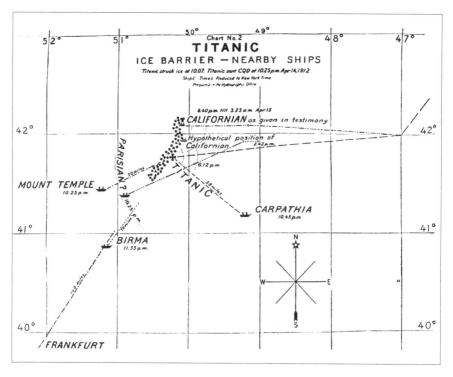

Knapp's chart No. 2, which is full of inaccuracies.

A further reference to the chart will show, midway between the plotted positions of the *Californian* and *Titanic*, a plotted 'hypothetical position of the *Californian*'. With the hypothesis that the *Californian* was in this plotted position, a dotted line is drawn on a bearing SSE given by the Master of the *Californian* as the bearing in which he sighted a large steamer. This dotted line is drawn to intersect the track of the *Titanic*.

A line parallel thereto is drawn to also intersect the track of the *Titanic* at a point at which the *Titanic* appears to have been at 10.06 p.m., New York time, 14 April – at 11.56 p.m. of that date by the *Californian*'s time – at which time the large steamer is testified to have been seen by Ernest Gill of the *Californian*.

It thus appears that the bearings of the steamer given by the Master of the *Californian* and the testimony of Ernest Gill of that ship will fix the *Californian*'s position near or about the hypothetical position shown on the chart, if the lights seen on that ship were those of the *Titanic*.

The thrust of Knapp's 'evidence' is to shamelessly force the *Californian* into an imaginary circle drawn between 7 and 16 miles from the *Titanic*. Seven miles, he believed, was the distance a ship's light could be seen by someone in a lifeboat. But he also believed, it seems incredible to relate, that the *Californian* could have seen the *Titanic*'s side lights – side lights, mind you – at a distance of 16 miles. Far-fetched indeed.

SIDE LIGHTS AT 16 MILES?

Knapp says (US Inquiry, p. 1118):

> ...16 miles [is] approximately the farthest distance at which... the side lights of the *Titanic* [could] be seen by a person at the height of the side lights of the *Californian*, or at which the side lights of the *Californian* could have been seen by a person at the height of the side lights of the *Titanic*.

This is complete claptrap, if we look at the stated evidence of *Titanic's* prime surviving witness. Not even those on the *Titanic's* bridge that night, high above the waterline, could see anything like such a distance. Fourth Officer Boxhall was recalled to the US Inquiry, having previously given evidence, and was questioned closely about a theory that the *Californian* was 14 miles away – a figure plucked from the air, and suspicious in itself (p. 914):

> Senator Smith: We have been figuring the distance the *Californian* was away from the *Titanic*, and from the positions given we have concluded – that is, we have evidence to support the theory – [the Senators were now sitting in Washington DC, where Knapp was based; had he already conveyed his theory?] that the *Californian* was but 14 miles distant from the *Titanic*. Do you think that under those circumstances you could have seen the *Californian*?
> Boxhall: I do not know, sir. I should not think so. [Not the answer they wanted!]
> Sen. Smith: You should not?
> Boxhall: No. Five miles is the distance the British Board of Trade requires masthead lights to show – that is, the white steaming lights of the steamer – but we know that they can be seen farther on such a clear night as that. [Masthead lights, being the highest and brightest, could obviously be seen much further away than side lights]

Boxhall had now given evidence twice. But at the conclusion of this public session, he was questioned yet again – the same evening – in separate evidence taken by Senator Burton. Here is how that brief third session concluded (US Inquiry, p. 934):

> Boxhall: ...I have already stated, in answer to a question, how far this ship was away from us, that I thought she was about 5 miles, and I arrived at it in this way. The masthead lights of a steamer are required by the board of trade regulations to show for 5 miles, and the [side lights] are required to show for 2 miles... I could see quite clearly.
> Sen. Burton: You are very sure you are not deceived about seeing these lights?
> Boxhall: Not at all.
> Sen. Burton: You saw not only the mast light but the side lights?
> Boxhall: I saw the side lights. Whatever ship she was, she had beautiful lights. I think we could see her lights more than the regulation distance, but I do not think we could see them 14 miles. [Adjourned]

Why did the US Inquiry, at its last gasp with Boxhall, suggest that he could be deceived, especially in relation to the distance of side lights specifically, as suggested by the final question so forcefully pressed? The suspicion must be that they already had Knapp's briefing claiming that side lights could be seen for a giant distance, even though Knapp would not give evidence for some days yet. But on all the evidence (rather than theory), it appears clear that Knapp is utterly out of touch when he expects side lights to be visible at up to 16 miles.

Meanwhile, where did this mysterious '14 mile' figure come from? Who provided what Senator Smith called the 'evidence' of this? The truth emerges from geometry. Although the distance between his 'hypothetical position' of the *Californian* and the SOS position of the *Titanic* was never explicitly mentioned by Knapp, when his chart is scaled up with all its intersecting arcs and radii, the distance is precisely measurable. The hypothetical distance on his chart is *exactly* 14 miles. That this concoction was taken as scientific fact by Senator Smith long before he retired to write his report is confirmed by what he confidently told witness Jack Binns – the wireless hero of the 1909 *Republic* rescue, who appeared after Boxhall, but before Knapp (US Inquiry, p. 1035):

> Senator Smith: Let me call your attention to the fact that the *Californian* was but 14 miles from the *Titanic* when it sank…

Fact? Boxhall of the *Titanic* had repeatedly rained on this theory just three sitting days previously. Boxhall saw the side lights – he knew how close she was. Nonetheless Knapp located his hypothetical *Californian* towards the outer limit of his 7 to 16 mile 'radius of visibility', implicitly estimating her to be 'fourteen' miles from the *Titanic*, since he confidently opined (US Inquiry, p. 1119):

> The *Californian*, if located in the hypothetical position shown on the chart, certainly could have reached the *Titanic* in a little over an hour.

This nonsense (let us remember, it could have been any ship whimsically placed anywhere on Knapp's chart) was loosely erected on the evidence of Gill, as seen above. Thus we have a 'castle in the air' and one paradoxically built on sand, for Gill's evidence is assuredly unreliable in the extreme. Not only this, but Knapp, like everyone else in officialdom in 1912, succumbs to the conviction that the *Titanic* really was where she said she was. In fact she sank many miles further to the east of the SOS position. But as can be seen above, Knapp accepted her invalid SOS position and tracked the *Californian* to where she hypothetically may have been in order to agree with a sighting by Gill that may not have taken place! The result is that it might agree with Gill, but it conflicts with every other sighting.

The hydrographer's confident testimony may have seemed impressive to the senators, but his brazenly unsupported speculation is destroyed when one examines his sole 'factual' reference in his foregoing musings. Knapp asserts that the master of the *Californian* saw a 'large steamer'. *Nowhere* does Lord say he saw a large steamer; in fact he testifies repeatedly to the exact opposite. She was instead 'something like ourselves' (6752).

Knapp's confabulations could fall on any one of a number of fronts. But they collapse from the moment of conception – which lay in desiring a particular outcome and then producing a theory to make it fit. And since the 1985 discovery of the *Titanic's* wreck we know for sure that it does not fit.

ONE MAN'S TIME OF IMPACT

Meanwhile another fatal blow is dealt to Knapp's chart by an inscription he has placed upon it, which proclaims: '*Titanic* struck ice at 10.07'. This is a reduction to New York time, based on the US Inquiry's belief that *Titanic* time was one hour and thirty-three minutes ahead of New York. This stems from evidence given by Lightoller and Boxhall, and a Marconigram from the *Carpathia*. Here is the fourth officer (US Inquiry, p 918):

> Senator Smith: Mr Boxhall, you seem to be the one upon whom we must rely to give the difference between ship's time and New York time; or, rather, to give ship's time and give the New York time when this accident occurred?
> Boxhall: At 11.46 p.m., ship's time, it was 10.13 Washington time, or New York time [*Titanic* – plus one hour thirty-three minutes]

This shows why Knapp has quoted a New York time of 10.07. It is deemed to be the same as 11.40 p.m. *Titanic* time, when most witnesses said their ship collided with the berg. *Titanic* Second Officer Charles Lightoller claims: 'I am only going by what I have heard. I do not know. About 20 minutes to 12, I believe' (US Inquiry, p.432); Steward George Crowe says: 'About 11.40 there was a kind of shaking of the ship and a little impact…' (US Inquiry, p.614); passenger James McGough states: 'I was awakened at 11.40 p.m., ship time' (US Inquiry, p. 1143); Wireless Operator Harold Bride says: 'Twenty minutes to 12' (US Inquiry, p.905). Senator Smith concludes: 'At 11.40; everybody seems to be agreed on that' (US Inquiry, p.905).

We know from Captain Lord that *Californian* time was one hour fifty minutes ahead of New York time. This does not mean we know categorically how *Californian* time related to that on *Titanic* – we do not, although Boxhall and Lightoller spoke of their ship sinking at 5.47 GMT, which converts to one hour thirty-three minutes ahead of New York time. There is little corroboration and it is a fraught point.

Yet the decision of the US Inquiry to accept this *Titanic* conversion means that *Californian* time is, by Lord, seventeen minutes *ahead* (and by his wireless operator, Evans, twenty-two minutes ahead) of *Titanic* time in every comparison. The British got out of this trap by deciding both ships had the same time, when we know at least that they did not. Knapp worked from Captain Lord's noon calculation, meaning a seventeen minute time difference with Boxhall's time (*Californian*'s wireless operator gave a NYT difference of one hour fifty-five minutes, but we have seen that this is longitudinally inappropriate).

But for now be aware that Knapp has built his ideas solely on Ernest Gill. The hydrographer testified this about his hypothetical position for the *Californian* (US Inquiry, p. 1118):

A line… is drawn to… intersect the track of the *Titanic* at a point at which the *Titanic* appears to have been at 10.06 p.m., New York time, April 14 – at 11.56 p.m. of that date by the *Californian's* time – at which time the large steamer is testified to have been seen by Ernest Gill…

Knapp thus accepts that *Californian* time was one hour fifty ahead of New York. But in accepting Boxhall's time-conversion for *Titanic* to New York, Knapp has built a time-bomb for his own argument… only he is too stupid to realise it, as we are about to see. Knapp – naturally – swallowed Gill's evidence in its entirety. He accepts that the *Titanic* was the steamer conjured up by the donkeyman.

Now let us recap Gill's sworn affidavit with its precise times (p.152):

At 11.56 I came on deck… I looked over the rail and saw the lights of a very large steamer… I watched her for fully a minute. It was now 12 o'clock and I went to my cabin [and told my mate] I saw a big vessel going along full speed.

How interesting; Gill came on deck at a time that the US Navy hydrographer insists is 11.39 p.m. *Titanic* time, because Knapp himself has accepted a conversion that puts the *Californian* seventeen minutes ahead of the White Star's brand new maiden voyager (one hour fifty less one hour thirty-three). Gill comes on deck at 11.56 *Californian* time (supposedly 10.06 New York), which is seventeen minutes ahead of *Titanic*, such that *Titanic* time is actually 11.39 p.m. (or 10.06 plus one hour thirty-three).

That is fine. Except that the *Titanic* collides at 11.40 her time, or 11.57 *Californian* time, by Knapp's reasoning.

This is the precise period when Gill looks over the rail. For 'fully a minute' between 11.56 and midnight (three minutes after *Titanic* collision, according to Knapp) Gill says he looked at a very large steamer charging at 'full speed', moving very rapidly when the *Titanic* was doing no such thing. This is the problem for Knapp in trusting Gill's precisely-timed affidavit. Gill also said his large liner was moving rapidly some 10 miles away from his ship, while Groves and Lord saw a ship some 5 miles away which had stopped at 11.30 (Lord) 11.40 (Groves) – or twenty minutes to half an hour before a full-speed and very large steamer streaks across the background unseen by anyone except Gill.

It is no good abandoning Gill to save Knapp's theory, because it is built on Gill. Knapp draws a line to intersect the *Titanic* track, leading to a place where *Californian* 'must have been' (hypothetical) in order to have seen her… except of course for the bitter truth, revealed in 1985, that the *Titanic* never reached the SOS position, never passed that way at all, and yes, concrete proof again, that Gill just didn't see her.

Nor is it any good trying to re-work the times – Knapp's quagmire gets even worse. If the British 'solution' is attempted, that of regarding *Titanic* and *Californian* times as identical, Gill is still seeing a runaway steamer when the *Titanic* has long been battered to a standstill by the power of nature.

Another theory, erroneous as we have seen, is that *Californian* time was twelve minutes behind *Titanic*. This would have Gill's goliath zooming about at up to 12.12 a.m., instead of sending out an SOS.

Perhaps it is no wonder that the US hydrographer hides behind New York times in his chart. Because his chart means that *Titanic* struck and began sinking one minute after Gill walked on deck. It would mean that Gill would then return to the deck for a smoke forty minutes after his first vision and not see a 'very large steamer' that should be sinking where she stopped in front of him. He instead sees rockets 'far away' – suggesting the ship kept steaming at full speed for much of those forty minutes – when Knapp himself, at the top of his very own chart, tells us the *Titanic* has been blocked and stopped.

Did Knapp know this in 1912? He had the evidence before him which showed that his chart was contradictory. He accepted *Titanic* evidence as true (Boxhall) which proved Gill to be a liar. Either he did not comprehend it – in which case he is merely an imbecile – or he realised all too well and villainously chose to hide it through reductions to New York time.

This is a man whose pseudo-science has so impressed Senator Smith into accepting his theories as fact. Meanwhile he will reveal more gaps in his understanding in the manner in which he dismisses the 'Third Ship' possibility.

AN INTERVENING SHIP?

Senator Smith asks (US Inquiry, p. 1120):

> Captain, are you able to state to the committee whether there was any vessel between the position of the *Titanic* just preceding and following the accident and the position of the *Californian* at that time?

Let's just look at the question for a moment. Knapp was at home in Washington – dry, and probably in bed at the time of the sinking. He was not in any position to state whether there was another vessel between the *Californian* and the *Titanic* and should have said so. Instead he again far exceeds his powers (US Inquiry, p. 1120):

> From being present at hearings before your committee, and from reading the printed testimony of witnesses examined by the committee, I am led to the conclusion that if there was any vessel between the *Californian* and the *Titanic* at the time referred to she does not seem to have been seen by any of the ships near there on the following morning, nor have there been any reports submitted to the Hydrographic Office which would indicate that there was any such steamer in that locality.

This answer is equivalent to saying: 'Not from what I read in the newspapers'. They might as well have asked the shoe-shine boy outside the Inquiry hall. Clearly Knapp did not read the evidence well enough; several other unknown vessels were indeed seen by the *Mount Temple*, *Californian* and *Carpathia* the following morning. They included:

1. A small two-mast steamer – seen by *Californian*, *Carpathia* and *Mount Temple*.
2. A schooner that raced across the path of Captain Moore and the *Mount Temple*.
3. A pink-funnel steamer heading north or north-west, seen by *Californian* on the west side of the ice barrier.
4. A steamer showing a red side light which crossed the *Carpathia*'s path at 3.15 a.m.
5. *Californian*'s yellow-funnel steamer seen to southward, east of the ice barrier, 4 a.m.–6 a.m.

Five ships, just for starters, that eluded investigation and certainly eluded Captain Knapp. Such a pity they did not forward reports about themselves to the Hydrographic Office.

Part of the problem was that the US Inquiry simply did not bother seeking evidence from a sufficient number of witnesses to make any kind of finding about the *Titanic*'s mystery ship. The senators did not call Stewart and Stone, who, like Lord, clearly saw a (yellow-funnel) ship in an arguable 'Third Ship' position from 4 a.m.–6 a.m. that morning. We have touched on some of these other unidentified ships before in this assessment. Two we have not yet mentioned, Captain Moore's schooner and Captain Rostron's 3.15 a.m. steamer, should now perhaps be looked at briefly:

CAPTAIN MOORE'S MYSTERY SCHOONER

Moore gave the following evidence (US p.761/2):

> Moore: I stopped the ship. Before that I want to say that I met a schooner or some small craft, ['I reckon it was shortly after 3 o'clock'] and I had to get out of the way of that vessel, and the light of that vessel seemed to go out.
> Senator Smith: The schooner was between you and the *Titanic*'s position? — Yes, sir.
> Sen. Smith: Was this schooner coming toward you? — I was steering east and this green light was opening to me.
> Sen. Smith: Was he evidently coming from the direction in which the *Titanic* lay? — Somewhere from there, sir. Of course, had he been coming straight he would have shown me his two lights, sir… I should say this light could not have been more than a mile or a mile and a half away, because I immediately put my helm hard a-starboard, and I ordered full speed astern and took the way off the boat.
> Sen. Smith: You think the schooner was within a short distance of the *Titanic*? — I thought she was within a short distance of us, because I put the engines full astern to avoid her.

Meanwhile Captain Rostron's 3.15 a.m. steamer, in a similar close encounter, was coming from a direction in which we now know the *Titanic* sank, and she sank just an hour earlier than *Carpathia*'s sighting, making her most interesting. This vessel was ignored in 1912 because she seemed to be steaming from the east towards the SOS location, whereas it was entrenched in the official mind that the mystery ship was located further west of the SOS location.

Yet since the wreck discovery in 1985, this steamer seen by *Carpathia* must be at least a candidate for the mystery ship because she was actually coming from the place where the *Titanic* is now proven to have sunk.

She was on a similar vector, in broad terms, to that of the *Parisian*, illustrated on Knapp's chart.

CAPTAIN ROSTRON'S MYSTERY STEAMER

25552. [The Attorney General] Does that state all the vessels that you saw? I think [you] stated two steamers [being *Mount Temple* and the two-master]? — No; I saw one more, but it was during the night previous to getting out [to] the *Titanic's* position. We saw masthead lights quite distinctly of another steamer between us and the *Titanic*. That was about quarter-past three.

25553. The masthead lights? — Yes, of another steamer, and one of the officers swore he also saw one of the side lights.

25554. Which one? — The port side light.

25555. Do you know of any identification of that steamer at all? — No; we saw nothing but the lights. I did not see the side lights: I merely saw the masthead lights.

25556. [The Commissioner] You did not see the additional lights yourself, the side light? — I saw the masthead lights.

25557. Did you see the lights your officer spoke of? — I saw the masthead lights myself but not the side light.

25558. What time was it? — About a quarter past three.

25559. And how was the light bearing? — About two points on the starboard bow.

25560. On your starboard bow? — On my starboard bow; that would be about N 30, W true.

But our dear Captain Knapp of the Hydrographic Office, convinced that because no nearby steamers had come to his blinkered attention in Washington then none could possibly exist, finally blundered to his conclusion – one that excluded all ships from the equation but *Titanic* and *Californian*: 'The evidence does not indicate to me that there was any such third steamer in those waters' (US Inquiry, p. 1120).

THE ICE BARRIER

It is immensely obvious that Knapp's chart also deliberately fudged the facts on where the *Titanic* had gone down in relation to the ice barrier. He declared to the senators: 'The ice barrier, from all reports… was impassable to a vessel proceeding to the westward'

(US Inquiry, p.1120). He accordingly located the *Titanic* on the east side of the barrier, having run right into it. But in fact the *Titanic* hit a lone berg far short of the ice barrier and no such barrier could be seen by anyone aboard her at the time. Knapp therefore engineered his ice barrier representation to run from north-east to south-west so the *Titanic* could be shown to have reached the far westerly SOS position and sunk there. In other words, he has forcibly pulled one section of the ice barrier to the west, in order to allow the *Titanic* to arrive at the SOS position.

But this neat solution to the 'impassable' solution, achieved by Knapp simply holding back the curtain of ice to allow the *Titanic* to get to where she was supposed to have sunk, actually flew in the face of all the evidence given to the US Inquiry. And in the face of all the ice-barrier reports sent to his own Hydrographic Office! The hydrographer was again depending on Gill, the donkeyman with the 'open sesame' icefield.

Knapp's chart and evidence was given on 18 May. Three weeks earlier two British newspapers had carried a very different chart from his, being that provided by Captain Ludwig Stulping of the SS *Birma*, who produced a detailed sketch of the icefield as he and his crew had found it. Stulping wrote:

> About 7.30 a.m. we were on the [SOS] scene of the wreck. There we saw some immense icebergs to the East, beginning from NE to S; and as far as the eye could reach, there lay pack-ice with icebergs, so that it was out of the question to proceed through the ice, and it was quite clear that the *Titanic* could not have been at that spot [that is, have passed through the ice to the western side].

And Captain Moore of the *Mount Temple* specifically testified that the SOS position was to the west of the barrier, and that in his opinion the *Titanic* sank farther east. Captain Lord made the same point, and both men were correct, as we know today, because the real wreck site is more than 13 miles further to the east and south. The ice barrier *was* impassable: it blocked off access to the SOS position to vessels coming from the east. Knapp has 'moved the goalposts'. Here is what Moore said about the ice field or barrier: 'Of course it extended as far as the eye could reach, north and south, sir' (US Inquiry, p.765). No mention of any 'slant' in a barrier of the type created by Knapp. Moore further proves the 'north to south' nature of the field as against Knapp's 'north-east to south-west' with these comments (US Inquiry, p.767):

> I searched for a passage to get through this pack, because I realised that the *Titanic* could not have been through that pack of ice, sir. I steered away to the south-south-east true. [Such a course would have taken him straight into Knapp's imaginary barrier. But Knapp was not there that night or morning]

Captain Lord's limited comments to the US Inquiry on the nature of the icefield supported Moore's assessment. Lord referred to going through the barrier to reach the west side and then going south to the SOS position ('the position she was supposed to have been in'), finding nothing and then having to cross the barrier a second time to reach the east side once more before noticing wreckage. But he was absolutely categorical in his British evidence:

> 6773. Did the ice extend at all to the eastward or westward of you? — It seemed to me to be running more north and south…
>
> 6774. From north to south was the field? —Yes.

Yet there is something more. If Knapp put a 'large steamer' into Lord's mouth, he also managed to mislocate the Russian Asiatic steamer *Birma* by a whole degree of longitude. This makes for a further gross error, but one that has other implications.

The *Birma*, eastbound, changed course after hearing the SOS before she had reached 52° W. The chart offered by Knapp showed her close to 51° W… and significantly does not follow through on her bee-line to the SOS position. Why not?

When *Birma*'s north-east course is imposed on to the chart offered by Knapp to the US Inquiry, it shows her smashing into Knapp's depicted ice barrier on its western side – and having to drive through it for at least 15 miles for it to reach the SOS position. But the *Birma*, steaming from the west, reached the SOS position through open seas with no ice. She only saw the ice barrier later, and further east. Her on-the-spot account is further evidence that Knapp's ice barrier portrayal is wrong, along with everything else. However Knapp's 'mistake' in placing the *Birma* one full degree closer to the SOS position might barely allow the steamer to skirt his icefield to the east. So is this indeed an error, or is it an intentional distortion? In any case, Knapp has ignored the eyewitness accounts of Captain Stulping (in British newspapers) and Captains Moore and Rostron of the *Mount Temple* and *Carpathia* (both in evidence at the US Inquiry), not to mention the strong insistence of Captain Lord, in order to arrive at his own magic solution from an office in Washington.

Taken in by Knapp's specious reasoning (should we call it the hypnosis of hypothesis?) and encouraged by Gill's extraordinary tale, Senator William Alden Smith, chairman of the US Inquiry, now equally felt fully qualified to write a damning indictment of the *Californian* in his final report (author comments bracketed):

> *Titanic* fired distress rockets… the officers of the *Californian* admit seeing rockets in the general direction of the *Titanic* [they actually saw them SSE, *Titanic* was supposedly SW)… while several of the crew of the *Californian* testify [several? The US Inquiry heard only from Gill, Lord and Evans] that the side lights of a large vessel going at full speed [only Gill – one man, not several – said he saw a large steamer going at full speed. He did not say he could see side lights] were plainly visible from the lower deck of the *Californian* at 11.30 p.m. ship's time [Gill claims to have seen a full-speed steamer only at 11.56] just before the accident…

The above paragraph, laden with amazing and reckless distortions of the truth, immediately preceded this conclusion:

The Steamship *Californian*'s Responsibility

The committee is forced to the inevitable conclusion that the *Californian*, controlled by the same company, was nearer the *Titanic* than the 19 miles reported by her Captain, and that her officers and crew saw the distress signals of the *Titanic* and failed to respond to them in accordance with the dictates of humanity, international usage, and the requirements of law.

The only reply to the distress signals was a counter signal from a large white light, which was flashed for nearly two hours from the mast of the *Californian*. In our opinion, such conduct, whether arising from indifference or gross carelessness, is most reprehensible, and places upon the commander of the *Californian* a grave responsibility.

The wireless operator of the *Californian* was not aroused until 3.30 a.m., New York time, on the morning of the 15th, after considerable conversation between officers and members of crew had taken place aboard that ship regarding these distress signals or rockets, and was directed by the Chief Officer to see if there was anything the matter, as a ship had been firing rockets during the night.

The enquiry thus set on foot immediately disclosed the fact that the *Titanic* had sunk. Had assistance been promptly proffered, or had the wireless operator of the *Californian* remained a few minutes longer at his post on Sunday evening, that ship might have had the proud distinction of rescuing the lives of the passengers and crew of the *Titanic*…

19

THE BRITISH INQUIRY

Captain Lord and the *Californian* were at sea when the US Inquiry reported. When they arrived in Liverpool they were drawn into new proceedings: Britain's own formal investigation. The British Investigation was certainly more exhaustive than its US counterpart, but it seemed the offer of the *Californian* as scapegoat (seized on for sacrifice by their transatlantic cousins) was too tempting to turn down.

Unlike the initial scattergun approach of the American sittings, the British investigation had little interest in any other ships but the *Californian* that night, apart from the subject at hand, of course. Senator Smith may have enquired about the whereabouts of a number of differing vessels, but his opposite number in London, Lord Mersey, had scant such interest. He was determined to run the *Californian* fox to ground. And while the evidence at the British Inquiry has already been extensively examined, it is perhaps instructive to just observe some of Lord Mersey's interruptions during his own proceedings. They show a man with his mind made up from an early stage.

The *Californian* issue was examined as early as Day 7 of the twenty-eight-day Inquiry, before any of the *Titanic*'s surviving officers had been called to the stand, nor anyone from the White Star Line! It seemed the Inquiry wanted to strike while the iron was hot. Captain Lord was the first *Californian* witness called. He was called strictly as a witness, not as defendant. He would have no opportunity to comment on the testimony of the other witnesses called thereafter. Yet less than one-quarter way through the evidence of Lord as the first *Californian* witness, we have this staggering exchange (British Inquiry, p.148, question 6804–5):

> [The Commissioner] What is in my brain at the present time is this, that what they
> [*Californian*] saw was the *Titanic*.
> [The Attorney General] I know.
> [The Commissioner] That is in my brain, and I want to see whether I am right or not.
> [The Attorney General] It certainly must have been very close.

A brain already filled with a prefabricated hypothesis. And the Attorney General, whose role should be to keep the focus on the straight and narrow, not only loses this opportunity to nudge Mersey towards due process, but actually encourages what is prejudice in its purest sense (Mersey's entry in the *Dictionary of National Biography* mentions a 1904 case in which counsel for the defendant was said to resent His Lordship's 'unjudicial hostility' towards his client).

Captain Lord's testimony began its climb uphill in these circumstances and soon encountered further determination on the part of the court to slot home its readymade conclusion:

> 6805. [The Attorney General to Captain Lord] Can you tell us whether you saw one or two masthead lights [on the unknown vessel that stopped nearby]? — I only saw one.
> 6806. You only saw one? — The Third Officer said he saw two.
> [The Attorney General] Now that is important.
> [The Commissioner] That is very important, because the *Titanic* would have two.
> 6807. [The Attorney General] Yes, that is it – two masthead lights.

Actually there is an ongoing debate as to the number of masthead lights carried by the *Titanic*. Now look at this next breathtaking piece of reasoning by the Attorney General, Sir Rufus Isaacs:

> 6807. [Attorney General to Lord] You only saw one, but the Third Officer [Groves] said he saw two? — And the Second Officer [Stone] said he saw one.
> 6818. [The Attorney General] If he did see two lights it must have been the *Titanic*, must it not? — It does not follow. [Of course not!]

By question 6847, Lord Mersey's displeasure at resistance to his own favoured version of events was becoming evident. Here he is talking to Lord:

> [The Commissioner] You do not give answers that please me at present. You said just now as plainly as possible that you answered the Third Officer, I think it was, and said, 'The only passenger steamer near us is the *Titanic*'. You now suggest that you do not remember whether you said that or not? — I do not recollect saying anything to him about it, my Lord.

Lord had earlier made it clear that he did not recollect any such statement as alleged by Groves. He had not said 'as plainly as possible' that he had answered the third officer in this manner. The captain's evidence was continuing when the Attorney General and Lord Mersey next produced this *coup de théâtre* (British Inquiry, p.149, question 6885–6):

> [The Attorney General] My Lord, I think it very desirable that the other witnesses from the *Californian* should be out of Court whilst this witness is giving evidence.
> [The Commissioner] By all means.
> [The Attorney General] If your Lordship will direct it.

[The Commissioner] Where are the other witnesses from the *Californian*? [The officers and men of the *Californian* stood up in court] Well, gentlemen, I think you had better leave the court at present.

One can imagine as they trooped out what they were thinking, and what must have run through the minds of the audience left inside. A serious turn of events is taking place – and someone is going to hang!

Even at the close of Lord's evidence, when he was being sympathetically examined by counsel for the Leyland Line, Mersey could not resist delivering a jibe dressed up as a misunderstanding:

7407. [Counsel Robertson Dunlop to Lord] Could you have navigated with any degree of safety to your vessel at night through the ice that you, in fact, encountered? — It would have been most dangerous.
[The Commissioner] Am I to understand that this is what you mean to say, that if he had known that the vessel was the *Titanic*, he would have made no attempt whatever to reach it?
7408. [Mr Dunlop] No, my Lord, I do not suggest that.

Dunlop would later mildly rebuke the Commissioner when touching on the evidence of Charles Victor Groves, the *Californian*'s third officer and the third *Californian* witness after Lord, in his closing submission to the Inquiry (p.834):

[Dunlop] Groves, the Third Officer, was the gentleman who was on watch from 8 till midnight. When he was pressed at the end of his evidence, I will not say by whom, to say he thought it was the *Titanic*, my Lord, he answered…
[The Commissioner] Did I press him?
[Mr Dunlop] Your Lordship asked the question.
[The Commissioner] I thought so.
[Mr Dunlop] Up to that moment, my Lord, he had not the courage to say that she was the *Titanic*, but, thus stimulated, he said this: 'From what I have heard subsequently I do, but I do not put myself forward as an experienced man'.

Lord Mersey's interruption (question 8838) during the evidence of *Californian* Chief Officer George Stewart was also most revealing: 'The previous officer told me, in answer to a question… that he was satisfied that it was the *Titanic* and at present I do not mind telling you that is my attitude of mind. You may perhaps change it'. And Mersey's highly coloured interruptions grew more opinionated. By Day 16 he was daring to be even more transparent in his antagonisms. Here, J. Bruce Ismay, managing director of White Star Line gives evidence:

18584. …If you will excuse my saying so, I do not think it was a steamer at all; I think it was a sailing ship we saw.

18585. [The Commissioner] Am I to understand that you do not think it was the *Californian?* — I am sure it was not.

18586. [The Commissioner] I am rather sorry to hear that…

Also on Day 16, Alfred Crawford, first class bedroom steward gave evidence:

17847. And before you left the ship's side did Captain Smith give you any directions with regard to a light? —Yes, he pointed to a light on the port side, the two masthead lights of a vessel, and told us to pull for there and land the people and return to the ship.

17848. Did you see those lights yourself? — I did.

17849. And what did you think they were? — I thought they were a vessel with two masthead lights.

17850. A steamer's masthead lights? —Yes.

[The Commissioner] Is there anyone here representing the *Californian?* [Immediately equating the *Titanic's* Mystery Ship with the *Californian*]

[Mr Cooper] Mr Dunlop will be here in a few minutes.

[The Attorney General] Somebody will be here, because we are calling somebody from the *Californian* today, and we have given them notice of it.

17851. [Mr Butler Aspinall, to the Witness]: I do not know whether you are a judge of distance of lights at sea, but what would you say? — I should say she was 5 to 7 miles away from us.

17852. The Captain gave the directions? —Yes, he pointed the ship out.

17853. Having got down to the water's edge did you obey that direction as well as you could? —We did.

17854. And rowed in the direction of that light? —Yes, we pulled all night in the direction of the steamer.

[The Commissioner] Does 5 to 7 miles away agree with the information from the *Californian* as to the position she took up when she anchored? [Anchoring in mid-Atlantic!]

[Mr Butler Aspinall] It is widely different, my Lord.

[The Commissioner] That is what I was thinking. The distance would be about 20 miles, would it not?

[Mr Butler Aspinall] Yes, 19 was in my mind – 19 to 20.

[The Commissioner] We have had the log of the *Californian.*

[Mr Butler Aspinall] We have.

[The Attorney General] The point your Lordship is upon is one which wants a little clearing up. Our attention has been directed to the same point.

[The Commissioner] Very well, I will not say anything more about it now.

But he did, when Crawford was giving evidence:

17976. And should those lights have been seen by the steamer towards which you were pulling? —Yes.

17977. Those rockets should have been seen? — Yes, I think they ought to have been seen.

[The Commissioner] Well, we know they were, Mr Harbinson. [Again appearing to equate the mystery ship with the *Californian*, the only ship to admit seeing rockets]

And later, also during Crawford's evidence:

18000. At what time was it you first saw her? — Just after one, when the Captain pointed it out.

18001. And how long had you her under observation? — Nearly all the night.

18002. What happened to her afterwards; did she come nearer to you, or did she disappear? — I could not say. We saw the *Carpathia* coming up, and we turned round and made for that one.

18003. [The Commissioner] Your interest in the *Californian*, if it was the *Californian*, ceased as soon as you saw the *Carpathia*? — Yes, my Lord.

[The Commissioner] Very naturally.

This naked display of Mersey's views during the examination of a *Titanic* steward's account of a ship he had seen is almost casual. By 18003, he barely manages the figleaf afterthought – 'if it was the *Californian*' – to disguise what is plain to see.

By Day 30, Lord Mersey had reinterpreted the law to put the burden of proof on to the 'defence', a reversal of basic principles of criminal law. But Mersey's was not a criminal court, and Captain Lord and the *Californian* were not in the dock. Lord was merely a witness, present to help Lord Mersey determine the cause of the marine casualty *Titanic*. Here is Mersey's statement (p.749):

[The Commissioner] I do not want to stop you, but I think the onus of proof in this matter is upon the *Californian*. I think for myself – I do not speak with absolute certainty for my colleagues – that it will be for the *Californian* to satisfy us that those were not the signals of the *Titanic*. Whether they will succeed I cannot say, but I think you may leave it.

On Day 24, after all the *Californian* evidence, the British Inquiry abruptly decided to change its terms of reference. It simply opted to give itself the power to make an adverse finding against the *Californian*, even though no part of its brief related to venturing into anything other than the circumstances of the loss of the White Star vessel. It was the Attorney General, Sir Rufus Isaacs, who delicately addressed what would otherwise be an obstacle to the apparent pre-formed intention to attach blame to the *Californian* (British Inquiry, p.611):

At the end of the evidence, according to the practice, it would be my duty to submit to your Lordship any further questions which ought to be put in addition to those I placed before the Court at the beginning of the Inquiry.

According to my view at present – and I do not think anything is likely to occur which will alter it – the only question which should be added is one relating to what I may call compendiously the *Californian* incident. There is no question in the twenty-six before you which would cover that.

It does occur to me, and my friend the Solicitor General associates with me in it, that it is important that the question should be specifically put and that your Lordship should take it into account, and that it ought not to be passed over merely as a matter throwing some general light upon the Inquiry. It has been already examined into, and my friend Mr Dunlop has been here representing the *Californian*, and, therefore, we ought to put the question and ask your Lordship to answer it.

If Mersey did not know this was coming, he was not in the least discomfited by the retrospective legal somersault and its implications for fairness. Isaacs, in legalese, had invited him to blame the *Californian* and not to merely 'pass over' the issue. Mersey caught the suggestion to make it central – and immediately sought guidance on how far exactly he could go (British Inquiry, p.611):

[The Commissioner] Quite so. I do not suppose I have any jurisdiction to direct that the Captain's [Lord's] certificate should be interfered with?
[The Attorney General] No, I think that only arises in a collision between two vessels. Then there is jurisdiction.
[The Commissioner] Assume that I take a view adverse to the conduct of the Captain of the *Californian*, all I can do is to express an opinion about it?
[The Attorney General] Yes.

Ten days later, at Day 34, Mersey was again publicly voicing possibilities – yet this time finally recognising realities about the inherent unfairness of what was about to be perpetrated against Captain Lord (British Inquiry, p.861):

[The Commissioner] …What I am pointing out is this, that Captain Smith could not be here; he is dead. He could not have been cited. But the Captain of the *Californian* is here really merely as a witness. He has not been cited to answer a charge of negligence, and I have great reluctance to find people guilty of negligence when they are not cited and charged with it, and have not had a proper opportunity of answering the charge.
[The Attorney General] I will deal with Captain Lord's case, my Lord.
[The Commissioner] Later on. I am only suggesting that there is an analogy between the two cases; I may be wrong, you know, but that is what I am suggesting.

In the event Mersey's final report would make no finding of negligence against Captain Smith, the man whose vessel ran into an iceberg at 22 knots. But the verdict on Captain Lord would be very different. This is the damning last paragraph of Mersey's finding on the *Californian* (British Inquiry Final Report, p.46):

These circumstances convince me that the ship seen by the *Californian* was the *Titanic*, and if so, according to Captain Lord, the two vessels were about five miles apart at the time of the disaster. The evidence from the *Titanic* corroborates this estimate, but I am advised that the distance was probably greater, though not more than eight to ten miles. The ice by which the SS *Californian* was surrounded was loose ice extending for a distance of no more than two or three miles in the direction of the *Titanic*. The night was clear and the sea was smooth. When she first saw the rockets the *Californian* could have pushed through the ice to the open water without any serious risk, and so have come to the assistance of the *Titanic*. Had she done so, she might have saved many, if not all, of the lives that were lost.

ALTERNATIVE NONSENSES

Lord Mersey in his final report chose to completely reject the body of evidence from *Titanic* witnesses stating that the mystery ship seen from the White Star Liner was 5 to 6 miles away. Instead he preferred to believe that she was from 8 to 10 miles away, an arbitrary increase of two-thirds to the mean distance cited by *Titanic* witnesses (British Inquiry Final Report, p.46):

> …according to Captain Lord, the two vessels were about five miles apart at the
> time of the disaster. The evidence from the *Titanic* corroborates this estimate, but I am
> advised that the distance was probably greater, though not more than eight to ten miles.

Read the above paragraph carefully! Mersey is equating the *Titanic*'s mystery ship with the *Californian*, and he accepts that the overwhelming thrust of the evidence from the *Titanic* witnesses is that the distance to their mystery ship (whatever her identity) was 5 miles.

Lord Mersey accepts the *Titanic* evidence of 5 miles, and Captain Lord's estimate of 4–5 miles' separation between his ship and a nearby stranger should simply copper-fasten an obvious conclusion, if indeed the *Californian* sees *Titanic* and vice versa. If they see each other, and both say 5 miles, then it should be 5 miles. Indeed the Attorney General, in his closing speech, said as much (British Inquiry, p.900):

> If you compare the *Titanic* evidence with the *Californian*, it is abundantly plain that
> the distance between them must have been comparatively small, that is to say certainly
> within five to seven miles…

But Lord Mersey's Report not only rejected his own Attorney General's submission on distance, but more importantly discarded the most common estimate of *Titanic* witnesses, who certainly had no reason to lie about their impressions. He openly proclaims that he is satisfied *Titanic* witnesses in the main are wrong, and that he is instead correct to rely on the advice of his nautical assessors. These are his assistants, who sat with him in London during the Inquiry, who certainly were nowhere near the North Atlantic that night, but who knew best. Why do they know best? Only four witnesses in total, from both inquiries, gave evidence supporting the British Report's final stretching of the nearest distance to what would become the officially endorsed range of 8 to 10 miles. They included two sailors, a nightwatchman and a female first class passenger. AB William Lucas says: 'It was about eight or nine miles; it was right on the horizon' (1585). Nightwatchman James Johnson states: 'I should consider it would be about eight or ten miles off' (3486). AB George Symons: 'Roughly between five and ten miles away when they fired the rockets' (11468). And passenger Mrs J. Stuart White claims: 'Oh, it was 10 miles away, but we could see it distinctly'. (US Inquiry, p.1008). Steward Alfred Crawford did say 'not farther than 10 miles' in his US evidence, but was more specific and circumspect in his British evidence: 'I should say she was 5 to 7 miles away from us' (17850). The main 8–10 mile 'barbershop quartet' is countered however by *all* of the RMS *Titanic*'s surviving officers, each an experienced and trained observer. Second Officer Charles Herbert Lightoller suggests: 'Certainly not over 5 miles away' (14150). Third Officer Herbert Pitman says: 'I thought it was about five miles' (15062). Fourth Officer Joseph Boxhall states: 'I judged her to be between 5 and 6 miles when I Morsed to her, and then she turned round' (15409). Fifth Officer Harold Lowe says:

> 15825 …I glanced over in that direction casually and I saw a steamer there.
> 15826. What did you see of her? — I saw her two masthead and her red side lights.
> [Implying closeness because side lights had to be seen a regulation two miles]

Incidentally, in a 1913 court case, *Ryan* v. *Oceanic Steam Navigation*, Boxhall reiterated that the mystery ship was approximately 5 miles away. Officer Lowe, judging the distance for the first time in evidence, said it was 4 miles away. Officer Pitman now estimated only 2 miles. These officers notably did not change their minds in accordance with Lord Mersey's findings!

Not only all the surviving *Titanic* officers, but crew members thought the same. A representative sample:

> QM Robert Hichens: 'about five miles away' (1162).
> Lookout Reginald Lee: 'five or six miles' (2719).
> AB John Poingdexter: 'A matter of four or five miles' (3089).
> Fireman Charles Hendrickson: 'A ship, five or six miles ahead of us' (11076).
> QM Walter Wynn: 'About seven or eight miles' (13340).
> AB George Moore: 'Two or three miles away, I should judge' (US Inquiry, p.564).
> AB Edward Buley: 'I should judge she was about three miles' (US Inquiry, p.611).
> QM George Rowe: 'Four or five miles' (17659).
> Scullion John Collins: 'About 4 miles; I am sure, three or four miles' (US Inquiry, p.629).
> QM Arthur John Bright: 'Possibly four or five miles away' (US Inquiry, p.836).

We shall not include any passenger observations to counter Mrs White's 'ten miles' above, since passenger estimations are unreliable in general, but will cite just one account to indicate that their guesses ranged widely: Passenger Mrs Imanita Shelley stated in a deposition to the US Inquiry: 'Right after the *Titanic* began to sink a steamer was sighted about two miles away, and all were cheered up; as it was figured that they would all be picked up inside an hour or so; however, their hopes were blighted when the steamer's lights suddenly disappeared' (US Inquiry, p.1148). The average mileage here – among nineteen estimates cited above from 1912 – works out at 5½ miles.

No-one can tell how far those ships were apart in reality, but the statistical truth is that she was 5½ miles away, and this is indeed in accordance with the figures cited most often. In this respect the Attorney General is correct when he asserts that the evidence proves (being proof in its legal sense) that the separation was 'certainly within five to seven miles'. So why did Lord Mersey's nautical examiners stay his hand?

Simple. They knew, as seagoing men, that the *Titanic* at 5–7 miles would look enormous to the *Californian* at such an 'easy distance', to quote the Attorney General. Captain Lord had previously seen the *Olympic*, the *Titanic*'s sister ship, at 5 miles, and had this to say: 'A ship like the *Titanic* at sea is an utter impossibility for anyone to mistake' (6991). The layers of brightness of the *Titanic* at that distance, her famous length – advertised as the size of a skyscraper laid on its side – could plainly not have given rise to the impression of a tramp with a few minor lights. And not only would her rockets have illuminated the night sky at such a close separation, but the associated detonations might have woken even a sleeping officer of the watch on a nearby vessel! The injection of nearly double the distance in the British findings is now easy to understand. Furthermore, the court must have belatedly realised that a distance of 5–7 miles represented only half an hour's steaming to the *Californian*. The Attorney General made this very point in his closing speech (British Inquiry, p.900):

> This vessel, [*Californian*] … could steam as much as 13 knots, but was certainly able to steam 11 knots, and putting it even further than the five to seven miles, it still gave her ample time to get there…

Yet it took the *Californian* five times as long as it should have done, by the Attorney General's own certainty (established on weight of *Titanic* evidence), to reach the scene next morning. The *Californian* quite simply took two and a half hours (from 6 a.m. to 8.30 a.m.) to reach the *Carpathia*'s side, although admittedly she went the long way – and still did not reach the actual sinking site.

We can also see a massive contradiction contained in these next remarks from the Attorney General about the *Californian*'s necessary proximity if the ship she sees is to be the *Titanic* – compared to the British Inquiry's later anxiety that she should be pushed further away (British Inquiry, p.900): 'She [*Titanic*] must have been within an easy distance in order that her masthead lights and her side lights were seen, as they were, by the *Californian*…' There are no two ways about it. But Lord Mersey was determined to have his double-indemnity insurance. He would apply arguments from one scenario against difficulties arising in the other, and vice versa, fleeing from one refuge to another as pressure arose.

If *Californian* was close to *Titanic*, why did the latter ship not appear like the giant she was? If they were far, how could each ship see the other's side lights (must be seen at 2 miles)? If they were close, why were the rockets low-lying? If they were far, how could they see a flickering masthead light and skylights, open windows, alleyways? If they were close why could they not hear the rocket explosions? And so on.

Yet there is another factor here too, which arises since the discovery of the *Titanic* wreck, found over 13 miles east of her SOS position – it is this: if the *Titanic's* mystery ship is seen at 5 or 6 miles to the north-west of the wreck site, this being the actual sinking spot (because the *Californian* saw rockets to the south-east), and if the insistence remains that this enigma is the *Californian*, then the *Californian* is not stopped at the ice barrier. She is nowhere near the ice barrier, but still in miles and miles of open sea. And yet the *Californian* was stopped by the field ice! But let us experimentally accept Mersey's distance of 8–10 miles, which was adopted purely and selfishly for the protection of the court's judgement in its damning verdict.

Let us agree with Mersey that 8–10 miles was, in fact, the separation. It remains an enormous distance for either vessel to see coloured side lights, but let that pass. We now have a situation in which it is argued that the *Titanic* came to rest at 11.40 p.m., her time at a distance 8–10 miles from the stationary *Californian*. The *Titanic* had been doing 22 knots before she was halted. In the previous half hour, back to 11.10 p.m., she would therefore have steamed 11 nautical miles.

If she was 8–10 miles from the *Californian* at 11.40, then she was 19–21 miles from the *Californian* at 11.10 p.m. – when she was first seen by Groves (who specifies both times, from first noticing his 'obliquely approaching' steamer until she stopped in front of the icefield). The figure of 19–21 miles is reached by factoring in *Titanic's* speed over the half an hour when Groves saw an approaching vessel, backtracked from Lord Mersey's determination that the final gap between *Titanic* and mystery ship at 11.40 p.m. was 8–10 miles.

If this is true, then Groves was first seeing his oncoming vessel at a distance that was many miles over the *Californian's* visible horizon. He could *not* have seen her light at 19–21 miles. *Titanic's* speed until she stopped shows she made 11 nautical miles between 11.10 p.m. and 11.40 p.m. (half an hour at 22 knots). But Groves himself said this ship made only 5 miles in that half an hour – a *Titanic* trudge!

> 8384. You said when you first saw the ship she appeared to be about ten miles from you?
> — Ten to twelve, I said.
> 8385. When she came to a stop what was the distance? — Well, I should think about five to seven miles. [A declination of 5 miles]

By Lord Mersey's own account, Groves could not have seen an approaching ship at 19–21 miles away at 11.10 p.m. But he did see a ship, as Lord had seen her forty minutes earlier, when he says he first discussed with Groves whether it could be a star. Even at 10.55 p.m. – fifteen minutes before Groves says he 'noticed her first' – the approaching ship light was being discussed on the *Californian* by Captain Lord, Evans, and Chief Engineer W.S.A. Mahon. Three witnesses, although Mahon was not called. Lord says he noticed her first at 10.30 p.m. *Californian* time and that she stopped at 11.30 p.m. (Groves claims 11.40 p.m. stop, *Californian* time). In an hour, the *Titanic*, wherever she is, will have steamed 22 nautical miles (she was powering along at 22 knots before she hit her berg at 11.40 p.m. her time).

But we must still add in Lord Mersey's 'stop-gap' of 8–10 miles in order to get the *Titanic*'s distance from the *Californian* when Captain Lord first saw a light so low on the south-east horizon that it might have been a star – until it later resolved itself into a steamer. This means, according to Mersey's final figures, that Captain Lord would have first seen the *Titanic* – for that is what Lord Mersey says she was – at a massive distance!

The *Titanic* did 22 miles to the west on a course of S 86 W in the hour to 11.30 p.m. She did at least 3 miles more for the extra ten minutes to 11.40 p.m., since that is the *Californian* time that Officer Groves said she stopped, and which Lord Mersey chose to accept for obvious reasons. That is a distance of 25 nautical miles from 10.30 p.m. until 11.40 p.m. stop. She is then said to bear 8–10 miles south-south-east of the *Californian*, making two sides of a triangle where the closing of a triangle against these two sides will give the direct distance that Captain Lord first saw her light at 10.30 p.m. If we apply trigonometry, assuming a 10 mile final separation, this works out at a gigantic and impossible 30.35 nautical miles. Lord cannot see anything like so far. This multiplies the *Californian*'s visible horizon (7.8 nautical miles) four times! And Captain Lord said he watched the light not from the flying bridge, but from a lower vantage point: 'I was just noticing it casually from the deck' (6718). Even using the lowest parameter of 8 miles as the stop-gap, Captain Lord is seeing his light at 29.2 nautical miles (29.76 at 9 miles). This means that *Titanic*, with its great height, ought to have seen the stationary *Californian*, if she was the mystery ship, for an eternity prior to the crash!

Of course, *Titanic* did not see anything, and neither was *Californian*'s nearby stranger doing anything remotely resembling the *Titanic*'s speed, else Lord could not have seen her so early and for so long. The approaching light was nothing like the distance away that Lord Mersey must assume, since Captain Lord next estimates her distance at 11 p.m., half an hour before he says she stopped, and thirty minutes after he had first seen her: 'At 11 o'clock... I suppose she was six or seven miles away. That is only approximately' (6731–2). Captain Lord also testified that, at some stage between 11 p.m. and 11.30 p.m., this vessel was 'about five miles' away (6761). Lord added later, in a further response, that when she stopped his vessel was 'about four or five – four to five miles' off (6960). The stranger has come down from 6–7 miles to 5 miles, and then to 4–5 miles. By Lord's account she has travelled a maximum of 3 miles (a speed of 6 knots) in this half hour from 11 p.m. to 11.30 p.m.

This then, is a steamer that is proceeding slowly, as indeed it may have done because it had seen the ice in the vicinity. Lord's 6 knots stands miserable comparison to the *Titanic*'s 22 knots, but it bears comparison to Groves' separately observed slow speed.

Lord Mersey might be inclined to dismiss Captain Lord's early sighting as falsehood, were it not for the fact that Captain Lord independently discusses the approaching ship with his wireless operator and chief engineer before Groves notices it. Evans' 11 p.m. Marconigram and testimony both prove a ship was seen long before Groves cottoned on. Yet Lord Mersey totally relies on Groves. Unfortunately for him, if Groves is correct about an oblique approach, then that ship is too slow to be the *Titanic*, and she is also steering a bizarre course to which *Titanic* witnesses never testified.

If Captain Lord is correct about the ship first being seen in the south-east and steaming on a course close to due west, then his ship is also far too slow to be the *Titanic*. Captain Lord's stop position for his own ship, with which Groves did not disagree, would also put this ship, if the *Titanic*, more than a dozen miles out of her track! In short, if either man is correct, the ship cannot be the *Titanic*. And surely both men – Lord and Groves – cannot be wrong about a ship that was 'in fact' the *Titanic*.

The actual *Titanic* was behaving in a wholly different manner to that which these men observed. It cannot be possible for Captain Lord and Officer Groves (separately and together) to fail to notice what the *Titanic* actually did, and to describe instead something else entirely! Thus it is utterly impossible for the *Californian* to have seen the RMS *Titanic*, largest moving object ever built to that point – the ship that the British Inquiry so desperately wanted her to see. It is equally impossible that the *Californian* was another ship in turn, the *Titanic's* mystery ship, which the British Inquiry so earnestly desired her to be, even if the hanging judge should have decided to allow her so much 'extra rope' (in the form of extra mileage) in order that *Californian* witnesses might mistake a sea-going colossus for Lord, Gibson and Stone's modest tramp steamer.

20

CAPTAINS CONTRASTED

There is an obvious difference in the British Inquiry's treatment of two captains – Smith of the *Titanic* and Lord of the *Californian*. But there is a further glaring difference in its treatment of Lord of the *Californian* and Moore of the *Mount Temple*. It is no part of this assessment to attempt to 'divert' blame towards Captain Moore – far from it – but merely to show that there was yet another egregious double standard displayed by the British Inquiry.

We have seen the treatment meted out to Lord. Yet it is a fact that Lord's *Californian* was the first vessel to reach the side of the rescue vessel *Carpathia* the next morning, despite starting from a position much further away than the *Mount Temple*. Captain Lord crossed through the ice barrier three times; Captain Moore did not penetrate it once. Yet Captain Moore knew about the SOS emergency all night, while Lord did not. Lord first crossed the ice barrier westbound between 6 a.m.–6.30 a.m. before hurrying down to the *Mount Temple* at the SOS position. The *Californian* passed the *Mount Temple* thereabouts at 7.30 a.m.

The *Mount Temple* had been looking for a way through the ice shortly before, to the south, and had returned north to the SOS position, where she had previously been stopped at 4.46 a.m. She had moreover come to a stop even before first arriving at the transmitted location of distress. Moore says (US Inquiry, p.761):

> Moore: …At 3.25 a.m. by our time we stopped.
> Senator Smith: Where were you then; in what position was your ship?
> Moore: I should say we were then about 14 miles off the *Titanic's* position.
> Sen. Smith: Can you tell me just what your position was; did you take it?
> Moore: I could not; I could not take any position. There was nothing – I could not see…

Why did the *Mount Temple* stop when a ship was sinking 14 miles away according to its best information? Moore claims (US Inquiry, 762–3):

> Moore: …after 3 o'clock… I stopped her on account of the ice getting so thick, sir. As a matter of fact, I did not stop her altogether; I simply stopped the engines and let the way run off the ship and then proceeded slowly.

And here is Moore at the British Inquiry:

> 9238. Later on, I think, about 3.25, did you meet pack ice? —Yes; I had met scattered ice
> before that, but that was the time I met the heavier ice.
> 9239. I think from that time onwards you continued to meet heavy ice? — Oh, yes.
> 9240. And at about daylight [4.30 a.m.] did you come up to the [SOS] position? — In
> the vicinity of that position.
> 9242. Did you see any signs of wreckage? — None whatever.

Moore also states: 'I reached the *Titanic's* position. I reckon I was very close to that
position, either that position or very close to it, at 4.30 in the morning sir' (US Inquiry,
p.764). And elsewhere: 'Half past 4, sir; that is, I reckoned we were at that position at half
past 4, sir' (US Inquiry, p.766).

At 4.30 a.m. therefore, and certainly at 4.46 a.m. when it is known from a wireless
transmission that she was stopped, the *Mount Temple* was at the SOS position. But she did
nothing, even though she quickly realised the *Titanic* must have struck on the other side of
the ice barrier. The survivors were still in lifeboats. The last *Titanic* lifeboat, No.12, would
not be picked up by the *Carpathia* until 8.30 a.m. Here is Moore:

> 9243. And were you, as you were proceeding to get there, getting messages from various
> steamers as to this disaster? —Yes.
> 9244. And I think shortly before 8 a.m. you came in sight of the *Carpathia* and the
> *Californian*? —Yes.

What had Moore and the *Mount Temple* been doing for over three hours while human
beings died of exposure in lifeboats less than an hour's steaming away? Effectively nothing.
Here is Moore's reason why:

> 9262. Just tell us what your instructions are? — Those instructions we usually get [are]
> that we are not to enter field ice, no matter how light it may appear.
> 9263. Not even in daylight? — At any time. We are not to enter field ice at any time, no
> matter how light it may appear...
> 9405. Your instructions seem to be that you are not to enter field ice? — Not to enter it
> on any account.

No matter what the overriding requirements of the dictates of humanity?

The author has uncovered another reason for what may seem like excessive caution
(*The Spectator*, Nova Scotia, December 1907):

STEAMER CRASHES ON ROCKS
Terrible Catastrophe Narrowly Averted

Seven hundred and thirty-two persons stared death in the face yet came through the ordeal unscathed when the C.P.R. liner, *Mount Temple*, driven far out of her course in a blinding snow storm was wrecked on Ironbound Island, at the mouth of the LaHave river on Sunday night.

It was between 11 and 12 o'clock when the steamer went ashore. For several hours she had been in shoal water and immediately she struck, a tremendous sea swept her broad-side on against the rocks. Sea after sea swept over her and when the frightened emigrants, who were chiefly Austrians, Russians, Poles, Gallicians, and Jews, rushed up from below, the decks were waist deep in water.

Pandemonium broke out. In an instant the frightened foreigners were panic stricken and cries and shrieks arose above even the howling of the gale and the crash of the waves as they surged over the ship.

Quickly the officers and crew calmed the frenzied passengers; life preservers were served out and a line shot ashore, while the old order, the first thought of a British sea-man, '*Women and children first!*' rang out.

There were about one hundred women and children on board and these were sent ashore in the breeches buoy while the men were transferred in boats. Only a portion of the passengers could be landed during the night as the seas were running very high.

Those that did get ashore spent a very uncomfortable night. Fires were lit and the lightkeeper and his family did everything in their power to relieve their sufferings, but nevertheless the night proved a terrible hardship to many. In the morning assistance was received from Lunenburg fishermen and local steamers.

A *Reuters* telegram from Halifax, Nova Scotia, dated 3 December says (the *Times* of London, 4 December 1907, p.8):

The Government steamer *Laurier* has landed 500 passengers of the *Mount Temple* here. They spent the night on a barren island sleeping on the snow, protected by mattresses and blankets from the wreck. Huge camp fires made the winter weather endurable. The steamer is in a bad position, but she may be saved if the weather continues fair. All the holds are full of water, there being 18ft in the forward hold.

Just four years and four months earlier, in other words, the *Mount Temple* had almost been lost. Captain Hubert Boothby, commander on that occasion, was sacked by Canadian Pacific even though he had been exonerated and even praised by a court of inquiry.

By April 1912, the memory of her striking resilient objects and having holds full of water must have been horribly fresh in the mind. At the same time however, the *Mount Temple* and her new captain were not in the slightest doubt about the gravity of the *Titanic's* situation. The *Mount Temple*, according to the evidence of her wireless operator, John Durrant, had known the *Titanic's* engine rooms were getting flooded since 1.27 a.m. But he noted at 4.46 a.m., that is a quarter to five in the morning ship's time: 'All quiet. We are stopped amongst pack ice' (9573).

The *Californian* would not make her first call for information for another twenty-five minutes! And the *Californian* responded immediately on learning the news, steaming into the pack ice, whereas the *Mount Temple* would only belatedly begin to skirt down to southward looking for a way through. Moore says: 'I went to the southward later on in the morning, when it got daylight' (US Inquiry, p.764). The *Mount Temple* never did venture into that ice. Ever.

Moore states: 'I went a little farther, and I turned around because it was getting far too heavy to put the ship through' (US Inquiry, p.764). But British Solicitor General, Sir John Simon, was later curiously gentle with the *Mount Temple*:

9589. [The Solicitor General, to Wireless Operator Durrant] I think you heard about 8 o'clock in the morning, your ship's time, from the *Carpathia,* that she had rescued? — Twenty boat loads.

9590. And, of course, as we know, your ship did her best but could not get to the spot in time? — No.

One can say that the *Californian* made every effort – that Captain Lord risked his ship twice to cross the ice barrier, to the west and then the east, in order to reach the *Carpathia's* side at 8.30 a.m. Critics would naturally say that the *Californian* was trying to make up for her guilt in seeing rockets the previous night and doing nothing about them.

Meanwhile an affidavit had been given to the US Inquiry by a medical doctor stating that the *Mount Temple* had actually seen the *Titanic* (US Inquiry, p.1098):

DOMINION OF CANADA, Province of Ontario, City of Toronto:

Dr F. C. Quitzrau; being first duly sworn, deposes and says that he was a passenger, travelling second class, on steamer *Mount Temple*, which left Antwerp April 3, 1912; that about midnight Sunday, April 14, New York time, he was awakened by the sudden stopping of the engines; that he immediately went to the cabin, where were already gathered several of the stewards and passengers, who informed him that word had been received by wireless from the *Titanic* that the *Titanic* had struck an iceberg and was calling for help.

Orders were immediately given and the *Mount Temple* course changed, heading straight for the *Titanic*. About 8 o'clock New York time, 2 o'clock ship's time, the *Titanic* was sighted by some of the officers and crew; that as soon as the *Titanic* was seen all lights on the *Mount Temple* were put out and the engines stopped and the boat lay dead for about two hours; that as soon as day broke the engines were started and the *Mount Temple* circled the *Titanic's* position, the officers insisting that this be done, although the Captain had given orders that the boat proceed on its journey.

While encircling the *Titanic's* position we sighted the *Frankfurt* to the northwest of us, the *Birma* to the south, speaking to both of these by wireless, the latter asking if we were in distress; that about 6 o'clock we saw the *Carpathia*, from which we had previously received a message that the *Titanic* had gone down; that about 8.30 the *Carpathia* wirelessed that it had picked up 20 lifeboats and about 720 passengers all told, and that there was no need for the *Mount Temple* to stand by, as the remainder of those on board were drowned.

Dr F. C. QUITZRAU

Subscribed and sworn to before me this 29th day of April, 1912. [Seal]
William James Elliott, Notary Public for the Province of Ontario.

Moore was asked about this affidavit, but the doctor's claims certainly were not pursued with the same vigour as those of Gill (US Inquiry, p.767):

Senator Smith: Some passengers on your vessel, Sunday night about midnight, claim to have seen these rockets from the decks of the *Titanic*. Have you heard anything about that?
Moore: I have read it in the papers, sir; but as a matter of fact, I do not believe there was a passenger on deck at 12 o'clock at night. I am positive, because they would not know anything at all about this, and you may be sure that they would be in their beds. I know the steward tells me there was nobody on deck; that is, the night watchman at the aft end. At the forward end there was nobody on deck. The man in what we call the permanent steerage that passes under the bridge deck – we have a permanent steerage there, and the other, of course, is a portable one we can take down – and nobody saw a passenger on deck, sir…

And slightly later (US Inquiry, p.769):

Senator Smith: Do you wish to be understood as saying that you did not see, on Sunday night or Monday morning, any signal lights from the *Titanic*?
Moore: I can solemnly swear that I saw no signal lights, nor did my officers on the bridge see any signal lights.

And that was it. He also denied he could have seen the *Carpathia*'s rockets, which were seen in the *Titanic* lifeboats at 3.30 a.m. and by the *Californian* in the extreme distance at 3.25 a.m. This was a time when the *Mount Temple* said she was still 14 miles to the west of the SOS position (US Inquiry, p.777):

Senator Smith: Let me ask you right there, did you see the rockets from the *Carpathia*?
Moore: I do not think it possible, sir, because if the *Carpathia* was farther away it is not likely you would see her rockets. But you see, this ship says she is sending rockets up. So it is possible that other ships may have seen them. I do not know. I thought of sending rockets up, but I thought it far better to let it alone, because if other ships thought they saw them they might be coming to me, and I had not seen anything of the *Titanic* and did not know exactly where she was; because I think, after all, the *Titanic* was farther east than she gave her position, or, in fact, I am certain she was.

The British Inquiry, which followed the senatorial hearings, asked precisely *no* questions about Quitzrau's allegations or about the *Mount Temple* seeing rockets. His deposition is assuredly flawed, but there were many similar claims from other *Mount Temple* passengers aired in the Canadian and American press, all of them overlooked. Instead there was this ringing declaration from Lord Mersey in the early part of Wireless Operator Durrant's evidence:

> [The Commissioner] This boat, the *Mount Temple*, was never in a position to render active assistance.
> [The Solicitor General] It was 49 miles away, and it was making for her.
> [The Commissioner] She could not possibly have reached her.
> 9486. [The Solicitor General] No, not possibly. She was doing her best.

The *Mount Temple* was 49 miles away at 12.30 a.m. Her top speed was something over 11 knots. She got to the empty SOS position at 4.30 a.m. But it is in regard to the four hours of daylight thereafter, until 8.30 a.m. when *Carpathia* picked up the last lifeboat, that questions should be asked. The British Inquiry had, after all, awarded itself an additional question to answer after hearing witnesses: 'What vessels had the opportunity of rendering assistance to the *Titanic*, and if any, how was it that assistance did not reach the *Titanic* before the SS *Carpathia* arrived?' (p.839). The answer in the official report was stark: 'The *Californian*. She could have reached the *Titanic* if she had made the attempt when she saw the first rocket. She made no attempt' (British Inquiry Final Report, p.71). This finding made no mention of any other vessels. It did not mention the *Mount Temple*, nor the ice barrier that prevented Moore from joining the *Carpathia*.

Let it be remembered that the *Californian* took an hour and a half to get from her drifted overnight stop to the supposed disaster scene – the location given by the *Titanic's* SOS, which was wrong. If Lord had been told enough, or had somehow divined the situation at 1.15 a.m. (when Stone first whistled down the speaking-tube) his vessel would have reached the SOS position (empty!) at 2.45 a.m. by the earliest (although inevitably much later because she would have been travelling in darkness instead of daylight).

The earliest possible arrival would have been half an hour after the *Titanic* sank. But there would have been no lifeboats even if she had reached there, because the *Titanic* herself gave out the wrong position. Another trip through the ice would have been required, even though just *one* such trip was beyond Moore and the *Mount Temple* in all circumstances (US Inquiry, p.783):

> Moore: …My instructions from my company are that I must not enter field ice, no matter if it seems only light. Those are my explicit instructions from my company.
> If I was to go through ice and my ship was damaged I would have pointed out to me that those were the instructions, that I was not to go into any ice, no matter how thin. As a matter of fact, I would not attempt to go through field ice if it was thick. The usual thing, on approaching ice, at night, is to stop and wait until daylight.

And Moore states: 'I assure you that I did everything that was possible, sir, consistent with the safety of my own ship and its passengers' (US Inquiry, p.785).

The *Californian* did the 'usual thing' on encountering ice at night: she stopped, drifting until daylight. She had no direct knowledge of the SOS transmission until five hours after the *Mount Temple* (5.11 a.m. as against 12.11 a.m., both *Mount Temple* time). And the *Californian* did risk her own safety, in Moore's description, dashing twice through the ice barrier to reach first one scene and then the other. She got no thanks for it.

21

MISSING LOGS

A log of the hours of the middle watch when the *Californian* saw rockets ought to have been kept by the officer of the watch – in this case, Second Officer Herbert Stone, in line with standard procedure. Industry-wide practice was that the officer of the watch kept notes on a 'scrap log' – often a torn-out sheet of paper – which would then be written up into the official log by the chief officer – in this case, George Stewart. It was the role of the chief officer on every vessel to keep the official log.

Titanic's chief officer, Henry Wilde, was responsible for that vessel's official log. He died in the sinking and the official log was never recovered. The *Californian's* official log was produced to the British Inquiry, but it turned out that the vessel's scrap log for the night in question had been destroyed. Lord Mersey in his Final Report chose to lay particular emphasis on the absence of the scrap log (p.43):

> The Master told the Court that he made [the *Californian's* overnight stop] position to be 42° 5' N, 57° 7' W [sic – actually 50° 7' W]. This position is recorded in the log book, which was written up from the scrap log book by the Chief Officer. The scrap log is destroyed. It is a position about 19 miles N by E of the position of the *Titanic* when she foundered, and is said to have been fixed by dead reckoning and verified by observations. I am satisfied that this position is not accurate.

Mersey has linked three things together: the claimed overnight stop position (50° 7' W, not 57°), the absence of the scrap log, and his satisfaction that the claimed overnight stop position is 'not accurate'. The sinister implication of Mersey's construction is clear: the *Californian's* scrap log was destroyed because its information did not concur with the position that *Californian* later relied upon, and which Mersey concluded was 'not accurate'.

We have seen in previous treatment why Mersey could believe the *Californian* standpoint to be 'not accurate' (a carefully-chosen phrase indeed), with his wrong-headed ideas about 'speeding' wreckage and the emerging evidence that the *Titanic* and *Californian* positions could not both be correct, which was indeed true. The missing scrap log now allows Mersey to convey shadows of dark conspiracy in further support of his judgement, and indeed the missing log has been cited many times since as a basis for the belief that the *Californian* falsified her position.

Unfortunately for such theorists, the truth is rather more plain and prosaic. Virtually all vessels, including the *Titanic*, used the scrap log system. And all such vessels routinely disposed of the scraps after their contents had been transferred into the official log. Therefore Lord Mersey is simply not entitled to equate the routine disposal of an out-of-date scrap of paper with a conspiracy, or an organised suppression of evidence. We will examine what was said about the *Californian's* scrap log by the witnesses to the British Inquiry.

It is a fact, however, that Second Officer Herbert Stone did *not* offer any mention of the unusual rockets in his personal notes for that midnight–4 a.m. duty. It is odd that he was never asked about his failure to record those signals. Nor was Stone ever recalled, in the light of other witness evidence, to answer questions about his omission. Instead it was left to others to do their best to explain his actions. Lord was asked:

7331. Is it not usual to record these things in the log? — We never realised what these rockets were, my Lord. If they had been distress rockets they would have been mentioned in the log.

7332. But the next morning you knew the *Titanic* had gone down? — Yes.

7333. Did you make no record then in your log of the signals that you had seen? — No.

7334. Why not? — We never took them to be distress rockets. The Second Officer's explanation to me of these rockets was that they were not distress rockets.

7335. Why was all reference to these rockets left out of the log? — If we had realised they were distress rockets we would have entered them, my Lord.

Chief Officer Stewart was also questioned on the issue:

8658. It is your business to write up the log-book from the scrap log? — Yes

8659. Who keeps the scrap log-book, and where is it kept? — It is just kept for the day, that is all.

8660. I am not sure that I understand. You do not mean there is a new scrap log-book for every day? — It is all bits that are torn out and destroyed. The [official] log-book is written up every day and the officer signs it.

8661. Do you mean that at the end of the day when you have written up your log from the scrap log-book you tear out the page of the scrap logbook and destroy it? — Yes.

8672. [The Solicitor General] Why do you do that? — Because we only keep the one log.

8673. But why? — By the company's instructions.

8674. [The Commissioner] I never heard of this. Are you instructed by your owners to destroy the scrap log as the voyage goes along? — Yes my Lord.

8675. [The Solicitor General] Day by day? — Yes.

8676. [The Commissioner] Does your steamer belong to the same company that practically owns the *Titanic*? — We belong to the Leyland Line, my Lord.

8677. Yes, I know, but is that part and parcel of the International Marine? — A part of it, my Lord.

8678. That is to say, it belongs to the same company that the *Titanic* belonged to? — I cannot say as to that, my Lord.

8679. I daresay you do not understand the arrangements between them but you are part and parcel of the International Marine? —Yes.

8680. And the *Titanic* was part and parcel of the International Marine? —Yes, my Lord.

8681. Am I to understand that those instructions are given to all the steamers, controlled by that company, that is to say to the White Star, the Leyland Line and others? — I cannot say that, my Lord.

Mr Andrew Laing (member of the advisory committee to the Board of Trade) offers clarification (questions 8686–7):

I can tell your Lordship what the practice is. The practice, so far as the White Star vessels are concerned is that the scrap logs are not to be kept. They are torn off a block, or pad, day by day. What is called the Chief Officer's log is kept, and handed in as soon as completed to the owners, but the scrap logs are not kept.

Further questions are put to Stewart:

8721. Now, I should like to follow this. As far as your memory serves you, did you enter into that log book everything that you found on the scrap log sheet [of Second Officer Stone]? —Yes.

8722. You observe there is nothing at all in your log book about seeing distress signals? —Yes.

8723. Is there anything? — No, nothing.

8724. Nothing at all? — No.

8725. No reference to any of these events of the night at all? — No.

8726. [The Commissioner] Does that convey to you that there was no reference to those events in the scrap log? —Yes, my Lord...

8733. [The Solicitor General] The scrap log-book is intended to be kept at the time, is it not, as the things happen? —Yes, Sir, but they generally write them up at the end of the watch.

8734. And you were there at 4 o'clock at the end of the watch? —Yes.

8735. And Mr Stone told you then at 4 o'clock that he had seen these signals? —Yes.

8739. Did not it occur to you that it was odd that there was nothing entered on the scrap log-book? — I did not notice the scrap log-book at that time.

8741. You made entries on the same sheet of paper between four and eight o'clock, didn't you? — Not till eight o'clock.

8743. Didn't you notice it then? — I noticed there was nothing on it then.

8744. But by that time you had had the message that the *Titanic* had sunk? —Yes.

8747. Then you did at eight o'clock notice there was nothing in the scrap log-book about what had happened between midnight and four? —Yes.

8748. And you have told us, in your view, it would be right to make such entries? —Yes.

8749. Did you ever speak to the Second Officer about it? — No.

8750. Never? — No.

8751. [The Commissioner] Or to the Captain? — No.

8752. Or to anybody? — No, my Lord.

8753. [The Solicitor General] This piece of paper, whatever it was, in the scrap log-book for 15th April, would be used until midnight on the 15th, wouldn't it? — Yes.

8754. Then would you write the entries into the log-book from the scrap log-book? — Yes.

8755. And do you say you then destroyed the record for April 15th? — Yes.

8756. When you destroyed it did you notice then there was no record on it about these distress signals, didn't you notice that? —— No, I just copied it off as it was.

Stewart says Stone had written up nothing for his watch. Stewart only made his own notes at the end of his watch at 8 a.m. Stewart says he himself destroyed the scrap log – which was completely insignificant in itself, since the scrap log was blank on this issue.

Commissioner Mersey later shows himself to grasp that the issue (if any) lies not in whether the scrap log was destroyed or preserved, but in the fact that no sightings of rockets were entered by Stone (8923):

> [The Commissioner] …I may tell you that the effect of these things on my mind is this – that it is the practice to tear out the sheets of the scrap log from time to time and destroy them. But, you know, that does not get over my difficulty that apparently, if this evidence is true that has been given in the box, there was no entry of any kind in that scrap log of these rockets having been seen.
> [The Solicitor General] I understand, my Lord.

Yet look at Mersey's Final Report, referenced earlier. He does not rely on the absence of any mention of rockets in the log – scrap or otherwise – as a plank of argument. He instead relies on the fact of destruction of the scrap log as a tool for a quite different suggestion – that of a conspiracy in relation to the *Californian's* position.

Yet Mersey knew (when he crudely wielded the destruction of the scrap log as a weapon in another context) that it was, in his own words, 'the practice… to destroy… the scrap log'. He chose to deliberately misrelate the evidence for his own ends. The scrap log is clearly being misused as a crutch for Lord Mersey's declared satisfaction that the overnight stop position is 'not accurate'.

Yet Stone, who certainly might have entered the rockets he saw, would not have had any reason to include the *Californian's* position in his scrap log notes. He came on the bridge for the middle watch after midnight. Groves was serving the previous watch from 8 p.m. to midnight (question 8115), with the *Californian* stopping midway through at 10.21 (although Groves thought it was 10.26). These details should have been recorded in Groves' scrap log. And this is what Groves had to say about the reported stop position, it is worth recalling:

8425. In the log book it is stated that when you stopped your ship in the ice the position of the ship was 42° 5' N and longitude 50° 7' W. Is that accurate? — Well, it is bound to be accurate if the Captain put it in.

Groves, be it remembered, was the last officer of the watch. It was his responsibility to take the *Californian* due west on the Boston track. He oversaw compass, course and speed. He knew his ship was substantially separated from the *Titanic* on the separate, southern, New York track. There is no basis, therefore, for suggesting that Stone's scrap log would have contained any mention of a 'giveaway' *Californian* position. We know instead that Stone's scrap log was effectively blank.

To be the mystery ship, *Californian* would have to have travelled at least 14 miles to the south (42° 05' minus 41° 46' is 19 minutes – 19 miles of latitude, less the average 5 miles separation from the *Titanic* cited by witnesses on the White Star vessel). Groves knew the *Californian* had not headed south. Because he was the one in charge at the time – it had been his duty to continue her progress due west!

Lord Mersey may have found it difficult to believe that scrap logs were routinely destroyed, until Mr Laing's intervention to point out that exactly the same position obtained on the *Titanic* and other White Star vessels. Here is Lightoller, second officer of the *Titanic*, in confirmation: 'The speed was taken down, I understand, in the log? — Yes, that would be kept in the scrap log' (14361).

And here is Pitman, third officer of the *Titanic* (US Inquiry, p.301):

Senator Fletcher: What officer had charge of the log of the ship?
Pitman: Well, the Fifth and Sixth usually keep that. Which log do you mean? We keep two or three. The scrap log is kept on the bridge; the Fifth and Sixth look after that. The Chief Officer's log is copied from that… which is really the official log.

Meanwhile Groves, the *Californian* third officer, who gave evidence to the British Inquiry about seeing a 'passenger steamer', told of the fate which befell every scrap log (including his own that night from his personal period on watch):

8507. Is the scrap log here? — No, it is not kept.
8508. [The Commissioner] Is it destroyed from time to time? — It is destroyed from time to time. There is one log always kept, of course, but the scrap log is destroyed from time to time.

Groves also told of opening a new scrap log, with pre-ruled pages to be torn out as required, for the *Californian*'s homeward voyage from Boston to Liverpool:

8530. Groves …We had evidently finished the old one, otherwise I should not have started it.

8531/2. Where is that old one? — I expect it was thrown away.

8533. ....I expect it went over the side.

The scrap log usually related to the *Californian's* own information, such as speed, course, weather, and so on. Groves' evidence shows that his own scrap log, prepared just before Stone took over after midnight, contained no mention whatsoever of his 'passenger steamer' that came up and stopped nearby:

8550. As you were making entries in the scrap log book from 8 to 12 that night, do you know whether you made any entry as to any ship that you saw? — No, no entry whatsoever relating to any ship.

So how sinister now is Stone's failure to relate the rockets of another ship? Whether or no, the British Inquiry was inclined to make a great deal of the *Californian's* 'missing' log, notwithstanding the fact of *Titanic's* missing log and identical scrap system.

It meant that Robertson Dunlop, counsel for the Leyland Line, felt he had to address the climate of suspicion on the issue in his closing address to the Inquiry. He insisted that the *Californian's* official log, the master copy, contained all the information – or lack of it – that had been included in the source material (British Inquiry, p.833):

…It was not suggested to the Master, or the officers of the *Californian*, nor are there any grounds for the suggestion, that the log before your Lordship has been 'cooked'. The log on the face of it appears to be a perfectly genuine log.

[The Attorney General] I think you are putting that too high – you say there is no suggestion.

[Mr Dunlop] No question was put, my Lord, to the Master.

[The Commissioner] Just a moment, please. The scrap log is gone.

[Mr Dunlop] The scrap log is gone, and the explanation of that was given by the witnesses when they were asked about it.

[The Commissioner] And as far as I remember it was given in a way that satisfied me that it had gone.

One can see immediately that no suggestion or accusation of 'cookery' of the log was ever put to Captain Stanley Lord or any of the *Californian* witnesses. Yet this very smear was later outrageously inserted into the Final Report and placed in the public arena by Lord Mersey himself! Such a decision was a betrayal of Mersey's duty to elicit the truth. The scrap log simply had nothing whatsoever to do with whether the *Californian* could have been the *Titanic's* mystery ship. Note, too, the role of the Attorney General, legal adviser to the British Government, in his sly intervention to bolster Mersey's prejudice.

22

THE FINAL REPORT

The inquiries accepted the *Titanic*'s SOS position without question. The *Titanic*, we know, saw a mystery ship off her port bow and fired rockets. The *Californian* meanwhile saw rockets to the south-south-east. Therefore, if the *Californian* was the *Titanic*'s mystery ship, it follows, by 1912 acceptance of the SOS position, that she had to be located to the west side of the ice barrier, whereas we know she stopped to the east. And not only this – but it becomes necessary to argue that the *Titanic*'s head must also have been pointing to the north... thereby allowing not only the *Californian* to see rockets to the south-south-east, but for her be the *Titanic*'s mystery ship, seen to the north-north-west from the opposite point of view. The *Titanic*'s head must be pointing north in this model of fitting-the-*Californian* – because the mystery ship is seen off the port bow of the *Titanic*!

It will thus be grasped that all other thirty-one points of the compass favour Captain Lord's vessel *not* being the mystery ship! Those who accuse the *Californian*, therefore, are gambling all on just a 3.12 per cent chance in the uncertain sweepstake of how the *Titanic* was pointing her bows.

A crucial point to grasp is that the *Californian* has no such 'heading' needs, and she will always see rockets to the south-south-east once the *Titanic* is put back towards the place where her wreck was found, a location that is indisputable. *Californian* will still see rockets where she said she saw them, irrespective of how the *Titanic* might be pointing her bows, whether to north, south, east or west – because the rockets will rise from their point of origin, however the unseen ship (*Titanic*) might be deployed, swinging or spinning.

If the *Titanic* is on the east side of the barrier and firing rockets towards a mystery ship, then it equally does not matter where that mystery ship is located (in terms of the compass), once the *Californian*'s stop position is acknowledged as credible. And it *is* now highly credible, in the light of what we know since 1985. The discovery of the wreck has finally disposed of the SOS position sent by *Titanic*. Believing the *Californian*'s stop position now makes complete sense in a scenario that must involve two pairs of ships.

If the *Titanic* is in reality firing rockets at a completely different ship, and they are both over the visible horizon from the *Californian*, then the *Californian* can see those rockets to be lying low over her own nearby stranger, which Lord, Stone and Gibson agreed was a nondescript tramp. The *Californian* saw rockets to the south-south-east – on the same bearing as their nearby ship. This is a literal coincidence, as the rockets and the nearby ship coincide. Regarding rockets, Stone comments: 'I had seen white lights in the sky in the direction of this other steamer' (7829), 'immediately above this other steamer' (7832), which was bearing 'first south-south-east' (7940).

Again, this scenario does not at all require the *Titanic* to be aligned on the same vector with her mystery ship – meaning the four-ships-in-a-line idea often erroneously offered. If both the *Titanic* and her mystery ship are over the visible horizon from the *Californian*, they can relate to each other in any way at all, and it is irrelevant to the rockets. The only requirement for confusion aboard the *Californian* is for the rockets (from a distant *Titanic*) to show in the same direction as their own nearby ship. That ship of the *Californian*'s will eventually steam off to the south-south-west, and Stone will say that the rockets changed their bearing with her. But this description cannot mean that the *Californian*'s nearby ship was the *Titanic*, because the *Titanic* not only was not a tramp steamer, but did not steam or move anywhere after striking her berg.

It has been postulated that the angle of elevation of the rockets could have changed as the *Titanic* was sinking. Viewed from a great distance however, the lights can only appear largely the same, so the argument is flawed. It might be that Stone simply continues to link the rockets with the moving ship in his own mind. Or he may have realised at the Inquiry that to disconnect the later rockets from the near ship would have left him open to the charge of ignoring some other ship whose well-being he could not establish, since he could not see her.

Yet it is essential to keep in mind what we now know, beyond all dispute, which is that the *Californian*'s claimed stopping place in 1912 is 23½ nautical miles in a direct line (and on the correct 'rockets vector') from the centre of the *Titanic* debris field. This is massively beyond the horizon for *Californian* to see *Titanic* that night – and it is inescapable, because the *Titanic* had to sink where she was actually found!

This is what destroys the idiotic idea of some writers (based on Groves), who claim the wounded *Titanic* might have closed the gap by voyaging north after the collision, thereby getting closer to a stopped *Californian*. The *Titanic*'s track was along latitude line 41° 46' N (the same latitude given in the SOS), but after the impact she drifted south – and in fact sank in a latitude of 41° 43' N.

That's where the wreck site is today – 3 nautical miles south of the SOS latitude and the New York track *Titanic* was following. If the *Titanic* went any distance at all to the north by engines therefore, she would have to reverse the entire distance back to her starting point, and then reverse further to the south (to make up for lost time!) – because she always sank where she is today. Her wreck site, to the south of the track, conclusively disproves the claim.

Let us backtrack to 1912. The inquiries accepted that the *Titanic* sank in the SOS position transmitted, whereas the *Californian* claimed to be far to the north-east of that spot. If *Californian* were to the north-east of the *Titanic* (sinking at the SOS position), then she should have seen *Titanic*'s rockets to the far south-west, and not to the south-south-east. Remember our triangle '△', with *Californian* at the top.

So, if the *Californian* saw rockets to the south-south-east, as she said, and if her claim to be where she said she was is also true, then it would necessarily mean to the 1912 Inquiry (built on the cornerstone of the SOS position) that *two* ships were firing rockets at roughly the same period, these ships being the *Titanic*, whose rockets *Californian* thus did not see, and an unknown stranger (whose rockets she did). This idea, quite understandably, was rejected, leaving the British Inquiry with the simple choice to believe either the *Californian*'s position, or that of the *Titanic*. They had two separate positional claims which could not both be right.

It was not a difficult choice. The *Titanic* would have no reason to lie about something as crucial as an SOS position. The *Californian* could, however, have a motive for lying. The British Inquiry chose to rely absolutely on the *Titanic*'s SOS position, and once this was laid down as fact, then the *Californian*'s claimed position, in the absence of another rocket-firing ship, could no longer stand. It was thus a short journey of reasoning to place the *Californian* to the north-north-west of the *Titanic*, her confessed sighting of rockets to the south-south-east now dovetailing nicely with the *Titanic*'s sighting of a ship on the reverse bearing.

All of this, in the British Inquiry's view, allowed the *Californian*'s claimed stop position to be portrayed as false. And when added to Lord Mersey's erroneous deductions about 'speeding wreckage', it would appear the *Californian* was indeed peddling falsehoods. But it was the *Titanic*'s SOS position that was wrong. The wreck was found in 1985, 13 miles to the east of the SOS position, and east of the ice barrier. Now, when the *Californian* is returned to her claimed stop position of 1912, she is found to be on a correct line to see rockets to the south-south-east, as everyone had agreed she had seen them. And Stone said those rockets were 'very low-lying' (7921). To understand what happened, therefore, it is necessary that the *Titanic* be moved to the east, not the *Californian* to the west!

There is no absolute proof how far distant the White Star and Leyland liners were from each other in 1912, apart from their being at opposite ends of a line running north-north-west ('\') to south-south-east. But since the discovery of the *Titanic* wreck, we can at least say that the *Californian*'s repeatedly-cited 1912 stop position, which not only put her neck firmly in the noose at the time but virtually kicked open the gallows trapdoor, is no longer so easily imagined to be false.

Indeed, her claims must instead be considerably strengthened, given that the *Titanic*'s SOS position is proven to have been hopelessly in error.

TURN, TURN, TURN AGAIN

It has been seen that it is necessary for the *Titanic* to have been pointing generally north after her collision with the iceberg in order for the mystery ship appearing off the port bow to be the *Californian*, which sees rockets to the south-south-east. But there is no reliable evidence, at least in the Attorney General's opinion, as to how the *Titanic*'s head was pointing after impact. The change of heading from westward, as the *Titanic* had been driving, to a heading north, represents a fairly violent turn.

We know there was a violent turn to avoid the berg, but to port, not to starboard. This would leave the *Titanic* pointing momentarily south of west – but even still it was not enough because the berg impacted on the starboard bow. The helmsman at the time, Quartermaster Robert Hichens, specifically says:

> 1000. Then she comes round two points and then strikes. Is that right? — The vessel veered off two points, she went to the southward of west.

Now, it is claimed that what happened next was that the bridge ordered the wheel swung hard in the opposite direction, in order to swing the *Titanic*'s stern away from the berg. This was a second turn that would have the effect of a starboard manoeuvre. The contention is that this next turn would have the effect of leaving the *Titanic*'s head to the north. But the only problem is that such a long, extended turn to starboard is not convincingly attested in evidence!

Note that putting the helm hard-a-starboard meant to swing the ship's head to port, as the rudder orders were contrary to the intended direction of travel. Ordering hard-a-port would have the effect of sending the ship's head to starboard. Therefore a left turn to avoid the berg would involve a 'hard-a-starboard' command, while a command to swing to the right, to take the stern away from impact, would require 'hard-a-port'.

Here is Hichens:

> 948. Had you had any instructions before she struck? Had you been told to do anything with your helm before she struck? — Just as she struck I had the order 'Hard a starboard', when she struck.
> 949. Just as she struck, is that what you said? — Not immediately as she struck, the ship was swinging [to the left]. We had the order, 'Hard a starboard', and she just swung about two points when she struck.

Officer Boxhall said he overheard what First Officer Murdoch, in command at the time of impact, said to the captain to explain what had happened:

> 15355. What conversation took place between them? — The First Officer [Murdoch] said, 'An iceberg, Sir. I hard-a-starboarded and reversed the engines, and I was going to hard-a-port round it but she was too close'.

Note that carefully: 'I was going to hard-a-port round it'. It is implied by Boxhall's account that Murdoch did not have a chance to fully carry out the second manoeuvre to swing the stern out of the way – he was only 'going' to make the manoeuvre. In fact, he explicitly said this at the US Inquiry (p.230):

> Boxhall: Mr Murdoch also said, 'I intended to port around it'.
> Senator Smith: 'I intended to port around it'?
> Boxhall: 'But she hit before I could do any more'.

But the evidence is that some form of starboard twist, if not an outright turn, did happen. AB Joseph Scarrott recalls:

352. Was it close to? — No, it seemed the ship was acting on her helm and we had swung clear of the iceberg.

354. You speak of this ship as if answering her helm – as if answering under which helm? — Under the starboard helm – under the port helm.

355. Get it right? — Under port helm. Her stern was slewing off the iceberg. Her starboard quarter was going off the iceberg, and the starboard bow was going as if to make a circle round it.

356. She was acting as if under port helm, her head going to starboard? — That is correct.

However Hichens, at the wheel, denied this took place:

1314. You were given the order to hard-a-starboard? — Yes.

1315. Was that the only order you had as to the helm? — Yes.

[Mr Holmes] Because, if your Lordship will remember, the evidence of the witness Scarrott on Friday was quite the contrary, when he came up on deck. He said that the ship appeared to be under a port helm, and appeared to be going around the iceberg towards the starboard side.

Hichens had previously said that Sixth Officer James Moody (who was lost) called out the original hard-a-starboard (to go left, or south of west) to the first officer, who was in command:

1014. Then you had put the helm hard-a-starboard and Mr Moody had reported it hard-a-starboard to Mr Murdoch? — Yes.

1019. After she struck, did you notice at all what happened? — No.

1020. Did you notice whether the ship had stopped? — Oh, yes, the ship had stopped.

1021. Can you tell us how long it was after the collision that you noticed that the ship had stopped? — Immediately.

Hichens thus implies the other helm order, hard-a-port to save the stern, was not carried out – but Scarrott, who had rushed on deck, had some backing from Quartermaster George Rowe, who was on the aft docking bridge at the stern. Rowe saw the berg strike on the starboard side – but leave the starboard quarter untouched (US Inquiry, p. 522):

Rowe: It was so near that I thought it was going to strike the [aft docking] bridge.

Senator Burton: Did it strike the bridge? — No sir; never.

Sen. Burton: Only 10 or 20 feet away? — Not that far, sir.

Sen. Burton: Could you hear the ice scraping along on the boat where you were?

Rowe: No, sir.

Sen. Burton: So you do not know whether it was rubbing against the hull there or not?

Rowe: No, sir.

Sen. Burton: What is your best judgment about that?

Rowe: I do not think it was.

Sen. Burton: You are positive you heard no rubbing?

Rowe: Yes, sir.

Sen. Burton: Do you not think that if the helm had been hard a-starboard the stern would have been up against the berg?

Rowe: It stands to reason it would, sir, if the helm were hard a-starboard.

These are the only accounts of the helm movement at the time. Taken together, they suggest a turn to starboard was carried out in some form, inching the *Titanic's* starboard quarter away from the berg before stopping. It does not appear to have been a very pronounced turn – indeed time was short – which would account for Murdoch's sense of incompletion ('I was going to port round it') and Hichens' missing it altogether.

Quartermaster Alfred Olliver also insists such a turn happened, and that it was sharp (US Inquiry, p. 527–8):

Olliver: I know the orders I heard when I was on the bridge was after we had struck the iceberg. I heard hard a-port, and there was the man at the wheel and the officer. The officer was seeing it was carried out right.

Senator Burton: What officer was it?

Olliver: Mr Moody, the Sixth Officer, was stationed in the wheelhouse.

Sen. Burton: Who was the man at the wheel?

Olliver: Hichens, quartermaster.

Sen. Burton: You do not know whether the helm was put hard a-starboard first, or not?

Olliver: No, sir; I do not know that.

Sen. Burton: But you know it was put hard a-port after you got there?

Olliver: After I got there; yes, sir.

Sen. Burton: Where was the iceberg, do you think, when the helm was shifted?

Olliver: The iceberg was away up stern.

Sen. Burton: That is when the order 'hard a-port' was given?

Olliver: That is when the order 'hard a-port' was given; yes, sir.

Sen. Burton: Who gave the order?

Olliver: The First Officer.

Sen. Burton: And that order was immediately executed, was it?

Olliver: Immediately executed, and the Sixth Officer saw that it was carried out.

So, if there is a second turn, then the simplest argument, perhaps, is that these port and starboard turns cancelled each other out and left the *Titanic* still heading broadly westward – not northward. Yet even after the collision and the stopping of the ship, there is evidence that the *Titanic* moved on her way again – once in reverse, while also forward for a time.

This is consistent with testing for damage, or backing off an iceshelf. In this context, the *Titanic* might have experimentally resumed her normal heading (westward).

The following are the engine accounts that should give pause to the proponents of a collision-led northward facing. Here is Thomas Patrick Dillon (on duty in the engine room):

> 3719. You just heard it ring. Then a few seconds after that you felt a slight shock [berg collision]? —Yes.
>
> 3720. Was anything done to the engines? Did they stop or did they go on? —They stopped.
>
> 3721. Was that immediately after you felt the shock or some little time after? —About a minute and a half.
>
> 3722. Did they continue stopped or did they go on again after that? —They went slow astern.
>
> 3723. How long were they stopped for before they began to go slow astern? —About half a minute.
>
> 3724. For how long did they go slow astern? —About two minutes.
>
> 3725. Two or three did you say? —Two minutes.
>
> 3726. And then did they stop again? —Yes.
>
> 3727. And did they go on again after that? —They went ahead again.
>
> 3728. For how long? — For about two minutes.
>
> 3729. Then did they stop the boat after that? —Yes.

And this is Greaser Frederick Scott (also on duty in the engine room):

> 5609. …They rang down 'Stop', and two greasers on the bottom rang the telegraph back to answer it. Then they rang down 'Slow ahead'. For ten minutes she was going ahead. Then they rang down 'Stop', and she went astern, for five minutes.
>
> 5610. [The Commissioner] The orders were 'Stop', 'Slow ahead', and then 'Astern'? — No, it was 'Stop', and then 'Astern' [1. Stop; 2. Slow Ahead; 3. Stop; 4. Astern]. She went astern for five minutes. Then they rang down 'Stop'…
>
> 5613. [Attorney General] Did you hear the order about 'Astern'? — Well, it was on the telegraph.
>
> 5614. What was the order? — 'Go astern' – 'Slow astern'. Then they rang down 'Stop', and I do not think the telegraph went after that.

So, here are two engine room survivors who say the *Titanic* went gingerly both ahead and astern after coming to rest. Where is the necessary northward heading now (in order for her mystery ship to be the *Californian*)?

This is Boxhall in evidence:

> 15505. I also recollect that we have been told in the evidence that after the collision you went astern? — The engines were going full speed astern for quite a little time.
>
> 15506. Did you go forward after that? — Not that I know of.

And here is Third Officer Pitman (US Inquiry, p.313):

> Senator Smith: I want to know whether the engines were reversed and the ship was permitted to drift, or whether she kept under her power.
> Pitman: Oh, as far as I heard, she went full astern immediately after the collision.
> She reversed her engines? — She reversed her engines and went full astern.
> Sen. Smith: She reversed her engines, then, and receded from the point of contact? — She was past it then, I think. We brought the ship to a standstill.
> Sen. Smith: Did you ever see that ship move after it was brought to a standstill, except when it sank in the sea? — I did not, sir.

Others do not remember any such happening. Here is Second Officer Lightoller:

> 13757. When you came out on deck was the ship already stopped or slowing down through the water? — She was proceeding slowly, a matter of perhaps six knots or something like that.
> 13758. Were the engines still stopped? — I could not exactly say what the engines were doing after once I got up. It was when I was lying still in my bunk I could feel the engines were stopped.
> 13759. Can you help us as to whether the engines were put full speed astern? — No, I cannot say I remember feeling the engines going full speed astern.

And AB William Lucas:

> 1577. [Mr Rowlatt] We cannot tell how she was moving. Did you notice whether the *Titanic* moved at all after the collision? — No, I do not think she did.
> 1578. She lay pointing in the same direction? — Yes.

It is a recipe for confusion. But all the officer evidence, including Lightoller's, is that the *Titanic* was moving after the collision. The only other senior survivor, Fifth Officer Lowe, was not awoken by the collision. When he was later roused by voices, he saw passengers in lifejackets.

Passenger Lawrence Beesley, who wrote a 1912 book about the disaster, had meanwhile been to investigate: 'I stayed on deck some minutes, walking about vigorously to keep warm and occasionally looking downward to the sea as if something there would indicate the reason for delay. The ship had now resumed her course, moving very slowly through the water with a little white line of foam on each side' (*The Loss of the SS Titanic: Its Story and Its Lessons*, p.30). Other passengers also mention the ship starting again, and Quartermaster Alfred Olliver, the man who emphasised the post-collision hard a-port, related:

> Senator Burton. Were the engines reversed; was she backed?
> Olliver: Not whilst I was on the bridge; but whilst on the bridge she went ahead, after she struck; she went half speed ahead.

Sen. Burton: The engines went half speed ahead, or the ship?

Olliver: Half speed ahead, after she hit the ice.

Sen Burton: Who gave the order?

Olliver: The Captain telegraphed half speed ahead.

Sen. Burton: Had the engines been backing before he did that?

Olliver: That I could not say, sir.

Sen. Burton: Did she have much way on when he put the engines half speed ahead?

Olliver: No, sir. I reckon the ship was almost stopped.

At some stage, the *Titanic*, having been moving after the initial impact, finally came to rest for the last time and would never move again.

After all of this, how can we have any confidence in a northerly heading, immediately after the collision, that stayed that way? We can see that it must be unreliable in the extreme. The possibility exists that the *Titanic* was brought back onto her course line. Her captain was back on duty and had the compass (binnacle) as guide. He could see immediately what direction was west (to New York). Why on earth would he leave a busy shipping lane to journey north into No Man's Land, when the next major track, to Boston, was some 20 miles away?

How could he find help by leaving his well-worn path, and why would he suicidally choose to leave a latitude forming a key component of his ship's distress call?

Credibly and notably, Fourth Officer Boxhall thought she ultimately stopped facing west (US Inquiry, p.914):

Senator Fletcher: Apparently that [mystery] ship came within 4 or 5 miles of the *Titanic*, and then turned and went away; in what direction, westward or southward?

Boxhall: I do not know whether it was southwestward. I should say it was westerly.

Sen. Fletcher: In westerly direction; almost in the direction which she had come? —Yes, sir.

Crucially, he had earlier said of that mystery ship's appearance (US Inquiry, p.910):

Boxhall: She was headed toward us, meeting us.

Sen. Fletcher: Was she a little toward your port bow?

Boxhall: Just about half a point off our port bow.

Sen. Fletcher: And apparently coming toward you? —Yes.

Both these quotes, taken together, seem to indicate the *Titanic* was pointing westward, as she had been first. Boxhall will be supported in a westward heading by Third Officer Pitman, and by Steward Alfred Crawford.

The meaning of this argument, if the *Titanic* did indeed come to rest facing west, is that the oncoming vessel therefore ended up slightly south of west, whereas the *Californian*'s claimed stop position was to the north-north-west of where we now know the *Titanic* actually sank. Meanwhile *Titanic* Steward Alfred Crawford agrees the mystery ship was seen to the south-west:

Senator Fletcher: Did you move [your lifeboat] in the direction in which the *Titanic* was moving when she went down?

Crawford: No; we were the other way; that way [indicating].

Senator Fletcher: If the *Titanic* was moving west you moved south-west?

Crawford: Probably so.

Senator Fletcher: Toward the light?

Crawford: Yes, sir.

Senator Fletcher: And then the *Carpathia* appeared in what direction?

Crawford: She came right up around and started to pick up the boats.

Senator Fletcher: She came from the north-east from you, then?

Crawford: Probably so.

Senator Fletcher: Assuming you had been going south-west?

Crawford: Yes, sir.

Senator Fletcher: She appeared from the north-east…

Crawford's account is credible, given what we know today of the layout of the scene. It is a perception issue – Crawford's lifeboat leads the race to the mystery ship. He says that vessel was to the south-west. If his lifeboat line crosses the *Carpathia*'s diagonal course line (set north-west, towards the empty SOS position) in a kind of 'X', then when the lifeboat is in the lower left hand corner of the 'X', the *Carpathia* in the centre (heading to top left) will appear north-east of the lifeboat.

Here is Third Officer Pitman's corroboration of a final *Titanic* stop position that was heading to the westward:

Pitman: I saw one white light.

Senator Smith: Where?

Pitman: Away on the horizon. We could not make anything out of it.

Senator Smith: At what time?

Pitman: About half past one.

Senator Smith: While you were lying on your oars in the lifeboat?

Pitman: Yes.

Senator Smith: In what position was it?

Pitman: It was to the westward. Right ahead.

Senator Smith: Right on the course of the *Titanic*?

Pitman: Exactly.

Senator Smith: Did you hear the testimony of Mr Boxhall on that point?

Pitman: No, I did not. I have heard him speak about it.

Two surviving officers – Boxhall and Pitman – thus both say the RMS *Titanic* finished up facing to the west, not to the north! Second Officer Lightoller would write in private correspondence in December 1912: 'I have not the faintest idea how her head was'. Only one ranking crew member says her head finished north, and this Quartermaster George Rowe:

17667. When you saw this light did you notice whether the head of the *Titanic* was altering either to port or starboard? —Yes.

17668. You did notice? —Yes.

17669. Was your vessel's head swinging at the time you saw this light of this other vessel? — I put it down that her stern was swinging.

17670. Which way was her stern swinging? — Practically dead south, I believe, then.

17671. Do you mean her head was facing south? — No, her head was facing north. She was coming round to starboard.

When all is said and done, the evidence as to how the *Titanic* was facing when the mystery ship was seen, as the Attorney General divined, is utterly inconclusive. Yet she must be facing north if the *Californian* is to be the mystery ship, which was seen off the *Titanic's* port bow. All other points of the compass favour the *Californian* as not being the mystery ship. The odds, on this point alone, are with Captain Lord.

Now let us return to the treatment of the *Californian* in 1912 in the British Inquiry Report.

LORD MERSEY'S CONCLUSIONS

It is informative, in returning to the judgement of the British Inquiry, to look behind other aspects of Lord Mersey's Final Report as it touches on the *Californian*. Written in a way that immediately equates *Californian's* nearby stranger with the *Titanic*, Mersey subtly introduced the word 'proximity' into his report to imply at an early stage that the *Californian* was close to the *Titanic*. In fact she was merely closer than Cape Race, a wireless station many hundreds of miles away. This is from Lord Mersey's Final Report (p.43):

> At about 11 p.m. a steamer's light was seen approaching from the eastward. The Master went to Evans' room and asked, 'What ships he had'. The latter replied: 'I think the *Titanic* is near us. I have got her'. The Master said: 'You had better advise the *Titanic* we are stopped and surrounded with ice'. This Evans did, calling up the *Titanic* and sending: 'We are stopped and surrounded by ice'. The *Titanic* replied: 'Keep out'. The *Titanic* was in communication with Cape Race, which station was then sending messages to her. The reason why the *Titanic* answered, 'Keep out', was that her Marconi operator could not hear what Cape Race was saying, as from her proximity, the message from the *Californian* was much stronger than any message being taken in by the *Titanic* from Cape Race, which was much further off.

The effect on the reader calculated to be achieved by the previous extract is that the *Titanic* was the *Californian's* approaching light, and that the two vessels were close to each other.

Mersey does not trouble to explain Evans' concept of 'near us', nor his ready concession immediately after that remark (questions 8984–8985) that he never had the *Titanic's* position. Evans formed his impression thus:

9120. What basis had you for saying she was near you? — The strength of the signals...
9126. Would that indicate roughly a certain number of miles – that you must be within a certain number of miles? — By the strength of the signals I should say he was not more than 100 miles off us in the afternoon. I heard him working a long time before I got him.

So, to Evans, the word 'near' means within 100 miles. Up to nine hours' steaming away by the *Californian's* speed that afternoon. Evans said the *Titanic* wireless set had 'a good power', but added when asked:

9124. Would the *Titanic* be able to judge from the distinctness of your message that you were near them? —Yes, you cannot judge a distance accurately.

Clearly then, Evans' reference to 'near us' is of no assistance to anyone – except Lord Mersey.
  Next, Mersey skilfully, almost imperceptibly, will denigrate the character of the *Californian's* captain before anything has yet happened (Final Report, p.43):

The Master of the *Californian* states that when observing the approaching steamer... he noticed that about 11.30 she stopped. In his opinion this steamer was of about the same size as the *Californian*; a medium-sized steamer, 'something like ourselves'.
  From the evidence of Mr Groves, third officer of the *Californian*, who was the officer of the first watch, it would appear that the Master was not actually on the bridge when the steamer was sighted.

Mersey makes it appear Lord was lying about seeing the steamer, and about seeing her stop. In actual fact, Lord watched her from the lower deck, separate to the bridge but no less valid. He had actually noticed the light much earlier than Groves, who noticed it first at 11.10. Lord said he spotted a light at 10.30 p.m. which emerged into a steamer. The above shows how Mersey implies that Lord was lying about seeing the vessel, thereby casting doubt about whether the stranger was, as Lord said, a medium-sized steamer, or 'something like ourselves'.
  Note how Mersey now suggests that the *Californian's* stranger was undoubtedly a passenger steamer by linking the evidence of Groves and donkeyman Gill, even though their evidence is mutually exclusive (Final Report, p.43–44):

In fact Mr Groves never appears to have had any doubt on this subject: in answer to a question during his examination, 'Had she much light', he said, 'Yes, a lot of light. There was absolutely no doubt of her being a passenger steamer, at least in my mind'.

Gill, the assistant donkeyman of the *Californian*, who was on deck at midnight said, referring to this steamer: 'It could not have been anything but a passenger boat, she was too large'.

So Gill is used to validate Groves' passenger steamer. Gill is also used to transfer the idea of 'large' to Groves' steamer, even though Groves never once offered an adjective in relation to the size of his steamer. Groves simply never said whether she was small, medium or large. He only said that she was a passenger steamer. But what Groves did say was that the near vessel had 'put out' her lights for the night *before* Gill saw her. Groves also said his steamer was stopped, but note how Mersey somehow fails to mention the inbuilt flaw in Gill, which of course is that his supposed steamer was actively steaming, and at 'full speed'.

It is only after this altogether fraudulent use of Gill to reinforce Groves' passenger steamer claims that the unavoidable question of that steamer's lack of light is tackled (Final Report, p.44):

The Master came up and joined [Groves] on the bridge and remarked: 'That does not look like a passenger steamer'. Mr Groves replied 'It is, Sir. When she stopped, her lights seemed to go out, and I suppose they have been put out for the night'. Mr Groves states that these lights went out at 11.40, and remembers that time because 'one bell was struck to call the middle watch'. The Master did not join him on the bridge until shortly afterwards, and consequently after the steamer had stopped.

In his examination Mr Groves admitted that if this steamer's head was turning to port after she stopped, it might account for the diminution of lights, by many of them being shut out. Her steaming lights were still visible and also her port side light. The Captain only remained upon the bridge for a few minutes.

In his evidence he stated that Mr Groves had made no observations to him about the steamer's deck lights going out.

Captain Lord indeed denies that the conversation described by Groves took place, but Mersey obviously prefers Groves' account. It is noticeable that the captain's presence on the bridge for 'only... a few minutes' is introduced before his denial of the conversation. The subliminal message is that Lord was too lazy to care what was said to him by a conscientious officer.

But if Groves is right and it does not look like a passenger steamer at this time, how can it subsequently have been unmistakably a 'large passenger boat' to Gill more than ten minutes later?

And look at Mersey's line that 'Mr Groves admitted that if his steamer's head was turning to port after she stopped...' How can she turn after she stopped? A sudden rogue wave? The unreliable notion is that the *Titanic* turned to starboard to face north – not that Groves' vessel turned to port, which he did not say (another Mersey mistake).

Meanwhile, Lord Mersey has artfully arranged chosen slices of evidence in a new sequence to suit his own taste. He goes on (Final Report, p.44):

Mr Groves... remained on the bridge until relieved by Mr Stone, the Second Officer, just after midnight. In turning the *Californian* over to him, he pointed out the steamer and said:'she has been stopped since 11.40 p.m.; she is a passenger steamer'.

Again Mersey opts to believe Groves' account and not that of Stone who did not say it was ever suggested to him that the steamer he saw nearby was a passenger steamer. Stone could see for himself that she was a tramp.

Mersey's Final Report omits any mention of the rather salient fact that Stone and Gibson instead thought the steamer nearby was small to medium-sized, with nothing about her, in Gibson's words, to suggest a passenger steamer (Final Report, p.44):

When Mr Groves was in the witness-box the following questions were put to him by me:'Speaking as an experienced seaman and knowing what you do know now, do you think that steamer that you know was throwing up rockets, and that you say was a passenger steamer, was the *Titanic?*' — Do I think it?

Yes? — From what I have heard subsequently?

Yes? — Most decidedly I do, but I do not put myself as being an experienced man.

But that is your opinion as far as your experience goes? — Yes, it is, my Lord.

Mersey then goes on to declare:'Gill, the donkeyman, states that he saw two rockets fired from the ship which he had been observing' (Final Report, p.44). But Gill did not see them fired from a ship. He says he did not see any ship at the time of the rockets. Gill said his ship had gone, when clearly, if she was the *Titanic*, she should have been stopped. Mersey's phraseology would suggest that she was indeed stopped – 'had been observing' – whereas Gill suggested his magical midnight steamer, going full speed, had long since rushed off towards New York.

Enough. We can see which way Mersey's report is going. There is little point in further nit-picking over his artful phrasing and choices of whom to believe. Let us cut to the quick of his conclusions (Final Report, pp.45–46):

There are contradictions and inconsistencies in the story as told by the different witnesses. But the truth of the matter is plain.

The *Titanic* collided with the berg at 11.40. The vessel seen by the *Californian* stopped at this time. The rockets sent up from the *Titanic* were distress signals. The *Californian* saw distress signals. The number sent up by the *Titanic* was about eight. The *Californian* saw eight.

The time over which the rockets from the *Titanic* were sent up was from about 12.45 to 1.45. It was about this time that the *Californian* saw the rockets. At 2.40 Mr Stone called to the Master that the ship from which he had seen the rockets had disappeared. At 2.20 a.m. the *Titanic* had foundered.

It was suggested that the rockets seen by the *Californian* were from some other ship, not the *Titanic*. But no other ship to fit this theory has ever been heard of.

These circumstances convince me that the ship seen by the *Californian* was the *Titanic*...

Mersey's list of coincidences are, in reality, contrivances.

The *Titanic* collided with the berg at 11.40 p.m., but the vessel seen by *Californian* probably stopped significantly earlier. Times not identical.

The rockets sent up by *Titanic* were indeed distress signals, but what rockets *Californian* saw did not lead her observers to conclude that they were distress signals.

Although the *Californian* saw eight rockets, it must be extremely doubtful from the testimony that the RMS *Titanic* fired only eight rockets. If she did fire only eight, then they were not being fired at 'short intervals' – a requirement, under regulation, if distress was to be conveyed.

There is nothing convincing about alleged similarity in timing between the *Titanic* sinking and the *Californian's* stranger steaming away. The nearby ship seen by Stone began to move off from the time the second rocket was seen. *Titanic* had no power when sending rockets, and could not change her bearing, as described by Stone and related by Gibson.

Mersey suggests that there had to be two ships firing rockets at the same time that night if the *Californian's* account is to be believed. But this is not the case, given what we now know about the *Titanic's* actual position in 1912.

Meanwhile it would not even be true to say that no candidates have ever been suggested for another ship (the one visible to the *Californian)* while rockets were also being seen, in Stone's words, at a 'greater distance' (7845). It is no part of this assessment to identify particular ships as either the *Titanic's* mystery ship or the *Californian's* nearby stranger. But it was a busy shipping lane and there are many candidates.

Captain Lord was asked about the possible identity of *Californian's* stranger, with the first emphasis predictably and rather wearisomely on the *Titanic*:

> 6818. [The Attorney General] If [Groves] did see two lights it must have been the *Titanic*, must it not? — It does not follow.
> 6819. Do you know any other vessel it could have been? — Any amount.

Any amount have since been suggested, in the categories of both the *Titanic's* proximate vessel and the *Californian's* close visitor.

Lord in a 1959 affidavit said that while searching for survivors the next morning he saw 'the smoke of several steamers on the horizon in different directions'. The Board of Trade and Foreign Office expended much energy during and after the British Inquiry in 1912 in trying to identify the small steamer carrying a black funnel with 'some device in it' described by Captain Moore of the *Mount Temple*. They initiated hundreds of contacts in her pursuit. Yet because this vessel was eastbound, cutting across the *Mount Temple's* bows and apparently stopped on the western edge of the ice barrier later that morning, this vessel must be a red herring. She certainly could not have been the *Californian's* stranger and likely not the *Titanic's* mystery ship as that vessel was sighted too early the previous night and located much further to the east.

Any amount of perplexing ships... yet the US Inquiry singled out only one for blame. And in its wake, the British equivalent chose the same target and utterly refused to be deflected.

23

LORD'S REBUTTAL

Lord Mersey's Final Report was issued on 30 July 1912. It had found an answer to the highly irregular question it had given itself following the departure of Captain Lord and other *Californian* witnesses (p.71):

Q.24(b): What vessels had the opportunity of rendering assistance to the *Titanic* and, if any, how was it that assistance did not reach the *Titanic* before the SS *Carpathia* arrived? A: The *Californian*. She could have reached the *Titanic* if she had made the attempt when she saw the first rocket. She made no attempt.

In a special section on 'The Circumstances in connection with the SS *Californian*' (pp.43–46), Lord Mersey finished:

The ice by which the *Californian* was surrounded was loose ice extending for a distance of not more than two or three miles in the direction of the *Titanic* [accepting Gill's nonsensical idea of a vanishing icefield]. The night was clear and the sea was smooth. When she first saw the rockets, the *Californian* could have pushed through the ice to the open water without serious risk and so have come to the assistance of the *Titanic*. Had she done so, she might have saved many, if not all of the lives that were lost.

Within two weeks of these dismaying findings, Captain Lord had personally prepared his own rebuttal to the charges laid at his door. The counter-argument he was not allowed by the Inquiry took the form of a letter to the publication of his professional body, the Merchant Marine Service Association. The letter, dated 14 August 1912, was written the day after he was told by the Leyland Line that he would not be re-appointed to the *Californian* in light of the Inquiry findings. It was published in the September issue of *The Reporter*, the MMSA's journal, and is as follows (this author's comments in square brackets):

Sir –
    The issue of the Report of the Court, presided over by Lord Mersey, to inquire into the loss of the *Titanic*, ends a compulsory silence on my part on points raised in the course of

the proceedings which affect me as the late Master of the steamer *Californian*, and it is a duty I owe to myself and my reputation as a British Shipmaster, to do what I have hitherto been prevented from doing, for obvious reasons, in giving publicity to circumstances which the Inquiry failed to elicit, and at the same time to show that the deductions which have been drawn, reflecting upon my personal character as a seaman, are entirely unfounded.

The facts briefly and consistently are as follows: On the night of the 14th April I had been on the bridge from dark until 10.30 p.m., at that time having run into loose ice, and, sighting field ice ahead, I deemed it prudent for the safety of the life and property under my charge to remain stopped until daylight. My wireless operator had been in communication with a number of steamers up to 11.30 p.m., and he then retired for the night, after a full day's duty, but not before warning all ships in the vicinity, including the *Titanic*, of the dangerous proximity of ice.

Forty minutes after midnight I left the deck in charge of the Second Officer, with instructions to call me if wanted, and retired to the chartroom, where I lay down, fully dressed, boots on and with the light burning. At 1.15 a.m. the Second Officer informed me through the speaking tube that a steamer, which had been stopped in sight of us since 11.30 p.m., bearing SSE, was altering her bearing [in other words was steaming away] and had fired a white rocket.

Meanwhile for over an hour my Morse signals to this vessel had been ignored. The officer reported her to be steaming away, and I asked him, 'if he thought it was a company's signal, to Morse her again and report'. The evidence of my officers from this point is conclusive that I had gone to sleep. A later message, to the effect that she was last seen bearing SW a half W, proving she had steamed at least eight miles between 1 a.m. and 2 a.m. [*Titanic* did not move after midnight] I have no recollection of receiving, and subsequent events were not regarded by the officers so seriously as to induce them to take energetic means of ensuring my cognizance of happenings, which should, and would, most assuredly have had my earnest attention.

I did not hear of the disaster until daylight, and that only after it was deemed safe for my steamer to proceed.

The evidence is conclusive that none of the responsible officers of the *Californian* were aware of the serious calamity which had taken place. That any seaman would wilfully neglect signals of distress is preposterous and unthinkable – there was everything to gain and nothing to lose. The failure to adopt energetic means of making me aware of the gravity of the signals is conclusive of the fact that my officers did not attach any significance to their appearance.

The absence of any reply to the succession of Morse signals made from the bridge of the *Californian* is further evidence which is entitled to some consideration.

When I asked the Second Officer the next day why he had not used more energy in calling me, and insisted on my coming on deck at once, he replied, 'if the signals had been distress signals he would have done so, but as the steamer was steaming away, he concluded that there was not much wrong with her'. He was the man on the spot – the only officer who saw the signals, so I think I was justified in relying on his judgment, which ought to carry some weight.

The evidence of the *Titanic* officer who was firing her distress signals states the steamer he had under observation 'approached' – obviously not the *Californian*, as she was stopped from 10.30 p.m. until 5.15 a.m.

Captain Rostron of the *Carpathia* states, 'Whilst at the scene of the disaster at 5 a.m. it was broad daylight; he could see all round the horizon. He then saw two steamers north of where he was [the direction of the *Californian*]. Neither of them was the *Californian*; he first saw that steamer at about 8 a.m., distant 5 to 6 miles, and steaming towards the *Carpathia*.

Had the *Californian* been seen by the *Titanic* before sinking, she would have been plainly in view from the *Carpathia* at this time, as she was then on the same spot as when she stopped at 10.30 p.m. the previous evening.

The conversation between my Second Officer and Apprentice, when watching the steamer referred to, was that she must have been a tramp steamer using oil lamps, and that opinion was formed by them after keenly studying the situation, and before they had heard of any disaster.

My position at the Inquiry was that of a witness only, and a nautical man rarely makes a good witness. My position was Marconigramed to other steamers at 6.30 p.m., five hours before the accident, and also at 5.15 a.m., before I had heard of the position of the accident, proving my distance from the disaster as given by me to be correct.

I trust this lengthy explanation, which I ought to have made earlier, but for various reasons could not, will be the means of removing the undeserved stigma which rests upon me, and through me, upon an honourable profession.

I am Sir, yours truly,
[signed] Stanley Lord
(Late Master, steamer *Californian*)
Liverpool, 14th August, 1912

Lord has introduced two new elements here. One is his suggestion (agreed by Stone?) that the *Californian*'s neighbour had steamed away 'at least eight miles' over the course of an hour, far beyond the possibilities of drift or current swing. This is a speed of at least 8 knots, compared to the 11 knots *Californian* had been doing before she stopped earlier that night. It may also suggest the *Californian*'s visible horizon.

The second new idea is the suggestion that Evans transmitted the *Californian*'s stopped position at 5.15 a.m., before receiving the *Titanic*'s SOS position, thus eliminating the possibility of subsequent invention of the *Californian*'s position. Such a transmission, however, was not explicitly stated at either Inquiry. However the possibility is there, since Evans gave evidence in Washington of sending a service advice message to the *Virginian* the next morning, seeking the distress position for the *Titanic*. Service advice messages, carrying an MSG prefix, commonly carried the transmitting vessel's position before giving body text. Evans testified:

I sent them [*Virginian*] a message of my own, what we call a service message, that an operator can always make up if he wants to find out something. I sent a service message, and said, 'Please send me official message regarding *Titanic*, giving position'.

A section of the letter sent by Captain Lord to the Board of Trade on 10 August 1912. He writes: 'My employers, the Leyland Line, although their nautical advisers are convinced we did not see the Titanic, *or the* Titanic *see the* Californian, *say they have the utmost confidence in me, and do not blame me in any way, but owing to Lord Mersey's decision and public opinion caused by this report, they are reluctantly compelled to ask for my resignation, after 14½ years service without a hitch of any description, and if I could clear myself of this charge, would willingly reconsider this decision'.*

Evans' previous service message had been an ice warning the night before, and had carried the *Californian*'s longitude and latitude at the start. It read: 'To Captain, '*Antillian*', 6.30 p.m. apparent time, ship; latitude, 42° 3' North; longitude 49° 9' West. Three large bergs…'

Thus, the giving of *Californian*'s position at 5.15 a.m. may have happened as Lord says, but it was not corroborated in evidence. Captain Gambell of the *Virginian* did not testify, as we have seen, and neither did anyone else from that vessel – a great pity.

It will be remembered that Gambell had told reporters at Liverpool that when he first had contact with the *Californian* 'he was then 17 miles north of the *Titanic* and had not heard anything of the disaster'. How did Gambell know where the *Californian* was, if he had not been told? If he was told the *Californian*'s position by that ship at a time when the *Californian* herself 'had not heard anything of the disaster', does it not once more exonerate Captain Lord's vessel of being the *Titanic*'s mystery ship?

In a handwritten letter to the Board of Trade on 10 August 1912, Lord had notably declared: 'April 15th, about 5.30 a.m.,I gave my position to the *Virginian* before I heard where the *Titanic* sunk; that gave me 17 miles away. I understand the original Marconigrams were in court' (National Archives documents MT9/920E, M23448, Kew).

The implications of these claims are naturally enormous. But they were never officially tested, such as by examination of the Marconi originals and *Virginian* PV, or wireless record. Gambell was not interviewed, and neither was his wireless operator.

Meanwhile Captain Lord had also begun contacting the newspapers with a view to vindicating his reputation. This is an example (*Weekly Irish Times*, Saturday 24 August 1912):

TITANIC DISASTER
Statement by the Captain of the *Californian*

Capt. Stanley Lord, late master of the liner *Californian*, last Friday [August 17] issued a statement regarding his action in connection with the *Titanic* disaster, which, he trusts, will remove the undeserved stigma that rests upon him.

The remainder of this long story consists of the same facts and phrases published a month later in the publication of Captain Lord's professional association. Similar accounts appeared in other newspapers, including the *Times*, showing he had mounted a spirited, if futile, campaign.

In an affidavit prepared many years later, Lord meanwhile told what had happened when he returned to Liverpool, after giving evidence, in order to rejoin the *Californian*. There now also follows an account of his later life, with one paragraph relocated for clarity, together with an editorial note and sub-headings to aid the narrative.

RELIEVED FROM DUTY

I returned to Liverpool on the evening of May 15th, being due to sail in the *Californian* on the 18th. However, after my return home I was verbally informed by the Marine Superintendent that I was to be relieved and I accordingly removed my gear from the ship.

Initially I had been assured by the Liverpool management of the Leyland Line that I would be reappointed to the *Californian*. However, I was later told privately by Mr Gordon, Private Secretary to Mr Roper [Head of the Liverpool office of the Leyland Line] that one of the London directors, a Mr Matheson KC, had threatened to resign if I were permitted to remain in the company, and on August 13th I was told by the Marine Superintendent that the company could not give me another ship.

I then saw Mr Roper, who said that it was most unfortunate but the matter was out of his hands and public opinion was against me. I was therefore compelled to resign, up to which time I had been retained on full sea pay and bonus.

I [had] first read the findings of the Court of Inquiry in the Press, and while naturally not at all pleased at the references to myself, I was not unduly concerned as I was confident that matters would soon be put right. I immediately approached the Mercantile Marine Service Association, of which I was a member, and a letter putting my side of the case was published in the September 1912 issue of the Association's magazine, *The Reporter*.

At a later stage, Mr A.M. Foweraker, of Carbis Bay, a gentleman whom I had never met, but who took a great interest in my case, supplied a series of detailed analyses of the evidence which were published in *The Reporter* and also in the *Nautical* Magazine under the title of *A Miscarriage of Justice* [April, May and June issues, 1913].

Albert Moulton Foweraker, whom Lord had 'never met' (and possibly never heard of) was a scientist and painter. Aged thirty-nine when he contacted Lord, he was a graduate of Christ's College, Cambridge, with a background in chemistry, engineering and journalism. Foweraker is chiefly remembered however as a watercolourist. He died in 1942 at the age of sixty-eight.

Foweraker was convinced Lord had been the victim of a miscarriage of justice. From his contacts with Captain Lord, he appears to have obtained the basis for this sketch of the field of ice that the *Californian* encountered that night. We know Captain Lord drew a sketch of his own, the apparent precursor to Foweraker's version. Lord told as much to the British Inquiry in April 1912:

> 7385. [Mr Dunlop] Did you prepare a rough sketch to show the position of the ice and also the course which you took from 6 a.m. to 8.30 a.m.?
>
> [Lord] Yes, I did; I drew a rough sketch of it.
>
> [Dunlop] I would like your Lordship to see the sketch he has made.
>
> [The Commissioner] Hand it up. [The sketch was handed in]
>
> [Lord] It is not to scale or anything.
>
> 7389. [The Commissioner] Where did you draw this thing? — I drew that in Boston, my Lord.

Subsequent questions elicited that Lord had prepared it alone, aboard ship, before being summoned to give evidence at the US Inquiry. He said that after Gill's statement in the papers 'that we were supposed to have ignored the *Titanic* signals, I knew at once there would be an Inquiry over it' (7396). The questions continue:

> 7397. You drew it for the purpose of showing that you had not ignored the signals? — I did it for the purpose of showing where we were, and the course we travelled on our way down to the ship.

Mersey, who said 'You must leave this sketch with me', also noticed a long statement in pencil on the reverse that Lord's own counsel had not seen. It was Lord's private notes made at the same time.

> 7411. Are these notes supposed to tell the story from your point of view? — Yes, private notes I made.

Lord Mersey, noticeably, immediately handed the sketch to the Attorney General. A moment previously Leyland Line counsel Robertson Dunlop asked Lord:

> 7406. Assuming that [*Titanic*] sank somewhere between 2 and 3, could you, in fact, if you had known at 1.15 a.m. in the morning that she was in distress to the southward and westward of you, have reached her before, say 3 a.m.? — No, most certainly not.

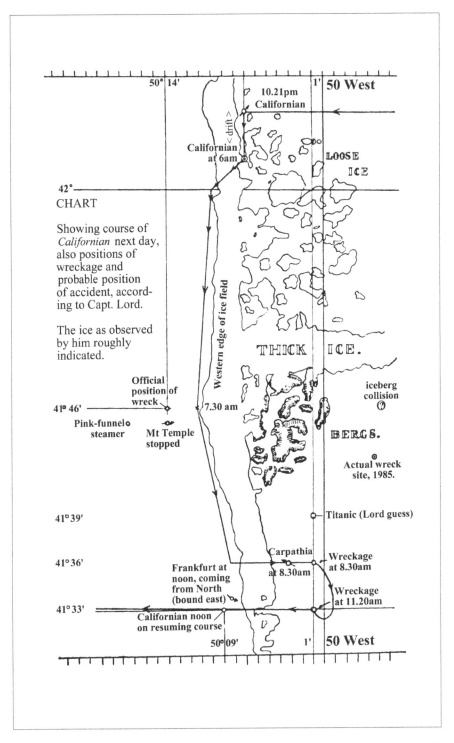

Chart showing the course of the Californian on 15 April, with the positions of wreckage and probable position of the accident according to Captain Lord (re-lettering, 1985 wreck site, collision point by author).

Lord Mersey, as we have seen however, concluded the exact opposite – that she could have saved all aboard.

The sketch, 'not to scale or anything', shows the course that Lord discussed and confirmed in evidence, down to his sighting of the *Mount Temple*, a pink-funnel steamer, and the *Carpathia*.

It also showed the 'probable position of the accident according to Captain Lord'. This was marked with the legend '*Titanic* struck 11.40 p.m.', which has been changed in this book to reflect the fact that it was Lord's guess in 1912 as to where the *Titanic* foundered. Lord specified a spot at 41° 39'N, 50° 01'W. The location of the actual wreck site has been added to the sketch, to show where the debris was found in 1985 – at 41° 43'N, 49° 56'W. Lord was out in his estimate by just four minutes of latitude and five minutes of longitude. Put another way, his guess was wrong by only 5 nautical miles for a ship he had never seen, compared with both the *Titanic* and the British Inquiry being wrong by 13 nautical miles in their adherence to the SOS position. The record shows the accuracy of Lord's instincts. The present author has also added an indication of where the *Titanic* might have been at the time of iceberg impact – somewhere to the north and east of the debris field to allow for sinking drift.

We can compare Lord's icefield sketch to the similar guesses of the captain of the SS *Birma* and the US Naval hydrographer, John J. Knapp of Washington DC.

A tale of three icefields... this sketch (shown opposite) brings together the plotted positions of the floe ice according to US hydrographer John Knapp, left, Captain Lord, middle, and Captain Ludwig Stulping of the SS *Birma*, right. Clearly both Captains Lord and Stulping disagreed with Knapp, and unlike him were there at the time.

A position given for the southern extremity of the icefield, 41° 20' N, 50° 02' W, later given by Captain Gambell of the *Virginian*, also contradicts Knapp, who had the field much further west to 'allow' the *Titanic* to reach the SOS position. Similar contradictions of Knapp were given by the *Mount Temple* and *Carpathia*.

Added material to the amalgamated chart shows the actual location of the wreck, discovered in 1985, a fraction over 13 miles to the east and south of the SOS position. It is shown in the centre of the *Birma* sketch, with a deduced *Titanic* collision point to indicate where the iceberg may have been at its highest possible latitude. *Californian's* 1912 stop position would seem roughly equidistant between this point and the SOS position (between 19½ and 20 nautical miles away by Lord's evidence. Lord's account of post-disaster developments now continues.

REQUESTS FOR REHEARING REFUSED

Letters were addressed to the Board of Trade both by the MMSA and by myself requesting a rehearing of that part of the Inquiry relating to the *Californian*. This request was consistently refused. The MMSA also sent a letter to the Attorney General [Sir Rufus Isaacs] requesting an explanation of the comment in his closing address that 'perhaps it would not be wise to speculate on the reason which prevented the Captain of the *Californian* from coming out of the chartroom' on receiving the Second Officer's message at 1.15 a.m. This obvious reflec-

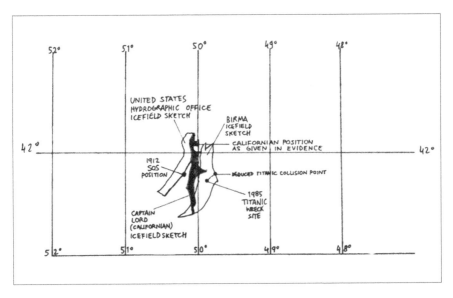

A tale of three icefields. This sketch brings together the plotted positions of the floe ice according to US hydrographer John Knapp, left, (see his chart no. 2), Captain Lord, middle, and Captain Ludwig Stulping of the SS Birma, *right.*

tion on my sobriety I greatly resented, for it was my invariable practice to refrain from taking alcohol in any form while at sea, quite apart from the fact that no previous reference to such a possibility had been made during the course of the Inquiry. The only reply received was that Sir Rufus was on holiday and must not be troubled with correspondence.

MOUNT TEMPLE

I received a letter dated August 6th, 1912, from a Mr Baker, who had served in the *Mount Temple* on her return voyage from Quebec. This appeared to indicate that she was the ship seen to approach and recede from the *Titanic*. Although this letter was brought to the attention of the Board of Trade, no action was taken… Through Mr Baker, I met Mr Notley, the officer referred to in Mr Baker's letters who had been taken out of the *Mount Temple*. He confirmed that he would give his evidence if called on to do so, but could not volunteer information because of the adverse effect this might have upon his future employment – a conclusion with which I quite agreed.

CORRESPONDENCE AND RE-EMPLOYMENT

I also corresponded with others whose evidence and opinion might prove of assistance to me and received letters from Captain Rostron of the *Carpathia*; Mr C.H. Lightoller [second officer of the *Titanic*]; and Captain C.A. Bartlett, Marine Superintendent of the White Star Line.

Captain Lord's correspondence with Lightoller, the senior surviving officer of the *Titanic*, drew these compassionate replies:

October 12th 1912 (on board RMS *Majestic*)

Dear Capt. Lord,

I can truly assure you that you have my sincerest sympathy, and I would have written to you before to that effect had I known your address. I sincerely hope that your efforts may be successful in clearing up the mystery of which you speak.

That another ship or ships might have been in the vicinity is quite possible and it seems a strange attitude for the B ofT [Board ofTrade] to take. I quite see how horribly hard it is for you – in fact that has been my feeling all along – and it must be doubly so with this other ship in your mind. I certainly wish you every success in clearing the matter up. Believe me, yours very sincerely,

C. H. Lightoller

And later:

December 16th 1912 (on board RMS *Majestic*)

Dear Capt. Lord,

We have so little time at home that my letters have to wait till I get to sea. I have read your enclosure with great interest – it certainly does seem extraordinary. All the same those *Mount Temple* chaps might have volunteered the information when it would have been of some use to you.

I am awfully sorry but I have not the faintest idea how her head was. You see, I just turned out and went straight to the boats, and beyond what came out in the evidence I know absolutely nothing about it or I would gladly let you know.

With regard to the steamer seen – I saw a light about two points on the port bow and could not say whether it was one or two masthead lights or a stern light – but it seemed there about 5 or 6 miles away. I did not pay much attention to it beyond calling the passengers' attention to it for their assurance.

I really do hope you will be able to clear the matter up. As to the BT [Board ofTrade], their attitude towards you is as inexplicable as in many other things – I don't hold any brief for them.

Wishing you success. Believe me, sincerely yours,

C.H. Lightoller

assurance.
I really do hope
you will be able
to clear the matter
up. As to the B T
their attitude towards
you is as inexplicable
as in many other
things — I dont
hold any brief
for them
Wishing you success
Believe me
sincerely yours
C H Lightoller

Scan of the last page of a letter sent by the senior surviving Titanic *officer, Charles Lightoller, to Captain Lord from aboard the* Majestic *and dated 15 December 1912. He wrote that he had 'not the faintest idea how her head was' in reference to the direction in which the* Titanic *came to rest. Shown here are his concluding remarks.*

Lord goes on:

I continued my endeavours to obtain what I considered to be the justice due to me but without success, although I personally visited the House of Commons on October 23rd 1912, and engaged in correspondence with the Board of Trade during 1913.

Toward the end of 1912, I was approached by Mr [later Sir] John Latta of the Nitrate Producers Steamship Co. Ltd [Lawther, Latta & Co.], who had apparently been approached on my behalf by a Mr Frank Strachan, United States agent for the Leyland Line, who had throughout done everything possible to assist me.

After a visit to London to meet Mr Latta, I was offered an immediate command with the company and entered their service in February 1913. I served at sea throughout the First World War, and as the aftermath of the *Titanic* Inquiry in those days was not such as to affect me personally or professionally in any way, I decided to let the matter drop.

I continued to serve in Lawther Latta's until ill-health compelled me to retire in March 1927. Sir John Latta's opinion of my service as a shipmaster is given in the reference I received from the company.

After my retirement I was unaware of any adverse reference to the *Californian* in respect of the *Titanic* disaster, as I have never been a filmgoer and was not attracted towards any books on the subject. Latterly my eyesight also began to deteriorate and the amount of reading I could do was consequently considerably curtailed. However I noted some extracts from a book called *A Night to Remember* in the Liverpool evening newspaper, the *Liverpool Echo*, although the brief extracts which I read – which did not contain any reference to the *Californian* – did not impress me.

In the summer of 1958 however, I became aware that a film, also called *A Night to Remember*, apparently gave great prominence to the allegation that the *Californian* stood by in close proximity to the sinking *Titanic*. I therefore personally called on Mr W.L.S. Harrison, General Secretary of the Mercantile Marine Service Association, of which organisation I had remained a member without a break since 1897.

24

LORD'S LAST TESTAMENT

Eighty-two-year-old Captain Lord now felt driven to make a final personal testament. The year was 1959, and nearly half a century had elapsed since that freezing night in April on the North Atlantic when so many died. Yet he felt compelled to revisit the issue for the last time. In three further years he was dead.

What follows is Lord's affidavit, prepared in support of his ultimate effort, through the MMSA, to obtain a review of his case. It must be borne in mind that forty-seven years separate his August 1912 letters of rebuttal and this final commentary by an elderly man in failing health, yet the detail in the affidavit is still sharp, since it is based on personal notes dated 21 May 1912, and retained by Lord in the years thereafter:

Affidavit of Captain Stanley Lord

I went to sea in 1891 as a cadet in the barque *Naiad* owned by Messrs J.B. Walmsley. After obtaining my Second Mate's Certificate of competency I served as Second Officer in the barque *Lurlei*. In February 1901 I passed for Master and three months later obtained my Extra Master's Certificate.

I had entered the service of the West India and Pacific Steam Navigation Company in 1897. This company was bought by the Leyland Line in 1900 and I continued in their service, being appointed to command in 1906 at the age of twenty-nine.

In April 1912, I was in command of the liner *Californian*, having sailed from London for Boston, USA, on April 5th. On April 13th, noon latitude by observation was 43° 43' North: On 14th April, the noon position by observation was 42° 05' N, 47° 25'W, and course was altered to North 61° West [magnetic] to make due West [true]. I steered this course to make longitude 51° West in latitude 42° North on account of ice reports which had been received.

At 5 p.m. on April 14th, two observations of the sun taken by the Second Officer, Mr H. Stone, to check the longitude were reported to me. These gave a run of 60 miles since noon, which was much ahead of dead reckoning. Another observation which I caused to be taken at 5.30 p.m. gave 64 miles since noon.

At 6.30 p.m. we passed three large icebergs 5 miles south of the ship. These I caused to be reported at 7.30 p.m. by wireless to the SS *Antillian*, the message being as follows: '6.30 p.m. apparent ship's time, latitude 42° 5' N, longitude 49° 9'W, three bergs five miles southwards of us, regards, Lord'. [Wireless Operator Evans transmitted error of 42° 3' N]

A little later I was informed that a routine exchange of signals with the *Titanic* showed that she had also received the message sent to the *Antillian*. These would appear to have been the same icebergs sighted and reported by wireless during the day by the *Parisian* in position 41° 55' N, 49° 14'W.

At 7.30 p.m. the Chief Officer, Mr G.F. Stewart, reported to me a latitude by Pole Star of 42° 5½' N. This with the previous observation for longitude gave me proof that the current was setting to WNW at about 1 knot.

At 8 p.m. I doubled the lookouts, there being a man in the crow's nest and another on the fo'c'sle head. At 8.05 p.m. I took charge on the bridge myself, the Third Officer, Mr C.V. Groves, also being on duty.

The weather was calm, clear and starry.

At 10.15 p.m. I observed a brightening along the western horizon. After watching this carefully for a few minutes I concluded that it was caused by ice. At 10.21 I personally rang the engine-room telegraph to full speed astern and ordered the helm hard a-port. As these orders came into effect, the lookout men reported ice ahead. Under the influence of the helm and propeller going astern the ship swung round to ENE by compass [NE true].

The ship was then stopped surrounded by loose ice and from one-quarter to half a mile from the edge of a low ice field. As I could not see any clear place to go through, I decided to remain stopped until daylight. Allowing S 89° W [true] 120 miles from my noon position, and also taking into account the latitude by Pole Star at 7.30 p.m., I calculated my position as being 42° 5' N, 50° 7'W.

At 10.30 p.m. as I was leaving the bridge, I pointed out to the Third Officer what I thought was a light to the eastward which he said he thought was a star.

I went down to the saloon deck and sent for the Chief Engineer. I notified him that I intended to remain stopped until daylight but he was to keep main steam handy in case we commenced to bump against the ice.

I pointed out to him the steamer I had previously seen approaching from the eastward and southward of us and about 10.55 p.m. we went to the wireless room. We met the wireless operator coming out, and pointing out the other vessel to him I asked him what ships he had. He replied: 'Only the *Titanic*'. I thereupon remarked, judging from what I could see of the approaching vessel, which appeared to be a vessel of no great size and comparable with our own: 'That isn't the *Titanic*'. I told him to notify the *Titanic* that we were stopped and surrounded by ice in the position I had calculated, and he left at once to do so. [Claims Evans had *Californian's* position when told to 'Keep out!' by *Titanic*]

Later I noticed the green [starboard] light of the approaching vessel, also a few deck lights in addition to the one masthead light previously seen.

At 11.30 p.m. I noticed that the other steamer was stopped about 5 miles off, also that the Third Officer was Morsing him. I continued watching and noticed that she didn't reply.

At 11.45 p.m. I went on the bridge, casually noticed the other vessel and commented to the Third Officer that she had stopped and wouldn't reply to our Morse signals. He answered in the affirmative.

At ten minutes after midnight, it now being April 15th, the Second Officer came on to the saloon deck. I drew his attention to the fact that we were stopped and surrounded by ice and that I intended to remain stopped until daylight. I pointed out the other steamer to him, told him that she was stopped, and that he was to watch her and let me know if we drifted any closer to her. He then went on to the bridge to relieve the Third Officer, and I went to the chartroom.

I sat there reading and smoking until 12.40 a.m., when I whistled up to the bridge through the speaking-tube and asked the Second Officer if the other ship was any nearer. He replied that she was just the same and I told him to let me know if he wanted anything as I was going to lie down on the chartroom settee.

I then did so, being fully dressed with boots on, etc., and with the electric light on. I left the watch on deck to the Second Officer with every confidence, as he was the holder of a British Board of Trade First Mate's Certificate of competency (foreign going) and my standing orders, which were well known to every officer, stated categorically that I was to be called at once in all cases of doubt.

At about 1.15 a.m. the Second Officer whistled down to say that the other steamer was altering her bearing to the south-west and had fired a white rocket. I asked him whether it was a company's signal and he replied that he didn't know. I thereupon instructed him to call her up, find out what ship she was, and send the apprentice, James Gibson, down to report to me.

I then lay down again in the chartroom, being somewhat relieved in my mind at the news that the other ship was under way and removing herself from her earlier relatively close proximity. For some time I heard the clicking of the Morse key, and after concluding that the Second Officer had succeeded in communicating with the other ship, I fell asleep.

Between 1.30 a.m. and 4.30 a.m. I have a recollection of Gibson opening the chartroom door and closing it immediately. I said: 'What is it?' but he did not reply.

At 4.30 a.m. the Chief Officer called me and reported that it was breaking day and that the steamer which had fired the rocket was still to the southward. I replied: 'Yes, the Second Mate said something about a rocket'.

I then went on to the bridge and was for some little time undecided as to the advisability of pushing through the ice or turning round to look for a clearer passage to the south-east. However, as daylight came in I could see clear water to the West of the ice-field, so put the engines on stand-by at about 5.15 a.m.

About this time the Chief Officer remarked that the steamer bearing SSE from us was a four-master with a yellow funnel and asked me whether I intended going to have a look at her. When I asked him why, he replied that she might have lost her rudder. I said: 'She hasn't any signals up, has she?' He replied that she had not, but that the Second Officer had said that she had fired several rockets during his watch. I told him to call the wireless operator and see what ship it was.

He did so, but fifteen or twenty minutes later came back and reported that the *Titanic* had struck an iceberg and was sinking. Some delay was then experienced before we received an authoritative message giving the estimated position of the disaster, but about 6 a.m. the following signal from the *Virginian* was handed to me: '*Titanic* struck berg wants assistance urgent ship sinking passengers in boats his position lat 41° 46', long 50° 14', Gambell, Commander'.

This position I calculated to be about S 16 W, nineteen and a half miles from our own estimated position. I immediately got under way and proceeded as quickly as possible on course between S and SW, pushing through about 2 to 3 miles of field ice. A lookout man was pulled in a basket to the main truck, given a pair of binoculars and instructed to look out for the *Titanic*.

At 6.30 a.m. I cleared the field ice and proceeded at full speed (70 revolutions). At 7.30 a.m. approximately, we passed the *Mount Temple* stopped in the reported position of the disaster. As there was no sign of any wreckage I proceeded further South, shortly afterwards passing a ship having a pink funnel and two masts, bound North, which turned out to be the *Almerian*.

A little later, I sighted a four-masted steamer to the SSE of us on the East side of the icefield, and received a verbal message from the wireless operator that the *Carpathia* was at the scene of the disaster. I steered to the south until the steamer was nearly abeam when I altered course and proceeded through the icefield at full speed, making for the other steamer. She proved to be the *Carpathia* and I stopped alongside her at about 8.30 a.m. Messages were exchanged regarding the disaster and subsequent rescue operations.

At about 9.10 a.m. the *Carpathia* set course for New York and I continued the search for survivors, the ship steaming at full speed with the Second Officer and a lookout man in the crow's nest. While carrying out this search, I saw the smoke of several steamers on the horizon in different directions. We passed about six wooden lifeboats afloat, one capsized in the wreckage; with the exception of two small trunks in a collapsible boat, the others appeared to be empty.

At about 11.20 a.m. I abandoned the search and proceeded due West [true] through the ice, clearing same about 11.50 a.m.. The *Mount Temple* was then in sight a considerable distance to the south-west of us and heading to the westward.

The noon position was 41° 33' N, 50° 09' W; the latitude was taken under the most favourable conditions by the three officers and reported to me. I did not personally take an observation this day. From this observation I placed the wreckage in position 41° 33' N, 50° 01' W, being about SSE, 33 miles, from the position in which the *Californian* had stopped at 10.21 p.m. the previous evening.

I later called for written reports on the events of the night from the Second Officer and Apprentice. In amplifying his report, the Second Officer stated that the rockets he saw did not appear to be distress rockets, as they did not go any higher than the other steamer's masthead light nor were any detonations heard which would have been the case under the prevailing conditions had explosive distress signals been fired by a ship so close at hand.

In addition, the ship altered her bearings from SSE at 0.50 a.m. to SW a half W at 2.10 a.m.; assuming her to have been 5 miles from the *Californian* when she stopped at 11.30 p.m., the distance she must have steamed to alter her bearing by this amount I calculated to have been at least 8 miles. While on passage to Boston, wireless messages about the disaster were received from Captain Rostron of the *Carpathia,* the American newspapers *New York American*, *Boston Globe*, and *Boston American, Boston Post,* a passenger in the *Olympic* called Wick, and the Leyland Line.

After our arrival at Boston at 4am on April 19th, I was summoned with the Radio Officer to appear before the United States Congressional Inquiry in Washington. I gave my evidence there in accordance with the above facts. Subsequently, I never had an opportunity to read a transcript of the proceedings or findings of this Inquiry, nor was the matter referred to by those I met on subsequent visits to American ports.

After the return of the *Californian* to Liverpool, I reported to the Wreck Commissioner and to the Marine Superintendent of the Leyland Line, Captain Fry. While in the latter's office, Mr Groves, the Third Officer, volunteered the opinion that the ship seen from the *Californian* on the night of April 14th was the *Titanic.* This was the first occasion I had heard him make such a statement and I duly commented to this effect to the Marine Superintendent.

I was summonsed by telegram to appear before the British Court of Inquiry in London on May 14th and travelled down from Liverpool the previous evening. When I arrived in Court, Mr Roberts, manager of the Leyland Line, introduced me to Mr Dunlop and told me he was watching the proceedings on behalf of the owners and officers of the *Californian.* Apart from the questions asked by Mr Dunlop when I was in the witness-box, I had no further conversation with him nor at any time was I afforded an opportunity to discuss the proceedings with him or to suggest what navigational and other technical facts might be brought out which would verify the truth of the evidence which I had given.

Evidence which Captain Lord would have called:

Had I at any time been clearly warned – as I consider I should have been – that adverse findings in respect of the *Californian* were envisaged, I would have taken all possible steps during the Inquiry to call evidence to prove beyond doubt:

(a) That the *Californian* was completely stopped, with full electric, navigation and deck lights burning, from 10.21 p.m. to 6 a.m. Additional evidence to prove this conclusively could have been provided by the production of the engine-room log books covering that period and by the testimony of the Chief Engineer and those engineer officers who kept watch during the night.

If the Court could have been satisfied that the *Californian* was indeed stopped all night, then inevitably they would have had to conclude:

(1) That the *Californian* must have been beyond the visual range of the actual position of the disaster, for in perfect visibility no other ship's lights were seen by the two lookout men and the two officers of the watch on the *Titanic* either before or immediately after she struck the iceberg, nor was the *Californian* in sight of the survivors as day broke. Additionally, none of the green flares burnt in the *Titanic's* boats which were seen at extreme range from the *Carpathia* were seen from the *Californian*.

(2) That the *Californian* could not have been the ship later sighted from the *Titanic* which led to the firing of rockets, for this ship was clearly seen to be underway; to approach from a hull-down position, to turn, and to recede.

(b) That from the navigational evidence the *Californian* must have been at least 25 miles from the position of the disaster. Additional proof could have been supplied from the engine-room log books to show how far she steamed from the time of getting under way at 6am to reaching the wreckage at 8.30; in addition, further detailed consideration should have been given to the relative movements, positions and astronomical observations of the *Californian*, *Carpathia*, *Mount Temple* and *Almerian* from before noon on the 14th to the evening of the 15th April in an endeavour to fix as accurately as possible the actual, as distinct from the estimated, position in which the wreckage and survivors were found.

A further point to which the Court gave no consideration was the fact that the area in which the *Californian* lay stopped all night was covered with field ice extending as far as the eye could see; the area in which the *Carpathia* found the *Titanic's* lifeboats contained very many large icebergs.

If the Court could have been satisfied that during the night the *Californian* was indeed at least 25 miles from the scene of the disaster, they would have had to conclude that even if the distant rocket signals beyond the nearby ship which were apparently seen from the *Californian* had been correctly identified as distress signals, and news of the disaster confirmed by wireless at the earliest possible moment, it would still have been quite impossible for us to have rendered any useful service, for bearing in mind the time taken to reach the wreckage in daylight, under the most favourable conditions, we could not have reached the survivors before the *Carpathia* did.

Finally, I would have submitted for the Court's consideration the following two important points:

(c) That had I or the Third Officer any reason to conclude that the ship seen approaching from 10.30 p.m. onwards was a passenger ship steaming towards an icefield at 21 knots, then instinctively as practical seamen either one of us would have taken immediate action to warn her that she was standing into danger.

(d) That it was perfectly reasonable for the Second Officer to decide that no emergency action was called for when a ship which had been so close to the *Californian* as to cause concern, and which had completely failed to respond to persistent attempts to call her up by Morse light, got underway and passed out of sight after substantially altering her bearing.

This positive action was more than sufficient to nullify any previous concern which might have been created by her apparently making use of confusing rocket signals of low power reaching only to mast height, and lacking any explosive content or detonation such as was customarily associated with a distress rocket and which should have been perfectly audible in the calm conditions then obtaining.

I was also in Court on May 15th. I clearly recall that when Lord Mersey, the President, pressed Mr Groves, the Third Officer, to express his opinion that the ship seen from the *Californian* was the *Titanic*, Lord Mersey commented that this was also his opinion – a comment which does not appear in the official record of proceedings.

Detail hereafter referring to his suspension at Liverpool, resignation, and subsequent career has been included previously. Lord ends the account with:

…I am making this sworn statement as a final truthful and authoritative record of what occurred when I was in command of the *Californian* on the night of April 14th, 1912.

[Signed] Stanley Lord

Sworn by the above-named deponent Stanley Lord at 13 Kirkway, Wallasey, in the County of Chester, on this twenty-fifth day of June, 1959, before me, Herbert M. Allen, Notary Public.

25

THE 1992 REAPPRAISAL

Despite the matter being taken up by the Mercantile Marine Service Association, Lord was to have no rehabilitation by the time of his death in 1962, half a century after the disaster.

The matter was only reopened after 'new evidence' emerged with the discovery of the wreck site in 1985. Maddeningly, in an attempt to keep the location secret, explorer Robert Ballard stated publicly soon after his success that the position of the wreck indicated that the *Californian* was much closer to the *Titanic* than she had claimed in 1912 – but this was a wilfully deceptive statement; Ballard later admitted that he had simply invented this claim to throw wreck-site pursuers off the scent. Once again it seemed that Captain Lord was fair game. The real position of the wreck immensely strengthens, if not utterly verifies, all of the *Californian* contentions.

The *Titanic's* exact co-ordinates, despite Ballard's best efforts, emerged within two years. As a result of their widespread circulation, the British Government in 1992 acceded to requests to re-examine the '*Californian* Incident' in light of the now-established scientific fact that the *Titanic* was 13 nautical miles (mostly to the east but also a little further south) of where she thought she was. This was also why the wreck had eluded discovery for so long.

Captain Lord meanwhile was thirty years dead and beyond redemption.

The case was referred to the Marine Accident Investigation Branch (MAIB) of the British Department of Transport. But because it was 'outside the ordinary run of MAIB investigations', an outside inspector – retired nautical surveyor Thomas Barnett – was appointed to the reappraisal. When his report was returned, it did not satisfy the Chief Inspector of Marine Accidents, Captain Peter Marriott, who did not agree with the findings. He considered further examination was required, and appointed his most senior colleague, Captain James De Coverly, the Deputy Chief Inspector, to undertake the task once more. That task was to find answers to four key criteria: the positions of the *Titanic* and *Californian*, and the distance between them from collision to sinking; to consider whether the *Titanic* was seen by the *Californian* during that period; whether distress signals from the *Titanic* were seen by the *Californian*, and if so, whether proper action was taken; and to assess the action taken by Captain Stanley Lord during that night and next morning.

The final answers amounted to the first official vindication of Captain Lord since 1912. They were:

a) The *Californian* was between 17 and 20 miles from the *Titanic*, most likely 18 miles.

b) It is more likely the *Titanic* was not seen by the *Californian*.

c) The *Titanic's* distress signals were seen, yet proper action was not taken.

d) The message from Gibson 'did not get through' to Captain Lord. Instead, Second Officer Stone was 'seriously at fault'.

The original, outside inspector - whose findings had been rejected by MAIB – felt that the *Titanic* and *Californian* were between 5 and 10 miles apart whilst they lay stopped, and probably nearer 5 miles. The Deputy Chief Inspector however instead found that the separation was 'substantially greater, probably about 18 miles'. The two inspectors disagreed substantially on the effect of drift. The first, retired surveyor Barnett, considered that a current (contrary to that setting west-north-west, identified by Captain Lord) had been affecting the *Californian* since noon on 14 April, so that she was considerably further south than she believed. Since the *Titanic* and *Californian* 'would not see each other even on a very clear night at a distance greater than 8 to 10 miles' (p.9), this original assessor considered that the *Californian* was indeed the *Titanic's* mystery ship.

This conclusion overlooks some rather obvious facts – such as the repeated celestial observations taken by the *Californian* to establish her position that evening, her positions transmitted in wireless messages, the captain's own reckoning of the stop position, and its verification by Chief Officer Stewart. All would require serial mistakes if the first inspector were to be correct. Also the visual identification of the *Titanic* at 5 miles by Lord, Stone and Gibson as being simply a modest tramp steamer goes unexplained.

Meanwhile the Deputy Chief Inspector listed his own several reasons why it was a 'most unlikely' theory that a pronounced southerly drift would go unnoticed by the *Californian* for almost ten and a half hours before she stopped, as the original inspector's findings would suggest. They can be briefly summarised as follows:

1) A southerly current in the region of the accident was unusual. It would have been progressively more unusual – and more noticeable – the further east one places it, such as to the *Californian's* eastern noon position.

2) The pole star sight taken by Stewart at 7.30 p.m., having been steaming due west, agreed in latitude with the noon observation of the same day. 'It follows that the net effect [of current] was nil', at least until 7.30, the Deputy Chief Inspector declares, unless the observations were in error or false evidence was given.

3) The positional evidence given before the accident occurred, in a wireless message to the *Antillian* about icebergs. The *Californian* cannot deliberately give 'false' evidence as to early drift long before any disaster has begun. The *Californian* can only be correct or in error. The Deputy Chief Inspector concluded that the latitude given to the *Antillian* 'adds weight... to the evidence against a southerly set' of drift earlier in the day and evening.

4) The icefield lay in a roughly north/south direction close to the 50th meridian. It seems clearly reasonable to associate this field with a southerly current; but if such a current was to be found much further east, why was no ice there?

Thus the Deputy Chief Inspector dismisses the odd reasoning of the outside consultant. It appears, however, that the DCI was unaware of other evidence that the current before the *Californian* stopped was setting not to the south, as the outside assessor imagines, but to the north. In the first place, there is the fact that Lord was steering slightly south of due west and relying upon the prevailing current to bring him back up to due west so that his latitude remained the same throughout. The *Californian* had also that evening transmitted this message to the *Antillian*, overheard by the *Titanic*: '6.30 p.m. apparent ship's time, latitude 42° 03' N, longitude 49° 09' W, three bergs five miles southwards of us, regards, Lord' (03' N is an error – the actual observed latitude of 42° 05' N was entered in the *Californian*'s log).

In his 1959 affidavit, Lord said of these bergs that they 'would appear to have been the same icebergs sighted and reported by wireless during the day by the *Parisian* in position 41° 55' N, 49° 14' W'. In other words the bergs had drifted north from 41° 55' to 42° – and not to south – if Lord's impression is correct that these were the same three bergs. They had also drifted east, as all the ice was doing. North and east is a Gulf Stream effect.

Titanic Fourth Officer Boxhall exactly explained the point (US Inquiry, p.917):

Senator Newlands: How about the ice in the locality in which you placed it on the chart? Was it likely to drift; and if so, in what particular direction?

Boxhall: Yes; we should expect it to drift to the northward and to the eastward.

Sen. Newlands: And not toward the south?

Boxhall: Not to the southward, as a rule; not in the Gulf Stream.

Sen. Newlands: So that, as you proceeded along the track after you had charted this ice, your assumption would be that the ice would drift farther away from your track rather than drift toward it?

Boxhall: More to the northward and eastward; yes, sir.

Lord meanwhile stated in the same affidavit that a Pole Star observation at 7.30 p.m., together with a previous observation for longitude 'gave me proof that the current was setting to WNW at about 1 knot'. Again we have a northern flavour to the current before *Californian* stopped, and not a southern one. The current may then be showing the influence of meeting the Labrador current. Even without this additional material, the DCI cannot agree with the outside assessor that the *Californian* and the *Titanic* were close enough to see each other, as a pronounced and long-term (yet somehow unnoticed) southerly drift since noon would have it. The DCI says:

> In my opinion, *Titanic* was not seen by *Californian*, nor vice versa, except possibly at a range much greater than the ordinarily visible horizon (8–10 miles) owing to abnormal refraction.

Even if this were so, the DCI stated that he had 'no need nor cause to discount *Californian*'s evidence' as to her stopping place. The only adjustment required after *Californian* came to rest, he wrote, was for the then drift of current – i.e. after 10.21 p.m. He then went on to deduce what he thought to be the likely drift obtaining. The DCI calculated the current by using the distance between the site of the *Titanic* wreck on the sea bed and the position where Captain Lord said he 'left the wreckage' at 11.20 a.m. The problem here is that Lord appeared to mean 'broke off the search' at that point, and clarifies in his last testament that the location refers to where he left the area, having earlier seen wreckage in the vicinity of the *Carpathia*.

Thus misled, the DCI then divided this distance by the number of hours – nine – that had elapsed since the sinking time (2.20 a.m.). From *Titanic* wreck (41° 43' N, 49° 56' W) to Lord's point of departure from the wreckage search (41° 33' N, 50° 01' W) is 10.7 nautical miles. This distance, 10.7 miles, divided by nine hours, gives a drift of 1.19 knots, but the DCI erred in rounding-up when he referred to a drift of 'about 1.3 knots' (p.9), instead of 1.2 as indicated by his own calculations. Then, on the same page, he again changes his mind with a reference to 'a current setting about south by west at something like 1.25 knots'. But this rate of drift is massively at variance with estimations given by witnesses to the 1912 Inquiries. These are the only estimations of drift from the American and British Inquiries and they all suggest the same rate of half a knot per hour. Captain Moore states: 'From about 12.30… until half past 4, there would be a drift there of perhaps, say, half a knot an hour' (US Inquiry, p.780). Sir Robert Finlay says: 'allowing for a drift of only half a knot that ice must have got to the southward of the track' (British Inquiry, p.769). Knapp states: 'The Labrador Current, which brings both berg and field ice down past Newfoundland, sweeps across the banks in a generally south to southwest direction… with a set of about 12 miles a day [½mph]' (US Inquiry, p.1121).

Then there is the *Californian* evidence about drift which is non-specific as to speed, but which hardly suggests drift of as much as 1 knot per hour – Gibson with his gradually changing bearings of the other steamer, Stone with his twice-declared observation (7969 and 8058) 'we were slowly swinging', and Groves, who emphasised: 'We were swinging, but very, very slowly' (8150).

Meanwhile we have seen that Captain Lord's wreckage position was not taken where he found anything necessarily, but was a retrospective estimate of the point where he resumed his course to the west, based on a noon observation taken by his officers forty minutes later. Such a misunderstanding over wreckage would then completely invalidate the DCI's calculations as to morning drift (meanwhile, the *Titanic's* wreck site is, significantly, 3 nautical miles below track, which would also appear to suggest a rate of drift slightly too rapid... One could could speculate about her going to the south and west after her attempt to avoid the iceberg, but idle speculation has cursed this story).

Look again at Lord's guessed place for the wreck site and its actual location... the wreckage from the actual site could in all likelihood not have drifted so far down as to find itself in his search circle. That distance is 10.7 miles – virtually an hour's steaming at all-out full working speed for the *Californian*.

The explanation may lie in the possibility that Lord was actually searching in a position too far south and west of the actual sinking site to see any waterlogged bodies, of which there were many hundreds for days afterwards, as seen by passing liners (*Northern Whig*, 2 May 1912, p.7):

BODIES AND WRECKAGE SIGHTED. Boston, Wednesday – The Captain of the steamer *Sagamore* reports having sighted two bodies and a considerable quantity of wreckage about five miles north of the spot where the *Carpathia* rescued the *Titanic's* survivors. – *Reuter.*

Lord naturally thought he was searching in the immediate area of the wreck and would later locate his guessed location of the foundering within short miles of where he had encountered the *Carpathia*.

Essentially the suggestion is that Lord's reference to 'the position where I left the wreckage' is a loose one, and that there may not have been actual main wreckage in the position where he turned back. Thus the actual drift would not be what the British Government's Deputy Chief Inspector of Marine Accidents calculated (on the basis of Lord's wreckage-leaving remark). Putting this location aside would substantially slow the rate of drift, in keeping with ALL the evidence to the British and US Inquiries, which instead uniformly agreed a drift of half a knot.

Let us accept however, for the sake of argument, the DCI's estimation of 1.3 knots. He uses this to calculate drift of the *Californian* between her own stop and *Titanic* stop. This would be over the hour and twenty minutes between 10.21–11.40 p.m., the Deputy Chief Inspector assuming for convenience that both times are contemporaneous. So, 1.3 miles for the hour, plus one-third of 1.3 (0.433) for the twenty minutes, is 1.73 miles. But the DCI again rounds up the 1¾ mile southward drift of the *Californian*, assuming the current is stronger again at up to 2 miles in that time: 'While stopped, she [*Californian*] would have drifted further, for some 2 miles up to the time *Titanic* hit the berg', the DCI writes. He admits that this is maximum drift, and indeed we have seen he has increased what already seems to have been a very much excessive drift calculation. We know that the *Californian* stop position is 23½ miles from the wreck site. Taking away the 2 mile drift reduces the separation to 21½ miles.

But the *Titanic* drifted also during her two hours and forty minutes of sinking (from 11.40 p.m. to 2.20 a.m.). Such drift too must be taken out of the 21½ mile separation.

This period is twice the one hour twenty minutes between *Californian* stop (10.20 p.m.) and *Titanic* stop (11.40 p.m.). Doubling the 2 mile drift found in the latter case means the 21½ miles are reduced to a 17½ mile separation during the sinking.

This is the absolute minimum distance between them, allowing for maximum drift, according to the DCI's calculations. And the Deputy Chief Inspector says as much: 'I therefore consider that the *Californian* was between 17 and 20 miles from *Titanic* at the time of collision, bearing about north-west by north from her... Between the collision and the sinking, both ships will in all probability have drifted similarly so that their position relative to each other would not appreciably change' (p.11).

Meanwhile, if the DCI had instead trusted to the ½ knot rate cited by those who gave drift evidence in 1912, the gap between the *Californian's* stop position and the wreck site decreases from 23½ miles to 22.83 miles in respect of the time when the *Californian* was drifting alone (½ knot multiplied by 1.33 hours equals 0.67 miles).

The separation then falls further, from 22.83 to 21½ miles, as a result of the *Titanic's* drift (½ knot multiplied by 2.66 hours equals 1.33 miles). In other words, 21½ miles is the putative maximum distance between the *Californian* and the *Titanic* at the time of impact, according to testimony the DCI has overlooked.

WAS THE RMS *TITANIC* SEEN BY *CALIFORNIAN*?

The DCI writes:

> To my mind, the question posed is answered conclusively by evidence of what was seen – and by what was not seen – from the *Titanic*... *Titanic's* speed, maintained until collision at 11.40 p.m., suggests that if at that time she was five miles from the *Californian*, then at 11 p.m. she will have been nearly 20 miles away, which is a very long way off for her to be seen [the *Californian's* stranger was seen as a light by Lord at 10.30 p.m., and noticed by Groves at 11.10 p.m.]... What is significant, however, is that no ship was seen by *Titanic* until well after the collision... watch was maintained with officers on the bridge and seamen in the crow's nest, and with their ship in grave danger the lookout for another vessel which could come to their help must have been most anxious and keen... It is in my view inconceivable that *Californian* or any other ship was within the visible horizon of *Titanic* during that period; it equally follows that *Titanic* cannot have been within *Californian's* horizon.

He continues:

> In his closing speech at the formal investigation, Mr Robertson Dunlop (on behalf of *Californian*) clearly drew attention to the marked inconsistency between what was seen by the two ships. It is no part of this reappraisal to criticise the Court, but it must be remarked as surprising that no consideration of what he said appears in their Report...

There are two possible explanations for what *Californian* saw. The first and most obvious is that a third ship was present which approached from the east, stopped on meeting the field ice, and then after a period steamed away to seek a break in the ice. This is very far from unlikely; the North Atlantic trade was busy in 1912 and a number of other ships are known to have been in the area... The second explanation, which was first advanced some years ago in an unpublished document, is that *Californian* did actually see *Titanic* but at a very much greater range than her horizon because of abnormal ('super') refraction. Against this theory, it requires a long period during which *Californian* could see *Titanic*, but not vice versa...

There are two further objections to the super-refraction theory, he adds, before discussing side lights and *Titanic's* heading and changes in bearing. In the end however, the DCI declines to reject super-refraction absolutely, and instead reports:

In sum, I do not consider that a definite answer to the question 'was *Titanic* seen?' can be given; but if she was, then it was only because of the phenomenon of super-refraction, for she was well beyond the ordinary visible horizon. More probably, in my view, the ship seen by *Californian* was another, unidentified, vessel.

WERE THE *TITANIC'S* ROCKETS SEEN?

Yes, they were, the DCI concludes. The possibility that they were company signals is 'quite unrealistic'. But he adds (p.14): 'In those days, before wireless was common at sea, rockets were much more used than is now the case for reasons other than indicating distress... Given the amount of shipping in the area, it must be very probable that *Californian* was not the only ship to see the signals'. Yet he goes on to state that the use of rockets, while much more common in 1912 than today, 'was certainly not so ordinary an event that their sighting, particularly in an area where ice was about, required anything less than all practicable positive measures to establish the reason for them being fired'. The DCI says Second Officer Stone should have called Captain Lord, and if he did not immediately respond, should have reported to him in person. The DCI continues:

Captain Lord's recollection of what he was told by Mr Stone is somewhat at variance with what that officer recalled; and he had only the vaguest memory, according to his evidence, of Mr Gibson's call... This seems to me entirely consistent with a common condition when a man is called while he is sleeping heavily; there is a state of somnambulism quite often experienced in which the subject appears to respond to a call but the message given does not break the barrier between sleep and consciousness... Commonly, when the subject does wake he has no recollection of the call until he is told of it, when there is some memory but only in a very hazy sense. In plain language, I think the message from the bridge simply did not get through... This inevitably points to weakness on the part of Mr Stone... one can readily imagine (him) on the bridge, knowing in his heart what ought to be done but trying to persuade himself that there was no real cause for alarm... I sympathise with Mr Stone, but it must be said that he was seriously at fault.

CONCLUDING COMMENTS

Even if the *Californian* had responded immediately she confirmed a second rocket, and if her wireless operator had been roused, and if the difference between the SOS position and the place where the rockets appeared to be coming from was resolved so that the *Californian* then headed straight for the actual *Titanic* and not for her mistaken SOS position, Lord's ship could not have saved any extra lives, the DCI concludes:

> The effect of *Californian* taking proper action would have been no more than to place on her the task actually carried out by the *Carpathia* – that is, the rescue of those who escaped... I do not think any reasonably probable action by Captain Lord could have led to a different outcome to the tragedy. This of course does not alter the fact that the attempt should have been made... The *Titanic* disaster led to a number of changes improving provisions for emergency at sea, but it was not until 1948 that the rules for distress signals were amended to make the requirement that they be red. Had that rule been in force in 1912, when it was much more needed than now, Mr Stone would surely not have remained passive.

26

CONCLUSION

The *Oxford Companion to Ships and the Sea*, edited by Peter Kemp, (Oxford University Press, 1976), first published nine years before the discovery of the wreck, had this entry under '*Californian*':

A 6,233-ton Leyland liner whose captain, Stanley Lord, was blamed by two Inquiries into the loss of the *Titanic* on 14/15 April 1912 for failing to come to the rescue of the liner's passengers and crew although within eight to ten miles of the sinking ship and in sight of her distress rockets.

This is based on ship's lights seen from the sinking *Titanic* at 1am, and rockets seen from the *Californian* at about the same time. However the evidence from both Inquiries is clear that the 'mystery' lights moved first towards and then away from the *Titanic*, and the *Californian* did not move her engines all night as there was an ice barrier ahead which Captain Lord did not want to negotiate in darkness. The alleged rockets seen by her watch officers were low in the sky, did not make the detonations normally associated with distress rockets or shells, and were not regarded as distress signals until after the news of the *Titanic*'s loss; company recognition lights and flares were common at the time.

It is probable, from all log book evidence, that the *Californian* was 19 miles from the sinking liner, and it is certain that her radio operator was off watch. Many think the late Captain Lord was made the scapegoat for the *Titanic* disaster for he never received a fair hearing, appearing at both Inquiries only as a witness, with no charges against him, and thus unable to defend himself against the accusations finally levelled by the courts of inquiry.

Note that '19 miles' refers to the SOS position. The actual wreck site had not been discovered.

The Marine Accident Investigation Branch added sixteen years later in the last lines of its 1992 reappraisal: 'The simple fact [is] that there are no villains in this story; just human beings with human characteristics'. But it had missed one of the most relevant factors: the importance of the transmission of the *Californian*'s location at 6.30 p.m. In the nearly four hours thereafter to 10.21, when she stopped, *Californian* was steaming west at 11 knots.

She in fact covered 43 nautical miles when the positions are compared. Applying this 43 miles towards the *Titanic* where she was later sinking (41 nautical miles away) means the *Californian* could have got there, but would have had to alter course sharply to the south-west immediately after 6.30 p.m., and stay plunging a remorseless diagonal for the next four hours. But it was the duty of 'whistleblower' Groves for most of that time, and he was in charge of a course of due west.

But the *Californian* had no reason to go south-west or south at all, as she was not troubled by ice at any stage during those four hours. This is one of the most simple, and yet most compelling of the arguments against her being the *Titanic's* mystery ship. No new wireless report about ice from the *Californian* for four hours shows that she held her course to the west – staying north. She simply had no reason to head south towards the *Titanic*.

Lord Mersey was a man who might have deserved censure in 1912. He escaped with the neglect of evidence adduced in his own court. Mersey was seventy-one at the time, having been two years *retired* from the bench. Yet he was hand-picked for the *Titanic* Inquiry.

When this was announced to the House of Commons by Prime Minister Herbert Asquith, Sir Edward Carson provoked ironic cheers by asking whether Lord Mersey would be influenced by the Board of Trade. Asquith told him it was an insult to suggest it. But perhaps Carson recalled that Mersey had made it a point throughout his career never to miss the Annual Dinner of the Chamber of Shipping. On St Valentine's night, Friday 14 February 1908, a scant four years before he would preside at the *Titanic* Inquiry, the learned judge gave this typically grandiloquent toast to that Chamber (*The Times*, Monday 17 February 1908):

> Mr Justice Bigham [later Lord Mersey], in proposing *The Shipping Interest*, said that those connected with the industry had to see that nothing was done by legislation, or in other ways, which would decrease the carrying power of this great country.

Mersey was thus advocating nothing less than a freemasonry of big shipping, whose adherents should act in the industry's sole interest at all times. The following year he dined with Lord Pirrie of *Titanic* builders Harland & Wolff, with his Liverpool contemporary, J. Bruce Ismay of the White Star Line, and with others at a function hosted by a guild known as the Shipwrights Company (source: *The Times*, 10 June 1909, p. 8). Less than three years later, this man had sole control of the ramifications of the *Titanic* sinking. He later became Viscount Mersey, having presided over the 1914 *Empress of Ireland* and 1915 *Lusitania* Inquiries (privately describing the latter as 'a very dirty business', with First Lord of the Admiralty Winston Churchill having secretly urged that William Turner, captain of that torpedoed vessel, be extensively blamed; Mersey also found that the *Lusitania* had been hit by two torpedoes when British intelligence already knew from German intercepts that only one had been fired). When Mersey died suddenly at a Littlehampton beach hotel in 1929, the *Times* recorded, in an uncommonly negative obituary, that he was 'too apt to take short cuts; and by no means free from the judicial fault of premature expression of opinion or bias, nor always patient with counsel whose minds did not work on the same lines as his own'.

Mersey's son Charles, who had been secretary to his father's *Titanic* Inquiry seventeen years earlier, succeeded to the Viscountcy. But when Stanley Lord died, his son, also called Stanley, was left to carry a tarnished name.

Lord Mersey, with a modicum of care and the application of his professional skills, might have cut through the vengeful fog to come to the aid of a British seafarer in grave difficulties in 1912. He did not do so.

Benjamin Kirk, who went up in a coal basket shackled high to the mainmast of the *Californian* on the morning of 15 April 1912, asked to go there in order to better scan the horizon, had this to say in 1969 of his former captain, who had died seven years earlier: 'I always found Captain Lord very understanding and a good Master to serve under'. By their deeds ye shall know them. And Kirk was there that night and morning.

Also there, in the wider vicinity, was another party; a ship that approached to within 5 miles of the *Titanic*, turned and stopped. A ship that both saw and heard the giant White Star liner's distress rockets, yet instead of coming to assist, decided instead to depart the scene.

Her identity remains one of the last secrets of the sea.

APPENDIX 1

Original statement of Herbert Stone, Second Officer, SS *Californian*, prepared at Captain Lord's request, 18 April 1912:

On going up to the bridge I was stopped by yourself at the wheelhouse door, and you gave me verbal orders for the watch. You showed me a steamer a little abaft of our star[board] beam and informed me that she was stopped. You also showed me the loose field ice all around the ship and a dense icefield to the southward. You told me to watch the other steamer and report if she came any nearer, and that you were going to lie down on the chartroom settee.

I went on the bridge about eight minutes past twelve, and took over the watch from the Third Officer, Mr Groves, who also pointed out ice and steamer and said our head was ENE and we were swinging. On looking at the compass I saw this was correct and observed the other steamer SSE dead abeam and showing one masthead light, her red side light and one or two small indistinct lights around the deck, which looked like portholes or open doors.

I judged her to be a small tramp steamer and about 5 miles distant. The Third Officer informed me he had called him up on our Morse lamp but had got no reply. The Third Officer then left the bridge and I at once called the steamer up but got no reply. Gibson, the apprentice, then came up with the coffee about 12.15. I told him I had called the steamer up and the result. He then went to the tapper with the same result. Gibson thought at first he was answering, but it was only his masthead lamps flickering a little. I then sent Gibson by your orders to get the gear all ready for streaming a new log line when we got under weigh again.

At 12.35 you whistled up the speaking tube and asked if the other steamer had moved. I replied 'No' and that she was on the same bearing and also reported I had called him up and the result. At about 12.45 I observed a flash of light in the sky just above that steamer. I thought nothing of it, as there were several shooting stars about, the night being fine and clear, with light airs and calms.

Shortly after I observed another distinctly over the steamer which I made out to be a white rocket though I observed no flash on the deck or any indication that it had come from that steamer, in fact, it appeared to come from a good distance beyond her.

Between then and about 1.15 I observed three more the same as before, and all white in colour. I, at once, whistled down the speaking tube and you came from the chartroom into your own room and answered. I reported seeing these lights in the sky in the direction of the other steamer which appeared to me to be white rockets.

You then gave me orders to call her up with the Morse lamp and try to get some information from her. You also asked me if they were private signals and I replied 'I do not know, but they were all white'. You then said: 'When you get an answer let me know by Gibson'. Gibson and I observed three more at intervals and kept calling them up on our morse lamps but got no reply whatsoever.

The other steamer meanwhile had shut in her red side light and showed us her stern light and her masthead's glow was just visible. I observed the steamer to be steaming away to the SW and altering her bearing fast. We were also swinging slowly all the time through S and at 1.50 were heading about WSW and the other steamer bearing SW x W.

At 2 a.m. the vessel was steaming away fast, and only just her stern light was visible and bearing SW a half W. I sent Gibson down to you and told him to wake you and tell you we had seen altogether eight white rockets and that the steamer had gone out of sight to the SW. Also that we were heading WSW.

When he came back he reported he had told you we had called him up repeatedly and got no answer, and you replied: 'All right, are you sure there were no colours in them', and Gibson relied: 'No, they were all white'.

At 2.45 I again whistled down again [sic] and told you we had seen no more lights and that the steamer had steamed away to the SW and was now out of sight, also that the rockets were all white and had no colours whatever.

We saw nothing further until about 3.20 when we thought we observed two faint lights in the sky about SSW, and a little distance apart. At 3.40 I sent Gibson down to see all was ready for me to prepare the new log at eight bells.

The Chief Officer, Mr Stewart, came on the bridge at 4 a.m. and I gave him a full report of what I had seen and my reports and replies from you, and pointed out where I thought I had observed these faint lights at 3.20.

He picked up the binoculars and said after a few moments: 'There she is then, she's all right, she is a four-master'. I said: 'Then that isn't the steamer I saw first', took up the glasses and just made out a four-master steamer with two masthead lights a little abaft our port beam, and bearing about S; we were heading about WNW. Mr Stewart then took over the watch and I went off the bridge.

Herbert Stone, Second Officer

APPENDIX 2

Original statement of James Gibson, Apprentice Officer, SS *Californian*, prepared at Captain Lord's request, 18 April 1912:

It being my watch on deck from 12 o'clock until 4 o'clock, I went on the bridge at about 15 minutes after twelve and saw that the ship was stopped and that she was surrounded with light field ice and thick field ice to the southward.

While the Second Officer and I were having coffee, a few minutes later, I asked him if there were any more ships around us. He said that there was one on the starboard beam, and looking over the weather-cloth, I saw a white light flickering, which I took to be a Morse light calling us up.

I then went over to the keyboard and gave one long flash in answer, and still seeing this light flickering, I gave her the calling-up sign. The light on the other ship, however, was still the same, so I looked at her through the binoculars and found that it was her masthead light flickering. I also observed her port side light and a faint glare of lights on her after deck. I then went over to the Second Officer and remarked that she looked like a tramp steamer. He said that most probably she was, and was burning oil lights.

The ship was then right abeam. At about 25 minutes after twelve I went down off the bridge to get a new log out, and not being able to find it, I went on the bridge again to see if the Second Officer knew anything about it. I then noticed that this other ship was about one point and a half before the beam. I then went down again and was down until about five minutes to one.

Arriving on the bridge again at that time, the Second Officer told me that the other ship, which was then about three and a half points on the starboard bow, had fired five rockets and he also remarked that after seeing the second one, to make sure he was not mistaken, he had told the Captain through the speaking tube, and that the Captain had told him to watch her and keep calling her up on the Morse light.

I then watched her for some time and then went over to the keyboard and called her up continuously for about three minutes. I then got the binoculars and had just got them focussed on the vessel when I observed a white flash apparently on her deck, followed by a faint streak towards the sky which then burst into white stars.

Nothing then happened until the other ship was about two points on the starboard bow when she fired another rocket. Shortly after that I observed that her side light had disappeared but her masthead light was just visible, and the Second Officer remarked, after taking another bearing of her, that she was slowly steering away towards the SW.

Between one point on the starboard bow and one point on the port bow I called her up on the Morse lamp, but received no answer.

When at about one point on the port bow she fired a rocket, which, like the others, burst into white stars. Just after two o'clock, she was then about two points on the port bow, she disappeared from sight and nothing was seen of her again.

The Second Officer then said, 'Call the Captain and tell him that that ship has disappeared in the SW, that we are heading WSW, and that altogether she has fired eight rockets'.

I then went down below to the chartroom and called the Captain and told him and he asked me if there were any colours in the rockets. I told him that they were all white. He then asked me what time it was, and I went on the bridge and told the Second Officer what the Captain had said.

At about 2.45 he whistled down to the Captain again but I did not hear what was said.

At about 3.20, looking over the weather-cloth, I observed a rocket about two points before the beam [port], which I reported to the Second Officer.

About three minutes later I saw another rocket right abeam, which was followed later by another one about two points before the beam.

I saw nothing else and when one bell went, I went below to get the log gear ready for the Second Officer at eight bells.

James Gibson, apprentice

APPENDIX 3

MYSTERY SHIP CLAIMS

Over the years there has been no shortage of nominations for the identity of the *Titanic*'s mystery ship. There have been far fewer suggestions as to the identity of the *Californian*'s nearby stranger. The hunt began in 1912 when the British Board of Trade and other arms of HM Government launched a determined attempt to track down one particular candidate they deemed worthy of attention. Harbourmasters, port authorities and customs agents in several countries were contacted to establish whether any vessels matching a 'Wanted' description put in or out of port around the time of the disaster.

The steamer they were looking for was one mentioned in evidence by Captain Moore of the *Mount Temple*. Captain Moore said that he encountered a steamer crossing his bows to the southward at a time between 1 a.m. and 1.30 a.m. as he made his way to the SOS location:

> 9257. …I saw her afterwards in the morning, when it was daylight. She was a foreign vessel – at least, I took her to be a foreign vessel. She had a black funnel with a white band with some device upon it, but I did not ascertain her name.
> 9260. Was she going west? — She was going east.

The British poured huge resources into ascertaining the movements of any vessel matching this identification. Moore at the US Inquiry had estimated her to be a tramp of 4,000–5,000 tons, specifying once more the 'device', but this time saying the funnel was black, not mentioning a white band. He also said he could see this steamer at 9 a.m. on 15 April 1912.

Saturnia

It has been suggested that this vessel was the Anchor-Donaldson Line's *Saturnia* (8,611 tons), which indeed had a black funnel with a white band. She was westbound from Glasgow to St John, New Brunswick, when she heard the *Titanic*'s distress signal and turned around. She was later stopped by heavy ice, supposedly 6 miles from the scene.

It may have been a pointless hunt by the British authorities however, because Moore's steamer was to the west of the ice barrier, whereas we now know the *Titanic* sank to the east. Whomever she might be, if the black-funnel steamer (with the device in a white band) was indeed heading east all the time, as Moore said, then she is likely not the *Titanic*'s mystery ship.

At the British Inquiry, counsel for the Leyland Line, Robertson Dunlop, named other vessels likely to have been in the vicinity, not by way of accusation, but to illustrate that the net for a culprit could be widely cast, citing westbound ships from Lloyd's Weekly Shipping Index.

Trautenfels

The *Trautenfels* was a two-masted black funnel steamer ('with red stripes', added Mr Dunlop, meaning hoops around a white band in mid-funnel) belonging to the Hansa Line of Bremen. A petroleum carrier, she had no wireless. Her registered tonnage was a mere 2,932. She was bound from Hamburg for Boston, the same destination as the *Californian.*

Dunlop read into the record of the British Inquiry (p.838) a report to Lloyd's saying the *Trautenfels* on 14 April was in latitude 42° 01'N, longitude 49° 53'W, when she sighted 'two icebergs fully 200 feet long and 50 feet high' (a latitude within 4 miles of the *Californian's* stop position).

The report added: 'Soon after, heavy field ice was encountered which extended for a distance of 30 miles and made it necessary for the steamer to run in a south-west direction for 25 miles to clear it. In the field ice 30 bergs were counted, some very large. In the Northward no clear water was seen, so that the Captain estimated that the ice in that direction must have extended fully 30 miles'.

Dunlop declared: 'We do not know at what time she was in this latitude. All we do know is she was there at some time on the 14th April, and she did what the witnesses from the *Californian* described the vessel which they saw did. They saw a vessel encounter ice and then run in a SW direction until she went out of sight'.

The Attorney General spoke up at this point to say that the British authorities had been making some enquiries about the *Trautenfels* in consequence of the colour of her funnel. A letter from the US customs at Boston to superiors in Washington, dated 23 May 1912, stated that the *Trautenfels* arrived in port early in the morning on 18 April. The *Californian* got there a day later.

In a report to the US Hydrographic Office, received on 19 April, Captain Hupers of the *Trautenfels* stated that he had passed two icebergs of 200ft in length, mentioned at the British Inquiry, at 5.05 a.m. on 14 April. Over the next three hours, to 8 a.m., the *Trautenfels* moved south-west, 'passing along a field of heavy, closely packed ice, with no openings'. The icefield could be seen extending far to the northward. During this time she sighted thirty large bergs.

Lindenfels

The *Trautenfels* and *Californian* were followed into Boston by a sister ship of the Hansa Line vessel. The two-masted tanker *Lindenfels* (built 1906; 5,476 tons) made port on 20 April.

She was reported to the British authorities by US customs at Boston because she was deemed to have a funnel resembling that specified in the alert – black with a white band – while she also fulfilled another part of the description by having a heraldic device in the middle of the band in the shape of a Maltese cross.

The Attorney General said he had been informed that the voyage from the SOS location to Boston took from three to five days. He opined that the *Trautenfels* would 'probably not have been in that locality on 15th April'. Captain Hupers' ice report said she had been there on the morning of 14 April instead.

Clearly however, the timeframe may have suited the *Lindenfels*. No statement is known to have ever been made by her captain or crew.

Paula

Mr Dunlop also cited the *Paula*, a three-masted oil tanker of 2,748 tons gross with a black funnel with a yellow band upon it containing a red R. She belonged to the Deutscher–Americana Petroleum Company of Hamburg.

Oil tankers of the time often had their superstructure aft, behind the funnel. Gibson of the *Californian* suggested the ship he was observing had shown a glare of light in her afterpart. There was this exchange about the *Paula* (British Inquiry, p.840):

> The Commissioner: She is a petroleum ship?
>
> Dunlop: Yes.
>
> The Commissioner: She is not likely to look like a passenger boat?
>
> Dunlop: No, she would look more like what the Master and Second Officer and Gibson say, a medium-sized vessel, apparently a tramp, not having the appearance of a passenger steamer.
>
> The Commissioner: Would she have her funnel aft?
>
> Dunlop: That I do not know, my Lord; I think not. [In actual fact she did]
>
> The Commissioner: I am told a tank steamer always has its machinery and funnel aft?
>
> Dunlop: Well, your Lordship is informed about that.

The *Paula* reported being in the locality at some time on 14 April. Dunlop argued that she too was a steamer going to the westward and then apparently steaming in a south-westerly direction in order to avoid the icefield.

The Attorney General once more offered information. A reply to enquiries by the Board of Trade on 27 May from the US customs revealed that the *Paula*, skippered by a Captain Rieke had put into Sabine, Texas, on 29 April. The report declared: 'The Master stated that he passed through the icefield on Sunday a few hours before the *Titanic*, and finding the ice cutting worse, changed course directly to the South for 25 or more miles'.

An ice advisory had been received from the *Paula* by the US Hydrographic Office. She reported that on 14 April at 5.30 p.m. she saw heavy pack ice and thirty large icebergs in one field, from latitude 41° 55' N, longitude 50° 13' W, to latitude 41° 40' N, longitude 50° 30' W. She was still in the area when the *Titanic* sank.

In addition to the above vessels, Dunlop also drew the court's attention to the *Memphian* (6,833 tons, Leyland Line), the *Campanello* (9,291 tons, Harding Line), and the *President Lincoln* (18,168 tons, Hamburg–Amerika Line). He put his estimates of their positions on a chart submitted to the British Inquiry. The *Campanello* and the *President Lincoln* both had Marconi apparatus.

Yet another German oil tanker, the fourth associated with the tragedy, would make her way into the reckoning in 1938. A first mate named Hoffman claimed that the vessel *Niagara*, owned by the same company as the *Paula*, had been journeying between New York and Hamburg when he and others saw a passenger liner to the north-west on the night of 14/15 April 1912.

As they passed some distance away, they saw lights at a tilted angle. They later saw rockets and formed the impression they were witnessing 'a celebration on board'. It was thought to be nothing unusual. On reaching Hamburg they learned of the disaster.

The similarities with the *Paula* are striking, but in fact the *Niagara* at the relevant time was operating in the Far East. Hoffman is either mistaken about which German tanker he was aboard, or was inventing the story – which formed part of an unpublished manuscript before the Second World War. The account was finally published in a German maritime magazine in 1976.

The number of ships investigated by the British in 1912 meanwhile grew to bewildering levels. It is pointless to list them all. But some, like the *Parisian* (5,395 GRT, Allan Line) and *Etonian* (6,438 GRT, Leyland Line) passed over the *Titanic*'s route.

As set out earlier, the Dow Jones news agency of New York reported before 9 a.m. on 17 April that the *Etonian*, not equipped with wireless, had docked in the North River the previous night. She reported that 'a number of fishing boats were in vicinity of the disaster at the time'. So too did *Ultonia*.

Interestingly, sealing vessels also operated in the vicinity of the Grand Banks. These had a custom of firing rockets and blowing whistles to summon back their dories from clubbing seals on pans of ice. Such a vessel, seeing rockets, or even hearing *Titanic* steam blown off, might imagine it was another sealer recalling hunting parties.

Parisian

The *Parisian* passed virtually over the spot where we now know the *Titanic* sank. Bound for Boston via Halifax, she was ahead of the *Californian* and in wireless contact with both that vessel and the *Carpathia*.

The *Parisian*, on the afternoon of 14 April, passed on to the *Californian* the message: '41° 55' N, 49° 14' W, passed three large icebergs'. The *Californian* would later herself see those bergs and record where they were at 6.30 p.m.

Captain William Hains of the *Parisian* sent a later report to the US Hydrographic Office at Boston in which he described his whereabouts:

April 14th, 4.30 p.m., latitude 41° 55' N, longitude 49° 02' W, passed first iceberg, 8 p.m. Latitude 41° 42' N, longitude 49° 55' W, passed last iceberg. Between positions passed 14 medium and large icebergs and numerous growlers.

It can be seen that the *Parisian* moved south of west. As she travelled fifty-three minutes further west, she also dropped 13 miles down from the north.

Her latter position is virtually on the exact spot where the *Titanic's* wreck was found seventy-three years later. Ironically, it can be seen on US hydrographer Knapp's chart, labelled '6.12 p.m.' to reflect New York time.

The wording of the *Parisian* report is unclear, but if the last position was taken at 8 p.m., it would mean that six hours before the *Titanic* went down the *Parisian* was at 41° 42' N, 49° 55' W. The *Titanic* sank at 41° 43' N, 49° 56' W. Thus the *Parisian* was only one minute of longitude further east and one minute of latitude further south than the *Titanic*. If she had still been there five hours later, she would have been a model for the mystery ship.

The *Parisian* at 8 p.m. was less than a mile from where the *Titanic* would eventually sink. She had been travelling that day at 12 knots. Her top speed was 13 knots, which she apparently ran to after 9 p.m. If she then encountered no ice to slow her, it would appear she was 55–60 miles from the *Titanic* at the material time when the mystery ship was around. The *Parisian* learned of the disaster only next morning when Wireless Operator Sutherland resumed duty.

Frankfurt

Almost every ship in wireless contact with the *Titanic* during the disaster has fallen under suspicion at one time or other. They include the *La Provence*, *Mount Temple*, *Baltic*, *Amerika*, *Antillian*, *Ypiranga*, *Caronia*, *Celtic*, *Virginian*, *Mesaba*, and *Prinz Friedrich Wilhelm*. Most can be discounted, but the number and names of ships in the vicinity was never properly established.

As early as 24 April 1912, the *Brooklyn Daily Eagle* reported that Boston and Portland dispatches indicated that besides the *Californian*, 'the freight steamship *Lena* and the tramp steamship *Kelvindale* and other ships were at points ranging from 20–30 miles from the ill-fated White Star liner [meaning the SOS position, possibly far less from actual site]'.

One writer stretches credulity to blame the *Frankfurt*, a Norddeutscher Lloyd vessel of 7,431 tons. The drawback is that she supplied her position to a sinking *Titanic* very early in the night – and could not have been preparing an alibi in advance. This transmission was overheard by the *Caronia*, *Mount Temple* and *Carpathia* at around 12.38 a.m. *Titanic* time, according to the British Inquiry. From that position, the *Frankfurt* was a monumental 140 miles away. Although she turned around, Captain Hattorff did not reach the disaster scene until all was over. The *Californian* met her the next morning as Captain Lord's vessel was leaving the vicinity.

Victorian

The *Victorian* was an Allan liner of 10,757 GRT. The following letter appeared in the members' forum of the April 1986 issue of the *National Geographic*:

> My father, now almost 89 years of age, left England in early April 1912 to come to Canada aboard the liner *Victorian*. He claims, and has claimed for years, to have witnessed the flares from *Titanic*. This ship may well have been the mystery ship and closest witness to this tragedy.
> Geraldine Hamilton
> Calgary, Alberta

This interesting statement follows a mere snippet in the *New York Times* of 21 April 1912, about the *Victorian*, which was indeed westbound to Canada from Liverpool at the time:

KEPT BAD NEWS SECRET
Victorian's Passengers Not Told of Disaster Until They Landed

HALIFAX, N.S., April 20 — Not one of the 1,424 passengers on board the Alan [*sic*] Line steamer *Victorian* knew of the *Titanic* disaster until they reached here today. The *Victorian* sailed from Liverpool April 12. The reason given by the officers for keeping back the information was the fear of causing uneasiness on board.

The news of the disaster was received by the *Victorian* eight hours after it occurred. The persons on board who knew of the message received were the wireless operator and Captain Outram. The news was received from the *Carpathia*, via the *Baltic*, on Monday, and the dispatch gave the number of lost and saved.

Captain Outram said no bodies or wreckage were sighted, although a lookout was kept. He said he had to go very far south to avoid collisions with icebergs. Thirteen large icebergs were passed at one time, and an apparently limitless stretch of heavy field ice.

Samson

The case of the *Samson* is a candidature that has provoked much discussion and controversy.

She was a barque of just over 500 tons, and 148ft long – or just one-third the length of the *Californian*. Featuring an impressive bowsprit, she was essentially a sailing vessel operating from Norway, although she did have auxiliary donkey engines and a funnel on her deck amid the masts.

Author Per Kristian Sebak in his book (*Titanic: 31 Norwegian Destinies*) tells how the story of the *Samson* is essentially that of one man – ice pilot and officer Henrik Naess, who was aboard the vessel in 1912.

In May and June 1912, a rumour started to circulate that the *Samson* had seen the *Titanic's* rockets and had left the scene. Commodore Sir Ivan Thompson of the

Cunard line remembered hearing the story in a Texan port at this time. It grew in the telling until an American newspaper account dismissed it as a 'Norwegian fairy story' in 1913.

Naess would later declare however that he had told a Norwegian consul in Iceland that the *Samson* had been operating as a sealer off Newfoundland on the night when the *Titanic* went down. During his watch he noticed two big stars to the south which looked peculiar. A lookout on the masthead reported that they were not stars but 'lanterns and a lot of lights'. A short time later several rockets were seen.

Naess said: 'We feared we might be taken for violating territorial borders and the lights out there meant there were Americans in the area. When the lights went out this probably meant that we had been observed, the rockets being maybe signals to other ships. We therefore changed course and hurried northwards.'

On arriving in Iceland and hearing of the disaster, he checked the *Samson*'s log and found that the date and location fitted: 'We had been ten miles away when the *Titanic* went down. There we were with our big excellent ship and eight [life]boats in calm, excellent weather. What might we not have done, if we had known? Alas we had no radio on board.'

In 1921, a Norwegian yearbook reported that the *Samson* had been in the vicinity and could have had the opportunity of rescuing many 'if the people on board had known what was taking place nearby'. Naess was not directly quoted.

The story did not substantially emerge however until 1928 when Naess achieved a certain fame as an ice pilot taking charge of a vessel in the attempted rescue of the crew of the airship *Italia*, which had crashed somewhere in the Arctic after a flight to the North Pole. Norway's famous son, Roald Amundsen, the first man to reach the South Pole, would be lost forever on a similar venture to find the lost crew of the *Italia*. It was in this undertaking, which became an international mercy mission, almost a race, that Naess was mentioned by his home town newspaper, the *Arbeideravisen* of Trondheim. In this interview, sixteen years after the *Titanic* disaster, Naess mentioned that he had seen rockets from the sinking White Star vessel, but that he and his captain, Carl Johann Ring, believed them to be flares from American patrol boats exchanging signals.

Captain Ring was a maritime victim of the First World War. Naess thereafter became a captain himself, and would achieve recognition as 'one of Norway's most famous arctic explorers'. Naess worked with Baden Powell and Fridtjof Nansen, and was awarded the Royal Order of Merit by Norway for his discovery of valuable coalfields on Spitsbergen. He died in 1950.

The case of the *Samson* returned to international attention in 1962, when the Norwegian state broadcaster aired a documentary to mark the fiftieth anniversary of the *Titanic* disaster, highlighting Naess's claims. Several detailed accounts of the incident, composed by Naess, eventually came to light. At least one version had the *Samson* seeing both the *Titanic* and her rockets. Naess said the *Samson* had been sealing illegally off the Grand Banks and it was feared the rockets might have been a signal to heave to and await a search party from an official vessel. The *Samson* instead fled the scene by engines. Sealing was indeed carried on in the area of the *Titanic* sinking, mainly by Canadian vessels. But the area is on the 'high seas' and no territorial limits applied so far from land, so there was no question of any illegality. The sealing season started in March as millions of newborn seals and their parents drifted south on frozen floes – with vessels venturing out to land clubbing parties on to the ice for pelts and blubber. Stealing the spoils of others was common.

Cassie Brown in her book *Death on the Ice*, an account of the great Newfoundland sealing disaster of 1914 in which 132 men were stranded on an icefield for two days and nights, two-thirds of them dying, declared: 'Piracy was almost a recognized part of the game'. It is noteworthy perhaps that one of the vessels involved in that 1914 disaster, the *Florizel*, had taken a peripheral part in *Titanic* body recovery two years earlier. It may also be worth noting that Third Officer Groves of the *Californian* saw seals he thought were bodies on drifting ice as his vessel searched the area on the morning of 15 April 1912.

The author Leslie Reade has cast doubt on the *Samson* story. A revenue book he uncovered for the Icelandic port of Ísafjördur lists harbour charges against the *Samson* for 6 April and 20 April 1912, seeming to suggest the vessel was in port on those dates. Since Ísafjördur is about 1,500 miles from the scene of the sinking, it would require the *Samson* to make 300 miles a day, or a steady pace of 12½ knots to make port five days after the disaster.

Charles McGuinness, chief officer of the *Samson* in her later incarnation as an exploration vessel, was not impressed with her speed. In his book *Sailor of Fortune* (Macrae-Smith, 1935) he writes: 'In a dead calm the engines propelled the clumsy barque at a rate of six knots per hour' (p.244).

It seems scarcely possible for her to have been on the scene and made port again – yet US researcher David Eno insists that the revenue book shows *prepayments* and is not a harbour log as such. A charge relating to the *Samson* appears among vessels listed from 20–23 April.

The *Californian*, having spent the entire morning of 15 April searching the scene, arrived in Boston at 4 a.m. on 19 April, a distance some 1,000 miles from the tragedy. The *Carpathia* had arrived in New York on 18 April at 9 p.m.

Meandering at half the rate of those vessels, the *Samson* would have taken 10½ days to reach Iceland, a journey 500 miles further. It seems the earliest she could have put in at Ísafjördur would have been the afternoon of 25 April.

Naess, however, does not mention the *Samson* being in Iceland before May. It is known she was there that month because of a fight involving her crew and locals, which was reported in the press.

Despite the apparent contradictions in her account, the *Samson* was evidently a tidy ship. She was bought by the American Antarctic explorer, Admiral Richard Byrd, for use in polar expeditions – on the recommendation of Roald Amundsen – and renamed the *City of New York*. She had a hull 3ft thick, a metal-plated bow, and saw plenty of icebergs in a sea-going career that lasted more than seventy years. She was exhibited at the Chicago World's Fair in 1933, and became a total loss off Nova Scotia twenty years later.

What benefit, meanwhile, the respected Naess could have hoped to gain by continuing in later life to freely connect his vessel with the sinking *Titanic* is not clear.

Premier

The *Premier* was a fishing schooner of just 374 tons, out of Gloucester, Massachusetts. She was 155ft long and captained by a Billy Morrison.

The American magazine *Sea Classics* reported in 1970: 'According to the recent report of a former *Premier* crew member [surnamed Rose], the *Premier's* 22-man crew saw the gradually sinking *Titanic* about five miles distant but failed to realise she was in distress'. The *Premier*, like all schooners of her day, had no wireless. The crew's reaction to the *Titanic's* distress rockets is unknown. Rose said they noticed a great deal of debris on the water the next morning but did not realise its significance until learning of the disaster in Halifax several days later.

The magazine suggested that the *Premier* might have been the mystery schooner with which the *Mount Temple* had a close encounter. It said crew members had 'admitted witnessing the *Titanic* in her death throes'.

A similar story is offered about the *Dorothy Baird*, another Gloucester schooner, of three masts and 241 tons. She was 118½ft long, and reported to have been in the area by the *Etonian*. Also mentioned in dispatches are vessels named *Bruce*, *Dora*, *Kura* and *Pisa*.

Almerian

The *Almerian*, just short of 3,000 tons, was another Leyland liner, like the *Californian*, except 100ft shorter. She was bound to the east, with a cargo from Mobile, Alabama. At 3 o'clock in the morning on 15 April, forty minutes after the *Titanic* sank, she stopped on the western side of the icefield. Another vessel was similarly stopped on the *Almerian's* port quarter, according to a report later given to Captain Lord.

When signalled by Morse lamp, all that could be made out of her reply were the letters '…ount…', according to the account retailed in the book *A Titanic Myth*, by Leslie Harrison, based on paper's in Captain Lord's possession, now in Liverpool Maritime Museum.

At daybreak, the *Almerian* could see that she was confronted by field ice. She began to go northwards to search for a way through the floes, and the vessel she had seen earlier got underway too. It was then they were able to read her name – *Mount Temple*.

On the other side of the ice could be seen a large four-masted steamer with her derricks deployed (presumably the *Carpathia*). Continuing north, the *Almerian* – which had no wireless – saw smoke shortly afterwards, which on nearer approach was seen to be coming from a ship of the same line (presumably the *Californian*). Before they got up to her on the western side of the ice, she changed course to the eastward and steamed through the ice in the direction of the four-master on the other side.

A curiosity about this story is that the *Almerian*, which was heading east, did not then follow her sister ship through the path she had negotiated, but continued north (paradoxically in the direction from which the ice was drifting down), and only found a way through the ice at 10 a.m. The *Almerian* knew nothing of the tragedy, completing her passage to Europe.

The explanation for the *Almerian* not following the *Californian* seems to be that the story is apparently in error on at least this detail – Captain Lord implied that he *passed* a pink-funnel steamer, which was heading northwards, *before* making his cut through the ice. Captain Rostron of the *Carpathia* gave evidence (question 25551):

> At 5 o'clock it was light enough to see all round the horizon. We then saw two steam-ships to the northwards, perhaps seven or eight miles distant. Neither of them was the *Californian*. One of them was a four-masted steamer with one funnel, and the other a two-masted steamer with one funnel.

If these vessels then become the *Mount Temple* and *Almerian* respectively, and the *Almerian*, already 7 or 8 miles north of the *Carpathia* next heads further north, then it is impossible for the Leyland liner she encounters, the *Californian*, to cross her bows. They must pass before Lord's descending vessel makes a sharp turn to port to head for the *Carpathia*. Captain Lord stated at the British Inquiry:

> 7400. Was there another vessel near the *Mount Temple*? — There was a two-masted steamer, pink funnel, [Leyland liners had pink funnels, including both the *Californian* and *Almerian*] black top, steering north down to the north-west.

Lord did not draw any further unwelcome attention to the Leyland Line, formally naming the *Almerian* only in 1959, but clearly that vessel was where he said she was, and at a most material time. Her reported story is intriguing and she has many unanswered questions of her own.

It will be remembered that the captain of the *Mount Temple* said his vessel stopped at 3.25 a.m., some time later than the *Almerian* claims to have received '...ount...' from a stationary steamer, judged in daylight to be the *Mount Temple*.

Mount Temple

Claims about the *Mount Temple* have been persistent. Moore said that when he first stopped, at 3.25 a.m., he estimated his vessel to be 14 miles from the *Titanic's* transmitted SOS position, which was incorrect. This estimate, however, finds a curious echo in a letter Captain Lord received in August 1912 from a W.H. Baker, written on board the Canadian Pacific liner *Empress of Britain* (see 'Lord's Rebuttal'). Baker stated that he had filled a vacancy as fourth officer on the *Mount Temple* for her return journey across the Atlantic immediately following the *Titanic* tragedy. He wrote:

> The officers and others told me what they had seen on the eventful night when the *Titanic* went down, and from what they said, they were from ten to fourteen miles from her when they saw her signals.
>
> I gather from what was told me that the Captain seemed afraid to go through the ice, although it was not so very thick.

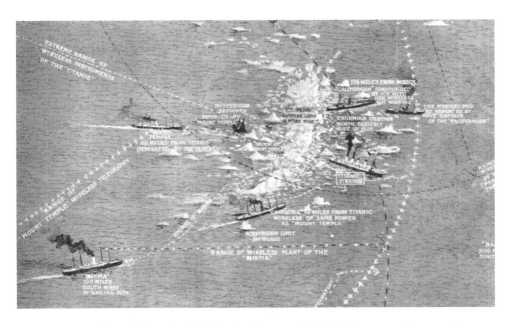

A drawing of the overall scene by G. H. Davis which appeared in The Sphere *on 4 May 1912 – long before any* Californian *witnesses were called before the British Inquiry. It correctly locates the* Titanic *sinking on the east side of the ice barrier, whereas* Mount Temple *arrived at the transmitted SOS position on the west side and found the ice impassable in front. While the map mistakes the location of the* Carpathia *and leaves out some other ships in the vicinity, it still stands as an indictment (before the fact) of the British Inquiry's conclusions.*

They told me that they not only saw her decklights but several green lights between them and what they thought was the *Titanic.* There were two loud reports heard, which they said must have been the finale of the *Titanic;* this was sometime after sighting her, I gathered.

The Captain said at the inquiry in Washington that he was 49 miles away but the officers state he was not more than fourteen miles off. I must tell you these men were fearfully indignant that they were not then called upon to give evidence at the time, for they were greatly incensed at the Captain's behaviour in the matter.

The doctor had made all preparations and rooms were turned into hospitals, etc, and the crew were standing by ready to help, on deck, watching her lights and what they said were the green lights burnt in the boats.

On our arrival in Gravesend the Captain and Marconi officer were sent for, also the two log books, scrap and Chief Officer's. What they wanted with the scrap log I cannot understand, for there was only about a line and a half within of what occurred during the four hours, and quite half a page in the Chief's book! I saw this myself. These fellows must feel sorry for you, knowing that you could not, in the face of this, have been the mystery ship.

Baker was verifiably aboard the *Mount Temple* as a replacement officer on the crossing in question, and other references in his letter prove accurate, yet the main aspects are admittedly hearsay, apart from what he claims to have personally seen.

Lord made efforts to follow up this letter but found the *Mount Temple*'s fourth officer A.H. Notley (the man replaced by Baker), and the *Mount Temple*'s doctor, W.A. Bailey, both unwilling to go on the record. Bailey suggested Lord seek evidence from the officers aboard at the time who 'saw certain things'.

In October 1912, Lord submitted what he had, including Baker's letter, to the Board of Trade. Baker alone appeared willing to give evidence, but the Board of Trade at the beginning of December replied merely that it would give 'the most careful consideration to any signed statements' from witnesses who had served in the *Mount Temple* on the night in question.

The *Mount Temple*, built in 1901 at Newcastle, was 8,790 tons. She was sunk by the German raider *Moewe* in 1916. The many claimants about her conduct on the night the *Titanic* sank are documented in the author's separate work, '*Titanic* Scandal: The Trial of the *Mount Temple*' (Amberley, 2009).

FURTHER READING

The transcripts of both official inquiries make fascinating reading; *The Loss of the SS* Titanic, *Report, Evidence &c*, can be ordered in a 972-page tome from the Public Record Office: PRO Publications, Ruskin Avenue, Kew, Surrey, TW9 4DU, United Kingdom (ISBN: 1 873 162 707). The 1,162-page American report (paradoxically much shorter in verbiage than the British equivalent, is today entitled *Titanic Disaster 1912 Hearings* and is available from Documents on Demand (1800-227-2477, or from outside North America 1-301-951-4631), email: cisdod@lexis-nexis.com. DoD is an arm of the Congressional Information Service, Inc., 4520 East-West Highway, Bethesda, Maryland 20814–3389 USA.

Both transcripts are available in a CD-ROM produced by the British National Archives at Kew (incorporating the Public Record Office) entitled '*Titanic*: The True Story' (see: http://www.nationalarchives.gov.uk/). They are also available on the internet via the Titanic Inquiry Project at http://www.titanicinquiry.org/

The report 'RMS *Titanic* – Reappraisal of Evidence Relating to SS *Californian*' (1992) by the Marine Accident Investigation Branch at the Department of Transport can be ordered through the HMSO, PO Box 276, London, SW8 5DT, England (ISBN: 0 11 551111 3).

Books specific to the *Californian* controversy include:

Harrison, Leslie, *A* Titanic *Myth* (William Kimber & Co, 1986)
Molony, Senan, Titanic: *Victims and Villains* (History Press, 2008)
Padfield, Peter, *The* Titanic *and the* Californian (Hodder & Stoughton, 1965)
Reade, Leslie, *The Ship That Stood Still* (Patrick Stephens Ltd, 1993)

Other books referenced in this volume include:

Beesley, Lawrence, *The Loss of the SS* Titanic (William Heinemann, 1912)
Bisset, Sir James, *Tramps and Ladies* (Angus & Robertson, 1959)
Gracie, Colonel Archibald, *The Truth About the* Titanic (Mitchell Kennerley, 1913)
Groves, Charles Victor, *The Middle Watch*, unpublished manuscript, 1957
Lightoller, Charles, Titanic *and Other Ships* (Nicholson and Watson, 1935)
Molony, Senan, Titanic *Scandal: The Trial of the Mount Temple* (Amberley, 2009)
Rostron, Sir Arthur, *Home From The Sea* (Macmillan, 1931)

INDEX